INDIGENOUS AND AFRICAN DIASPORA RELIGIONS IN THE AMERICAS

INDIGENOUS AND AFRICAN DIASPORA RELIGIONS IN THE AMERICAS

Edited by Benjamin Hebblethwaite
and Silke Jansen

UNIVERSITY OF NEBRASKA PRESS   LINCOLN

© 2023 by the Board of Regents of
the University of Nebraska

All rights reserved

The University of Nebraska Press is part of a land-grant institution with campuses and programs on the past, present, and future homelands of the Pawnee, Ponca, Otoe-Missouria, Omaha, Dakota, Lakota, Kaw, Cheyenne, and Arapaho Peoples, as well as those of the relocated Ho-Chunk, Sac and Fox, and Iowa Peoples.

Publication of this volume was assisted by University of Florida College of Liberal Arts and Sciences and Center for the Humanities and the Public Sphere (Rothman Endowment).

Library of Congress Control Number: 2022043571

Set and designed in Charis by N. Putens.

CONTENTS

List of Illustrations · vii

Acknowledgments · ix

Introduction: Multidisciplinary Approaches to Indigenous and African Diaspora Religions · 1
BENJAMIN HEBBLETHWAITE AND SILKE JANSEN

1. Meeting Grounds in Saint-Domingue and the Emergence of Haitian Vodou: An Ecological Approach · 61
LEGRACE BENSON

2. The Many Faces of Marie Laveau and Voudou in Nineteenth-Century New Orleans · 83
ELEANOR A. LAUGHLIN

3. Shamanic Healing, Initiation, and Ritual Technique in a Kwak'wala Narrative from the Boas-Hunt Corpus · 111
DANIEL J. FRIM

4. Language and Rituals of the Brotherhood of the Holy Spirit of the Kongos of Villa Mella · 145
JOSÉ MARÍA SANTOS ROVIRA

5. A Joyful Place: Baniwa Jaguar Shamans' Songs and
   Historical Change   173
   ROBIN M. WRIGHT

6. Embodying, Reshaping, and Combining the Past and the
   Future: A Mapuche Shaman's Historical Agency in Chile   203
   ANA MARIELLA BACIGALUPO

7. Other Knowledges: Tensions and Negotiation between
   Religion, Knowledges, and School in a Wixárika Community   233
   IRITAMEI FRANCISCO BENÍTEZ DE LA
   CRUZ AND ITXASO GARCÍA CHAPINAL

8. It's the Song That Cures: Healing, Music, and Ayahuasca
   in Brazil's Santo Daime Churches   257
   DERECK DASCHKE

9. Finding Orisha in New Places   281
   JEFFERY M. GONZALEZ

Contributors   319

Index   323

ILLUSTRATIONS

FIGURES

1. *Marie Laveau* portrait by Frank Schneider — 86
2. *Un bal de Signares (mulâtresses) à St. Louis (Sénégal)* — 89
3. *A Voudoo Dance* by John Durkin — 99
4. *Marie Laveau* by E. W. Kemble — 102
5. *Marie Laveau* by Sallie Ann Glassman — 104
6. A church in Villa Mella — 150
7. A house in Villa Mella — 151
8. Arriving at Villa Mella — 153
9. José María Santos Rovira talking with some *villamelleros* — 154
10. Meeting place of the Brotherhood of the Holy Spirit of the Kongos — 155
11. A ceremonial dance in Villa Mella — 157
12. Graph depicting the Cosmos (*Hekwapi*) — 177
13. Yoopinai spirits of the forest — 179
14. The Spirit of Sickness, Kuwai — 185
15. The Spirit of Power, Dzuliferi — 185
16. Graph depicting Wixárika and Spanish language use in primary school — 247
17. Yewa River, Idogo, Nigeria — 287
18. Ogun River, Abeokuta, Nigeria — 288
19. Olókun's Well, Ile-Ife — 288
20. Sogidi River in Awe, Nigeria — 289

21. Ogun shrine, Ilaro, Nigeria — 290
22. Arugba next to Ogunleki statue, Ibadan, Nigeria — 291
23. Carrying offering to the Ogunpa River, Ibadan Nigeria — 292
24. Our Lady of the Regla, Regla, Cuba — 293
25. Olókun drums, Matanzas, Cuba — 294
26. Olókun offerings at the sea, Matanzas, Cuba — 295
27. Festival in 1950 — 295
28. Bahia in 2012 — 296
29. Rio de Janeiro in 2019 — 296
30. Worshipping at ocean near Miami, 2014 — 297
31. Drumming and singing at estuary of Oleta River State Park, 2017 — 297
32. Oloshas United, Miami, 2017 — 298
33. Cabrillo Beach, California, 2017 — 299
34. Shrine of Yemọja, Ilaro, Nigeria — 300
35. Casa Yemanja, Bahia, Brazil — 300

MAPS

1. West and Central Africa — xii
2. Haiti and the Dominican Republic — xiii
3. Mexico — xiv
4. South America — xv
5. United States and Canada — xvi

ACKNOWLEDGMENTS

The initial spark for this edited collection was ignited through the generous teaching and research fellowship received by Benjamin Hebblethwaite and Silke Jansen from the German Academic Exchange Service (Deutscher Akademischer Austauschdienst) in 2016–17. This allowed Hebblethwaite to teach at Friedrich-Alexander Universität in Erlangen, to learn from his new German students, and to pursue conversations with Jansen on the analysis and comparison of Indigenous and African diaspora religions in the Americas.

Our DAAD-funded workshop "Vodou and Shamanic practices in the Americas" on February 24, 2017, with Michel Weber and Maria van Daalen, served as a springboard for the call for papers that subsequently became the basis for the chapters in this volume.

The National Endowment for the Humanities Collaborative Research award (RZ-51441–12) for "The Archive of Haitian Religion and Culture" (www.dloc.com/vodou) is gratefully acknowledged for their support on this book project. We also express our thanks to the University of Florida College of Liberal Arts and Sciences and Center for the Humanities and the Public Sphere's Rothman Endowment for a subvention that supported this publication.

We thank Houngan Michelet Tibosse Alisma, Manbo Marie Alisma, Houngan Emanuel, and Houngan Marcus Saint-Pierre at Société Linto Roi Trois Mystères in Miami for welcoming us in their ceremonies.

We remember our friend, the photographer and anthropology librarian Richard Freeman, z"l, who traveled to Miami, Haiti and Cuba, working on the NEH grant. May peace be upon him.

We thank Akíntúndé Akínyẹmí, Robin M. Wright, Mariana Past, Judy Shoaf, Kole Odutola, Joe Aufmuth, Jenny Freeman, Kevin Meehan, Manbo Maria van Daalen, Andrew Tarter, Terry Rey, Patrick Bellegarde-Smith, Celucien Joseph, Matt Statler, Parker Van Hart, Magnus Fischer, Guido Mensching, Rob de Rooij, Kola Thomas, Richard Kernaghan, Romi Gutierrez, Lauren Phillips, Carlos de la Torre, Anthony Baxter, Sean MacDonald, Pamela Haines, Geoffrey Fletcher, Rori Bloom, Youssef Haddad, Roxana Walker-Canton, and Alioune Sow for their help and accompaniment on this project.

Matthew Bokovoy, Heather Stauffer, Tish Fobben, Erika Rippeteau, Ann Baker, Leif Milliken, and the staff at the University of Nebraska Press shared generously of their time and talents throughout the publication process. We thank the four peer reviewers who painstakingly read, commented on, and corrected our drafts. We express our deep appreciation for Emily Shelton's meticulous copyediting on our project.

I am thankful for the love and support of my parents, John (1940–2022) and Meredith Hebblethwaite. To my wife, Julie Rhee, and my daughters, Chloe and Ellie, 너무 사랑해요!, I give thanks for their love and support. — Benjamin Hebblethwaite

I am grateful for the support, enthusiasm, and curiosity of my many friends and family members, especially Marisa and Bernd. — Silke Jansen

INDIGENOUS AND AFRICAN DIASPORA RELIGIONS IN THE AMERICAS

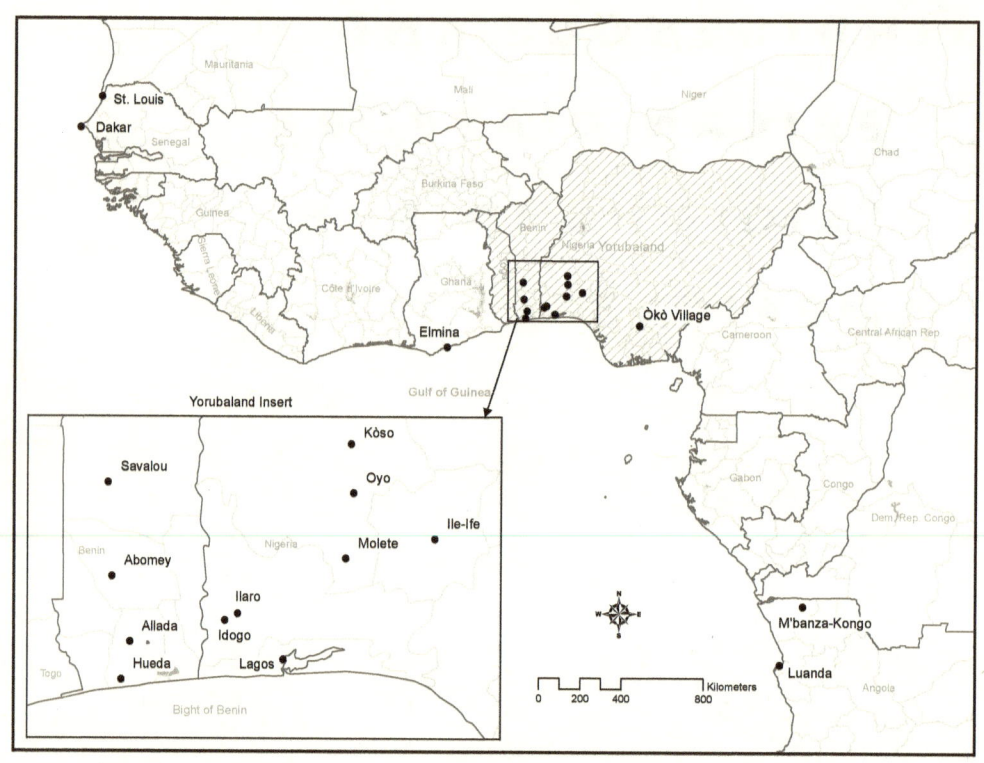

M1. West and Central Africa. Cartography by Joe Aufmuth.

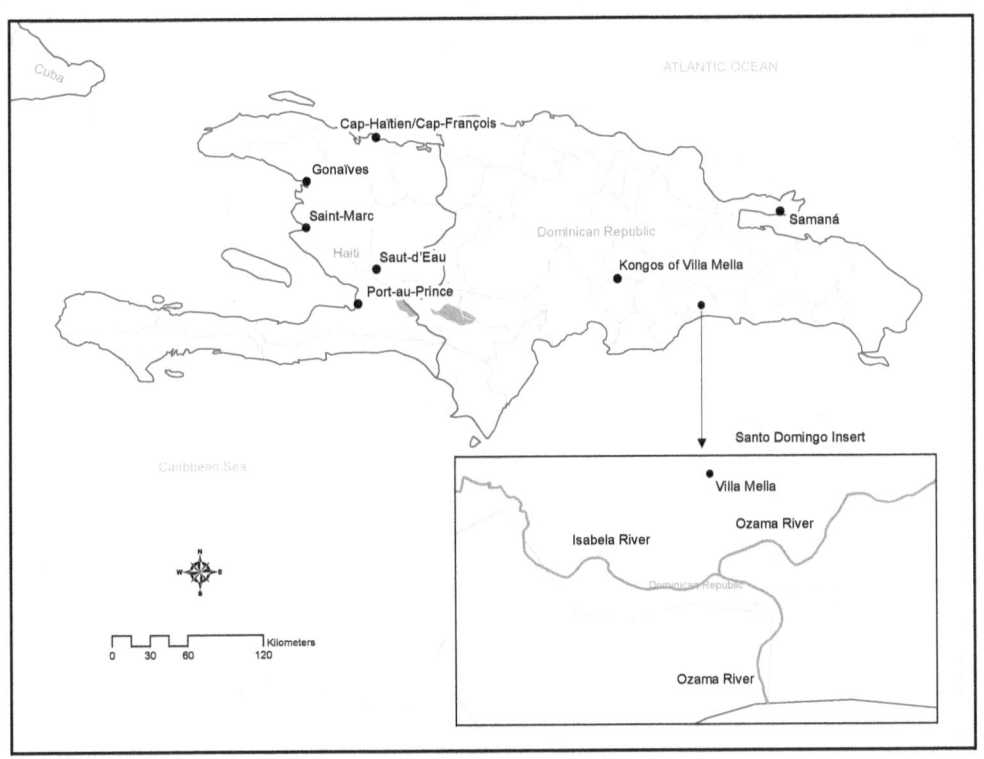

M2. Haiti and the Dominican Republic. Cartography by Joe Aufmuth.

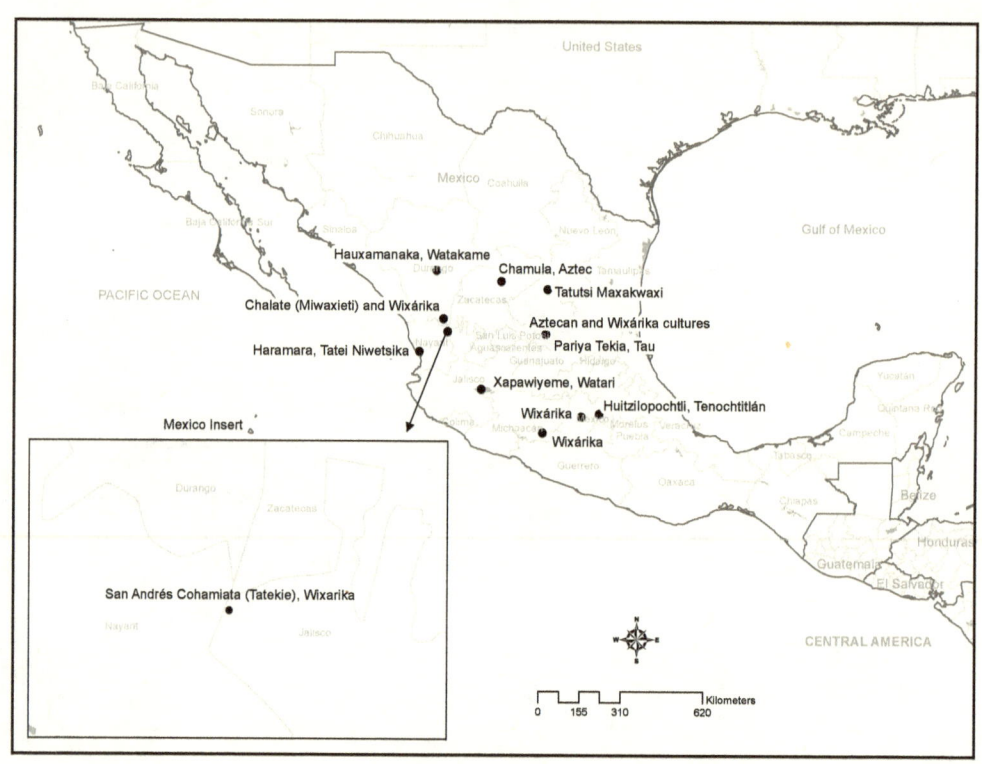

M3. Mexico. Cartography by Joe Aufmuth.

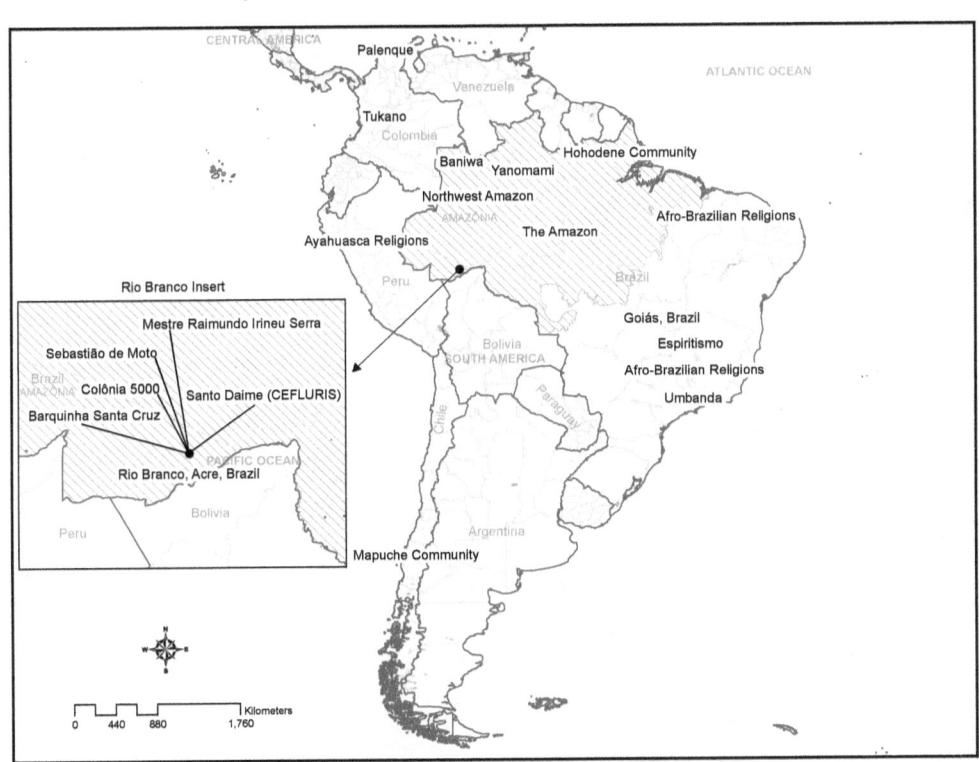

M4. South America. Cartography by Joe Aufmuth.

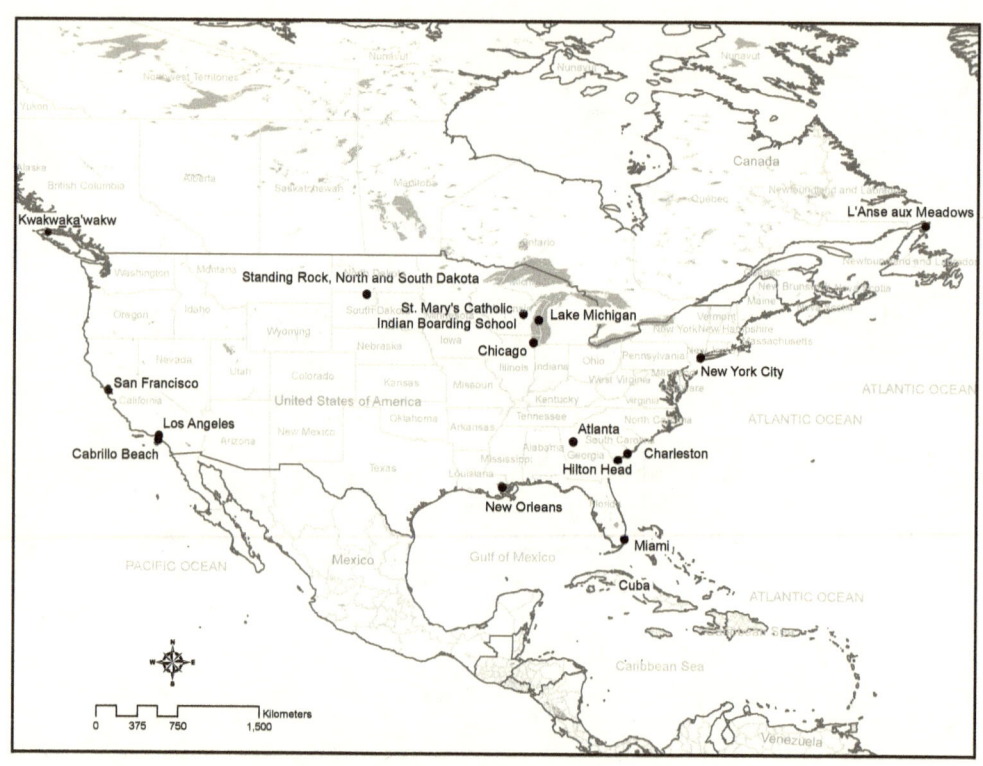

M5. United States and Canada. Cartography by Joe Aufmuth.

INTRODUCTION

MULTIDISCIPLINARY APPROACHES TO INDIGENOUS AND AFRICAN DIASPORA RELIGIONS

Benjamin Hebblethwaite and Silke Jansen

American Indigenous and African diaspora religions appear in manifold expressions in the Americas of today. Their antecedents predate European colonization by centuries. As reservoirs of ancient and recent history and knowledge, the study and documentation of these traditions assists in preserving humanity's vulnerable cultural, historical, and linguistic memories. Our effort is to discover and remember religious and spiritual traditions that reflect intimate and profound aspects of contemplative thought centered on the nature of being.

Despite ethnic, linguistic, and historical distinctions, American Indigenous and African diaspora religions are cultural systems that share typological similarities. These similarities relate—with some regional variations—to service to spirits, initiation rites, drums, the sacred rattle, singing and dancing as worship, rituals around the axis mundi, and communication with spirits through dance, song, possession experiences, and dreams. They can partly be explained by shared experiences, often in the same geographical and social spaces, under European and white colonialism. Nevertheless, American Indigenous and African diaspora traditions have been separated in scholarship on disciplinary, ethnic, linguistic, geographical, or historical grounds, largely because disciplinarian academics are trained to compartmentalize traditions and to dig in as deep as possible. Against this backdrop the comparison between intellectual, cultural, material, symbolic, historical, and structural features of Indigenous and

African diaspora religions is a significant desideratum and appears as a highly promising academic endeavor because it can shed light on mutual intelligibility and similarity between seemingly disparate human inheritances while revealing fascinating differences.

This collection of chapters explores spirit-based religious traditions across vast geographical and cultural expanses. It gathers a variety of chapters rooted in participant-observer fieldwork and book-based historical, critical, and social approaches to religion. Its goal is to profile these religions using interdisciplinary research methods to a) expand our knowledge of a curated selection of these traditions; b) compare and highlight the convergences in these traditions; and c) challenge colonial erasures of these traditions. The joint consideration of spirit-based traditions from a hemisphere presents an inclusive typological approach. The individuals and communities studied here serve spirits through ritual, singing, instruments, initiation, contact with spirits via possession or trance, veneration of nature, and, among some Indigenous people, the consumption of ritual psychoactive entheogens. Before delving into comparisons, it is important to understand how the terms "Indigenous" and "African diaspora" have evolved and changed over five hundred years of colonial history and to define how they will be used in our collection.

PROBLEMS WITH "INDIGENOUS" AND "AFRICAN DIASPORA"

The term "Indigenous," as well as its near synonym "Native," suggests a strong and naturally given tie of a population and their cultural manifestations to a territory, which is established by birth (OED). In accordance with this, Indigenous religions of the Americas are often considered to be cultural practices anchored in communities that are place based and have a strong focus on descent and ancestry. This view largely ignores the fact that ethnic and territorial belongings are dynamic and, to a certain extent, negotiable in many Indigenous societies. For example, some groups of the northwest Amazon traditionally led a nomadic lifestyle, which caused heated debates among Western scholars in their efforts to exactly trace the geographical boundaries of each group's territory. Likewise, the principle of linguistic exogamy (i.e., the obligation to marry someone outside one's own linguistic group) practiced in this region enhances geographic, cultural, and linguistic mobility (Fleming 2016). Before the colonial period, the Timucuans in Florida, for example, also made seasonal visits to hunt, fish, and gather shellfish along the St. John's River to the Atlantic coast (Worth 1998).

While it is true that place plays an important role in some American Indigenous cultures and religious practices, its role is more dynamic and versatile than might be expected. The distribution of domesticates like peach palm landraces suggests that Arawak and Tupi migrations have five thousand years of recognizable history, with vast histories of upheaval, resettlement, integration, and conquest implied in this timeline (Alexiades 2009, 20). The Arawak people, who form the largest language family in South America, have sociocultural practices like "topographic writing" that directly link their mythologies to the geography they inhabit (Santos-Granero 2002, 47; Erikson 2011, 273; Wright 2013, chapter 4). Elements of the landscape such as waterfalls, mountains, or rivers, as well as human-made landmarks such as graves, petroglyphs, and battlefields, are interpreted as cultural signs that function as mnemonic devices to remember important events and people of the society's historical memory. Often these so-called topograms are connected to ceremonial song, culture, religion, and mythology (Eriksen 2011, 273; Santos-Granero 1998, 140ff; 2002, 47). Several "topograms" can be combined to form a wider semiotic system of landscape signs (i.e., topographs). When Arawak shamans and traders spread Arawak culture to foreign territories and integrated them into their prestigious sphere, topographic writing served as a means of cultural appropriation of geographical space, transforming land into Arawak territory (Eriksen 2011, 278). European observers have often misunderstood these complex place-making practices, beginning with Christopher Columbus's journal and other late fifteenth-century texts from the Antilles in which the authors mistakenly interpret Arawakan topographic markings as literal geographical description (Keegan 1996, 23).

While Indigenous people and their religions are not thought of as being linked to the experiences and memories of settlers or colonial migrants from another homeland, their existences have been utterly upended by the former (Stewart 2018, 740). Different types of mobility have always created diasporas in the Americas, including among Indigenous people.

For example, the Aztec or Mexica people migrated from today's northern Mexico or southern United States to the Central Mexican Highlands, probably at the beginning of the fourteenth century. Their mythical tradition reports that their patron deity Huitzilopochtli ordered them to leave their homeland, Aztlán, and led them to the Lake Texcoco after many years of traveling. There they founded Tenochtitlán (today's Mexico City), which would later become the center of the Aztec Empire. As noted in Laack (2019, 86), the Aztlan migration myth was an important part of Mexica identity. Accordingly, the Spanish chronicler Diego Durán reports that the Mexicas' ritual performances, like the ones led by the shamans who served Moctezumah I, centered on the quest for the mythical homeland (Laack 2019, 161, 268). Thus, the huge and powerful Aztec Empire was built on a diasporic identity.

The so-called Island Caribs or Kalinago people from the Lesser Antilles are another example, as they viewed the Carib South American mainland as their ancestral homeland and culturally identified with the Kalina people, whom they considered to be their ancestors (Taylor 2012, 21). Although it is not clear to what extent this origin myth corresponds to a historical reality or was inferred by colonial interlocutors, Kalinago language and culture is indisputably a product of centuries-old mobility between the South American continent and the Eastern Caribbean islands (Jansen 2020). This led to the emergence of an etymologically "mixed" linguistic repertoire with gendered patterns of language usage: originally speaking an Arawak language, the Kalinago incorporated a high number of words into their repertoire that originally belonged to the Kalina (Cariban) people of the Guyana region. Among the Kalinago these elements were restricted to men, probably because they indexed prestigious activities associated with masculinity such as trade and war that brought the Kalinago in contact with the Kalina (Jansen 2020; Taylor 1976, 98). Likewise, the Kalinago lifestyle and religious practices more closely resemble that of Cariban groups than what has been called the "Arawakan cultural matrix" (Santos-Granero 2002).

The later history of the Kalinago people holds even more challenges for the traditional understanding of "indigeneity." In the seventeenth and early eighteenth century, the Kalinago society integrated Africans through cultural fusion and intermarriage. These were enslaved people who escaped various shipwrecks near St. Vincent (Taylor 2012, 22; Forbes 2011, 82ff), or were captured in Kalinago raids against the Spanish colonies (Petitjean Roget 1980, 503ff; Hofman et al. 2019, 364). In 1797 British colonists deported the non-European population of St. Vincent to British Honduras (today's Belize), from where they spread over large parts of Central America (Whitehead 2002, 67; Hofman et al. 2019, 363). Today the descendants of these people, now known as Garifuna, still speak a language that goes back to the islands' fusion of Carib and Arawak mentioned above, including retaining vestiges of male and female speech (Taylor 2012, 22), with a few African influences. In the Garifuna diaspora they call out in song to "Youroumaÿn," their St. Vincent homeland (Greene 1998, 172; Taylor 2012, 17).

Given that the Aztec, the Kalinago, and the Garifuna people (to mention just a few examples) developed a diasporic identity, which they expressed via ritual and multilingual practices, as well as in other ways, how can they factually be called Indigenous groups, in contrast to people of African or European descent who populated the Antillean space in colonial times?

Equally complex are the "African diaspora" religions of Haitian Vodou, Cuban Santería, Trinidadian Ṣàngó, or Bahian Candomblé. How could anyone say they are not now indigenized wherever they are practiced in the Americas? How do they manage to retain diasporic status centuries after forced migration? They became Indigenous over time in a process that transferred African linguistic and cultural knowledge into Creole, Spanish, or Portuguese linguistic molds. In rare cases complete songs or sentences from an African language like Fon, Yoruba, or Kikongo have been retained, but in general the cultural content—especially the names of rites, spirits, leadership, and rank—has been rendered intelligible to the local language and culture. In many instances this cultural transfer is nearly direct, with only minor modifications to the conceptual, historical, and lexical core, while in other instances noticeable shifts and syncretism point to degrees of accommodation and adaption.

For example, in the case of Haitian Vodou, a syncretistic orientation of the creators allowed them to combine disparate religious traditions to create Sèvis Ginen, revealing a stunning expansiveness, with its inclusion of the religious traditions of roughly twenty-one African ethnicities. Even without wars of independence like the one that led to Haitian independence in 1804, African diaspora religions have become Indigenous in the colonial and postcolonial societies where they have been practiced for generations.

Weighed against these facts, the word Indigenous suffers from an overgeneralizing essentialism, since Indigenous people have themselves been migrating, integrating, conquering, falling to conquest, and becoming diasporic from before colonialism until today. As a Eurocentric and colonial concept, the term construes the enormous American space as a container, and it posits Indigenous people in direct opposition to Europeans and Africans. Differences between continents are essentialized while cultural diversity and mobility within the Americas is erased. The term "Indigenous" also establishes the year 1492—the only moment in time when it could reasonably be used to distinguish the local population from the foreign invaders—as a reference point for the definition of ethnic identities. After Columbus, the Native Americans forced by the U.S. military to march on the Trail of Tears to Oklahoma reservations in the nineteenth century also became diasporic in relation to their southeastern homelands of Mississippi or Alabama.

Similarly, the descendants of Europeans and enslaved African people became Indigenous people themselves. Over time people of different backgrounds mixed with each other. Generations lived and died forming bonds to new places, people, and their identities. Few people living in the Americas can trace their ancestry back to one national or even continental group alone. This is poignantly illustrated in Creole-language colonies where enslaved people created languages, religions, and cultures that took from but contrasted with the languages, religions, and cultures of the colonists. In the Haitian context, the process of indigenization was forged by the forces of linguistic and cultural creolization, the emergence of a Creole Vodou that reflected syncretized African traditions, and the aspiration to land ownership and self-rule (Trouillot, Past, and Hebblethwaite 2021, 54).

Further complicating any idealization of hermetic traditions, American Indigenous and African diaspora peoples have also fused aspects from Western societies into their belief systems, such as biblical mythology, Freemasonry, and Catholic saints, especially their chromolithographic images, which now depict spirit traditions. From colonial times to our days, the simultaneous exercise of Catholicism and spirit-based religious traditions has been common in the Americas and is generally not felt to be a contradiction. Sometimes European and local traditions may have influenced each other—for instance, in rituals with palm fronds in the Taíno religion, as well as Haitian Vodou's Rada Rite cycles for Ayizan, although ritualizing with palm fronds is also common in the Bight of Benin (Rouget 2001). The *vèvè* ground designs still traced in Haitian Vodou ceremonies by *oungan* priests and *manbo* priestesses may have been a point of contact. Objects like Taíno stone trigonal icons, arrowheads, and *cemíes* are incorporated into Haitian Vodou altars as *pyè tonnè* (lightning stones sent and inhabited by spirits), illustrating the way archeological objects that are symbolically powerful can pass from Indigenous people to the traditions of enslaved Africans in the colonial context (Waldron 2019, 256, 243). Against the backdrop of centuries-long coexisting and blending between European, Indigenous, and African traditions, the same spiritual entity can receive different readings in different religious systems. For example, the Catholic saint Jerome, who is often depicted with a big cat that he tamed, is interpreted by the Lancandon (Maya) people of Mexico as Father Jaguar, whereas he is interpreted as the metallurgical *lwa* Ogou in Haitian Vodou (Capper 2016, 147; Plathoff 2015, 5). Haitian lwa and Cuban *orixas* are generally identified with the pictorial representations of one or more Catholic saints, but not their biographical traditions.

Although terms like Indigenous, African diaspora, and Western can have legitimate social and political functions, they often indefensibly extend beyond appropriate limits, negating the intersections that traditions share because of the "coloniality of reality," which are the colonial aspects of postcolonial societies (Burman 2016).[1] Diasporic (from *dia speiro* 'to sow over') communities arise from enslavement, exile, as well as migration, suggesting that associating the term with ethnic or racial groups suffers from essentialism. The asymmetrical "inter-community adoption" of American Indigenous, African diaspora, and Western ideas raises doubts about treatments of these traditions as hermetically evolved phenomena (Oakdale 2018, 257). Instead, five centuries of asymmetrical inter-community contact, adjustment, and opposition have deeply changed Indigenous and African diaspora traditions (as well European ones). Contrasting Indigenous and African diaspora cultures with Western cultures provides important historical context for understanding where traditions originated. However, centuries of conquest and imbrication negate reductionistic analyses, instead generating hybridity within and around us.[2] Against this backdrop we use the terms "American Indigenous" and "African diaspora" not as descriptive terms for an allegedly preexisting reality but as instances of academic strategic essentialism that will allow us to precisely deconstruct essentializing views on religious practices in the Americas.

WORKING WITH SPIRITS

Working with spirits is a central feature of religious expression throughout the Americas. The term "spirits" in Indigenous and African diaspora traditions refers to immaterial beings remembered through mythology, songs, prayers, stories, dreams, light, possession experiences, and entheogenic plants (Beauvoir 2008a; Kopenawa and Albert 2010). Spirits live within people and repose in the land, forests, rivers, sky, animals, and sparkling light and lightening. Spirits may have human ancestral, animal, plant, or natural attributes, and they are frequently imbued in mythology with qualities of "peoplehood" that render them familiar.

Spirits watch over, protect, and punish humankind. Practitioners of spirit-based religions serve, pray to, and propitiate spirits for preservation, healing, socialization, and community involvement. Ritual specialists primarily serve and call on spirits to assist and integrate their communities. Unlike New Age spiritualists who delve into Indigenous and African diaspora religions, shamans and priests are primarily motivated by community work, not by a personal quest for spiritual enlightenment (Kehoe 2000, 86). The spirits have supernatural, human, animal, and natural attributes that make them both uncanny and familiar. They specialize in enhancing human pursuits in areas like work, love, death, healing, self-defense, war, agriculture, farming, hunting, language, the ocean, bees and pollination, the priesthood, and other universals. Indigenous and African diaspora people in white colonies encountered norms of intolerance that drove their communities and religions into extreme hardship—a matter examined next.

SURVIVING APOCALYPTIC CONDITIONS

For the practitioners of Indigenous and African diaspora traditions, existence itself devolved into apocalyptic conditions of deracination, displacement, enslavement, servitude, disease, forced assimilation, and experiences of alienation in the centuries since the Norse (briefly after 1021) and the Spanish (after 1492) arrived on the shores of this continent and its islands. Indigenous and African diaspora people experienced dehumanization and total loss through conquest, enslavement, erasure, or forced migration. Those who survived have dealt with generations of racist legacies and social fragmentation. Colonial lawmakers alternated between denying that Indigenous people or African diaspora people had any religion whatsoever—referring to their practices as "superstition"—and attacking spirit-based traditions (McNally 2020, 34; Ramsey 2011, 24). Practitioners of African diaspora and Indigenous religious traditions have opposed, adjusted to, accommodated, camouflaged themselves behind, or been snuffed out by European invaders. Kopenawa and Albert (2010) demonstrate how this process continued unabated into the 1970s as the Yanomami people encountered the Brazilian army, road builders, Catholic missionaries, and unlicensed gold diggers as well as epidemics like measles that the invaders brought with them. There is no doubt that this process continues in 2021, with Amazonian deforestation so extensive that it has created a devastating feedback loop in which a megadrought expands due to shrinking sources of forest humidity (Spring 2021).

Spanish colonists called Indigenous Caribbean people "savages" for several reasons. They did not wear European clothing; according to Amerigo Vespucci (1505), they engaged in cannibalistic rites; and the Taínos and Caribs fought aggressive territorial disputes (Duviols 2017, loc. 7). While some Europeans believed that the Indigenous people had a perfectible humanity, others like Fernández de Oviedo and Ginés de Sepúlveda believed they were incapable of acquiring European civilization. By the second journey of Columbus, the travel accounts of doctor Diego Álvarez Chanca and Michele da Cuneo, and shortly after the travel accounts of Amerigo Vespucci, with their depictions of anthropophagy, contributed to the circulation of the idea of Indigenous people as "primitives," a topos that persisted for centuries (Duviols 2017). The travel accounts of Hans Staden (1525–76),

André Thevet (1516–90), and Jean de Léry (1536–1613), who lived with or close to Indigenous people, tended to confirm the racial prejudices of Europeans (Duviols 2017, loc. 9). This barbarization and dehumanization of the Indigenous people set the stage for enslavement, genocide, land invasion, and theft.

The Spanish Crown authorized the colonists to enslave Indigenous people if they resisted evangelization (Taussig 1986, 84). Although the Spanish colonial laws called the Leyes de Burgos or Ordenanzas Reales para el buen regimiento y tratamiento de los Yndios (1512) were issued to abolish slavery and protect the Indigenous people of Hispaniola from exploitation in plantations and gold mines, they also organized the conquest and conversion of Indigenous people and dismissed Indigenous religious and cultural practices as inferior compared to European ones (Stone 2021, 55). During colonization the extirpation of Indigenous religious practices was a central concern for the Spanish colonial empire, and stigmatization continues to this day, as several chapters in this book show.

The French colonial Code noir (Black code) of 1685 explicitly "forbids" all religious practice besides the "Roman, Catholic, and Apostolic Faith" in which the newly arrived enslaved people were required to be "instructed and baptized." So important was Catholic exclusivity in the eyes of the code's composers that they inserted these instructions at the very beginning, in articles 2 and 3. Explicitly anti-Vodou laws are documented from 1727 in Saint-Domingue until their elimination in 1987 in Haiti (Ramsey 2011, 32). In the eyes of colonial law, Indigenous and African diaspora religions were dangerous practices with threatening political and military potentialities. Enforcers of colonial traditions have used legal measures to harm Indigenous and African diaspora practitioners and to enact special privileges for the Catholic and Christian religions of the colonists and their descendants. The Washington National Cathedral is just one example of how the conquerors enshrined Christianity's privilege in the capital of the United States.

The enslavement, genocide, displacement, containment, and erasure of Indigenous and African diaspora people in the United States reflects an immense, century-spanning process. The enslavement of primarily Africans and African Americans began around 1620 in the thirteen British colonies and continued in the United States until 1865. Over the same period imperial-minded U.S. citizens waged war on Native Americans. The Indian Removal Act of 1830 legalized and institutionalized the forced displacement of Native Americans from the eastern to the western United States between 1830 and 1847. Native American "reservations" are still scattered all over the western United States. In 1883 the U.S. commissioner of Indian affairs, Hiram Price, published the Code of Indian Offenses, which outlawed Indigenous religious practices like the "sun-dance," the "scalp-dance," and the "war-dance" (article 4) as well as the "practices of so-called 'medicine-men'" (article 6), including the "arts of a conjurer" (Price 1883). Opposition to Indigenous language, culture, and religion also drove another nineteenth-century policy of separating Native American children from their families. Between 1860 and 1978, thousands of Native American children were sent to Native American boarding schools operated by Christian organizations with the goal of Anglo-Americanizing them and erasing their Indigenous languages and identities (Pember 2019). Many crimes and abuses took place at schools like St. Mary's Catholic Indian Boarding School on the Ojibwe Reservation in Odanah, Wisconsin, well into the latter part of the twentieth century (Pember 2019; Smith 2007).

Illustrating how a prototypical prejudice replays across colonial time, the example of U.S. occupiers (1915–34) like Beale Davis (1925) accusing Haitian Vodouists of cannibalism to justify the United States's military occupation stands out because there is scant evidence of anthropophagy in Haiti or Africa. Likewise, the managers of Brazilian rubber companies accused the Indigenous people of the same, exploiting centuries of colonizer folklore to justify their brutality (Taussig 1986, 85). In the Dominican Republic, the practice of Vodou exacerbates discrimination against Haitian migrants due to negative stereotypes that have been transmitted by mainstream society, the Catholic Church, and media (Ferguson 2003, 7). At least until the middle of the twentieth century, Garifuna people were accused of killing children for cannibalistic rituals (Taylor 1951, 132). As a result of this hostility, many religious traditions have disappeared, and those that have survived into the contemporary period persist because there is a concentration of settled people from common ethnic groups who practice together but nevertheless face great socioeconomic obstacles.

In the case of the Taíno Indigenous people of Hispaniola or Puerto Rico, survivors of the Spanish conquest mixed with African and European cultures to create various Creole cultures. Words of Taíno origin like *zemi* (or *cemí*, statue or figure of divinities), *ranmak* (hammock), or *gwayav* (guava) persist in Haitian Creole while "barbecue," "maize," "potato," "canoe," and "hurricane" are Taíno words that have been transferred through early American Spanish into English and many other languages of the Caribbean region and beyond. Taíno people fled Europeans if they could and resettled where they were able to, including in South America and on the island of Grenada, where seventeenth-century Taíno refugees buried cemíes in fields to improve harvests (Stone 2021, 164). What we know about the Taíno is archaeological but no less important for that.

Practitioners of African diaspora traditions have inherited oppressive circumstances enforced by the descendants of colonizer peoples. In Black majority states like Haiti, independent since 1804, Vodouists still face dire economic conditions and persecution from Christian extremists, both foreign and domestic. Perceptions of Vodou and other ecstatic traditions have been dominated by defamatory pop-culture stereotypes. While African diaspora spirit-based religious traditions are more stable in Salvador, Bahia (Brazil), Port-au-Prince, or, in the United States, Miami, many practitioners face serious economic and societal hardships. The situation among practitioners of Indigenous spirit-based traditions is equally critical. Invasion, genocide, epidemics, deforestation, mining, industrialization, pollution, large-scale monoculture agriculture, forest fires, slash and burn farming, and forced displacement have devastated Indigenous peoples and their traditions from Alaska to Georgia to the Amazon and Patagonia, as well as every place in-between (Anderson 2014; Bacigalupo 2016; Haveman 2016; Kopenawa and Albert 2010; Ostler 2019; Stone 2021). Avaricious resource extraction and land thefts are still unfolding today in the Amazon basin, in Standing Rock, in North and South Dakota, and in Southern Chile, among countless other locales.

Amid the imperial nations of the Americas, cultural transfer, hybridization, and opposition to colonial societies opened new spaces for the survival and transformation of spirit-based traditions. Forced and voluntary migration—for example, in the context of slavery and marooning—created spaces of encounter between different Indigenous and African diaspora groups. The African Americans who escaped slavery in the South and joined Seminole communities in Spanish Florida (1513–1763, 1783–1821) are one such group (Ortiz 2018, 36, 43; Sattler 1996). Methodist missionary observers in the 1780s on St. Vincent claimed that the Caribs and West Africans shared a culture of protective "charms," and that both chanted to ward off "evil spirits" and their malignancies (Taylor 2012, 97). John Baxter, Methodist missionary, was unable to influence the Black Caribs and left rapidly. By the 1790s English colonists were hatching plans to deport the Black Caribs so that they could reward fellow loyalist refugees from North America with stolen lands.

Throughout the Americas state-sanctioned land theft spurred opposition, war, defeat, and forced migration on foot of entire Indigenous nations that were thrust into areas with less arable land. As conquest and occupation expanded, many Indigenous and African diaspora people continued to worship their ancestral spirits, sometimes with the admixture of Christian practices or the renewal of African sources, as contact with Africa has increased. In this way traditions continue to evolve, develop, and rejuvenate themselves in the multilingual and multicultural colonial and neocolonial settings that encompass the Americas.

Spirit-based religious traditions have been present in the Americas across vast geographical and cultural expanses. Although differences exist between them, they deserve deeper examination. Exploring fundamental Indigenous and African diaspora ideas about *being* and *time*—ontology and history—offers resources for discovery, to which we now turn.

ONTOLOGY AND HISTORY IN DIASPORA TRADITIONS

Two interwoven emphases are important to examine in Indigenous and African diaspora traditions. Ontological and historical notions permeate the work of practitioners and scholars alike. The emphasis in published writing on being or ontology reflects the concern for understanding how people interpret the existence of beings, including theories about their constitutions and interdependencies. The emphasis in published writing on history is concerned with lived, remembered, and interpreted people and events. Practitioner historians preserve the cultural, ethnological, musicological, ritual, mythological, medicinal, and linguistic traditions of the community. Gaining a grasp on ontological and historical ideas in Indigenous and African diaspora traditions is essential for approaching the worldview of the peoples who practice them.

Indigenous ontologies are largely built on the idea of interdependence and reciprocity between different kinds of beings. In the Amazonian context, this holistic view has been described with the concepts of "multinaturalism" and "perspectivism" (Viveiros de Castro 1998). "Multinaturalism" means that people, animals, and plants are interrelated in dependencies and layers of similitude. This reflects the idea of the "unity of the spirit and the diversity of bodies" and the idea that "the universe is inhabited by diverse types of protagonists or subjective agents, human and non-human," who share a similar "soul" (Viveiros de Castro 2015, 350). Humans, spirits, animals, and plants are bound together through a common conceptual and volitional framework defined by the notion of "personhood," or "peoplehood," wherein the different "bodies" and "perspectives" coexist in a shared natural habitat of mutual dependencies (Viveiros de Castro and Skafish 2014; Oakdale 2018, 57).[3] "Perspectivism" refers to the point of view of spirits, humans, animals, the dead, and plants who are "intensively people, virtually people, for any of them can reveal themselves to be people" (Viveiros de Castro 2015, 383). The concepts of "personhood" and "perspective" reflect a common spectrum of degrees, contexts, and positions instead of the distinctive properties of a species (383). The principles of "multinaturalism" and "perspectivism" provide a basis for communication and metamorphosis between different kinds of corporeal forms (e.g., humans and animals), which is a core element in many American Indigenous religious traditions (Uzendoski and Calapucha Tapuy 2012, 10; Capper 2016, 164ff).

In line with this, Northern Amazon Yanomami shaman Davi Kopenawa speaks of "the spirits of the forest," "the spirits of the waters," "the animal spirits," and "the spirits of the bees" (Kopenawa and Albert 2010, 676). He also speaks of "animal ancestors" whose "images" visit him in dreams. All beings of the forest have an "*utupë* image" that is called down by the shaman (Kopenawa and Albert 2010, loc. 1355). These images are not the same as the flesh of the animals that people eat. In Yanomami ceremonies these animal spirits become *xapiri* spirits when they enter human bodies.

These praise performances illustrate the ritual enactment of ontological equivalency.

In Yanomami myth human ancestors had "animal names" in primordial times. These beings "metamorphosed" into animals, dressing themselves in animal "skins." These human ancestors are the prey of hunters to this day. The venerated animal ancestor spirits that dance as xapiri "spirits" descend in their "spectral" (*në porepë*) form, reflecting their true, nonphysical, and interior nature (Kopenawa and Albert 2010, loc. 1364). While the xapiri reflect human attributes like the healing arts, warfare, malevolence, or even race, they also link to nonhuman phenomena like thunder, dogs, and pollination (loc. 1545). The xapiri resemble humans in their predilection for nectar, ripe plantains, fruits, tobacco, and other plants (loc. 1605). However, the xapiri neither drink water nor eat meat, suggesting a degree of exceptionality from the natural plane.

The Arawakan Baniwa "ecology of the sacred" also reflects the interrelation and interdependency of various beings (Wright 2013, 21). The whole cosmos, as conceptualized by shamans, is populated by beings— "peoples"—from top to bottom, with varying degrees and qualities of spiritual power. Sky, earth, and water are the dwelling places of multiple kinds of living beings, visible and invisible, that interact with each other constantly. The fusion of the jaguar and the shaman in Baniwa ritual points to the personhood of powerful animals, and the fluent transition between the human and animal sphere.[4] Animals have souls that reside in "animal spirit worlds" located under the ground in small hills of the forest (142). According to Hohodene shamans, the demiurge Nhiãperikuli (the Eternal Master) has "a tribe of bee spirit-people" that produce a powerful healing honey, a concept that overlaps with Yanomami myth (224).[5] The Baniwa *pajé* (shaman) transforms into a cicada to "gain more knowledge" (36).

Another spirit animal, the harpy eagle, is the symbol of shamanic power throughout Amazonia and the Americas. This raptor nests atop the forest canopy, acting as the avian counterpart of the jaguar. The eagle's feathers are used to control weather, open cosmic portals, and induce lucid visions (Wright 2013, 174). In Baniwa ontology the eagle's feathers are imbued with power. The path of Baniwa ontological realization includes prolonged fasting and the consumption of the tree-based psychoactive substance called *pariká,* or DMT (26). After ingesting the DMT, the Baniwa shamans encounter the mythological figure of Kuwai, whose "blood" is said to be made of pariká (66). This meeting permits shamans to be the messengers of the great spirits. The Brazilian Kawaiwete (Tupi) shaman Prepori contacts spirits and totemic animals in the forest so that the shaman who hunts animals receives the blessing of the animals' spirit protectors (Oakdale 2018, 61, 65).

The Mapuche machi shamans of Chile and Patagonia also embrace an approach to ontology that reveals areas of comparability with Amazonian Indigenous traditions. Trees have a "power" that generates tree-cutting prohibitions (Bacigalupo 2016, 17, 157). The *rewe* is the "tree of life," and the axis mundi that assists machi possession (12). A large boldo tree conferred shamanic powers on machi Rosa Kurin and contained ancestral spiritual powers as well as the thunder spirit (17, 32, 156). Although native trees may possess spiritual power, non-native ones like eucalyptus and pine that the white settlers planted on monoculture plantations have led to ecological devastation from pest control and fumigation, an industrial process that destroys the "spirit masters of the native forest" (163). Power is obtained from thunderstones that encase spirits (22, 32). An evil serpent named Kaykay is associated with the deeds of wicked settlers, whereas a good earth serpent named Trengtreng is associated with machi Rosa, demonstrating not only the incorporation of mythology in the telling of history but also an ontology that embraces the peoplehood of humans and animals (36).

The ontology of the Indigenous Tupinambá (Tupi) shamans of Brazil reflects a path between people and spirits. The Tupinambá believe that a special person—mortal, but having traits of immortality—can become a deity (Fausto 2012, 274). Many famous spirits were once great shamans, pointing to enhanced ancestral veneration (274).[6]

The transition from great spiritual human being to spirit being is important in African diaspora traditions, as is the spectral dimension of forests. The approaches of Haitian, Cuban, Trinidadian, and Bahian specialists to ontology also centers on the idea that humans, ancestors, animals, plants, spirits, and natural phenomena participate in the "personhood of beings" (Viveiros de Castro 2016, loc. 379; Daniel 2005). In Haitian Vodou, Cuban Santería, Trinidadian Ṣàngó temples, and Bahian Candomblé, as in Indigenous traditions, spiritual categories are intensively and virtually "people" because they are revealed to be or are transformed into people in some degree, context, and situation (Viveiros de Castro 2016, loc. 379).

Communion with these spiritual categories is an important goal in African diaspora traditions (Daniel 2005, 55). "Social cohesion" with the living, the ancestors, and major spirits is established through ceremonial dance performances (55). In line with the principle of "personhood," specific personal information determines the dance performance for each *oricha* in Cuban Santeria (15).[7] The "personality and domain" (for example, love, war, agriculture, etc.) of the oricha guides the dance performance (15). Songs and dances are examinations of the ways the oricha behave. The mastery of the oricha system is a process completed by an initiation that imprints the spirits' personalities and traditions on the initiate (19).

Dance performance serves as a propitious setting for ritually encouraging the embodiment of lwa (Haiti), oricha (Cuba), òrìṣà (Trinidad), or *orixá* (Brazil) in the African diaspora traditions. Dreams, divination, contemplation of nature, or trauma are equally important contexts for contact with spirits. This embodiment—the possession performance—reflects the personification of the spirit, revealing knowledge about the entity's point of view (Viveiros de Castro 2016, loc. 422).[8]

Descriptions of the relationships of oungan or manbo with the lwa reveal dependencies among categories in Haitian Vodou. Many oungan and manbo assert that they are "almost lwa" or that they are "literally a lwa." The Vodouist has lwas that "represent various aspects of her or his personality" (Beauvoir and Dominique 2003, 89). This is illustrated in the observations that Vodouists make to identify spirits in the character of the people they know and themselves.[9] The Vodouist masters the layers of self and their rapport with the lwa, becoming assimilated with the personality of spirits through experiences of acculturation, possession, songs, dreams, liturgy, ceremonies, and prayer (89).[10]

In ceremonies, after the embodiment of the spirit in a human "horse," there is the greeting of the horse's rider, the spirit (Glazier 2009, 241–43). Members of the community form a line to greet the spirit in the formal salutation style of each tradition. The choreographed courtesies of the greeters emphasize the sacred character of the encounter (Daniel 2005,

25). The passing of sweat droplets from Legba's brow, for example, to the greeter's brow shows a unique encounter with the spirit's ceremonial personification.

In Bahian Candomblé the orixá are the diplomats of Olorun (the supreme being). Associated with nature and "mortal characteristics" of humans, the orixá must be "fed" and "loved" through ritual to appear in the bodies of their choice (Murrell 2010, 170). The orixá are matched up with the personal traits of their human servants for initiation (170). They also have "personality descriptors" that overlap with those of Catholic saints (170). Candomblé connects them to songs, rhythms, dances, colors, attire, liturgy, plants, pharmacopeia, food types, and sacrificial animals (Murrell 2010, 170; Daniel 2005). This symbolic system enhances the interrelation, dependency, and similitude of humans and spirits. Ṣàngó's devotees are concerned with his "personality traits and relationships between various members of the òrìṣà pantheon" (Glazier 2007, 233). In Trinidad the "personal relationships" of the òrìṣà Ṣàngó and his followers are symbolized in domestic altars, family, financial, and community matters (237).[11]

Haitian Vodouists keep close ties with their ancestors, as manbo Tansia explains to her initiate, Mimerose Beaubrun: "You must try to maintain a relationship with the *Zany* ("spirit, angel") of your family, with *Djèto a* (the ancestral soul)" (Beaubrun 2010, 78). The manbo adds that "personality is not your being" but "an image of yourself" that comes from concentration "on one aspect of your being," whereas "deep inside this image there is a being that no one knows, who is a mystery" (101). During her initiation a terrified Beaubrun is visited by a "spiritual snake" who manbo Tansia calls her *allié* ("spirit ally"), warning her that "you have perceived her as a snake because you have not changed position" (122). Manbo Tansia explains that "form is nothing but appearance," and if you change your perception, "the forms will change at the same time."[12]

Just as in Indigenous religious traditions, the animal world and the human world can fuse in African diaspora traditions. The serpent lwa Danbala and Ayida Wèdo are examples of spirits that blend human and animal attributes.[13] In Rada Rite ceremonies, initiates can transform into the serpent-spirits.[14] Here humans ritually and symbolically participate in the features of the serpent such as slithering on the ground horizontally and hissing. However, at the same time, the serpent-spirits provide their servants with advantages sought by people: protection, health, good luck, wealth, and fertility. Danbala's links to wealth and sexual health point to the lwa's traits of personhood.

Although the notion of the personhood of plants and nature, for example, seems to be less prominent in African diaspora religious traditions than in Indigenous ones, it can still be detected. In Haitian Vodou plants and leaves are consumed by candidates of initiation for the aim of achieving noticeable "effects" (Beaubrun 2010, 128). During the initiation, the spirit feeds leaves to the candidate (oungan Nelson Marcenat, personal correspondence, 2008). According to manbo Tansia, harvesting leaves and plants for the purpose of healing is akin to asking for the plant's "cooperation, to give a little of its energy through its leaf or bark, to grant pardon for having hurt it . . . for having made its blood run" (193). Under the lwa Gran Bwa's patronage, the *fèy lan bwa* (leaves in the woods) are picked for curing illness or inflicting harm (Jil and Jil 2009, 272). In a related vein, the Haitian water spirit Simbi is called upon to empower the Vodou priest and the healing leaves, suggesting their dependency on the spirits.[15]

The lwa, oricha, òrìṣà, or orixá are consulted through sacred leaves to connect to the sacred force, *ashe* (Murrell 2010, 132). Leaves, herbs, and trees are the natural basis of *ewe* (herbal) pharmacopeia, objects for ritual insignia, and symbols that guide people to the spirit world (Murrell 2010, 130–32). The title of Pierre Verger's 1997 book, *Ewe: The Verb and the Power of Plants among the Yoruba*, points to the vital power of plants. Cuban *santero* or *santera* diagnose and heal physical, mental, or interpersonal problems. The interactive energy between priests, plants, spirits, and patients produces "magical" healing (Murrell 2010, 132). Plants have "individual temperaments and personalities" that are connected to a specific spirit (132).[16] Plants are matched with spirits in ceremonies like initiation where the appropriate leaves are needed for purification baths and for seating the oricha (spirits) in the initiate's head (132). Healing and ritual plants accumulate ashe (divine energy) in ritual. In Amazonia and other parts of South America, *ayahuasca*, from Quechua *aya waska* 'vine of the dead', generally a mixture of the vine *Banisteriopsis caapi* and the bush *Psychotria viridis*, has a similar function of connecting people with spirits in ceremonies that combine religious, spiritual, and healing functions (Apud Peláez 2020, 17–18).

Various species of tree are considered sacred due to their impressive size, healing properties, and the impression they give of perpetuity. In Cuba, Haiti, Trinidad, Jamaica, and Brazil, the *ceiba pentandra* (silk-cotton tree, or *mapou*, in Haiti) is sacred, serving as an abode of spirits, a source for leaf medicine, and a natural temple for outdoor rituals (Séverin 2002, 52). Santeros and santeras believe that *bilongos* (spells) and *ebbos* (offerings) are buried at the foot of this tree. Haitian Vodou ceremonies, sacrifices, and libations frequently occur at the base of *pyebwa sèvi* (altar trees), the sacrificial blood connecting people, animals, nature, spirits and the universe itself (Beaubrun 2010, 128). In Lakou Souvenance near Gonaïves, people who have been unfaithful to the spirits are "held" in a temporary punishment by the protruding roots of the mapou tree (houngan Michelet Alisma, personal correspondence, 2014). According to Mayan cosmovision, a holy *ceiba* constitutes the axis mundi (Capper 2016, 150). Ceiba tree veneration is also common in Cuba and Jamaica, where it is generally considered to be an African diasporic element (Neill 2011, 362).[17]

In the African diaspora spirit-based traditions, the underlying sacred force called *ashe* (e.g., *ase*, *axé*) threads together humans, spirits, animals, and various species of plants and trees.[18] The traits of personhood in the categories reflect a common principle of ontology that structures African diaspora traditions. Historical concerns are significantly advanced in these traditions, and they are rarely severed from ontology and mythology.

The attention to *history* is a central concern of practitioners and researchers, including the chapters in this volume. Historical awareness is central due to its connection to the defense of identity and values in the face of European colonization, imperialism, and enslavement. Indigenous and African diaspora traditions conserve and make history in oral, textual, and recorded traditions, a few examples of which are given below.

Contemporary Baniwa shaman Mandu da Silva's transmission of his biography and teachings illustrates the importance he assigned to establishing personal and communal historical records. Sacred narratives, songs, and discourses provide sources for interpreting the emergence of Baniwa "visionary prophets" who guided the communities to recover from destructive colonial forces (Wright 2013, 91). The Baniwa tradition of the "prophet jaguar-shaman" dates from the mid-nineteenth century (134). Prior to colonization shamans formed a class of elite ritual specialists and priests (222). The jaguar shamans turned to prophecy to warn society about colonial threats to the continuity of traditions and to assure society that their spiritual power was greater than that forced on them by the invasive colonial society (229). This Baniwa prophetic development drew from the creation narratives in which the Creator overcame the violence and predation of enemy tribes. Baniwa oral histories from the mid-nineteenth century recount how the prophet jaguar-shamans outwitted the colonial forces that sought to annihilate them. More than ten Tukanoan and Arawakan prophetic traditions are attested in the nineteenth century as well as several from the twentieth century (139–40). Thus, prophetic religion is a means of cultural preservation and resilience in a colonial context, a matter to be discussed later.

Alongside the history-making of the prophet jaguar-shamans, the Baniwa shamanic concept of the "circuit of temporality that connects humans to their first ancestors" demonstrates how mythological historical memory relates to the sacred ancestral sources of community and family life (Wright 2013, 171, 174). This cyclical time that connects the present to the primordial times is experienced during rites of passage. The psychoactive pariká (N,N-Dimethyltryptamine), is the "instrument of time travel" to that primordial world (171). The tools of Indigenous ontology like pariká are also tools for primordial historical knowledge. To this Indigenous notion of time travel through layers of history, Bacigalupo (2013) adds the notion of "multitemporal knowledge."

The Mapuche shamans in Chile and Patagonia are concerned with history via multitemporal trance techniques. Machi shamans use dreams, visions, and trances to "experience different temporalities—past, present, and future" (Bacigalupo 2016, 3). The thunder machi journey to different worlds and time periods as they master various realities, using multitemporal knowledge to bring the present back into equilibrium and restore hope. The machi embodies multitemporality by partaking in multiple personhoods that originate in various worlds and time periods through possession trance.

These historical personhoods are ancestors like the machi of previous times. Machi notions about historicity are linear in their attention to the events and progression of the past, and they are cyclical in their attention to multitemporal practices like possession trance that involve people of the past who reemerge in the present. Historical memory of this kind allows machi to reactivate community power in the present. Machi understand Chilean "national history" as an ideological "weapon of repression and control" that is disseminated by the state and schools (Bacigalupo 2016, 7). The achronological narratives of the machi aim to undermine the Chilean "national history" espoused by right-wing white settlers.

The Chilean state has advanced historical methods on behalf of settlers, including secularist traditions as well as Catholic ideologies that undermine machi practitioners. The machi shamans challenge the secular version of history promoted by the colonialist institutions (Bacigalupo 2016, 8–12). The machi shaman produces or disremembers history through texts, ritual objects, spirits, embodied ritual experience, and oral biographies of their lineage of machi, employing "temporal simultaneity in altered states of consciousness" to reorder history (11). The narrative technique of dislocating time periods allows for a conflation of the events and people of the present with those of the colonial past and neocolonial present.

In the nonlinear telling of history and the moral order, the Mapuche people are spiritual champions of history. The possession of machi Francisca Kolipi by past shamans, like the spirit of her mentor machi Rosa Kurin, made possible the telling of past stories and teachings for the purpose of reshaping present and future experiences. Although a "before time" and a "today time" are distinct in machi presuppositions, shamanic narratives mingle them through possession (Bacigalupo 2016, 35). Central to this reshaping of historical narratives is resistance to the invasive force of white settler colonialism.

One of the main expressions of historical thinking in Indigenous studies is the biographical genre of significant shamans, as illustrated in Ana Mariella Bacigalupo's (2016) work with the Mapuche machi Francisca Kolipi, Bruce Albert's work with Yanomami shaman Davi Kopenawa (Kopenawa and Albert 2010), and Robin M. Wright's (2013) work with Baniwa shaman Mandu da Silva. The biography is a valuable methodology for historical preservation, since it examines a person's life in the social and historical context, shifting from local to global, preserving the ideas and experiences of the shaman and community (Bacigalupo 2016, 14). The biographies of great Mapuche, Yanomami, and Baniwa shamans help to create "shamanic historical consciousness" that "reshapes history" because they tell history from Indigenous perspectives (28, 35). The hardships of colonialism spurred a focus on historical narratives among the machi (190).

The historical "revisionism" of machi shamans advances moral projects that allow their communities to change attitudes and improve living conditions. For example, machi and *longko* (community leader) narratives analyze the Mapuche as civilized, respectful, and responsible people in contrast to marauding European settlers who steal land and murder Native people (Bacigalupo 2016, 194). Machi historical narratives have contributed to a shift in the attitudes of right-wing Mapuche. Instead of glorifying Chilean military traditions, Mapuche traditions are embraced as diplomatic, peaceful, and civilized. These historical narratives legitimate the Mapuche as a sovereign nation that is morally grounded.

The moral order in Mapuche shamanic history centers on calmness, responsibility, and seriousness and emphasizes egalitarianism, community labor, social contacts, parliamentarianism, care for spiritual teachers, and the acquisition of knowledge (Bacigalupo 2016, 196). These values are understood in opposition to the ecologically destructive ones like individualism, entrepreneurship, industrialism, and consumerism emphasized by European colonists. Mapuche historical revisionism opposes systems of control and repression like the military, the police force, the judicial system, and prisons (143).

Machi spirits are repositories of Mapuche history (Bacigalupo 2016, 221). Spirits, ancestors, and animals of past times reappear by possessing shamans. Possession reconnects people with knowledge about the past and empowers them in the present. The "reborn" spirits and ancestral machi act as "historical agents" who interpret from a Mapuche perspective, instilling resilience as well as strategies for living in the present (222). The machi and national spirits as well as the machi and local spirits are "resingularized" and "historicized" in remembering communities (223). In this process of machi becoming spirits, the sacred qualities of the collective spirits (*filew*) accrete to memories of the machi, transforming them into spiritual beings. This process reveals the interweaving of historical, ontological, and mythological thinking, trends that are equally central in African diaspora traditions.

Haitian Vodou and Bahian Candomblé illustrate historical concerns in African diaspora religions. Practitioners of Haitian Vodou's Sèvis Ginen "Ginen Service," centered in Léogâne and Port-au-Prince, rigorously preserve the history of Haiti's African religious legacies in a multirite system that stands out compared to the single-rite systems of temples around Gonaïves (e.g., Lakou Souvenance's Danwonmen Rite or Lakou Nan Badjo's Nago Rite). The creators of the Sèvis Ginen have included numerous leading African ethnonational religious traditions under a single umbrella, syncretizing diverse African traditions under one banner.

Oungan and manbo of Sèvis Ginen practice ceremonial rites (*rit*) such as the foundational Rada Rite (from Allada and Hueda), Nago Rite (from the Yoruba), Petwo and Kongo Rite (from the Kongo), Gede Rite (from the Gedevi people of the Abomey plateau), Ibo Rite (from the Igbo in eastern Nigeria), Danwonmen Rite (from the Fon people of the kingdom of Dahomey), Makaya Rite (from the Kongo), and the Wongòl Rite (from Angola), among others, preserving historical facts about the diverse African traditions they federate under the banner of 21 Nanchon Ginen (21 African Nations).

Oungan and manbo recall in oral and textual tradition extensive canons of spirits, their personalities, an encyclopedic range of songs, oral traditions, magical practices like spells, vèvè diagrams, and ancillary traditions related to Catholic Saints. The data sets and degrees of maturation associated with Sèvis Ginen are so demanding that the *kanzo* initiation has three rankings: beginner, intermediate, and priest or priestess. There are over 100 lwa in just the Rada Rite with historical antecedents in the Bight of Benin (Beauvoir 2008b, 187–96; Hebblethwaite 2021, 134–83). Over 1,700 Haitian Vodou songs are collected in Beauvoir's (2008a) corpus. The majority of lwa are organized into rites that mirror the regions of Africa from which they come. Hundreds of lexical items in the Haitian Vodou lexicon originate in Aja, Fon, Gedevi, Yoruba, or Kikongo languages and histories. The female lwa Èzili Dantò illustrates the historical linguistic dimensions of Haitian Vodou language. "Azili" (Èzili in Haitian Creole) is a rivulet near Abomey, the erstwhile capital of the kingdom of Dahomey, while "Danto" (Dantò in Haitian Creole) is a stream to the east of the town of Savalou, situated north of Abomey—two examples of how African toponyms can offer evidence about the origins of African diaspora religious traditions (Hebblethwaite 2021, 73; Verger 1957, 552).

The second example of the historical resources of African diaspora traditions is illustrated in the Xangô traditions of Bahia, Brazil. Xangô's connections to Ṣàngó's power in Yoruba history as well as his transformation into a powerful orixá in Bahia should be examined to understand how the orixá's followers contributed to building Bahian history. Ṣàngó's mythology connects him to thunder as well as an historical link to the Oyo Empire's supreme ruler, the Aláàfin. Traditions report that the historical Ṣàngó was one of the great Aláàfin who expanded the Oyo Empire by defeating the town of Òwu (Fọláránmí 2009, 158).

Details of Ṣàngó's historical existence are contradictory, but a few are repeated. Ṣàngó, who was the child of Odédé and grandchild of Òkànbí, lived in Òkò village and became a powerful ruler of the Oyo Empire. After a council of elders lost confidence in him, Ṣàngó hung himself in Kòso and was deified by his followers, as was the custom for the kings of Oyo (Akínyẹmí 2009, 190, 193). The themes of royalty, justice, malevolence, volatility, and vengefulness permeate the legends, songs, and personal qualities of Ṣàngó (Fọláránmí 2009, 174). Due to its royal status and prestige, the cult of Ṣàngó emerged as a means for Oyo's Aláàfin to secure the loyalty of the people, demonstrating the place of this òrìṣà tradition in Oyo's politics.

The attributes of royalty and justice are also pivotal in Bahia, where Xangô's devotees helped found several temples (Parés 2009, 250). "Ìyá-Nàsó"—the formal Yoruba title for a high priestess in Oyo—was also the name of a nineteenth-century priestess who freed herself from enslavement, returned to Africa, and then traveled back to Bahia to lend her strength to help build a prominent Xangô temple that fused people from Oyo and Ketu. Similarly, in São Luis, Brazil devotees of Xangô helped found a Casa de Nagô alongside the Casa de Mina, becoming one of the main traditions. Xangô's cultural importance in Bahia is also reflected in the wide adoption of the Yoruba *abatá* drums (253).

Parés (2009, 252) argues that Ṣàngó-Xangô's "symbolic representation as a king" and his status as an "icon of power, aristocracy, and leadership" capable of overcoming all sorts of adversities made him attractive to orixá devotees. As historical and symbolic king of Oyo, he was viewed as the king of kings. A "historical" and "humanized" tradition exists alongside a "mythological" one, and both invigorate the tradition with meaning (254). The instantiation of Xangô's influence is reflected in the multidivinity Nagô temples in which a "court" of orixá gather around the "king" Xangô (255). In mythology the Bahian Xangô is also connected through marriages and his children with a diversity of other orixá, revealing his role as an important node who aggregates a pantheon of divinities. Xangô in Bahia, as the symbol of kingship and leadership, forms an "ideal-type" or "brand" that symbolizes and consolidates the solidarity of African Brazilian practitioners (265). Service to Xangô, as to other lwa, oricha, òrìṣà, and orixá, contributes to making and preserving religious history in Haiti, Cuba, Trinidad, Bahia, and elsewhere.

Practitioners of Indigenous and African diaspora traditions envision humans, ancestors, spirits, animals, plants, and nature as interrelated in dependencies and layers of similitude. The relatability and efficaciousness of the categories depends on their peoplehood, the features of personality, volition, and a vital force—ase, ache, ashe, or axé. Both traditions are anchored in the historical and mythological traditions that encode ethnic, linguistic, identity, and organizational properties, and have played an important role as a means of cultural resilience and resistance in colonized communities. The next section intensifies the examination of convergences in Indigenous and African diaspora traditions.

CONVERGENCES OF SPIRIT-BASED TRADITIONS

The spirit-based traditions of North and South America may have been faintly shaped over the vast span of time by those of ancient Siberia and the Arctic. The African affinities of African diaspora spirit-based traditions are demonstrated straightforwardly. Robin M. Wright (personal correspondence, 2019) suggests that Indigenous traditions of the Americas possibly reflect an ancient Asian substratum dating from approximately 18,400 to 15,000 BCE, whereas the African diaspora traditions reflect a recent African influence dating from circa 1500 to 1850 CE.

Kehoe (2000, 69–70) points out that subsuming the practices of Siberians and South Americans under the label of "shamanism" is profoundly flawed. Entheogens are not necessarily used in Siberia, whereas their use is widespread in South America; the drum is common in Siberia but relatively uncommon in South America (65). For this reason the use of the term "shaman" in this volume typically denotes an Indigenous American healer who works with spirits and may or may not include entheogens in her or his practices. Likewise, the term "priest" in the context of Indigenous religions refers to a religious expert who in his or her work focuses on formal, memorized traditions of knowledge, including the lineage of priests and kings, canonical knowledge like songs and liturgies and the spiritual mythology of kings. The terms do not straightforwardly distinguish Indigenous leadership roles from African diaspora ones. The weakness of translated terms like "shaman" or "priest" is their lumping of healers and priests of unrelated traditions together into putative types when the overlaps and distinctions are immensely complex (102).

Commonalities between Indigenous and African diaspora traditions are significant. "Shamanism," "Vodou," "Santería," "Candomblé" and other equivalent terms refer to the shaman's or the priest's complete world of practices, including those relating to spirits, curing and therapeutic techniques, social welfare and governance, dream interpretation, the ownership of songs and intangible culture, and even warfare (Fausto 2012, 187–88). Shamans and priests *work* for patients and their community, and their work of struggling with spirits is exhausting (Kehoe 2000, 42).

Although "shaman" and "priest" are useful generalizations for academic delineation between the two traditions, it is not uncommon for Vodou priests to also consider themselves "shamans," just as we see priestly traditions in Indigenous societies (see Beauvoir 2008a). Shamans and priests defend the psychic integrity of their communities from demons, illnesses, and evil sorcerers (Eliade 1987, 8273). Some shamans and priests are confirmed through initiatory traditions. For instance, Davi Kopenawa's narratives on Yanomami shamanic initiation, Haitian Vodou's *deka* or kanzo initiations, or Santería's *kariocha* initiation, among many others, entail the journey of the initiate to a deeper relationship with her or himself and with spirits. Both Indigenous and African diaspora initiatory traditions include isolation, trials, and an encounter with spirit culture. Symbolic death and rebirth are fundamental traits of both initiatory traditions (as well as in Christian belief, albeit under different guises), and shamans and priests experience types of possession or trance. Through spiritual exploration, maturation, and a calling to public spiritual service, both work with spirits to impart advice in consultations and to restore balance among people.

One of the central shared functions of shamans and priests is their healing practice, where prayer combined with leaf medicine is the basis for cures and magic (Brown 2005, 3822; Wright 2013, 136). We find this combination already in Pané's description of Taíno practices, which was one of the historical substrates of Haitian Vodou. It also seems to be common for historical and contemporary southern Indigenous cultures (Roth 1924, 240ff) as well as for Garifuna people. Russell and Rahman (2015) note that tobacco is a leaf medicine that is smoked or mixed with other substances (such as ashes or salt) in the mouth for spiritual practices across Indigenous religious traditions, and it was also introduced in African diaspora practices since colonial times. Among many Caribbean and South American Indigenous groups, a substance called *yupa*, *ñopo*, or *kurupua* (*Piptadenia peregrina*) is used for ceremonial intoxication (Roth 1924, 243ff). Baniwa reverence for the spirit Nhiãperikuli includes chewing of the coca leaf (Wright 2013, 239).

An open disposition toward other traditions of knowledge often accompanies these practices. The Amazonian shaman Prepori and the Haitian Vodou priest Michelet Alisma, for instance, both embrace Western medicine, affirming that both their own as well as Western traditions may be appropriate depending on the type of sickness that is being dealt with (Oakdale 2018, 65; oungan Michelet Alisma, personal correspondence, 2014). For instance, *pajés* (shamans) believe that Western medicine can be helpful in treating ailments transmitted or sent by white people whereas Indigenous medicine treats ailments beyond the scope of Western medicine (Wright 2013, 20).

Shamans and priests recruit supernatural helpers or spirits that dwell within people, in rocks, rivers, crystals, trees, and impressive natural sites. Some shamans in South America get married to spirit-wives or spirit-husbands in a tradition comparable to the marriage of spirit Èzili Freda and devotee in African diaspora traditions, although being a priest is not a requirement in the latter (Furst 2005, 8290). For example, Baniwa shamans marry bird-spirit-wives and, with them, have children who are auxiliaries to the shamans; similarly, Yanomami shamans have relations with female water spirits (Wright, personal correspondence, 2020). A spirit wedding intensifies the relationship between devotee and spirit. Furthermore, spirits that cause or block illness are supernaturally sent or recalled in both traditions (Eliade 1987, 8272). Normative religion aims to heal and protect while nonnormative aims to harm and usurp, and both exist in religions worldwide.

Animal sacrifice in Mapuche ritual in Chile, for example, symbolizes transformation, restoration of the cosmic moral order, preparation for a feast, the containment and restructuring of violence, and the appeasement of the spirits and the dead—motivations relatable to sacrifice in African diaspora traditions (Bacigalupo 2016, 99). In Mapuche traditions sacrifice reinforces reciprocal relationships with ancestral spirits and the deity Ngünechen (82). In Cuban Santería, the blood of animal sacrifice "feeds" the orichas, and they reciprocally favor the people who offer the sacrifice (Ayorinde 2005, 215).

Another comparable feature shared by shamans and priests is their connection with "other worlds." Both types of practitioners access an "upper world" and an "under world" of spirits (Frese and Gray 1987, 9334). Trees are fundamental axes that serve as pathways from the sky to the earth and back again and sacred mediators in religions around the world. Spiritual power streams off powerful trees, which have symbolic manifestations such as the *potomitan* (center post) around which Vodou worshipers circulate, the ceiba in Middle American and Caribbean Indigenous and African diaspora traditions (Neill 2011; Capper 2016), or the Mapuche rewe (axis mundi) that includes branches of the foye and triwe trees around which machi Francisca Kolipi carried out rituals (Bacigalupo 2016, 68). Spirits and ancestors live in trees, sometimes represented by a given species (Brown 1991). The Amazonian Baniwa cosmos is understood as a world-tree that the shamans must ascend in their healing practices (Wright 2013). Shamans and priests employ trees to assert their powers to communicate with the celestial and chthonic worlds in their work to heal and transform the community. Trees provide bark, sap, roots and leaves for medicine as well as compounds for psychoactive drugs like pariká that the Hohodene Amazonian people find in the Great Tree of the deity Kaali (226).

Indigenous and African diaspora traditions alike use language as the bedrock for maintaining sacred culture. On the one hand, intelligible varieties of languages like Haitian Creole or Navajo are used in contemporary songs, prayers, and rituals (Beauvoir 2008a and 2008b; Gill 1981). On the other hand, special ritual languages or language fragments that are only understood by spiritual adepts are documented for several Indigenous and African diaspora communities. Archaic language that is unintelligible to uninitiated contemporary people includes the ritual language of the historical Island Caribs and their modern descendants, the Garifuna people (Taylor 1950, 116–17); Haitian Vodouists' use of *langaj* in fragments of speech (Beauvoir 2008b); Abakuá ritual language in Cuba (Cabrera, Miller and Gómes-Cásseres 2020); Kikongo in hymns maintained in Palenque, Colombia (Schwegler 1996); Yoruba in the Şàngó temples of Trinidad (Simpson 1962); or "ancient words" among the Chamula in Mexico (Wheelock 1987, 5303). Likewise, the use of ceremonial languages is a general feature of Amazonian Arawakan cultures (Santos Granero 2002, 31; Eriksen 2011, 250; Aikhenvald 2012, 365). Archaic ceremonial language reflects ancestral language that became extinct due to migrations, slavery, or colonization within the American hemisphere. Archaic words, expressions, and songs are retained in religious textual and oral traditions due to their proximity to revered ancestors and memories. Archaic language can provide valuable evidence about migration, as well as cultural change and assimilation in the past: for example, a spirit like Simbi provides a path into Haiti's Kikongo past while a spirit like Ogou provides a path into Haiti's Yoruba past. Likewise, the Chané and Tariana Indigenous groups of South America today speak Chiriguano (Tupian) and Tucano, but have maintained their ancient Arawak language in religious ceremonies (Eriksen 2011, 250).

Indigenous and African diaspora traditions describe the directional relationship with spirits in complex, complimentary, and contrasting ways. One notion that has been overemphasized by scholars is the supposed "directionality" of relations between spirits and specialists. The Indigenous shaman is said to travel to the world of the spirits where he or she "controls them" without serving as their instrument (Eliade 1987, 8269). In Kopenawa's account of his initiation into Amazonian Yanomami shamanism, however, the xapiri spirits actively visit people with a shamanic disposition via dreams, through the *yãkoana* (DMT) bark powder, and in healing ceremonies in which spirits detect and extract illness through a shaman (Kopenawa and Albert 2010, loc. 2458). The hallucinogenic bark powder entails a dramatic "journey" that the Yanomami imbiber undertakes to become a spirit (loc. 2422). Some experiences of taking yãkoana are described as journeys to the houses of the xapiri spirits. Once the imbiber or shaman returns from those inspirited worlds, they share words and alert their followers about what they discovered and learned (loc. 5611). Spirits and humans fluidly travel from this world to other worlds in Indigenous traditions for the purpose of gaining knowledge.

In African diaspora ceremonial contexts, the spirit travels to the specialist and *pran* (takes) or *monte* (mounts) the human "horse" in a possession performance or ritual. That journey may be from Ginen, from a tree where the spirit rests, or from deep within the individual's soul, where the spirits are latent (Beaubrun 2013). Adepts also travel to the world of spirits by "going under the sea" for special teachings (Brown 1991) or on pilgrimages to a natural altar of a spirit, like the waterfalls of Saut-d'Eau, Haiti, where the servants of the lwa Èzili congregate annually. Another example of a Vodou specialist "traveling" to the other world is the ritual, 366 days after the burial of a family member, in which a priest travels to the dead to retrieve the departed soul who returns through the priest to the gathered family members (Deren 1953).

Shamanic trance is sometimes described as "voluntary," while African diaspora trance is described as "involuntary" (Rouget 1990, 73). Critical thinking tends to shatter that reductionistic notion. In African Brazilian traditions, for example, the devotee in early phases of social integration experiences involuntary possession, but over time they become voluntary as the host "gains control of his or her spirit" (Crapanzano 1987, 8688). In the case of multidivinity traditions like Haiti's Sèvis Ginen, spirit possession tends to be sudden and intense, although it may be somewhat attenuated when the "horse" is a priest or priestess. The singing, lyrics, drumming, gestures, and ritual objects are codified, kinesthetic, and accumulative in Cuban, Haitian, and Bahian traditions (Daniel 2005, 19–20). A Haitian Rada Rite "cycle of salutation" for the lwa Èzili Freda, for instance, is a propitious time for the appearance of Èzili. Ritual combines rigid codification with accumulating enthusiasm driven by drumming, dancing, and singing.

The ecstatic trance of the shaman is mainly induced by means of psychotropic plants, and this is a significant difference from African diaspora traditions of ecstatic trance (Boomert 2000; Furst 2005, 8290). The Yanomami shaman encounters spirits after imbibing the yãkoana DMT bark powder. Baniwa pajés like Mandu da Silva consume pariká (DMT) and fall into "trance," which they call *maliume* (unconsciousness), going on journeys of the soul (including leaving the body) and retrieving sacred songs from the spirit Kuwai in the sky, where burning resin purifies their "body-shaped souls" (Wright 2013, 83). The most common scenario for ecstatic trance in African diaspora traditions, in contrast, occurs during danced, drummed, and sung ceremonies that are musically, symbolically, socially, psychologically, and culturally oriented to the embodied expression of a spirit that usually correlates with the ritual underway. In this light the directionality of the Indigenous shaman on a soul journey *to* the spirits contrasts straightforwardly with the spirit journeying *to* the human "horse" in African diaspora ecstatic trance.

The mythologies and traditions of spirits in Indigenous and African diaspora traditions share numerous similarities. Symbolic foods and drinks, either prescribed or prohibited, represent spirits and their congregations. Baniwa spirit Kuwai's death gave rise to the flutes made from the *paxiúba* palm tree while the Haitian Vodou spirit Ayizan carries the palm frond *ayizan* (Wright 2013, 170; Hebblethwaite 2021). Domains like metallurgy are connected to Omama in Yanomami mythology and Ogou across African diaspora congregations. Universal conditions like war and defense are the domains of Aiamori for the Yanomami and, again, Ogou for African diaspora congregations. Spirits are patrons of domains like hunting, love, death, work, and farming. Spirits are linked with nature, including the ocean, springs, leopards, jaguars, eagles, vultures, bees, and even pubic louses, in the case of Haitian Vodou's Gede spirits (Kopenawa and Albert 2010, loc. 3663; Hebblethwaite 2021, 205). Thus, in both American Indigenous and African diaspora traditions, spirits incarnate central aspects of fundamental human experiences. It should also be noted that religious traditions like Santo Daime (see Daschke in this volume) blend Indigenous consumption of psychoactive plants with service to African diaspora spirits.

In the traditional literature, it is asserted that some shamans become possessed, although it is considered exceptional (Eliade 1987, 8269). As we have seen, the shaman instead consumes an entheogen and travels on an ecstatic soul journey. At the same time, in the biographies of Yanomami shamans like Davi Kopenawa, readers discover that the xapiri (spirits) "dance" for people in ceremonies through shamans (Kopenawa and Albert 2010, 6881). Kopenawa's three hundred references to "dancing" consistently refer to the xapiris' "dances of presentation," which are ceremonial performances used to introduce the "image" of spirits (loc. 8178). Yanomami elders sang the songs of the spirits while dancing the dances of the xapiri, showing how Yanomami dance is a symbolic introduction to the world of spirits. Yanomami dances of presentation are reminiscent of Haitian Vodou dances like the serpentine spinal movements of the *yanvalou* dance for the Rada spirits Danbala and Ayida Wèdo, or the pelvic thrusting of the *banda* dance for the sexually knowledgeable Gede spirits. The dances provide symbolic instruction about the nature and class of different Vodou spirits, coding spirit culture kinesthetically and preparing the worshippers for the appearance of spirits in human vessels.

While the dances of presentation no doubt refer to Yanomami ceremonial religion, Yanomami shaman Davi Kopenawa frequently talks about how the shaman makes the "images" of the xapiri dance. The shaman is a specialist who sees the xapiri dance after consuming the yãkoana powder. The shaman, yãkoana, and the xapiri are bound together reciprocally in Yanomami religion (Kopenawa and Albert 2012, 1544–59). Yãkoana is the veritable food of the xapiri, so a shaman must imbibe it to feed the xapiri and keep them satisfied.

Similarities and differences in the experiences of coming into awareness of the spirits abound across traditions. This is described as the "clamor" of spirits who "take an interest in" and "show affection" for the person to work as a shaman or priest (Kopenawa and Albert 2010, loc. 790, 852, 972). In Haitian Vodou the calling can be experienced as a "mild sickness" (Richman 2005, 130) or in West African Vodun as "harassment" until initiation is completed (Le Hérissé 1911, 134). Both practitioners of Yanomami religion and Haitian Vodou talk about their journeys under the water, where the mysteries of the spirits are revealed. Kopenawa refers to the female "beings of the waters" (mãuyoma) who drew him to their dangerous aqueous "houses" (Kopenawa and Albert 2010, loc. 836, 1192). Since Kopenawa spent a lot of time on riverbanks, the "beings of the waters" incessantly captured his image "to make him dream" (loc. 851). The "beings of the waters" and the xapiri admire great hunters and potential shamans, desiring to take up residence in an altar near people they recognize (loc. 1026). Vodou manbo Mama Lola describes how the female spirit Lasirèn draws specialists under the water and back to Ginen, where they are trained in the "arts of diagnosis and healing" (Brown 1991, 224). Haitians say that people who seek answers in Vodou *mete pye nan dlo* (put feet into water). Analogously, worshippers are taken by the lwa after they submerge themselves in the waters at the pools at Lakou Souvenance or in the lwa Manbo Inan's river at Lakou Soukri (Saint-Lot 2003, 124). Water flows through Vodou rituals and symbols: the priest or priestess presents water to the cardinal points and a cup of it is always carried by a ritual assistant at her or his side in the Rada Rite.

Indigenous shamans and African diaspora priests either receive the spirits as an inheritance of the family, or they are called to service by the spirits at some point in their lives. The call of the spirits can be in infancy, adolescence, or adulthood, depending on when the spirit(s) call the individual, as understood within these cultures. Charismatic shamans and priests come to be recognized by a community for their leadership abilities, their ecstatic practices (possession or trance), their skillfulness in healing and divinatory arts, their knowledge of ritual and tradition, and their mastery of chants and songs. They are revered due to their excellence across a multitude of traditional arts (Eliade 1987, 8270).

In both traditions the acquisition of ecstatic and traditional practices is called "initiation," which entails a retreat guided by elders involving ceremonies, isolation from the community, fasting, visions, and the discovery of spirits. In Haiti alone several African diaspora initiations exist, including the approximately one week required to complete the kanzo initiation into Sèvis Ginen, or the shorter *deka* or *lave tèt* initiations associated with the Lakou traditions. They are expensive and mentally demanding formal entryways into membership in the various traditions.

Yanomami shaman Kopenawa, like the Vodou priest Michelet Alisma, began manifesting his vocation in childhood. The xapiri spirits would "frighten" Kopenawa in his sleep, whereas Alisma began healing people through the power of the lwa. Kopenawa's initiation occurred as he took up residence alongside his father-in-law, a respected shaman. Initiation is intimately connected with "drinking the *yãkoana*" and refining knowledge of the xapiri with the guidance of an initiating shaman who "gives" the initiate the xapiri spirits (Kopenawa and Albert 2010, loc. 1766). The initiator constantly blows the yãkoana into the candidate's nostrils, and he or she ensures that no person disturbs the spiritual journeys of the candidate. The candidate must retire from the world, avoid cold water, fast, endure thirst, cease sexual activity, and remain still as the xapiri feed the candidate "invisible food" (loc. 1791). For five days Kopenawa consumed exclusively yãkoana while the "wasp spirits" and "bee spirits" called *xaki* slowly devoured the fat on his body. Gradually, through the daily consumption of yãkoana, the candidate begins to see the xapiri "presenting themselves in dance" at night. The emaciation and hunger symbolize death and rebirth as "other," as "spirit," experiences confirmed vividly by yãkoana (loc. 1883, 2032). After the initiation the new shaman slowly begins to eat food again, avoiding salty or acidic foods and gaining weight.

The transition to shaman or priest is marked by important changes of behavior, both by those who inherit and by those who are called to the tradition. If the spirits called the future priest or priestess, he or she may be possessed from an early age. The specialist may begin a healing ministry while possessed by a spirit, regardless of age. Michelet Alisma, as mentioned above, was called to the priesthood through recurrent possessions at age seven, which attracted people for divination and healing. Likewise, the shaman may exhibit unusual behavior like self-isolation, emotional episodes, the occurrence of visions and dreams, bouts of unconsciousness, and extraordinary experiences (Eliade 1987). Among the Tupi people, shamans receive the songs of spirits through dreams and this mode of transmission during sleep is also common in African diaspora spirit religions (Fausto 2012, 277; Beaubrun 2013). For the Amazonian Tapirapé, dreams are the soul's journey out of the body to contact the spirits (226). In both traditions an illness can be interpreted as a sign from the spirits that an initiation is necessary (Richman 2005).

Priests, in addition to shamans, are also found in Andean cultures and in historic Amazonian cultures. "Priestly chanters" were distinct from "jaguar shamans" in Baniwa Arawak culture, for instance, although both were treated as *malikai* (powers). The priestly chanters served during life "transitions," and their knowledge was "canonical" rather than "ecstatic" (Wright 2013, 102). To cast Indigenous spiritual leaders as "shamanistic" and African diaspora leaders as "priestly" risks reducing diverse classes of religious authorities in both groups as well as diverse classes within specific societies. For example, Haiti's *bòkò* specialists deal with client-based divination, whereas the oungan and manbo specialists deals with congregations in communal religion.

Shamans and priests contribute to the social and political organization of their societies (Boomert 2000; Furst 2005, 8291). They may serve as advisers, confidants, diviners, oracles, and allies or opponents of powerful people. After contact with Europeans, prophetic shamans who denounced colonial violence arose in North and South America (Wright 2013). Shamans and priests mediate conflict, assume leadership in crisis, and are sought out to treat the sickest members of a community, contributing multivalently to social cohesion. In precolonial contexts leading Indigenous shamans and African Vodun priests were either aligned to political power or so distant from it that they were sold into slavery, as occurred with politically rebellious Vodun congregations in the kingdom of Dahomey (Bay 1998; Hebblethwaite 2021). People seeking political and economic power—as well as mere survival—patronize shamans and priests.

Religious specialists carried considerable social and political weight in the nineteenth century among the northern Plains cultures in the United States (Gill 1982, 164). As we saw with the Arawak Baniwa shamans, who arose as prophets after conflict developed with European Americans, millenarian movements led by prophets with revealed teachings simultaneously emerged among the Plains peoples. The Removal Act of 1830 and mounting military defeats drove an expectation for radical millennial transformation. A prophet among the Delawares in the eighteenth century foretold of divine intervention to return the land and to abandon alcohol. In the early nineteenth century, a Shawnee prophet advanced a reform agenda and worked to develop an "intertribal confederacy," but was killed in the

War of 1812 (164). Many Native American prophets came from backgrounds that exposed them to Indigenous as well as to settler traditions involving the Bible and Christian theology. A Paiute named Wovoka on the Walker Lake Reservation in Nevada combined the ancestor-affirming Ghost Dance movement with settler Christian traditions like Shaker religion during the 1880s.[19] During a health crisis Wovoka had a vision in which the dead gave him millennial instructions to prepare the Paiute people for the end times. They were to continue trance dances, live uprightly, and stop drinking and fighting. Combining the shamanism of his father with some settler traditions, his leadership reflected a bridging of cultures (Gill 1982, 165).

The Yanomami shaman Davi Kopenawa is an example of a practitioner with a global impact, mirroring the prophetic dimension of shamanism. He gives voice to Indigenous social and political concerns and crises, rendering comprehensible the apocalypse facing the Amazonian environment. Kopenawa and Albert (2010, loc. 3004) reveal the harrowing struggle of the Yanomami and other Indigenous peoples to survive the onslaught of *this* generation's "White" (les Blancs) invaders and the epidemics, pandemics, and violence they herald, followed by decimation, genocide, language extinction, deforestation, industrialization, new diseases, ecological collapse, the manufacture of machines, and the machines turning against people. Kopenawa describes the "ravaging of the forests" by unlicensed gold diggers seeking an "evil substance we had never heard of" (loc. 5640). "Cannibalistic epidemics" follow the roads, paths, smelteries, factories, and merchandise of the whites (loc. 6320). The whites' culture of accumulating merchandise further fuels "unlimited desire" (loc. 7004). The "words of merchandise" inspire the cutting of trees, the mistreatment of the land, and the soiling of the land (loc. 7005).

Between 1980 and 1990, Kopenawa visited several European nations and the United States, receiving the Global 500 Award for his environmental work. At a United Nations conference in 1992, he received legal recognition from the Brazilian state regarding a large tropical forest reserved exclusively for the Yanomami. Therein is illustrated his statecraft and skills in negotiation and conscience-raising, as recognized in 1999, when he was decorated with the Rio Branco by the president of Brazil (Kopenawa and Albert 2010, loc. 180).

In Haiti—as we learned during a visit there—Vodou communities have received government-funding for construction and the upkeep of facilities, like Lakou Souvenance during the René Préval government's second term (2006–11). Some politicians seek the blessing of important Vodou leaders in Haiti while campaigning or in power. Haitian president Jean-Claude Duvalier famously sought the advice of Vodou priests in 1986 as his rule was crumbling. They advised him to flee because his government had been "very, very bad" by ignoring the needs of the poor (Postlewaite 1985). After the assassination of president Jovenel Moïse in 2021, Haitian YouTubers described how he had served the lwa Bosou. Macolas Volmar's Vodou community Lakou 4 Drapo (Yard of 4 Flags) held a memorial ceremony seeking justice for the assassinated president (Ayiti Ayizan 2021). President Moïse's interment at the familial tomb was accompanied by a Vodou ceremony (News Haiti TV 2021). The footage reveals the profound concerns of Vodouists for the rule of law and legitimate political power, as well as their presence in rites of passage and ceremonies at the heart of Haitian social and political life.

The musical and spiritual instruments of the Indigenous shaman and the priest of African diaspora religion are similar, but we must keep in mind that drums and rattles are spread around the globe. In Indigenous and African diaspora traditions, sacred drums or rattles are used to call the spirits and to shift the consciousness of participants toward reverence, receptivity, and trance (Kopenawa and Albert 2010, loc. 42; Wilcken and Augustin 1992). In North American Inuit shamanism a sacred drum is beaten, and Lakota shamans use various drums. Although it has been claimed that drumming is not closely associated with South American traditions, in South American Mapuche shamanism, the *kultrung* (drum), the *kaskawilla* (sleigh bells), and the *wada* (calabash rattle) are used (Bacigalupo 2016, 3). The Baniwa pajé uses a sacred rattle called the *kutheruda* that represents his body and the gourd his head, but not a drum (Wright 2013, 91). The pebbles inside the pajé's rattle are named "celestial things." According to sixteenth-century sources, the Taíno people of the Caribbean used a drum called the *maguey* and *mayohabao*, or log drum (Martire d'Anghiera, *Decada* III, caput 7, 21, 392; Roth 1924, 466; Oliver 2021, 92). In the Guianas Indigenous and African diaspora people use similar kinds of rattles in dances and ceremonies, although it is not clear if they have the same historical origin (Roth 1924, 463–64). Drums were and are also widely used in South America (466ff), although they are more directly associated today with African diaspora religious expressions.

The gourd rattle, on the other hand, is a central instrument and symbol in South, Central, and North America in Indigenous and African diaspora religions. The fact of its small, handy size and portability, and the anthropomorphism by which it is represented, makes the rattle *the* most confederating instrument. Its handle represents the world tree, and the stones or seeds inside it invoke the ancestral spirits through shaking (Furst 2005, 8291). The salt song leaders of the Chemehuevi people of Southern California sing to the beat of a gourd rattle to bring "good medicine" to the people (Trafzer 2019, xv). For the Amazonian Baniwa, the rattle represents the shaman's body and soul in flight (Wright 2013, chap. 4). The maraca gourd rattle is retained in contemporary *ayahuasca* ceremonies in Europe (Goldstein and Labate 2018, 83).

In Haitian Vodou percussive instruments include the *manman* (mother drum), the *segon* (second drum), and the *boula* (small drum), in addition to a piece of iron called the *ogan*. Beaten together they produce an intense polyrhythmic sound texture. As for the manbo or oungan priests, she or he grips the *ason* (gourd rattle) with a bell, using them to direct the tempo of drummers, choreograph the dancers, and to activate, call, and send away spirits in the ason's shaking. To *pran ason* (take the rattle) is the highest honor in Vodou initiation. All initiates learn how to use the ason for personal use, but only the highest ranked initiates, the oungan and manbo can use one publicly in a ceremony. As Haitian Vodou drummers create a rhythmic foundation in services, the priest shakes the rattle and bell in her or his right hand. The drums provide the appropriate rhythmic foundation for the ritual in terms of rhythm style (e.g., *yanvalou* in Rada, *kongo* in Petwo-Kongo, *banda* in Gede), anticipating and hastening possession through intensification created not only via increasing the speed of the tempo but also via the *kase* (breaks) that jarringly disrupt the rhythm. After each cycle of salutation in a ceremony, the temple's main ason rattle is passed from one priest to another. She or he holds the ason in the air, directing the audience and the initiates to complete a *dogwe* (ground-touching ritual).

As the center of attention in Vodou ritual, the ason is a sacred priestly musical instrument and the most significant symbol of religious power conferred upon all Vodou initiates in the kanzo initiation.

Another similarity between shamans and priests is their identification with sacred animals. Across the American tropics, for example, the shaman identifies with the jaguar, the most powerful predator, as well as several other powerful animals, including the eagle, the anaconda, and the alligator or caiman, among others. Shamans, like those from the Tupi community, "transform into animals" like jaguars or harpy eagles, ritually pointing to the shared quality between humans and animals (Boomert 2000; Furst 2005, 8291; Fausto 2012, 289). From the multinaturalist point of view, they are reclaiming an aspect of peoplehood in a distinct guise. The shaman uses somersaults, jaguar teeth, pelts, and hallucinogens to represent the transformation into the spirit-jaguar. The Chemehuevi people of southern California sing ancient "bird songs" to bring about wellness and joy. These songs originate in a time when "people scattered like birds across the landscape" (Trafzer 2019, 5). Some of the main interlocutors of Amazonian Bororo or Tukano "horizontal shamans" are "animal spirits" who are frequent causes of sickness due to the "cannibal vengeance" the consumed animals inflict upon their human consumers (Viveiros de Castro 2014, 153–54).[20]

Jaguars are important in Indigenous shamanism because, as climbers, cave dwellers, and swimmers, they link the sky, land, and water. The Cubeo of the Northwest Amazon claim that the ferociousness of the jaguar has a human origin (Viveiros de Castro 2014, 69). Other symbolic species in shamanism include birds like eagles, vultures, parrots, macaws, and bats (Kopenawa and Albert 2010, loc. 2269). Eagle and hawk feathers, along with pipes and medicine bundles, were sacred among the Cahuilla people of southern California (Trafzer 2019, 45). Indigenous naming traditions in North America sometimes symbolically link powerful animals and their attributes to people such as "Blue Eagle," "Great Buffalo High Chief," "Sitting Bull," "Black Hawk," "Black Elk," "Lone Horn," "Spotted Elk," and "Crazy Horse" (Anthes 2014). Most Eastern Woodland nations, such as the Florida Seminoles, include clans named for "animal or plant totems," including wolf, deer, and bear (Fixico 2014, 264). Among Western Indigenous nations, "military societies" or "age-group societies" also had "clan totems" such as the Lakotas who had the "young bull society," the "old shields society," the "elk society," and the "old bull society" (264). These names that draw on fauna instantiate the Indigenous ontology that identifies and comingles the peoplehood of diverse beings.

Identification with animals and their attributes is also common in African diaspora religions. As discussed above worshippers possessed by the serpent spirit, Danbala Wèdo, slither like snakes on the ground, those possessed by Agasou become panthers, and those possessed by Agwe become fish-like by puckering their lips. Specialists of Vodou can even transform into owls or other birds, but this is considered an advanced practice (Beaubrun 2013). Danbala is described like the jaguar with respect to their shared dexterity on land, trees, and water. Animals and insects are rite-specific and reflect thematic emphases. Thus, symbols of fertility and life like serpents and fish populate the regal Rada Rite, whereas horrific and repellant insects populate the Gede Rite, which centers on death and sexuality, including sexually transmissible diseases. In that context Mòpyon Lakwa (Crabs of the Cross) and Ti Pis Lakwa (Little Flea of the Cross) are two irreverent Gede-related epithets (Hebblethwaite 2021, 203–5). The term *Lakwa* (The Cross) once again draws attention to Christian-Vodou hybridity, a topic examined in the context of chromolithographs below.

The hybridity or syncretism involving Catholic saints and their chromolithographs has marked the development of Haitian Vodou for more than three centuries. The Sen yo (Saints) in the chromolithographs primarily represent Vodou lwa due to symbolic attributes of the image. Saint Patrick stands in for Danbala Wèdo, the serpent lwa, because his chromolithograph includes snakes. Saint Lazarus stands in for Atibon Legba, the elderly lwa, because in his image the old figure holds a cane. The Black Madonna Mater Salvatoris stands in for Èzili Dantò, the maternal lwa, because of her scarifications as well as the infant she holds. Saint Ulrich stands in for Agwe Tawoyo, lwa of the sea, because he holds a fish.

The snakes, cane, the Black scarified mother and child, and fish denote the lwa, and, beyond recognizing their Catholic names, little of Catholicism is recognized in the saints. Once again the consequences of article 3 of the Code noir must be considered. Forbidding "any religion other than the

Roman, Catholic, and Apostolic Faith from being practiced in public" drove Vodouists to conceal their faith within the Catholic chromolithographic tradition (Dieudonné 1685). One cannot underestimate the influence of Catholic prayer books, songbooks, and the Bible among some Haitian Vodouists. Although many are drawn to the parallel Christian cultures of Haiti, other Vodouists reject Christian influences like the Catholic chromolithographs. Freemasonry and its thriving French-language literature are also popular among Vodou priests in Haiti and major bookstores like La Pléiade in Port-au-Prince have sections dedicated to the topic.

Syncretic interpretations and even new forms of religion have also arisen among American Indigenous peoples as a consequence of the European conquest. In colonial times the Catholic church made a considerable effort to erase the preconquest religions of the Indigenous peoples—for example, by destroying temples and meting out heavy punishment upon Indigenous people who refused to embrace the Catholic faith. However, ancient religious traditions survived under the guise of Catholic practices. Bernardo de Sahagún, a Spanish chronicler in sixteenth-century Mexico, reported that the Aztec goddess Tonantzin was identified with the Virgin Maria de Guadalupe del Tepeyac, San Juan Bautista with Telpochtli Tezcatlipoca de Tianquizmanalco, and Santa Ana with Toci de Chiauhtempan (Carrasco 1975, 200). This reinterpretation was a strategy of cultural survival and resistance that allowed people to worship ancient gods in public celebrations even under the Spanish rule (201). At the same time, Spanish missionaries contributed to intercultural identifications by condemning Indigenous spirits and deities as manifestations of the devil.

Until today Catholic saints have been reinterpreted in terms of Meso-American gods in popular religious expressions: for example, in contemporary Mexico, the archangel Michael can be identified with the Aztec rain god Tlaloc (Báez-Jorge 2013, 139), San Ramos with the wind god Ehécatl-Quetzalcóatl (161), or the Virgen de Guadalupe with the earth goddess Coatlicue (111). We find complex religious practices that combine and fuse elements from European and American Indigenous traditions in diverse ways. For example, the practice of *Costumbre* among Mexican K'iche Mayas in Guatemala combines "earth lords, Jesu Cristo, [Catholic] saints, and ancestors, a year-bearer cult recognizing four sacred mountains as the seats of alternating mayors of the solar year, and the 260-day diving almanac or Ch'olK'ij" (Cook and Offit 2008, 44). Interestingly, syncretic practices such as Costumbre are often criticized not only by purist practitioners of Catholicism but also by nationalist Indigenous movements that strive to keep their religion "pure" (47).

Contact between Catholicism and Freemasonry are important examples of syncretism; however, they do not match in significance the intra-African hybridity of the multiple national traditions that are brought into a unified orbit in Sèvis Ginen, which subsumes twenty-one diverse rites. European folk beliefs have also left their traces in Indigenous and African diaspora spirit traditions: for example, Garifuna spirits include elves (*duendu*, from Spanish *duende* 'elf'), as well as the Flying Hollander (*faia landia*, from the latter expression; Taylor 1951, 106). Haitian Vodou has also vodouized the word *dyab* (from the French *diables* 'devils') to refer to hot, fast-acting lwa. Indigenous and African diaspora traditions in the Americas are not immune to contemporary global influences, either: for example, traditional *Costumbristas* who reject Spanish or Catholic influences are quite open to integrating elements from astrology or new age (Cook and Offit 2008, 49), and a Protestantized or Pentecostalized form of Costumbre has emerged among ex-Catholic and ex-Protestant converts (55).

THE COLONIALITY OF REALITY

Indigenous and African diaspora religions offer ways to better understand how human societies have constructed their worldviews. Indigenous and African diaspora spirit-traditions and their ontologies of the interrelatedness of humans, spirits, ancestors, animals, and plants provide new mirrors not only for interpreting our existences but also for inspiriting a natural habitat that we otherwise pillage. European colonists have clashed with Indigenous and African diaspora people and their traditions since 1021, when the first Vikings built a camp in a place they called "Vinland" on the edge of Newfoundland, Canada. From the fifteenth century until recently, Indigenous and African diaspora peoples have orbited, in chains, the global capitalism of European-Americans, enduring multigenerational enslavement, land theft, and physical extinction, their existences under constant threat from states and colonists. Global forces forced practitioners into overlapping states of existence, a condition that extends over centuries and produces mixtures and hybridizations that vex essentialist reductions (Oakdale 2018, 58). The inextricable interactions of our cultures in the modern period render unreliable the strict connection of "Indigenous thought," "African diaspora thought," or "Western thought" to the peoples from which they derive.

The participant-observer engagement of many of this volume's authors likewise suggests degrees of entanglement between their thoughts and the Indigenous and African diaspora traditions that they write about. The "coloniality of reality" means that we navigate multiple ontologies, each stitched into our idea of self (Burman 2016). The coloniality of reality can mean that some of what is written about Indigenous and African diaspora traditions reflects academic traditions more than the cultural traditions purportedly under focus, but it can also mean that scholars and writers become blended into and accurately describe the traditions they examine.

Despite the ways that the coloniality of reality limits our ability to be objective, we strive as a community of authors to achieve consensus among practitioners and scholars about the Indigenous and African diaspora traditions we examine, and we seek to preserve and defend the peoples and cultures we learn from and study. A conventional separation of typologically related traditions on the basis of disciplinary, linguistic, ethnic, national, or geographical criteria would unnecessarily obfuscate the comparisons and contrasts that we undertake in our writings on these religious legacies, thereby inhibiting a deeper understanding of spirit-based traditions in the Americas. The chapters in this volume instead address spirit-based traditions on the scale of a continent and its islands, simultaneously revealing areas of overlap and divergence.

METHODOLOGIES AND ETHNOGRAPHIC PREPARATIONS

The authors implement a range of methodologies that draw from diverse experiences in ethnographic, social science, and humanistic research. We have organized the chapters in rough chronological order with the first chapters focusing on aspects of the colonial period and later ones addressing the contemporary period.

LeGrace Benson's chapter, "Meeting Grounds in Saint-Domingue and the Emergence of Haitian Vodou: An Ecological Approach," reflects the methodologies of ecological analysis, epistemology, and historiography while drawing on work in Haitian studies. Benson explores the ecosystem of the major slave port Cap François at the beginning of the eighteenth century, viewing the people who met in Saint-Domingue, together with the environments they had inhabited and in which they became relocated, as extended, dynamic and unitary continuities. These continuities formed the "long conversations" that bind past humans to the present. For travelers, expatriates, exiles, and captives, the diaspora was a condition of multiple consciousness. Scattered into the plantations, but finding ways to convene at secret meeting grounds, the captives created a powerful impetus for the assertion of the rights for all people that endures today.

Eleanor A. Laughlin's chapter, "The Many Faces of Marie Laveau and Voudou in Nineteenth-Century New Orleans," employs methodologies of archival research, historiography, and art history and criticism, as well as fieldwork in the Miami Haitian Vodou community, to explore Marie Laveau's representation in portraits. Analyzing portraits as well as information from primary periodicals, personal memoirs, and oral histories, the chapter examines how Laveau became recognized. Thanks to her agency as a free woman of color, and to her approach to combining folk Catholic, Indigenous, and African diaspora Voudou traditions for her clients, Laveau earned acceptance from a diverse community. However, writers who produced pop culture texts and images about her distorted her image instead of celebrating an assuring figure due to their ignorance surrounding her Voudou spiritual practice.

Daniel J. Frim's chapter, "Shamanic Healing, Initiation, and Ritual Technique in a Kwak'wala Narrative from the Boas-Hunt Corpus," utilizes methodologies in religious studies, textual and narrative interpretation, linguistic analysis, and historiography in order to assess Frantz Boas's ethnographic work and claims around "sleight of hand" healing techniques. Frim's analysis of perceptions of ritual techniques in Kwakwaka'wakw healing performances and initiation rituals excavates a single interpretation of sleight of hand and supernatural healing. The author argues that, while the narrative under analysis treats techniques of sleight of hand and supernatural power as separate conceptual categories, the text illustrates how both techniques are legitimate as harmonized mirror images of each other.

José María Santos Rovira's chapter, "Language and Rituals of the Brotherhood of the Holy Spirit of the Kongos of Villa Mella," focuses on a community in the Dominican Republic, using humanistic and social science methodologies, including ethnomusicology, historiography, and linguistic analysis. Santos Rovira describes the ethnographic fieldwork he carried out in one of the few surviving Black spiritual brotherhoods in the Dominican Republic. Located north of Santo Domingo, this community of Villa Mella descends from African enslaved people. Over time Haitian immigrants migrated to the settlement and contributed to the development of a syncretic religion that combines African, Dominican, and Haitian spirit-based traditions along with Catholic traditions.

Robin M. Wright's chapter, "A Joyful Place: Baniwa Jaguar Shamans' Songs and Historical Change," builds on ethnographic work in the Northwest Amazon that uses humanistic and social science methodologies, including ethnomusicology, lexical analysis, and historiography, to reveal the meanings of Baniwa songs. Wright investigates the cosmology of the Baniwa shaman, Manuel da Silva, and the "people" he communicates with. "People" refers to "other-than-humans" that take animal, spirit, plant, and ancestral forms; thus this chapter goes into further depth about the ontological system discussed in this introduction. Wright explores the place of song in mediating between the patient, shaman, and the worlds of primordial peoples that advise and guide shamans.

Ana Mariella Bacigalupo's chapter, "Embodying, Reshaping, and Combining the Past and the Future: A Mapuche Shaman's Historical Agency in Chile," examines the multitemporal ritual actions of Mapuche shamans in their service to personal, social, and political struggles in the present. Bacigalupo's methodology is built on decades of work as a research assistant to shaman Francisca Kolipi, participant-observer experiences that shape her historical, anthropological, and social science approaches to Mapuche shamanism.

In their chapter "Other Knowledges: Tensions and Negotiation between Religion, Knowledges, and School in a Wixárika Community," Francisco Iritamei Benítez de la Cruz and Itxaso García Chapinal reflect upon lengthy lived experiences, fieldwork in the community, comparative epistemology, and social science methodologies to understand the Indigenous Wixárika community in Miwaxieti, Mexico. The authors analyze tensions between Wixáritari religious beliefs and world knowledge in the context of state-operated primary schools in Miwaxieti, a community situated north of Jalisco, and they examine festivals, customs, religious beliefs, and the mythology of Wixárika deities, including Niwetsik, Tatewari, and Tatutsi Maxakwaxi, drawing from ethnographic, humanistic, and social science methodologies.

Dereck Daschke's chapter, "It's the Song That Cures: Healing, Music, and Ayahuasca in Brazil's Santo Daime Churches," employs participant-observer and social science methodologies to examine the rituals, songs and mythology of Santo Daime. The author's engagement with the Santo Daime churches and rituals reveals the intersections of community, ayahuasca drinking, and communal singing in a process that heals and transforms the self. Additionally, the study of a handful of Santo Daime hymns draws from ethnomusicology and language documentation.

Jeffery M. Gonzalez's chapter, "Finding Orisha in New Places," employs the methodologies of historiography, photography, social science, and humanistic methods, as well as participant-observation fieldwork. The chapter spans the contemporary festivals and sacred spaces of Yorubaland and the Orisha diaspora in Cuba, Brazil, the United States, and Trinidad, where new sacred spaces were gradually discovered as waves of enslaved people become established in the West. Drawing on archival research and his own photography, Gonzalez sheds light on his fieldwork and social networks in his analysis of Orisha culture's dissemination into the African diaspora.

Editor Benjamin Hebblethwaite has taught courses on Haitian Creole and Vodou religion for more than twenty years and visited Vodou communities in Haiti and Florida, attending services and recording, transcribing, and interpreting songs. Hebblethwaite et al. (2012), *Vodou Songs in Haitian Creole and English*, and Hebblethwaite (2021), *A Transatlantic History of Haitian Vodou*, reflect fieldwork, research, and thinking about the Haitian Creole songs of Vodou and their African sources. Editor Silke Jansen has published on the Spanish Caribbean and has conducted in-depth ethnographic and linguistic fieldwork in the Dominican Republic and Cuba. She has studied processes of linguistic and cultural hybridization among

Indigenous, African, and European influences since colonial times, with a special focus on contact scenarios between French and Creole as well as the Spanish Caribbean.

This multidisciplinary collection provides diverse perspectives on Indigenous and African diaspora religious traditions. The selection of chapters represents an inclusive approach to spirit-based religions modeled on religious typology rather than ethnic or national groupings. In their attention to historical and ontological issues, the chapters scrutinize questions of how to speak of the past, present, and future, and how to describe the nature of being in the context of the "peoplehood" of humans, ancestors, spirits, animals, and plants. Concerns central across chapters are the ways that practicing and preserving the spirit religions enhances their chances of survival in a hemisphere dominated by neocolonialism, Christianity, and technoscience.

This volume works toward decolonizing knowledge through its focus on producing scholarship that reflects consensus among the authors and practitioners. Yet colonial and neocolonial mental structures influence our minds, and our sources and interpretations must err in places. As Kehoe (2000, 42) notes, persistent myths about shamanism in the West include the portrayal of shamans (or priests) as individuals fulfilling personal spiritual callings rather than working as servants of their communities.

For Miami-based Vodou priest Michelet Alisma, nothing is more exhausting than the weeks of labor required for planning and holding the demanding kanzo initiation that his candidates of initiation undertake at his home and temple. The kanzo demands a "surrender of self" and "rapid regression" that mold the candidate into a state of "uncertainty and dependence" so that they can receive the lessons of initiation, central among them being the surrender to "trance" (Brown 1991, 352). Initiations, healing rituals, and ceremonies in Indigenous and African diaspora religions reflect *work* that is oriented to individuals in the community. The shaman's or priest's goals are not the fulfillment of a personal quest for enlightenment, although that may be attained through service to others.

The ethoses of invasion, colonization, settlement, forced Christianization, enslavement, the denial of human rights, racism, mechanization, industrialization, militarization, capitalism, and consumerism have impacted all the cultures of the Americas. If not driven to extinction, Indigenous and African diaspora communities are still at a disadvantage, marked by historical and contemporary traumas that have inflicted immense harm. Disproportionate structural and institutional violence against Black and Indigenous people has been a feature of the West since 1492. Today military industrial domination, mass incarceration, the war on drugs, food deserts, addiction to opiates, alcoholism, income disparities, and other afflictions signal unchanged disparities and corruption. The essentialist and racist thinking of the contemporary period are connected to the recent past. Idealizing the "non-ordinary realities" of Indigenous and African diaspora traditions for personal healing and gain while ignoring the "ordinary realities" of collective impoverishment and higher rates of sickness and death experienced in those communities is a vain attempt to silence a deafening past (Kehoe 2000, 100).

Catholic orders and Protestant clergy have provided religious services for primarily colonists since 1492. Catholic evangelism focused on the urban elite until Vatican II in the 1960s, shifting the church's emphasis to the educational and spiritual well-being of the poor (Greene 1993, 132). Overall, little has changed in Catholic and Protestant domination of land, resources, schools, and influence in the regions this collection examines. When Christians did interact with Indigenous or African diaspora people outside of colonization, their attitudes were often belittling. In the late nineteenth and twentieth century, Protestants and Catholics opened more than 150 state-sanctioned boarding schools to assist in the eradication of Indigenous culture through the inculcation of Christianity and English proficiency (Smith 2021). Evangelical crusades in the 1960s and 1970s undermined Amazonian shamanism in ways comparable to the actions of the Haitian state and the Catholic church in their "anti-superstition" (i.e. anti-Vodou) campaigns of the 1890s and 1940s (Wright 2013, 24; Beauvoir and Dominique 2003; Ramsey 2011). Acknowledging the crimes of colonialism in this volume is only one aspect of a rational response. The authors also demonstrate how scholars can help *document, preserve,* and *learn from* sacred traditions like songs, prayers, rituals, teachings, and mythologies, and they show the roles of fieldwork, book learning, language documentation, and interpretation informed by comparing related traditions.

Shaman-activists like Davi Kopenawa (Kopenawa and Albert 2010) and oungan-scholars like Max Beauvoir (2008a and 2008b) illustrate the important trend involving insiders who document and publish sacred knowledge in texts of hitherto understudied traditions. Beyond the unique new knowledge they collect, these works illustrate an exciting trend of Indigenous and African diaspora practitioners who publish books, sacred texts or narratives in combination with important editorial and academic foundations. Kopenawa and Albert and Beauvoir turn their atttention to the hymnology, mythology, and theology of their traditions, advancing our understanding of ontology and culture in both traditions while providing original texts to assist long-term preservation and even the expansion of the respective traditions.

Research comparing, contrasting, and comingling Indigenous and African diaspora traditions deserves more attention, since the effort reveals cross-cultural insights into the nature of humanity. Dividing research on Indigenous traditions from African diaspora traditions compartmentalizes strikingly relatable systems. Breaking free from racial, ethnic, and disciplinary separation not only will facilitate dismantling structural barriers to mutual understanding but may also lead to unprecedented discoveries that draw human cultures even closer than we imagined.

Common points among the traditions include the service to spirits; trance possession; reverence for the ancestors; animal sacrifice to placate ancestors and spirits; plant-based healing practices; circumambulation around an axis mundi; initiation rituals involving isolation, ordeals, and symbolic resurrection; the use of plants in rituals; the playing of drums, aerophones (flutes), rattles, and bells; and the use of natural symbols and "found temples." The ontology in both traditions envisions personhood shared among humans, spirits, ancestors, animals, plants and natural phenomena. Despite these structural similarities, profound differences are found in mythologies, spirit attributes, names, themes, and rituals, as well as ethnobotanical practices, revealing how particularities accumulate within structures that retain much comparability.

The most significant difference between the traditions relate to the centrality of entheogenic drugs like DMT, ayahuasca, or peyote in Indigenous traditions and their scarcity in African diaspora ones. The example of *vomitivos* (emetic wands) common in ancient Taíno religion, as well as among contemporary South American Indigenous groups (Roth 1924, 705), illustrates this important point. The emetic wands were the ritual implements of the Taíno *behiques* (shamans) who put the long, curved end into their mouth to induce vomiting prior to entheogenic rituals (Waldron 2019, 235). The purification of the vomiting enhanced the effects of the *cohoba* and prepared the behique for the encounter with spirits. Made of wood, stone, or from the rib of a manatee, these ritual implements were decorated with carved designs that resembled the ones on the calabash maracas shaken by the Taíno shamans (237). Although the Indigenous universe of entheogens represents a distinct dimension, the behique's maraca returns us to common ground.

The Indigenous and African diaspora practices focused on service to ancestors and spirits reflect ancient substrate patterns in religiosity. The rationale to separate them on disciplinary, ethnic, linguistic, geographical, or historical grounds evaporates in our interconnected world. Shared cultural, historical, and structural features of American Indigenous and African diaspora spirit-based traditions mutually deserve our attentions since the analyses and dialogues give way to discoveries about the deep commonalities as well as divergences in our cultural heritages. These readings make possible therefore journeys of recognition as well as discovery in Indigenous and African diaspora religions.

NOTES

1. It is revealing that we never talk about "mainstream" (colonial) American culture as the "European diaspora," which reflects a Eurocentric view.
2. The rise in Western cultures of the consumption of psychoactive plants called entheogens is historically rooted in the ritual psychedelic plant use of Indigenous South American cultures (Kehoe 2000, 65).
3. Robin M. Wright (personal correspondence, 2020) points out that the notion of multiple "peoples" of the environment is widespread throughout the Americas, and has been noted by anthropologists since at least the 1960s.
4. Being the most powerful predator in tropical America, jaguars play a key role in many Indigenous religious traditions. For example, in Mayan society, political leaders and shamans were considered to share souls with jaguars (Capper 2016, 155).
5. The peoplehood of bees is also faintly echoed among ecologists who warn of how their decline threatens humans.

6. The transition from great spiritual human to spirit being is important in African diaspora traditions, as is the spectral dimension of forests. See Beauvoir-Dominique and Dominique (2003) for information on the transition from being to spirit in Haitian Vodou. See Daniel (2005, 159) for information about religious rituals in forests in the context of an Odu Nago-Keto ritual for Oxossi in Bahia.
7. This is not the case in Haitian Vodou, in which several lwa share the same *yanvalou* rhythm (Daniel 2005, 15).
8. Part of this personification may entail the incorporation of a male or female spirit and their personality, reflecting an underlying emphasis on the gendered personhood of the entity. The vessel or "horse" of the spirit expresses the appropriate gender or species of the lwa, oricha, òrìṣà or orixá, and they are recognized as such in ritual (Daniel 2005, 23). In Cuba, as elsewhere, a *santera* possessed by Ogún is treated like a male while a *santero* possessed by Oyá is treated like a female (23–24).
9. For instance, a person's tenacious fighting spirit may reflect the Ogou lwa or a person's hard-working nature may reflect lwa Azaka Mede.
10. These ideas about the self are included within the Bantu etymon of the Creole word *moun* (people): "All the living and the dead, all the ancestors and the spirits living with us" (Beauvoir and Dominique 2003, 90; Mosquera 2020). The Garifuna people also use the word *mutu* to refer to a "living person" (Taylor 1951).
11. In Trinidad Ṣàngó is represented as a mixed-race person, whereas Ògún is portrayed as Black. The great military òrìṣà Ògún demands "absolute obedience" while the regal Ṣàngó is more "flexible," listening to all parties before judging (Glazier 2007, 245; Parés 2009, 251). Ṣàngó is quick to anger but does not hold a grudge (Parés 2009, 245). Ṣàngó may wear women's clothing; however, his polygamous household and love affairs mirror those of a sexually active man (Glazier 2007, 243). Today Ṣàngó serves as a patron of electronics, computers, and the internet (Parés 2009, 245).
12. The blood consumed by the jaguar is his beer and the maggots eaten by buzzards from a cadaver are the bird's grilled fish (Viveiros de Castro 2016, loc. 641).
13. In Vodou ceremonies people also transform into the aquatic spirit Agwe Tawoyo in the Rada Rite.
14. Bondye (God) created the serpent spirits at the beginning of creation. The *potomitan* (center post) is painted with their images. The servants of the lwa dance around the symbolic "serpent's tree" to summon the spirits (Jil and Jil 2009, 86). Hundreds of songs are dedicated to them (Beauvoir 2008a and 2008b). Danbala calls people to initiation by causing a mild illness, and he guides them through the ordeal (Richman 2005). Snake vertebrae representing the serpent spirits are strung around the ason rattle—a priest's or priestess's main symbol. The iconic vèvè diagrams for the serpent spirit are invariably traced at the foot of the potomitan before ceremonies.

15. For example, in the song "Fèy o" (Oh leaves) we learn about Simbi's role in healing: "Oh leaves save my life / Oh from the misery that I'm in / My child is ill / I ran to the gangan's house / Oh Simbi / If he's a good gangan / He'll save my life / Oh from the misery that I'm in" (297).
16. Plant individuality is expressed not only in multitudinous species but also in individual phenotypes within species. Any gardener knows that no two plants are identical.
17. Given the importance of the ceiba tree in Meso-American Indigenous cultures (Capper 2016, 150), a syncretic origin does not seem to be excluded.
18. One of the etymons, the Fon *sɛ*, refers to the "powerful and essential part of a being; vital principle; destiny; outcome; God; providence" (Segurola and Rassinoux 2000, 404).
19. Note that the Ghost Dance originates in the northwest area of the United States in the 1870s (Gill 1982, 164).
20. The "vertical shamans" instead are priestly chanters who derive authority from nonecstatic, canonical traditions, but nowhere do they predominate in Amazonian societies compared to "horizontal shamans" (Viveiros de Castro 2014, 154).

REFERENCES

Aikhenvald, Alexandra. 2012. *Languages of the Amazon*. Oxford: Oxford University Press.

Akinjogbin, I. A. 1967. *Dahomey and Its Neighbours, 1708–1818*. Cambridge: Cambridge University Press.

Akínyẹmí, Akíntúndé. 2009. "The Ambivalent Representations of Ṣàngó in Yorùbá Literature." In *Ṣàngó in Africa and the African Diaspora*, edited by Akíntúndé Akínyẹmí, Falola Toyin, and Joel E. Tishken, 187–212. Bloomington: Indiana University Press.

Anderson, Gary Clayton. 2014. *Ethnic Cleansing and the Indian: The Crime That Should Haunt America*. Norman: University of Oklahoma Press.

Anthes, Bill. 2014. "'Why Injun Artist Me': Acee Blue Eagle's Diasporic Performative." In *Native Diasporas: Indigenous Identities and Settler Colonialism in the Americas*, edited by Gregory D. Smithers, and Brooke N. Newman, 411–42. http://ebookcentral.proquest.com/lib/ufl/detail.action?docid=1666553 (accessed August 6, 2022).

Alexiades, Miguel N. 2009. "Mobility and Migration in Indigenous Amazonia: Contemporary Ethnoecological Perspectives—an Introduction." In *Mobility and Migration in Indigenous Amazonia: Contemporary Ethnoecological Perspectives*, edited by Miguel Alexiades, 1–47. New York: Berghahn.

Apud Peláez, Ismael. 2020. *Ayahuasca: Between Cognition and Culture*. Tarragona: Publicacions URV.

Ayiti Ayizan. 2021. "Yon Gwo Seremoni Vodou Fèt Nan (Lakou 4 drapo Macolas Volmar) pou jistis prezidan Jovenel Moïse" [A big Vodou ceremony that took place in Lakou 4 Drapo Macolas Volmar for justice for president Jovenel Moïse]. YouTube video, retrieved October 21, 2021. https://www.youtube.com/watch?v=5l2vz6nrXmE.

Ayorinde, Christine. 2005. "Cuba: Tradition and Transformation." In *Yoruba Diaspora in the Atlantic World*, edited by Toyin Falola and Matt D. Childs, 209–30. Bloomington: Indiana University Press.

Báez-Jorge, Félix. 2013 *¿Quiénes son aquí los dioses verdaderos? Religiosidad indígena y hagiografías populares*. Xalapa: Biblioteca Universidad Veracruzana.

Bay, Edna. 1998. *Wives of the Leopard: Gender, Politics, and Culture in the Kingdom of Dahomey*. Charlottesville: University of Virigina Press.

Beaubrun, Mimerose P. 2013. *Nan Dòmi, an Initiate's Journey into Haitian Vodou*. San Francisco: City Lights.

Beauvoir, Max. 2008a. *Le grand recueil sacré, ou, Répertoire des chansons du vodou haïtien*. Port-au-Prince: Edisyon Près Nasyonal d Ayiti.

———. 2008b. *Lapriyè Ginen*. Port-au-Prince: Edisyon Près Nasyonal d Ayiti.

Beauvoir-Dominique, Rachel, and Didier Dominique. 2003. *Savalou E*. Montreal: Les Éditions du Centre International de Documentation et d'Information Haïtienne, Caribéenne, et Afro-Canadienne.

Bacigalupo, Ana Mariella. 2016. *Thunder Shaman: Making History with Mapuche Spirits in Chile and Patagonia*. Austin: University of Texas Press.

Beck Kehoe, Alice. 2000. *Shamans and Religion: an Anthropological Exploration in Critical Thinking*. Prospect Heights IL: Waveland.

Boomert, Arie. 2000. "Trinidad, Tobago, and the Lower Orinoco Interaction Sphere, an Archaeological/Ethnohistorical Study." PhD diss., Universiteit Leiden.

Brown, Karen McCarthy. [1991] 2010. *Mama Lola: A Vodou Priestess in Brooklyn*. Los Angeles: University of California Press.

———. 2005. "Healing and Medicine: Healing and Medicine in the African Diaspora." In *Encyclopedia of Religion*, edited by L. Jones, 3821–24. Detroit MI: Macmillan Reference.

Burman, Anders. 2016. *Indigeneity and Decolonization in the Bolivian Andes: Ritual Practice and Activism*. Lanham MD: Lexington.

Cabrera, Lydia, Ivor L. Miller, and P. González Gómes-Cásseres. 2020. *The Sacred Language of the Abakuá*. Jackson: University Press of Mississippi.

Capper, Daniel. 2016. *Learning Love from a Tiger: Religious Experiences with Nature*. Oakland: University of California Press.

Carrasco, Pedro. 1975. "La transformación de la cultura indígena durante la colonia." *Historia Mexicana* 25, no. 2: 175–203.

Clastres, Hélène. 1975. *La terre sans mal: le prophétisme Tupi-Guarani*. Paris: Seuil.

Cook, Garrett, and Thomas Offit. 2008. "Pluralism and Transculturation in Indigenous Maya religion." *Ethnology* 47: 45–59.

Crapanzano, Vincent. 2005. "Spirit Possession: An Overview." In *Encyclopedia of Religion*, edited by Lindsay Jones, 8687–94. Macmillan Reference.

Daniel, Yvonne. 2005. *Dancing Wisdom: Embodied Knowledge in Haitian Vodou, Cuban Yoruba, and Bahian Candomblé*. Urbana: University of Illinois Press.

Davis, Beale. 1925. *The Goat without Horns*. New York: Brentano's.

Deren, Maya. 1953. *Divine Horsemen: The Living Gods of Haiti*. New York: Book Collectors Society.

Dieudonné, Louis (Louis XIV). 1685. *The Black Code*. New York: Roy Rosenzweig Center for History and New Media.

Duviols, Jean-Paul. 2017. "Premiers regards sur les sauvages (xvie siècle)." *América: Cahier du CRICCAL* 50: 13–25. https://journals.openedition.org/america/1789 (accessed August 5, 2022).

Eliade, Mircea. 1987. "Shamanism: An Overview." In *Encyclopedia of Religion*, edited by L. Jones, 8269–74. Detroit MI: Macmillan Reference.

Eriksen, Love. 2011. "Nature and Culture in Prehistoric Amazonia: Using G.I.S. to Reconstruct Ancient Ethnogenetic Processes from Archaeology, Linguistics, Geography, and Ethnohistory." Department of Human Geography, Human Ecology Division, Lund University. https://lup.lub.lu.se/search/ws/files/3626162/1890749.pdf (accessed August 5, 2022).

Fausto, Carlos. 2012. *Warfare and Shamanism in Amazonia*. Cambridge: Cambridge University Press.

Ferguson, James. 2003. *Migration in the Caribbean: Haiti, the Dominican Republic, and Beyond*. London: Minority Rights Group International.

Fixico, Donald. 2014. "From Tribal to Indian: American Indian Identity in the Twentieth Century." In *Native Diasporas: Indigenous Identities and Settler Colonialism in the Americas*, edited by Gregory D. Smithers and Brooke N. Newman, 473–96. Lincoln: Unversity of Nebraska Press.

Fleming, Luke. 2016. "Linguistic Exogamy and Language Shift in the Northwest Amazon." *International Journal of the Sociology of Language* 240: 9–27.

Fọláránmí, Stephen. 2009. "Art in the Service of Ṣàngó." In *Ṣàngó in Africa and the African Diaspora*, edited by Akíntúndé Akínyẹmí, Falola Toyin, and Joel E. Tishken, 157–86. Bloomington: Indiana University Press.

Forbes, Michelle Ann. 2011. "Garífuna: The Birth and Rise of an Identity through Contact Language and Contact Culture." PhD diss, University of Missouri.

Frese, Pamela R., and S. J. M. Gray. 2005. "Trees." In *Encyclopedia of Religion*, edited by Lindsay Jones, 9333–40. Detroit MI: Macmillan Reference.

Furst, Peter T. 2005. "Shamanism: South American Shamanism." In *Encyclopedia of Religion*, edited by L. Jones, 8290–94. Detroit MI: Macmillan Reference.

Gill, Sam D. 1981. *Sacred Words: A Study of Navajo Religion and Prayer*. Westport CT: Greenwood, 1981.

Glazier, Stephen. 2009. "Whither Sàngó? An Inquiry into Sàngó's 'Authenticity' and Prominence in the Caribbean." In *Ṣàngó in Africa and the African Diaspora*, edited by Joel E. Tishken, Tòyìn Fálolá, and Akíntúndé Akínyẹmí, 233–47. Bloomington: Indiana University Press.

Goldstein, Ilana Seltzer, and Beatriz Caiuby Labate. 2018. "From the Forest to the Museum: Notes on the Artistic and Spiritual Collaboration between Ernesto Neto and the Huni Kuin People." In *The Expanding World Ayahuasca Diaspora: Appropriation, Integration and Legislation*, edited by Beatriz Caiuby Labate and Clancy Cavnar, 76–94. New York: Routledge.

Greene, Anne. 1993. *The Catholic Church in Haiti: Political and Social Change*. East Lansing: Michigan State University Press.

Greene, Oliver N. 1998. "The 'Dügü' Ritual of the Garinagu of Belize: Reinforcing Values and Society through Music and Spirit Possession." *Black Music Research Journal* 18 (Spring-Autumn 1998): 167–81.

Haveman, Christopher D. 2016. *Rivers of Sand: Creek Indian Emigration, Relocation, and Ethnic Cleansing in the American South*. Lincoln: Univeristy of Nebraska Press.

Hebblethwaite, Benjamin. 2021. *A Transatlantic History of Haitian Vodou: Rasin Figuier, Rasin Bwa Kayiman, and the Rada and Gede Rites*. Jackson: University Press of Mississippi.

———. 2015. "Historical Linguistic Approaches to Haitian Creole: Vodou Rites, Spirit Names, and Songs: The Founders' Contributions to Asogwe Vodou." In *La Española-Isla de Encuentros / Hispaniola-Island of Encounters*, edited by Jessica Stefanie Barzen, Hanna Lene Geiger, and Silke Jansen, 65–86. Tübingen: Gunter Narr.

Hebblethwaite, Benjamin, with editorial assistants Joanne Bartley, Chris Ballengee, Vanessa Brissault, Erika Felker-Kantor, Andrew Tarter, Quinn Hansen, and Kat Warwick. 2012. *Vodou Songs in Haitian Creole and English*. Philadelphia: Temple University Press.

Heckenberger, Michael. 2006. "History, Ecology, and Alterity: Visualizing Polity in Ancient Amazonia." In *Time and Complexity in Historical Ecology: Studies in the Neotropical Lowlands*, edited by William Balée and Clark Erickson, 311–40. New York: Columbia University Press.

Hofman, Corine L., Arie Boomert, Alistair J. Bright, Menno L. P. Hoogland, Sebastiaan Knippenberg, and Alice V. M. Samson. 2019. "Ties with the Homelands: Archipelagic Interaction and the Enduring Role of the South and Central American Mainlands in the Pre-Columbian Lesser Antilles." In *Islands at the Crossroads: Migration, Seafaring, and Interaction in the Caribbean*, edited by Antonio Curet, 63–73. Tuscaloosa: University of Alabama Press.

Jansen, Silke. 2020. "Island Carib, Gender Indexicality, and Language Contact." In *Mundos Caribeños—Caribbean Worlds—Mondes Caraïbes*, edited by Gabriele Knauer and Ineke Phaf-Rheinberger, 141–68. Madrid: Iberoamericana/Vervuert.

Jil, Dyeri, and Jil, Ivwoz S. 2009. *Sèvis Ginen: Rasin, rityèl, respè lan Vodou*. Davi FL: Bookmanlit.

Keegan, William F. 1996. "Columbus Was a Cannibal: Myth and the First Encounters." In *The Lesser Antilles in the Age of European Expansion*, edited by Robert L. Paquette and Stanley L. Engerman, 18–32. Gainesville: University Press of Florida.

Kopenawa, Davi, and Bruce Albert. 2010. *La chute du ciel: paroles d'un chaman yanomami*. Paris: Plon.

Laack, Isabel. 2019. *Aztec Religion and Art of Writing: Investigating Embodied Meaning, Indigenous Semiotics, and the Nahua Sense of Reality*. Leiden: Brill.

Laguerre, Michel. 1980a. *Voodoo Heritage*. Beverly Hills CA: Sage.

Law, Robin. 1980. *The Kingdom of Allada*. Leiden: Centrum voor Niet-Westerse Studies.

Le Hérissé, Auguste. 1911. *L'ancien royaume du Dahomey, mœurs, religion, histoire*. Paris: Émile Larose.

McNally, Michael D. 2020. *Defend the Sacred: Native American Religious Freedom beyond the First Amendment*. Princeton NJ: Princeton University Press.

Marcelin, Milo. 1949. *Mythologie vodou (rite arada I)*. Port-au-Prince: Éditions haïtiennes.

———. 1950. *Mythologie vodou (rite arada II)*. Port-au-Prince: Éditions haïtiennes.

Martire d'Anghiera, Pietro. 2005. *De orbe novo decades: a cura di Rosanna Mazzacane ed Elisa Magioncalda*. Genova: Dipartamento di Archeologia Filologia Classica e Loro Tradizioni [1511–30].

Mosquera, Yair Andre Cuenu. 2020. "El Muntu en la literatura contemporanea: filosofia de la fuerza vital en Fe en disfraz (2009) de Mayra Santos-Febres." *Revista Poligramas* 51: 75–97.

Murrell, Nathaniel Samuel. 2010. *Afro-Caribbean Religions: An Introduction to Their Historical, Cultural, and Sacred Traditions*. Philadelphia: Temple University Press.

Neill, Paul. 2011. "El Templete and Cuban Neoclassicisms: A Multivalent Signifier as a Site of Memory." *Bulletin of Latin American Research* 30: 344–65.

News Haiti TV. 2021. "Ceremonie vodou sou sèkèy Ex prezidan Jovenel Moise tout manbo ak ougan reyini" [Vodou ceremony on the casket of ex-president Jovenel Moïse, all manbo and oungan meet]. YouTube video, 13:23, July 20, 2021. https://youtube/OgCyv5EhRKk.

Oakdale, Suzanne. 2018. "Brazil's 'March to the West': Memories of an Indigenous Shaman and Other 'Moderns.'" *Journal of Anthropological Research* 74, no. 1 (Spring): 54–73.

Oliver, José R. 2021. "The Vibrancy of Taino-Themed/Arts and Crafts Identity and Symbolism in Modern and Postmodern Borikén." In *Real, Recent, or Replica: Precolumbian Caribbean Heritage as Art, Commodity, and Inspiration*, edited by Joanna Ostapkowicz and Jonathan A. Hanna, 80–109. Tuscaloosa: University of Alabama Press.

Ortiz, Paul. 2018. *An African American and Latinx History of the United States*. Boston: Beacon.

Ostler, Jeffrey. 2019. *Surviving Genocide: Native Nations and the United States from the American Revolution to Bleeding Kansas*. New Haven CT: Yale University Press.

Oxford English Dictionary. 2000. Oxford: Oxford University Press.

Parés, Luis Nicolau. 2009. "Xangó in Afro-Brazilian Religion: 'Aristocracy' and 'Syncretic' Interactions." In *Ṣàngó in Africa and the African Diaspora*, edited by Akíntúndé Akínyẹmí, Falola Toyin, and Joel E. Tishken, 248–72. Bloomington: Indiana University Press.

Pember, Mary Annette. 2019. "Death by Civilization." *Atlantic*, March 8, 2019. https://www.theatlantic.com/education/archive/2019/03/traumatic-legacy-indian-boarding-schools/584293/.

Petitjean Roget, Jacques. 1980. *La société d'habitation à la Martinique: un demi siècle de formation, 1635–1685*. Paris: Champion.

Plathoff, Anne. 2015. "Drapo Vodou: Sacred Standards of Haitian Vodou." *Flag Research Quarterly* 7: 2–23.

Postlewaite, Susan. 1986. "Voodoo Priests Advised Duvalier to Flee." United Press International Archive, February 11, 1986. https://www.upi.com/Archives/1986/02/11/Voodoo-priests-advised-Duvalier-to-flee/5068508482000/.

Price, Hiram. 1883. "Rules Governing the Court of Indian Offenses." Wikisource. Accessed August 5, 2022. https://en.wikisource.org/wiki/Code_of_Indian_Offenses.

Ramsey, Kate. 2011. *The Spirits and the Law: Vodou and Power in Haiti*. Chicago: University of Chicago Press.

Richman, Karen E. 2005. *Migration and Vodou*. Gainesville: University Press of Florida, 2005.

Rodríguez Álvarez, Ángel, ed. 1498. *Relación sobre las antigüedades de los indios: Mitología taína o eyeri. Ramón Pané y la relación sobre las antigüedades de los indios: el primer tratado etnográfico hecho en América*. Ed. bilingüe (español-inglés), contiene una reprod. en facsímil de la versión en italiano del siglo XVI. San Juan: Ed. Nuevo Mundo.

Roth, Walter Edmund. 1924. "An Introductory Study of the Arts, Crafts and Customs of the Guiana Indians." *Thirty-eighth Annual Report of the Bureau of American Ethnology to the Secretary of the Smithsonian Institution* 38: 25–745.

Rouget, Gilbert. [1980] 1990. *La musique et la transe: esquisse d'une théorie générale des relations de la musique et de la possession*. Paris: Gallimard.

———. 2001. *Initiatique vôdoun, images du rituel: chants et danses initiatiques pour le culte des vôdoun au Bénin*. Saint-Maur-des-Fossés: Éditions Sépia.

Russell, Andrew, and Elizabeth Rahman. 2015. *The Master Plant: Tobacco in Lowland South America*. New York: Bloomsbury Academic.

Sattler, Richard. 1996. "Remnants, Renegades, and Runaways Seminole Ethnogenesis Reconsidered." In *History, Power, and Identity: Ethnogenesis in the Americas, 1492–1992*, edited by Jonathan D. Hill, 36–69. Iowa City: University of Iowa Press.

Saint-Lot, Marie-Jose Alcide. 2003. *Vodou, a Sacred Theatre: The African Heritage in Haiti*. Coconut Creek FL: Educa Vision.

Santos-Granero, Fernando. 1998. "Writing History into the Landscape: Space, Myth, and Ritual in Contemporary Amazonia." *American Ethnologist* 25, no. 2: 128–48.

———. 2002. "The Arawakan Matrix: Ethos, Language, and History in Native South America." In *Comparative Arawakan Histories: Rethinking Language Family and Culture Area in Amazonia*, edited by Jonathan David Hill and Fernando Santos-Granero, 25–50. Urbana: University of Illinois Press.

Schwegler, Armin. 1996. *"Chi mankongo" Lengua y rito ancestrales en El Palenque de San Basilio (Colombia)*. Madrid: Vervuert/Iberoamericana.

———. 2002. "On the (Sensational) Survival of Kikongo in Twentieth-Century Cuba." *Journal of Pidgin and Creole Studies* 15, no. 1: 159–64.

Segurola, Basilio, and Jean Rassinoux. 2000. *Dictionnaire fon-francais*. Madrid: SMA Société des Missions Africaines.

Séverin, François. 2002. *Plant ak pyebwa tè d Ayiti*. Port-au-Prince: Éditions Quitel.

———. 2007. *Ti zwazo kote w a prale*. Port-au-Prince: Société Audubon.

Simpson, George Eaton. 1962. "The Shango Cult in Nigeria and in Trinidad." *American Anthropologist* 64, no. 6: 1204–19.

Smith, Andrea. 2007. "Soul Wound: The Legacy of Native American Schools." Amnesty International. March 26, 2007. https://web.archive.org/web/20121206131053/http://www.amnestyusa.org/node/87342.

Smith, Peter. 2021. "US Churches Reckon with Traumatic Legacy of Native Schools." Associated Press. July 22, 2021. https://abcnews.go.com/US/wireStory/us-churches-reckon-traumatic-legacy-native-schools-78994651.

Spring, Jake. 2021. "Brazil Drought Crisis Linked to Global Climate Change, Minister Says." Reuters. July 8, 2021. https://www.reuters.com/world/americas/brazil-drought-crisis-linked-global-climate-change-minister-says-2021-07-08/.

Stewart, Georgina. 2018. "What Does 'Indigenous' Mean, for Me?" *Educational Philosophy and Theory* 50, no. 8: 740–43.

Stone, Erin Woodruff. 2021. *Captives of Conquest: Slavery in the Early Modern Spanish Caribbean*. Philadelphia: University of Pennsylvania Press.

Taussig, Michael. 1986. *Shamanism, Colonialism, and the Wild Man: A Study in Terror and Healing*. Chicago: University of Chicago Press.

Taylor, Christopher. 2012. *Black Carib Wars: Freedom, Survival, and the Making of the Garifuna*. Jackson: University Press of Mississippi.

Taylor, Douglas. 1951. *The Black Carib of British Honduras*. New York: Viking Fund.

Trafzer, Clifford E. 2019. *Fighting Invisible Enemies: Health and Medical Transitions among Southern California Indians*. Norman: University of Oklahoma Press.

Trouillot, Michel-Rolph, Mariana Past, and Benjamin Hebblethwaite. 2021. *Stirring the Pot of Haitian History*. Liverpool: Liverpool University Press.

Uzendoski, Michael A., and Edith Felicia Calapucha-Tapuy. 2012. *The Ecology of the Spoken Word: Amazonian Storytelling and Shamanism among the Napo Runa*. Urbana: University of Illinois Press.

Verger, Pierre. 1957. *Notes sur le culte des Orisa et Vodun à Bahia: la Baie de tous les saints au Brésil et à l'ancienne Côte des esclaves en Afrique*. Dakar: IFAN.

———. 1997. *Ewé, le verbe et le pouvoir des plantes chez les Yorùbá*. Paris: Maisonneuve et Larose.

Viveiros de Castro, Eduardo. 1998. "Cosmological Deixis and Amerindian Perspectivism." *Journal of the Royal Anthropological Institute* 4, no. 3: 469–88.

———. 2016. *Métaphysique cannibale*. Paris: Presses Universitaire Françaises.

Viveiros de Castro, Eduardo, and Peter Skafish. 2014. *Cannibal Metaphysics*. Minneapolis: Univocal.

Waldron, Lawrence. 2019. *Pre-Columbian Art of the Caribbean*. Gainesville: University of Florida Press.

Wheelock, Wade T. 2005. "Language: Sacred Language." In *Encyclopedia of Religion*, edited by Lindsay Jones, 5301–8. Detroit MI: Macmillan Reference.

Whitehead, Neil L. 2002. "Arawak Linguistic and Cultural Identity through Time: Contact, Colonialism, and Creolization." In *Comparative Arawakan Histories: Rethinking Language Family and Culture Area in Amazonia*, edited by Jonathan David Hill and Fernando Santos-Granero, 51–73. Urbana: University of Illinois Press.

Wilcken, Lois, and Frisner Augustin. 1992. *The Drums of Vodou*. Performance in World Music Series, no. 7. Tempe AZ: White Cliffs Media.

Worth, John. 1998. *The Timucuan Chiefdoms of Spanish Florida, Vol. 1, Assimilation; Vol. 2: Resistance and Destruction*. Gainesville: University of Florida Press.

Wright, Robin. 2013. *Mysteries of the Jaguar Shamans of the Northwest Amazon*. Lincoln: University of Nebraska Press.

1

Meeting Grounds in Saint-Domingue and the Emergence of Haitian Vodou

AN ECOLOGICAL APPROACH

LeGrace Benson

The human beings arriving at the quays of Saint-Domingue were carrying all the places where they had lived.[1] That is what human bodies do. Where we were is who we are. At the quay Cap François ships arrived from St. Louis, Dakar, Elmina, Luanda. Stevedores let down cargoes of traumatized human beings stripped of even the rags on their backs but bearing invisible remembrance of things past and hopes or fears of things to come. They transported the sight, and smell, the taste and feel of homelands not only as images but also in bone, muscle, and nerve.[2] Like all travelers, expatriates, exiles, and captives, they were in diaspora, a fundamental condition of consciousness stretched beyond habit to deal with endless novelties of the new place and time.

With no means by which to garner information about the undetermined future, such displaced persons struggle to do so with hindsight, reasoned predictions, and divinations. To be in diaspora is more than simply being in an-Other place, it is to be among an-Other people different from one's own family and community, usually with a sense of unwilling separation, of loss as painful as death. Everyone coming off the ship, landing at the meeting ground, was a dislocated stranger in a strange land, immediately confronting a briefly common condition and predicament. Everyone was separated from the beloved. Seafarers, missionaries, colonists, captive merchandise waiting to be sold were each there as points in the trajectory of their existences. Some had expectations of success, if not now then soon. The Africans were already burdened with expectations of continuing brutalization.

Seafarers had been in ports around the world. From 1709 throughout the eighteenth century, when all of Europe froze through the winter and continued to endure chill throughout the year, most ports were colder. Some were severely hampered by changes created by events of the "Little Ice Age." Every seafarer would be aware of this. Anyone coming from Europe would have been experiencing the coldest average temperatures in memory with severe crop failures and intricately imbricated economic conditions, almost certainly factors in the immanent fall of the French monarchy. The king was in debt. Many planters in Saint-Domingue were crop-rich but financially indebted.[3] Ensuing economic instability provided conditions for massive social change.

In Africa there was more rain than usual throughout the slave traffic era.[4] Weather and climate records for Saint-Domingue are scant, but long-term weather patterns and reports of travelers suggest more rain there as well. There were hurricanes distinctive to the Caribbean and so remarkable to outsiders that artists did engravings to report the "Terrible and Incredible Storm" back home.[5] Saint-Domingue, hot and humid, was a productive host vector for lethal diseases. For the captive cargo the climate was familiar. So was the year-round even division of day and night.

Everyone on the Cap-François quay was temporarily in the common ecosystem of the quay. Behind them and far to the horizon was the ocean. To their west rose mountains green with mahogany and pine; on the east plains, palms and hectares of crops; and in the near distance more mountains. Sounds of a busy trading city displaced those of ocean wind and water, masts groaning, sails cracking, and moaning in the packed slave bunkers. Smoke, sweat, rot, and the heavy perfume of tropical blossoms pervaded the air.

Into that new environment each person brought an embodied heritage of other places, other times: the personal knowledge, the personally carried common heritage (see Bacigalupo in this volume). African captives, the planters who bought their lives, and the Catholic missionaries there to spread the Gospel of Jesus Christ: each and all brought their distinctive long conversations, habits of attention, and styles of consciousness to the meeting ground at the Cap-François Port-au-Prince, Saint-Marc or Gonaïves quays. Every person that gathered at the meeting ground by coercion, will, or direction, every grouping of persons by immediate function and power position, found themselves in a foreign ecosystem. Every person there was an osmotic packet of knowing, remembering, breathing the air, gathering in the novel experience, and, in the encounter, changing the place, shaping its events.

Most attention was on the visible cargo, whatsoever planters wanted or needed and could either afford or stand for credit on the next sugar or coffee, mahogany or indigo crop: tools, furnishings, machinery, clothing, tomes on agriculture and veterinary medicine, and the European horses, cattle, and pigs that were devastating to local flora and fauna. Primarily planters' cargo of interest was the manual laborers who would work for mean lodgings they themselves would build, two lengths of cloth each year to make their own clothing, and a meager diet they would augment with whatever they could forage or grow in little plots beside their huts.

If there was a missionary on board, he would have his small allowance of clothing including ritual vestments; perhaps some simple household furnishings and utensils; altar goods, wine, and communion wafers; images of Jesus, Mary and the saints; and a supply of medicines. *Inventaire des biens* include bibles, psalters, missals, and other devotional literature.[6]

For the seafarers who manned the ship it was clothing, the last bits of food, sometimes little books of prayers or of magic such as *Petit Albert* and similar grimoires, and nearly always either Christian or folkish good luck amulets.[7] Richest of all their possessions were the spoken rumors and tales about the world beyond Saint-Domingue.

The captives had nothing but their invisible, untouchable long conversations, habits of attention, and styles of consciousness. In a magnificent series of paintings and sculpture, Haitian artist Edouard Duval-Carrié brings some of this reality into visibility. His *Migration of the Spirits* tells us that Ogou and Èzili, Danbala, Bosou, Ayizan, Azaka, Legba, Agwe, and Anansi came with the captives every league and every fathom of that murderous passage (see Gonzalez and Laughlin in this volume).[8] They say those who perished on the voyage went to blessed Vilokan under the sea where all the lwa and all the deceased ancestors live in peace and harmony.

Although few actual books arrived, there was always an unspecifiable store of information derived from books. Captives coming from Senegal and other Islamized regions were literate in Arabic. Many had memorized all or portions of the Quran.[9] (There appears to be no evidence of Qurans smuggled into Saint-Domingue in that era of state and papal exclusion and persecution of Islam.) The presence of books for all the Europeans and their absence among captives reminds us that the Europeans, even those who were illiterate, were "people of the book." This was especially true for the missionaries. Above all was the Bible in the Latin of St. Jerome with the Old and New Testament, including those sections that Protestants would denote as "apocryphal." Books—and, preeminently, the Holy Bible—were ingrained in the consciousness not only of the missionaries, but also as an inescapable environmental presence for all Europeans. The Bible, even when not read but heard, had shaped law and norms of social contract even when broken or reinterpreted for a burgeoning capitalism. From Athens to Edinburgh, Rome to Dublin, crossing the ocean to all the Americas, Bible stories told and retold in sermons and visual images of events and holy persons, together with the crucifixes in public squares and crossroads, meant that Europeans to one degree or another embodied at least bits and pieces of that book everywhere they set foot. Those who were literate and educated, which was most of the resident colonists, embodied or carried about as property a host of other literature as well (see Benítez de la Cruz and García Chapinal in this volume).

Literacy, or daily engagement in a social matrix where book knowledge, biblical or otherwise, has so pervasive a presence that it is a significant part of the long conversation, greatly directs habits of attention. It thus pervades styles of consciousness. Books are mediators of knowledge and understanding and in a sense also a meeting ground. A book is a material object—that is important—but it is a carrier of knowledge that must be mentally decoded, thus creating an illusion that the knowledge imparted is immaterial: "ideas" in a disembodied "imagination."[10]

In addition to the bible Psalters and missals, inventaire des biens include two other influential books: *Imitatio Christi*, by Thomas à Kempis, and *Exerctia spiritualis* by Ignatius Loyola. Quite possibly a missionary would also have an influential printed image, the Sacred Heart of Jesus and the

Sacred Heart of Mary as seen in visions by Margaret Mary Alacoque in 1672 (see Laughlin in this volume). The image rapidly spread as a devotional focus—both as idea and printed or drawn image in convents, monasteries and parish churches across Europe (Sauvy 1989). Meditation on the Sacred Heart with its crowning flames and thorny binding was meant to facilitate identification with the agony of Christ in order to withdraw from the things, people, and events of this world, even to the point of severe mortification of the flesh. The "mind" excised from its flesh should habitually turn attention away from materials, from desires (or needs in mortification of the flesh) to engage only the pure "spiritual."

Sacred Heart devotion had a dedicated feast day and weekly Thursday devotions. This habit of momentary withdrawal of attention from the environment in order to achieve special contact with spirits is highly congruent with certain Vodou practices as described from after the "tunnel period" forward.[11] This form of mental concentration in withdrawal is found worldwide, including in the homelands of the African captives, so such practice would have been doubly present long before the Concordat of 1860. The flaming, thorny heart probably arrived in Saint-Domingue with the earliest missionaries. With such lively engagement in the convents of Europe (Sauvy 1989), it would be especially surprising if the image were absent from the establishments of the holy women sent to the colony and even from the private chambers of some of the more pious of colonial women. At a date still unknown, the flaming heart of Jesus, as well as that of the Sacrum Cor Mater Dolorosa pierced by swords, began to be attributes of Èzili Dantò the Afro-Haitian lwa of all loves. Contemporary Vodou services often follow the opening paternoster with the Litany of the Sacred Heart of Jesus and the Sacred Heart of Mary. Further research may find evidence that these practices and images began as early as the late seventeenth century.

At the meeting ground, then, there were several combinations of mediated knowledge from books and immediate knowledge from direct engagement with the things and energies of this world. Most planters were schooled, had treatises and books referring to aspects of managing a farm or plantation, and understood numerical accounting methods. They coupled book learning with all the know-how—what Michael Polanyi has called nonquantifiable "personal knowledge" (Polanyi 1958) and more recent researchers call "embodied cognition"—that emerges from physical engagement with work and tools.

Many sailors were only partially literate, if at all, but had rich direct knowledge of seafaring work together with the ecology of seas and ports around the world. They were accustomed to a continuous displacement from one ecosystem to another. The music they sang as they worked held the rhythm of hauling sails and anchors and heaving cargo, and their songs and stories passed along real and exaggerated events, people, creatures, and places. (No fanciful exaggeration lacks an anchor in experienced realities.)

From what is known or can be deduced from evidence of their life histories, the missionaries were heavily invested in mediated knowledge. They may have grown up on a farm or learning a family craft or trade, the physical memories of which remained active although mostly peripheral to the main attention focus, but they had left it early to go into the seminaries and monasteries. There, all life, including active physical life, was concentrated on words and The Word. Brother Lawrence in the scullery framed even the humble immediacy of washing dishes into attention to praise words for his God.[12]

Above all, both as a metaphor and as a supposed reality, they believed that this world was not their home. The environment in which they in their impure bodies were situated was tainted—tinctured with temptations, most of its joys quite possibly the works of the Devil. From all we know of these missionaries, we ken that these beliefs were often honored in the breach. Imagine the ongoing tension of disparity between the gathering and use of information from the whole environment and the responses of a body evolved to do exactly that, but pulled and torn by the belief that both the call of the environment and the normal response to it was wickedness to be told to the confessor each Friday afternoon. Yet, for all that emphasis, it was not so simple. There was a curious kind of physical sensibility that found expression in the reported raptures of the exceptionally holy, their marvelous legends told in the little mission churches scattered out into the countryside beyond the port: Saint Theresa in ecstasy, Saint Francis communicating with birds and wolves and Brother Sun.

The captives on the quay, soon to be dispersed into the fields and habitations of that countryside, had their own treasure of tales and talents. Native or imported animals were mostly unfamiliar, but there were many plants they recognized as the same families as some back home. By the eighteenth century, crops transplanted from Africa—rice, sugarcane, and yams—and cared for by African captives were thriving. Most of all there were the stories, the songs, and the instructions. This lightest of all ship's cargo would come to have the weightiest presence in the development of a vision of human worth, culminating on the one hand in the creation and establishment of the world view, Vodou, and on the other in the astonishing revolution and establishment of the free nation of Haiti (see the introduction in this volume). Long conversations, habits of attention, and styles of consciousness are complex and deep-seated in nerve and gut and muscle. Not readily available as information to be observed directly or described explicitly, they were nonetheless fully in action at the tropical port and in the looming dispersal of captives into plantation slavery.

EMBODIED CONSCIOUSNESS

"Long conversations," "habits of attention," and "styles of consciousness" are shorthand phrases for three subtle, complex aspects of human perception, cognition, and interaction with humans, other animals, and, indeed, the entire ecosystem, locally, known of, and intuited or imagined (see Bacigalupo and Wright in this volume).[13] Here they are understood to encompass the conscious and the unconscious, including those aspects of a living being—like the flow of oxygen and carbon dioxide or the circuit of nerve impulses that are inaccessible to consciousness but nonetheless active and influential. Long conversations, habits of attention, and styles of consciousness are understood to be unitary, with distinctions between them but no divisions, of a piece with the whole living system. In other words, the discoveries of researchers in ecological psychology, biological evolution of consciousness, and embodied consciousness show that ideas and images are understood as materially real, bound to the corporal, in contrast to the positions taken following the dualism of mind and body posited especially and brilliantly by René Descartes. Long conversations, habits of attention, and styles of consciousness thus have no place for a zeitgeist—spirit of the times or ortgeist—spirit of place.[14] "Long conversations" refers to the continuity from early humans to the present by communicating to and from each other and other animals through gesture, song and speech, music, drawings, sculptures, and performances—"show and tell." Some of this conversation is summarized as ideas and images passed from one being to another, from one generation to the next, but more of it is what Michael Polanyi (1958) calls unspecifiable, unquantifiable "personal knowledge" and "tacit knowledge." It is the passing along of competencies as well as preserved images and verbal, symbolic, and written repetition of ideas, laws, and intimations of immortality.

Habits of attention are in their greater part formed by these exchanges. The family, society, and nation generate the tell and show and social enforcement that shapes what to look for, how to look, permissible or impermissible ways to communicate what has been attended to in repetitive or novel forms of the long conversation. Like these conversations, habits are in part explicit but in large measure tacit, largely unspecifiable except in the breach.

Styles of consciousness include both the conversations and the habits of attention. They are immediately recognized as personal, familial, regional, or larger geographical ways and means of expressive behavior. For example, it is possible to analyze words and phrases in texts to determine authorship and the religious community and something of the history that generated and used it—for instance, melodic lines or rhythmic structure to determine that this music is from France circa 1700, and this beat is from the Ibo people or the Congo people of western African lands. African and European styles of religious consciousness encountered one another in the era of colonial slave trade as though utterly incompatible (see the introduction; Bacigalupo; and Wright in this volume). Their separate, distinctive long conversations and habits of attention led them to understand themselves and the world in what seemed to be mutually incomprehensible styles of consciousness.

To summarize: *long conversations* are the interminable human communications, representations that began earlier than can yet be documented. They may have begun as moanings, cries, soothing little wordless hums, eventually forming into language. More than just talk, long conversations are also songs, pictures, dances, pantomimes, rituals, theater, and ways of food and eating. It is always about what is local to the person voicing or presenting a communication—hence, call and response to the enveloping ecosystem. This term refers to phenomena often called "roots," a metaphor that carries a sense of being in one place, like a great tree. The long conversation is transportable in space and time.

Habits of attention are the complicated personal and social experience of differentiating and making distinctions within what William James in his 1890 *Principles of Psychology* describes as the "great booming, buzzing confusion" that confronts us from birth. The evolutionary shaping of those habits is, like the source of them, ecological both from the standpoint of what is in the environment and how the individual, social unit or larger aggregation manages to live there. At the time of the trade in human beings, a shift of attention in literature and the visual arts toward heretofore overlooked or even disdained urban and rural lives was beginning to take place, and with it a consciousness that would soon lead to the Declaration of the Rights of Man in France and the outlawing of the slave trade in Great Britain. The colonists knew this and were setting their teeth against such eventualities. The African captives soon heard of the developments in their rapidly developing, common Kreyòl language. They turned their attention to means by which to ensure the shift.

Together long conversations and habits of attention of a place and times generate *styles of consciousness*. It is just here that its differentiation from the often-used notion of "zeitgeist," or spirit of the times, is crucial. A style of consciousness that is developed out of the long conversations and habits of attention of a specific population can be long enduring. Such styles can also be transported from one place and culture to another, but always with subtle to startling changes in response to new conditions. Of particular interest here are the styles of consciousness of those persons promulgating colonial empire and the accumulation of wealth; of those propagating a religion; of those ordinary folk who work on ships, sell goods, or render personal services; of those captives to be enslaved totally for the benefit of others as soon as they arrive on the quay.

Long before written histories, such long conversations included innumerable works of art permanently visible or performed time and time again for later generations. There are also ways of thought, languages—habits of attention—that become encoded as personal and social behavioral expectations. The memories and the passions are materially real. Every memory carried forward as the "spirit" or "soul" of the past is, as a matter of fact, physically present, albeit invisible, in the living bodies of descendants: bone, muscle, blood, nerve, and the unceasing traffic among them (see Bacigalupo in this volume). Memories *take place, take time*. The imagination of visible, touchable, tasteable, audible events already completed, or possible for now and the future, or seeming to be fantasies not possible outside the imagining body—all are enabled by that informed, constantly updated concatenation of the actualities of living bodies.

There were no ghosts inhabiting the bodies on the Cap-François quay. There was no determining zeitgeist or ortgeist ruling local personal or group actions. Instead, there were emerging processes and objects, never fully stable or fully determined. Real persons and social groupings acted with embodied memories, present conditions, and expectations, all encompassed in a continuing material and nested hierarchy of ecosystems. The continuous connections in this nesting are so far only beginning to be identified and are only lightly predictable within a massive cosmos wherein both perception and comprehension of the ends are out of sight: incomprehensible, indeterminable Alpha and Omega.

In the beginning was the mystery. The beginning is still a mystery: Alpha and Omega beyond kenning. But humans keep on learning how to hunt and fish, which plants to gather, how to make tools, how to make fire, how to herd animals, how to grow crops, how to make a machine that takes us to the moon and back, and how to fashion search engines that bring text treasures older than John Gutenberg's press to personal computer screens. Yet mysteries beyond mysteries remain to be understood. We are all urged toward answers, and, if not answers, then intuitions. It is how we survive.

That eighteenth-century gathering of people on the quay was collectively and individually working out solutions to the local mysteries and transcending mysteries using what was at hand. All techniques for survival, all sciences, technologies, and religions they discovered and used were here-and-now material. Individually each person existed as a living unit inseparable from the ecosystems that shaped them and that they shaped as they participated in the circulating flows of energy and information. Their dependable, predictable technical knowledge, the probing for more information of the energetically growing sciences of the era of Enlightenment and the probing further into the transcending incomprehensible that is still called "religions," were arising within and partaking of specific properties of the local ecosystems where they were living, moving and being, waking or dreaming. Each person on the quay meeting ground had a heritage—long conversations. All had habits of attention formed by individual interest and social direction. All had styles of consciousness—ways of being-here-in-this-world. Some of them had vague notions about where we come from, what we are doing here, and where we might be going after the last breath. Some held to doctrines that purported to answer those questions. Question and supposed answer were in the long conversations.

The predominant style of the colonists, and quite possibly of many ship captains, was shaped by the creation and ordering of an empire, imbued with winning and accumulating territory and wealth. Attention was on here-and-now appetites and the short-range future of their crops. They were already part of the shift taking place at that time that would separate newly forming empirical sciences from traditional speculative philosophies. Science was yielding useful information about crops and livestock and creating new tools to put to use immediately. There were certainly moments when one's eventual moral fate was under consideration; that momentary flash was usually shaped by the dominant Christian notions that were also being transformed by the new science and by thought and action of a developing global capitalism.

The predominant style of consciousness for missionaries was directed toward thought and action that abjured the "the world, the flesh, and the Devil" to focus on thought and action that would lead to being with God the Father, Son, and Holy Spirit in heaven. Priests' style of consciousness, so strongly shaped by an especially powerful assemblage of long conversations and habits of attention, was more developed and intense than most members of their congregations and markedly different from that of the excluded Protestants. The styles of the planters and the priests, although differing, were both in process of evolving in response to the new sciences and the developing economic system. They shared much, and both were radically different from styles of consciousness of the African captives.

Among the Africans there was a range of consciousness styles from ancient Indigenous ways, to sub-Saharan forms of Islam, to the Christianized Congolese. Most Western African peoples had a fundamental sense of an encompassing, integrated quotidian and transcendent ecosystem, inhabited by what was perceivable in the everyday local environment and invisible personages, powers, and forces pervading the continuous local and transcendent realms. This was the case even across Senegal and Mali, where Islamic monotheism was widespread. The whole kingdom of Congo was instructed and obliged to be Christian by the end of the seventeenth century, and there was a formal envoy to the Vatican.[15] Many, especially in rural districts, continued traditional habits of attention. Any Fulani nominal Muslim or Congolese nominal Christian on the quay had fashioned a working "double consciousness" already part of their long conversations and habits of attention. This reality had important implications for the formation of Haitian Vodou.[16]

Captured Congo *nganga*, *olorishas* of Yoruba land, imams, holy seers, healers, teachers and priestly mediators on the quay for sale as laborers had deep knowledge of homeland ecologies and their continuance into the wider cosmos. These leaders would evolve into the oungan and manbo of Saint-Domingue–Haiti. Their knowledge, like that of the Catholic priests, was more subtle and intense than that of the less dedicated population, but the latter were nevertheless aware of the presence and power of their knowledge and understood some degree of that knowledge themselves. The style of consciousness of the Africans, and very quickly of the slave oungan and manbo, consciously, tacitly, and unconsciously continued the traditional understanding of humans (and usually all other animals as well) as being-here-now in bodies evolved to cope successfully with earthly ecosystems, eyes facing the immediate environment and possibly that of tomorrow, able to discern the state of the environment as a whole and in the peculiar ecosystem of enslavement (see the introduction and Frim in this volume). At the same time, they continued the habit of attention consciously in touch with the transcendent, believed to be ordinary and present—in short, a form of panentheism.[17]

VISIBLE SIGNS AND INVISIBLE FORCES

On the quay meeting ground in Cap Haïtien there were experts with access to the sacred, among the seafarers, the missionary priests, and the captives. The Catholic priests, with duties to officiate in the transitions of life, were on the quay to perform the obligatory baptism of captives. Some captives, who had already undergone Christian baptism in Africa, would soon be singled out for special service with the missions. Those captives who were not holders of special knowledge and functions nevertheless had their personal sense of an inspirited environment, of the lines between the yet-to-be-born, the living, and those who had died; of dealing with conflict and conciliation in family and community; of collaborating in seedtime, cultivation, hunting and harvest; in loves and wars. They dealt regularly with practical matters, with transcendent matters, and with the crossroads between them, calling upon diviners and healers to deal with exigencies and the always contingent knowledge of the transcendent.

The manbo and oungan descendants of the African keepers of sacred knowledge from the time of Saint-Domingue to the present embody the long conversation from African lands, aware of the energies present in trees, water, rocks, human loves and hates. They knew and held fast their ancient names: Legba, Danbala and Danbala Wèdo, Ayizan, Azaka, Èzili Ogou. Disdained as "animism" by Europeans, naming was an affirming recognition of real energies and actual forces present without interruption throughout all creation. The names and the notions continued.

Seafaring workers, ever in transit, anonymous except in some ship manifests, often unremembered in records of their original communities, are thin shadows in the secular and ecclesiastical history books. Yet they, too, brought their personal cargo to the quay. In peril on the sea as often as not, everyday habits of attention included the loves and hates and errors of the past and a sharp and omnipresent fear of death. The daily rum ration was little comfort and no reassurance. Many kept amulets and lucky charms on their persons, believing that the amulet in touch with their body and supposed soul would transfer protection, thus keeping the two together. Some had crosses, little books of prayers, or grimoires.[18] These sailors' goods are the likely origin of certain objects still found today on Vodou altars.

The people gathered at the quay were also transporting much secular baggage including knowledge of how to manage account books, how to direct an agricultural project; how to "manage" the enslaved workers; how to garner the most allegiance and best financial support from parishioners; how to do blacksmithing, repair tools, and develop detailed agricultural expertise. There were Africans who were master agriculturists who knew what had to be done should it rain too much or not enough, and how to keep a herd of cattle healthy. There were literate men among the captives who knew the Arabic kitab of agriculture and husbandry by heart and by experience, down-to-earth expertise coupled with regard for the transcendent will of Allah.[19] One tantalizing evidence of this existed up through the early twentieth century outside a cul-de-sac farming village: carved doors of a granary that included incised Arabic writing (Fouchard 1988, 20).

It should be held in mind that alongside knowledge and techniques of the quotidian and the sacred there was the omnipresent consciousness of separation. For the Africans it was being wrenched and torn away from earth, land, and sky from parents, sisters, and brothers, and from their intangible but entirely real status, high or low, in a community: severed from Mother Africa until death. In Vodou that fostered belief in the return at death to Nan Ginen–Vilokan. In the twenty-first century some Afro-Haitians traveling to their ancestors' African homelands scoop up a vial of the earth in which Mother Africa resides to bring back to Haiti. The bit of earth is not a tourist souvenir but a holy presence cherished by the pilgrim. On the eighteenth-century quay, the consciousness of separation from all that had been home was about to be intensified by the obligatory separations of family members from each other and the splitting apart of cohorts from the same territory. Plantation inventaires de biens list slaves as a mix of such peoples as Mandinga, Wolof, Yoruba, Nago, Igbo, Coromanti, Congo, and Arada. For all the captives, the physical pain of whippings, hunger, sickness, fear, and the stripping of dignity were paramount. The sorrow of being wrenched from homelands to go forevermore into a strange land where one is an alien, dishonored being was another kind of beating. Recollection of unnamable ways things looked and smelled and tasted; the named recollection of places, special events, and relatives was a necessary anchor in sanity. Nago, Ibo, Congo, Rada (Arada) endure into the present as *fanmi* (family) or *nanchon* (nation) of Vodou spirits (lwa) and their associated rites and sacred objects.

The insistent holding to long conversations, habits of attention, and styles of consciousness of homeland and family has such authority that it has persisted into the twenty-first century and the contemporary diaspora. Karen E. Richman has meticulously documented this robust continuity of the *imaginaire* of African ways and how modern technology such as telephones, photography and, especially, cassette players have both preserved and evolved this heritage (Richman 2005).

DISPERSAL AND EMERGENCE

The separation out of Africa, out of the ship, off of the quay into the strangeness and estrangement of Saint-Domingue plantations was about to be completed at auction. But, first, the baptism. For Congolese it was water and words that they knew. For Ibo or Coromantin it was a puzzle. For the officiating priests it required a rearrangement of tenets of their belief. They had to reconstruct the message of "Love thy neighbor as thyself. Feed the hungry, minister to the sick and suffering, clothe the naked" to see enslavement as saving the Africans from supposed satanic captivity, the worship of false gods and debauchery, and to baptize them into the Kingdom of Heaven and the One True God. They washed away "ungodly" birth names to "grace" each enslaved person with a French sobriquet, or, ironically, with an un-Christian name of a Greek or Roman deity, general, politician or philosopher. Those are common names in Haiti to this day. Catholic priests had to believe they were saving invisible souls for eternal bliss despite the visible woes of the mortified flesh present in front of them. Many Vodou communities still require Catholic baptism as part of their initiation.

Africans had unmediated knowledge present as body, bone, muscle and nerve; in ears and mouths, stomachs, legs, arms, hands and the soles of their feet—ways of seeing, ways of being-here. They held the authority of experience, for which there is no substitute. As for the presence of the transcendent spirits everywhere, and the special manifestation of the coming down into the community, everyone had witnessed it. Even some of the children had directly experienced such manifestation of the real invisibles.

What came together both invisibly and visibly, audibly, palpably, actually soon scattered with the participants: return to the ship for the next voyage, return to the habitations to run the colonial agricultural and financial enterprise, return to the parishes to bring the Word of God, or go past point of no return into slave quarters, fields, and workstations to create the goods that made Saint-Domingue the colony that produced the greatest wealth in the world.

Whole libraries and archives exist consisting of writings about the early history of Vodou in Saint-Domingue. Moreau de Saint-Méry (1750–1819) is the most quoted witness source. Père Jean-Baptiste Labat (1663-1705) is also primary. Earlier descriptions of other French Caribbean colonies by Père Jean-Baptiste Dutertre (1610–87) are also informative. There are shorter reports from missionaries and other travelers from the time of Columbus that describe landscape, people, and commercial and religious activities in sufficient detail that it is possible to gain some sense of the often catastrophically changing ecologies from 1492 to the high colonial presence of the eighteenth century.

Leslie Desmangles (1992) traces the first African arrivals bringing their traditional religions to Hispaniola to circa 1612 and more intensely at the time of greatly increased imports after the 1697 Treaty of Ryswick. He notes that those earliest captives included the whole range of African societies including priests, and that in the turbulent, brutal world of the eighteenth-century plantations, "the domain of religion exhibited the strongest forms of continuity with Africa" (17–28). In addition to the work of Moreau de Saint-Méry he cites other sources from that era, including those describing Catholic missions, and goes on to focus especially on what he called the "symbiosis" of the two religions, "a symbiosis by ecology and by identification. The first suggests the juxtaposition of religious elements necessitated by environmental and geographical adaptation and the second suggests specifically the system by which, on the basis of similarity, Catholic Saints were identified with or 'transfigured into' Vodou gods" (8).

The ecological perspective suggests an expansion of Desmangles's proposition. Juxtaposition in biological symbiosis often evolves beyond simple juxtaposition, wherein each separate element coexists retaining a degree of distinctive characteristics, to achieve degrees of amalgamation or even mutation into something new. Geographical adaptation—the survival response to changing ecosystems—is often the tenacious driver of such rearrangements of energy and identity.

An ecological perspective can make use of the reports of such polymath missionaries as Dutertre and Labat, not for their harsh, erroneous judgment of Africans and their ways, but for the finely detailed descriptions and drawings of the environment. Their style of consciousness was to see each plant and animal and lay of the land categorically rather than as an interconnected whole, while the disdained Africans were at all practical and transcendent levels of their consciousness alert to the continuous flow connecting each to all. This understanding survived all attempts to obliterate it and endures into the present. Internet Vodou is now in process of greatly modifying this style of consciousness, as a quick search of "Vodou" or "Voodoo" will reveal.

SYMBIOTIC EVOLUTIONS

The symbiotic, evolutionary character of Vodou is more discussed than the symbiotic evolution that would more slowly take place over time in the Roman Catholic Church. Yet such intersection can be noted in early diocesan reports, such as those referred to by Père Antoine Cabon (1936) that the "superstitions" of Vodou were infiltrating the parishes in thought and deed and physical symbol. Anti-Duvalierist fervors of the later twentieth century found once banned and burned Congo and Rada drums accompanying hymns in parish churches and the once staid posture of processions relaxed into slightly bent knees and swaying shoulders, feet moving forward to drumbeats so different from the four-four European hymnody.[20]

The most intense gathering of sense of environment and of the need to collimate Kongo and Fulani, Yoruba, and Arada energy into focus to ram down the walls of colonial servitude would gather in scattered locales for ceremonies. These were at once worship and an invocation of all powers and forces into an extended meeting ground. Formation of a religious involvement responsive to the most local and immediate people and conditions, and at the same time fully gathered and oriented to the wider world and the transcendent future, depended absolutely on the long conversations from Africa. Refocusing their habitual attention to new ecologies and forming a revised style of consciousness, liberated Haitians became a bellwether for the slow unfolding of civil rights and respect for all creatures and creation that remains a work in progress.

Colonists did not comprehend a danced religion, much less the sensibility of the real presence of transcendent spirits coming down into ordinary people, into animals, trees, water, rocks, and human relationships, or that communicated messages for action in drumming and dancing was from the lwa (see the introduction; Bacigalupo; and Wright in this volume). They were slow to realize that the growing revolt of the enslaved was forming in what colonists initially saw as weekend parties where the "savages" indulged in orgies of relief from work. Colony-wide uprisings and poisonings finally got their attention, and ineffective suppressions were instituted.[21] The famous incident of Bwa Kayiman Vodou ceremony, variously reported and misreported from August 1791 to the present, marked the frontier of African and Afro-Creoles on one side and French on the other. The next meeting grounds would be battlegrounds.

Outnumbered and no match for guerilla tactics of a dispersed but cohesive people with a muscular consciousness of what it meant to be free and honored, the French retreated from the Battle of Vertières and from Saint-Domingue. Afro-Haitian long conversations, habits of attention responsive to immediate ecological circumstances, and a robust, evolving style of consciousness enabled the establishment of a religion and a nation that endure to this day. What the enslaved people understood with their worldview and religion oriented to survival, living well, procreating and becoming honored ancestors were the droits de l'homme—the rights of all human beings. This was and is accepted, even by many who violate it, as a universal idea or ideal. Viewed as words on a page and thought in the mind, the rights of humans were without material existence for the French. For the materially suffering enslaved Africans, this sacred ideal was the biological, ecological condition essential to the continued human physical survival. Thus they acted.

NOTES

1. Reading the first draft of this chapter I realized that the term and notion of "meeting grounds" was "in mind" to be used as a result of the scholarship of Dean MacCannell, especially his *Empty Meeting Grounds* (1992). While we have differences of approach, I must credit MacCannell with having significant influence on my own interdisciplinary methods.
2. There is a growing scientific literature on this topic as well as entire conferences devoted to various aspects of embodied memory. For examples, see abstracts for *Formation of Embodied Memory*, Deutsche Gesellschaft für Phänomenologyische Anthropologie, Psychiatrie und Psychoterapie, Heidelberg, 2017, http://dgap-ev.de/formation-of-embodied-memory/ (accessed August 8, 2022). Recent papers frequently cite inter alia Polyani, Merleau-Ponty, Gibson, and Varela. See the references for this chapter.
3. Archives d'Outre Mer in Aix-en-Provence includes a collection of Saint-Domingue notary files and inventories of goods as well as their admirably meticulous account books. Together these indicate many planters were, in today's business parlance, "highly leveraged."
4. "Study Reconstructs African Climate History," Historical Climatology, July 30, 2013, https://www.historicalclimatology.com/study-reconstructs-african-climate-history.html.
5. Theodore De Bry, "A Terrible and Incredible Storm," engraving, 1594, Special Collections, University of Houston Libraries, printed in *National Museum of American Indian* (Fall 2018): 19.
6. Inventaire des biens, initially in Bibliothèque Nationale, Paris, now in Archives d'Outre Mer, Aix-en-Provence, are highly detailed inventories of all property held by French inhabitants of Saint-Domingue. The massive collection of the complete papers of Moreau de St. Méry, including his frequently cited *Description topographique* are also in Aix. Aside from Moreau's *Description*, most documents are not yet digitized for access on the internet.
7. *Les Secrets merveilleux de la Magi Naturelle ou Petit Albert* and *La Poule Noire* were among the several treatises that came in from France and were reprinted in Saint-Domingue. Paperback copies are still to be seen in Haiti's outdoor bookstalls. Copies are on some Vodou altars at present.
8. *Migrations of the Spirit* installation at Figge Museum, Davenport, Iowa, 2005.
9. See Fouchard (1988) for an extensive study of slaves' literacy and its suppression.
10. The literature related to this position is at least as old as Spinoza; see references for recent scientific studies.
11. The tunnel period is 1804, when Haiti declared independence and was cut off from the Roman See until 1860, when the Concordat reestablished relationships, and missions returned.

12. *The Practice of the Presence of God* collects the thoughts and prayers of this seventeenth-century monk, noted for his humility and for understanding the presence of God in the most mundane of human daily actions. The book compiled after his death became and remains a major devotional book among Catholic Christians.
13. The author has developed these terms in earlier essays, based upon theories of ecological perception first proposed by James J. Gibson (1966, 1979) and carried into the present by subsequent researchers, used as applicable to the arts and religions.
14. The art historian Sir Ernst Gombrich on several occasions (in the late 1960s, when the author was present) while he was Distinguished Visiting Scholar at Cornell University firmly dismissed any notion of "zeitgeist" as a determinant of styles of art. He stressed that, although not all possibilities were available at any given moment in history, the individual always has undetermined possibilities of invention and new creation. Furthermore, this escapee from the Anschluß of Austria asserted that zeitgeist determinism leads to political authoritarianism. He especially noted this in a seminar to which he had been invited by this author, but we did not make a sound recording of his remarks.
15. For a detailed presentation of the relationship between Kongo Indigenous religion and Christianity see John Thornton's *The Kingdom of Kongo* (1983), especially 60–63, where he discusses the relationship between *nganga* religious leaders and Catholic priests. What Thornton calls "mental world" is in some ways equivalent to the notion here of "styles of consciousness."
16. W. E. B. Du Bois in *The Souls of Black Folk* (1903) spoke of a double *social* consciousness. Here we expand the doubling to encompass the wider ecosystem of geographical place and of the way time is measured and used.
17. Eighteenth-century philosophers arrived at this term as early as 1809, by Friedrich Schelling, but the belief itself is ancient and occurs in many locations around the world. A reading of eighteenth-century romantic poets provides many instances, tacit or overt. Many holding such sensibilities were Abolitionists who also favored the voice of the people in governance.
18. The grimoires sailors carried were small copies of books of magic rituals, incantations, and designs alleged to heal sickness, to insure ill luck or even death to enemies, and to bring good fortune to the holder who went through related rituals. Modern printings of these are still to be found in outdoor bookstalls stacked next to computer manuals.
19. The most likely agricultural kitab known to the Africans was the *Kitab al-filahal*, written by Ibn al-'Awwam of Seville in the twelfth century and widely used throughout the Mediterranean and upper Africa. It was not translated into French until 1864, so the French planters had access to this knowledge only through their expert slaves.

20. Father Pierre Augustine made efforts over a period of several years to bring the traditional African drums into Roman Catholic services, finally accomplished in the early 1980s.
21. Ramsey (2011) presents a detailed study of this highly complicated era.

REFERENCES

Cabon, Père Adolph. 1936. *Notes sur l'histoire religieuse d' Haïti*. Archevêché: Port-au-Prince, 1936.

Damasio, Antonio. 2018. *The Strange Order of Things: Like, Feeling, and the Making of Cultures*. Toronto: Random House.

Desmangles, Leslie. 1992. *Faces of the Gods: Vodou and Roman Catholicism in Haiti*. Chapel Hill: University of North Carolina Press.

Du Bois, W. E. B. 1903. *The Souls of Black Folk*. Chicago: A. C. McClurg.

Dutertre, Père Jean-Baptiste. 1654. *Histoire generale, des isles de S. Christophe, de la Guadeloupe, de la Martinique, et autres dans l'Amerique*. St. Genevieve: Chez Jacques Langlois.

Feinberg, Todd E., and Jon M. Mallatt. 2016. *The Ancient Origins of Consciousness*. Cambridge MA: MIT Press.

Fouchard, Jean. 1988. *Les Marrons du Syllabaire: quelques aspects du problème de l'instruction et de l'éducation des esclaves et affranchis de Saint-Domingue*. Port-au-Prince: Éditions Henri Deschamps.

Fuchs, Thomas. 2016. "Embodied Knowledge—Embodied Memory." In *Analytic and Continental Philosophy: Methods and Perspectives; Proceedings of the 37th International Wittgenstein Symposium*, edited by Sonja Rinofner-Kreidl and Harald A. Wiltsche, 215–30. Berlin: De Gruyter.

Gazzaniga, Michael S., ed. 1999. *Conversations in the Cognitive Neurosciences*. Cambridge MA: MIT Press.

Gibson, James, J. 1966. *The Senses Considered as Perceptual Systems*. Boston: Houghton Mifflin.

———. 1979. *The Ecological Approach to Visual Perception*. Boston: Houghton Mifflin.

Hurbon, Laënnec. 1987a. *Le barbare imaginaire*. Port-au-Prince: Imprimerie H. Deschamps.

———. 1987b. *Dieu dans le Vaudou*. Port-au-Prince: Éditions Deschamps, 1987.

———. 1993. *Les mystères du vaudou*. Paris: Gallimard, 1993.

———. 1995. *Voodoo: Search for the Spirit*. New York: Harry Abrams/Thames & Hudson.

Labat, Père Jean-Baptiste. 1742. *Nouveau voyage aux Isles de L'Amerique*. Paris: Chez Guillaume Cavelier.

Lakoff, George, and Mark Johnson. 1999. *Philosophy in the Flesh: The Embodied Mind and Its Challenge to Western Thought*. New York: Basic.

MacCannell, Dean. 1992. *Empty Meeting Grounds: The Tourist Papers*. London: Routledge.

Moreau de Saint-Méry, Méderic-Louis-Elie. 1797–98. *Description topographique, physique, civile, politique, et historique de la partie Française de l'isle Saint-Domingue*. Philadelphia: Chez l'auteur . . . chez Dupont . . . chez les principaux libraires.

Ramsey, Kate. 2011. *The Spirits and the Law: Vodou and Power in Haiti*. Chicago: University of Chicago Press.

Richman, Karen E. 2005. *Migration and Vodou*. Gainesville: University Press of Florida.

Thornton, John K. 1983. *The Kingdom of Kongo: Civil War and Transition, 1641–1718*. Madison: University of Wisconsin Press.

Polanyi, Michael. 1958. *Personal Knowledge: Towards a Post-Critical Philosophy*. Chicago: University of Chicago Press.

Sauvy, Anne. 1989. *Le miroir du coeur: quatre siècles d'images savants et populaires*. Paris: Les Éditions du Cerf.

Varela, Francisco J., Evan Thompson, and Eleanor Rosch. 1993. *The Embodied Mind: Cognitive Science and Human Experience*. Cambridge MA: MIT Press.

2 The Many Faces of Marie Laveau and Voudou in Nineteenth-Century New Orleans

Eleanor A. Laughlin

The Voudou legacy of Marie Laveau (1801–81) is a looming presence in the city of New Orleans.[1] Shop displays and pamphlets extol her renown, and reproductions of her portrait are available throughout the city and on the internet, connecting her name and image to the practice of Voudou. Actually, relatively little is known about nineteenth-century Voudou practices. An examination of primary periodicals, personal memoirs, and portraits reveals the historical context surrounding Marie Laveau and brings some clarity to these practices in New Orleans and the role she played in them. In this chapter I analyze four representations of Marie Laveau: a painted portrait, her home altar via descriptive oral histories in the Louisiana Writer's Project (LWP), a caricature of Laveau with her daughter, and a twentieth-century tarot card portrait.[2] I argue that each representation conveys different perspectives of Laveau's sociopolitical context, adding to our understanding of Voudou practices in nineteenth-century New Orleans, its reception outside of Voudou circles, and Laveau's hybrid approach to serving as a priestess, which helped her achieve agency across classes, races, and religions.

Marie Laveau was born in 1801, married Jacques Paris in 1819, and had two children. Shortly thereafter Paris died, and Laveau became known as the "Widow Paris." By 1826 she entered into a relationship with Charles Glapion, although the two were not allowed to marry because of antimiscegenation laws; Charles Glapion was white. Together they had seven children. Laveau lived a full and well-rounded life: she had a large family, was a respected hairdresser, attended Catholic Mass regularly, and participated in gatherings at Congo Square, a space designated for African American celebrations. Beyond this, in her later years, she devoted herself to volunteer work in hospitals and the prison system. Upon her retirement from her responsibilities as a priestess, another woman named "Marie Laveau" assumed her clients and performed the same services.[3] The two women were often mistakenly thought to be the same person, leading to a heightened perception of the original Laveau's longevity and power. Although old legends and contemporary lore attempt to make Laveau a sensational figure, my research indicates that her exceptionality existed in the subjecthood she achieved for the time period and her skillful use of religion as a means to help her clients and find acceptance among community members of various backgrounds.

In her lifetime Laveau saw a great shift in the ideologies that governed African American lives in New Orleans, including postcolonial transitions with growing numbers of Anglo-Saxon settlers early in the century, intense crackdowns on Voudou practitioners prior to the Civil War, and the increasing racist sentiments in the 1870s that led to Jim Crow laws. Before her birth the French and Spanish approaches to managing the colony allowed opportunities for enslaved people to buy or work toward their freedom. In fact Laveau was born a free woman of color. After the United States' purchase of Louisiana in her early childhood, the governance shifted from one that supported Catholic principles, which recognized Blacks as individuals with spirits, to one that did not acknowledge the spiritual needs of Black people and therefore did not allow them time off on Sundays (Long 2006, 10; Fandrich 2005, 84, 89; Bell 1997, 12). With one day of freedom each week under the colonial administrations, many enslaved people worked extra jobs and, by saving their profits, were slowly able to obtain manumission.[4] Because New Orleans was one of the few port towns in the United States formerly under colonial rule by France—or by Spain with its relatively liberal black code—a large percentage of Blacks were free, compared with other U.S. locations (Long 2006, 6, 14, 15; Bennett 2005, 137–42). Thus there were also a disproportionately larger number of free women of color, like Marie Laveau, who were negotiating the landscape of white domination, working to locate their sense of personhood within the Eurocentric habits of attention and styles of consciousness imposed upon them (see Benson in this volume).

Under the Spanish Cabildo (government), free women of color in New Orleans occupied numerous types of service positions including jobs similar to those done in slavery such as domestic labor, or working as shop vendors, laundresses, and cooks; or trade work that required a technical skill such as working as beauticians, hairdressers, nurses, seamstresses, or boarding house managers (Long 2006, 36; Fandrich 2005, 93–100). Rather than being an exception to the rule in New Orleans, Laveau was a fairly typical free woman of color, part of the most visible group producing Voudou priestesses in the city (Fandrich 2005, 115).

THE GEORGE CATLIN PORTRAIT OF MARIE LAVEAU

A portrait by Frank Schneider (1881–1935), copied from an original George Catlin (1796–1872) painting that was lost for some years, depicts a free woman of color identified as Marie Laveau by the Louisiana State Museum (fig. 1).[5] In the portrait Laveau sits against a dark background. She is wearing a black dress and is turned in three-quarter profile toward the viewer. She sits with her spine adroit, assured of her personal power. Her facial expression is one of indifference to being looked at. She neither smiles nor makes eye contact with the viewer, looking beyond them with an air of superiority. Over her shoulders she wears an elegant silk shawl, purportedly a gift from the Chinese emperor, with a fire-red floral design on a gold background.[6] The edges of the shawl are lined with red lace trim that brushes against her dress. Around her head she wears a cream-colored tignon (scarf), red-striped, in the Madras style.

The portrait identifies its subject as a woman with sufficient notoriety to attract the attention of George Catlin, an artist who sought to capture the life and culture of the American Indians. In pursuit of this endeavor, he traveled across the United States visiting numerous tribes and painting hundreds of portraits. While it is certain that Catlin traveled on the Mississippi River and within the vicinity of New Orleans in the 1830s, his travel accounts make no direct reference to Marie Laveau, or to any free woman of color he painted in New Orleans (Truettner 1979; Gurney, George, and

F1. *Portrait Identified as Marie Laveau* by Frank Schneider. Copy of the original by George Catlin (attribution now in question), ca. 1835. Oil on canvas. Courtesy of the Collections of the Louisiana State Museum #11537.

Heyman 2002).[7] If they did meet, their acquaintance may have been due to Laveau's partial Native American heritage and her interest in Indigenous spiritual culture and herbal healing practices, which she incorporated into her practice (Raphael Villère, interview by Hazel Breaux, LWP folder 25; Fandrich 2005, 192). Both the tignon and her herbal remedies are transcultural approaches to her self-representation and service as a priestess, respectively.

The tignon wrapped around Laveau's head was a visual marker of race originally required by the Edict of Good Government (1786), which became known informally as the "Tignon Law."[8] Enacted by governor Esteban Miró, the law was punishable if disregarded with the stated goal of creating a good colony. His recommendations included sartorial edicts to identify enslaved people and free women of color in public settings, because skin tones varied and therefore were not a true indicator of social status. The sumptuary law proscribed that women of African descent or with African blood "wear feathers nor curls in their hair, combing it flat or covering it with a handkerchief if it is combed high as was formerly the custom" (Tulane 2013; Long 2006, 20). The intention was to limit luxurious fabrics and jewels to the provenance of the upper class and relegate lesser-quality clothing materials and accessories to enslaved people and people with dark skin. However, women of color in New Orleans chose instead to wear brightly colored headscarves and to wrap them in inventive ways, drawing attention to their flair for everyday style; they incorporated jewels and ribbons into tignon wraps and used the finest-quality fabric available to them. Often high-quality madras cotton fabric dyed in a plaid pattern in India or Saint-Domingue, was the fabric of choice (Tulane University 2013).[9] This headscarf, imposed throughout the Caribbean, was often reinterpreted by its wearers as a sign of agency. In Martinique and Haiti the wrapping style of the tignon was encoded with secret messages: one knot might hold a ceremonial meaning, while two knots could mean the wearer's heart is taken (Tulane University 2013; New Orleans Public Library 2005). Although the tignon was no longer required by the time the portrait was made, head wrapping remained in style among women of African descent for several decades after the edict was enacted, as evidenced in the portrait of Laveau, and it remains popular in present-day Haiti and the Haitian diaspora.

Today, in Haitian Vodou, headscarves are obligatory for women, and in some temples for men as well. In all Vodou rites, whether Nago, Kongo, Rada, or Gede, women cover their heads. Wearing a head covering is at the heart of a female Vodouist's symbolic attire and is a feature of ceremonial practice. In Haitian Vodou the *mouchwa* (headscarf) represents a lwa with a symbolic color (i.e., purple and black are symbolic of Gede). Specific headscarf colors are worn for particular ceremonies; thus color-coding is absolutely central to the use of headscarves in Vodou. LWP interviews indicate that the color of Laveau's dress and tignon depended upon the kind of work she was doing rather than the spirits she called upon (Raymond Rivaros, interview by Hazel Breaux, LWP folder 25; Long 2006, 111). Although differences exist between Haitian Vodou and nineteenth-century New Orleanian Voudou, the tignon is a definitive visual marker worn by women in Vodou and in Creole culture more broadly.

Many people associate New Orleanian Voudou with Haitian Vodou, but Haitian practitioners did not settle in Louisiana in significant numbers until nearly a century after the first slave boats arrived in Louisiana in 1719. Rather, slave trade ship logs indicate that both Senegambia and Kongo had a stronger influence on the foundational culture, and by extension the initial Voudou practices in New Orleans than did Haiti (Hall 1992, 31, 34; Fandrich 2005, 42; Long 2005, 279; Long 2006, 5–6). During the early French colonial period in Louisiana (1682–1762), nearly two-thirds of the population was comprised of enslaved people from the Senegambian region—a particularly high percentage compared with other locations in the western hemisphere (Hall 1992, 35; Fandrich 2005, 40–41). The French enlisted the help of enslaved people from the Senegambian region due to the nature of the Louisiana landscape and the challenges they faced cultivating crops there. Over the centuries Senegambian agricultural specialists had developed expertise in the cultivation of rice and indigo, had built up resistance to tropical diseases like malaria, and were acclimated to the heat and humidity of Louisiana (Hall 1992, 31–37; Fandrich 2005, 41). And, not coincidentally, the tignon was a garment worn by choice in the Senegambian region of West Africa.

A group of Senegambian women of mixed African and French descent known as *signares* donned a head wrap similar to the tignon. The signare

F2. *Un bal de Signares (mulâtresses) à St. Louis (Sénégal). Côte occidentale d'Afrique* by Colonel Frey. 1890. Bibliothèque Nationale de France. gallica.bnf.fr/Médiathèque du musée du quai Branly–Jacques Chirac.

head wrap is taller than the New Orleanian tignon, resembling a cone in form, with a tie in the shape of a flower. The signare women were renowned for the power they were able to achieve, including land and slave ownership, amid the Atlantic slave trade (Brooks 1976, 20). Signares on the island of Gorée often married European men because the men found them particularly beautiful. Once married, signares helped their husbands handle business affairs and thus gained an elevated status within the community (Brooks 1976, 30). A nineteenth-century engraving titled *Un bal de Signares (mulâtresses) à St. Louis (Sénégal)* depicts a large group of women and men gathered around a small circle of women dancing with one man in European clothing at the center (fig. 2). The costumes of the surrounding onlookers vary and include other men wearing suits, African women in turbans, and those with elegantly braided hair. However, the tall, conical tignons of the signares stand out as the predominant head covering in the group. The image represents a ball with dancing, food, and socialization between those cultures living in the French colonial region.

Such a celebration may have been an occasion for signares to meet European men, as male attendance is highlighted in the foreground of the image. Similar balls were held in New Orleans to create opportunities for free women of color to mingle with potential partners (Long 2006, 38; Fandrich 2005, 110). These balls became the subject of poetry and song in nineteenth-century Louisiana (Cable 1886).

Although we have few details about the practice of Voudou in New Orleans during the nineteenth century, compelling similarities exist between the cosmologies found in the Kongo and Senegal River basins and that of New Orleanian Voudou. The Kongolese, Senegambian, Haitian and New Orleanian Voudou traditions all feature a high God and numerous ancestral spirits (though Haitian has more), rather than a focus on the Yoruba orisha, and Senegambian religions are noted for their practitioners' use of charms (Long 2006, 114–16; Fandrich 2005, 42). Like West African Vodunists, Marie Laveau was renowned for her ability to create gris-gris, or charms, on behalf of her clientele. In fact the creation of *gris-gris* is a hallmark of New Orleanian Voudou. The term "gris-gris" has its etymological origins in the Senegambian region with the Mende term *gergergys*, or "charm," connecting the New Orleanian charm to Senegambia linguistically, whereas in Haiti the term *wanga* is used for charms similar to gris-gris. A positive amulet is called *zinzin* in Bambara (a subgroup of the larger Senegambian Mende cultural family) and has exactly the same name in Louisiana Creole.[10] *Zin* (or *zen*) is also an important word in Fon, referring to a sacred receptacle for holding spirits (Fandrich, 2005, 41; Long, 2006, 94). In Louisiana the Senegambian and Kongolese cultures introduced African religions to Louisiana, while the influx of immigrants from the Haitian revolution, and new enslaved people from other regions of the United States and other parts of Africa, later influenced New Orleanian Voudou, layering their practices over time.

VOUDOU IN NEW ORLEANS

While the Catlin portrait raises many questions, it also provides information about the context surrounding Marie Laveau's life and Voudou practice in nineteenth-century New Orleans. The investigation of this portrait informs us about the origins of the blend of African cultures that led to the version of Voudou that is particular to New Orleans. Likewise, it speaks to a prevalence of free black women in Louisiana and their power as a group. In fact a sufficient number of portraits of free women of color dating to the nineteenth century exist to create a genre and is an area ripe for further research.

Perhaps the preponderance of portraits is due to the fact that free women of color in New Orleans were a notable sight to white visitors in the nineteenth century. Numerous primary accounts record observations of their beauty, their attention to their clothing, and their confidence when walking in the streets of the city. Although many free women of color may have been Voudou priestesses, they also made quite a showing at church, often outnumbering the men and praying dramatically. Voudou in New Orleans was practiced subversively, as the Code noir (Codigo Negro) and the Catholic Church did not officially permit the practice of other religions.[11] However, the rituals, symbols, and saints of the Catholic Church, along with the clergy's reluctance to implement the code in full force, provided opportunities for Voudouists to practice aspects of their faith in plain view, in some cases changing the expectations of what was appropriate Catholic practice in the city (see Benson in this volume). In 1819 Benjamin Henry Boneval Latrobe wrote, "Sunday in New Orelans is distinguished only, 1., by the flags that are hoisted on all the ships, 2., by the attendance at Church (the Cathedral) of all the beautiful girls in the place, & of 2 or 300 quateroons, negroes, and mulattoes, & perhaps 110 white males to hear high Mass, during which the two bells of the Cathedral are jingling" (1951, 35).[12]

Here, the author notes not only the number of women in the church compared to that of men but also the cultural mix that was present in the parish, and the fact that they all attended church together, without segregation. Church policies dating back to the eighteenth century were designed to assimilate the Black population with white parishioners, partially due to the scarcity of white women to pair with French soldiers and adventurers, despite the Code noir (Long 2006, 37–38; Bell 1997, 13). Such strategies supported the development of a relaxed regard for government laws that limited Black interaction and instead allowed interracial mingling, ultimately aiding the transition of the Black community into freedom (Long 2006, 14; Bell 1997, 15). During the nineteenth century, both the parish divisions in town and the method of seating in the Catholic Mass continued to act as a unifying force across lines of race, gender, and socioeconomic status (Long 2006, 38; Fandrich 2005, 70–71; Bennett 2005, 137–42). Travelers' accounts record astonishment at the fact that members of all races in the St. Louis Cathedral congregation shared the same benches week after week, singing and praying together. Father Antonio de Sedella (1748–1829), known as Père Antoine, led one of the most racially integrated parishes—or even places—in the country. The most actively visible members of the church were the free women of color. They dedicated their resources of both time and money to the church and received a measure of moral and social respect in return (Fandrich 2005, 71; Long 2006, 38).

> I have had a daily view of the ceremonies performed in the Church, & especially of those belonging to the funerals. There still remains here, in spite of the heretical apathy with which the ceremonies of the Church are stared at by strangers & neglected by the Catholic Creoles, much old-fashioned devotional practice among the women & especially among the colored part of the congregation. Among these devotional practices, that of vowing & presenting lighted tapers at the Shrine of the Virgin, or of St. Francis, to whom the side altars are dedicated, & even at the foot of the great altar, is very conspicuous. (Latrobe 1951, 164)

As he observes the congregation, Latrobe's eye is drawn to the Black women who focus on the rituals such as processing in funerals, lighting candles, and vowing, particularly at the altars of the Virgin Mary and St. Francis. This type of presentation with lit candles is typical in Haitian churches frequented by Vodouists in the present day. In the past it was likely a form of expression among the women of color in New Orleans that was related to Voudou practices and therefore supposedly banished to the private realm, but subversively and courageously practiced within the church itself as a public expression of cultural identity and spiritual subjectivity.

As enslaved people, and later refugees, from not only Senegambia and Kongo but also the region now known as Nigeria, Haiti, and other states within the union, they brought to New Orleans the Indigenous faiths and rituals from their homelands, some of which had already incorporated Catholicism. This mix of religions further blended with the Catholic tradition imposed in Louisiana to create a form of Voudou distinct to New Orleans and the surrounding area in the nineteenth century.[13]

Latrobe mentioned the special attention given to the Virgin Mary and St. Francis. Numerous historic accounts refer to saints favored in the Voudou mélange of Louisiana. The pantheon of saints is one aspect of the imposed Catholic tradition with which Voudouists were able to connect and from which they could appropriate elements for their own use. With few historic documents for reference, it is difficult to ascertain whether the saints camouflaged African beliefs, as is the case in Haiti, or whether nineteenth-century Voudou practitioners blended Catholic ideas with their own, leading to versions of a unique Creole pantheon of divine representation in Louisiana through the process of transculturation.[14] These figures vary in the forms worshipped and meanings held, depending upon the context for the Voudou worshipper. With respect to Catholic saints and Voudou, Robert Tallant says, "Voodooists still mix their beliefs with some perverted form of Christianity. In New Orleans it is still often blended with Catholicism, probably because the city has always had a large Roman Catholic population. They adopt many Catholic saints as their own and invoke them to aid in Voodoo work. Besides this they have special saints of their own, these changing from time to time, old ones fading and new ones coming into popularity" ([1946] 1974, 204).

Tallant's comments, Eurocentric in nature, are based on interviews conducted by the Works Progress Administration's Louisiana Writers' Project. His observation that Voudou practitioners utilized saints from two belief systems, and that these can change, appears to reflect the history discussed above, specifically the process of blending distinct religious traditions. Fundamentally, Voudou and its practice was (and will likely continue to be) dynamic and ever-changing in its neocultural formulation (Ortiz [1947] 1995, 103; Long, 2006, 11–12, 118).

In the 1930s Zora Neale Hurston set out to record the Voudou rituals and methods from the past, including those of Marie Laveau, to whom she devoted an entire chapter, "Hoodoo in America." One section of her study titled "Paraphernelia of Conjure" is a sort of pantry list of materials Voudou practitioners kept in stock for use with clients. Included are "pictures of saints":

> St. Michael, the Archangel. To Conquer.
> St. Expedite. For quick work.
> St. Mary. For cure in sickness.
> St. Joseph with infant Jesus. To get a job.
> St. Peter without the key. For success.
> St. Peter with the key. For great and speedy success.
> St. Anthony de Padua. For luck.
> St. Mary of Magdalene. For luck in love (for women).
> Sacred Heart of Jesus. For organic diseases. (1931, 413)

In this list Hurston makes no mention of distinctly African figures, but she does include St. Expedite, who has found particular favor in Latin America, and especially Brazil, the island of Réunion, and Louisiana, where there are cults who honor him. Although St. Expedite was a Roman martyr and canonized by the Vatican as St. Expeditus, he is also associated with Bawon Samdi in Haitian Vodou, due to the cross, the symbol of death he holds (Valdman et al. 2007, 71) and quite popular in and beyond the Voudou community in nineteenth-century New Orleans, as Tallant explains:

> Perhaps the most popular saint in the Voodoo world is St. Expédite, who, incidentally is a peculiar example of the bridge between New Orleans Voodooism and Catholicism. Though his authenticity is more than doubtful, statues of St. Expédite are in at least two Catholic churches in the city, one of them Our Lady of Guadalupe. . . . The church is a very old one and was originally the Catholic chapel from which all burial services were held. . . .
>
> Priests, questioned about St. Expédite remain noncommittal. Some will tell you they are certain he did exist. Others disagree entirely. There are no records. Some years ago Archbishop Shaw of New Orleans made a public and angry demand that these statues be removed from Catholic churches in New Orleans. But nothing was ever done, and the statues remain. Since then two Negro "Mothers" have opened St. Expédite temples.

> But, whatever the truth is about his history, many Orleanians know that St. Expédite is the most dependable saint in Heaven when it comes to getting things done in a hurry. You have only to say, "St. Expédite, do this now." It will be done. Then you go to his statue at Our lady of Guadalupe Church and pay off—sometimes by burning a candle before him and saying a prayer, but other times, if you're a genuine Voodoo, by leaving a slice of pound cake, a new penny or a sprig of green fern at his feet. Such articles are constantly being found before the image. ([1946] 1974, 105)

This passage reveals a view held by its author that although St. Expédite had "doubtful" authenticity, his statue was not only allowed to remain in two prominent Catholic churches in New Orleans—one devoted to a brown-skinned virgin— but also that the church turned a blind eye to offerings left for St. Expédite—Bawon Samdi in traditional and recognizable Voudou fashion. These perceived oversights of the Church speak to relaxed aspects of the Catholic approach in New Orleans to Voudou. Practitioners took this opportunity to express their faith within the broader community and in the process created a visual culture of Voudou-Catholicism unique to New Orleans that tourists still seek today.

Another story put forth by Tallant, and borrowed from the LWP interviews, is the testimony of Mary Ellis, which includes a recollection of the blending of saint names within Marie Laveau's practice:

> My aunt told me one time she had trouble wit' her landlord. He told her to git out of her house or he'd have her put in jail," Mary said. "He even sent a policeman after her. The next day she went to Marie Laveau and she told my aunt to burn twelve blue candles in a barrel half full of sand. She done that and my aunt never did have to move and she never went to jail in her whole life. . . . She was real good to my aunt. She even taught her a Voodoo song. It went like this:
>
> > St. Peter, St Peter, open the door,
> > I'm callin' you, come to me!
> > St. Peter, St. Peter, open the door . . .
>
> That's all I can remember. Marie Laveau used to call St. Peter somethin' like "Laba." She called St. Michael "Daniel Blanc," and St. Anthony "Yon

Sue." There was another one she called "On Za Tier"; I think that was St. Paul. I never did know where them names come from. They sounded Chinese to me. ([1946] 1974, 102–3)

Mary Ellis's memory reveals another level of symbolic meaning for the saints mentioned. Studies in Haitian Vodou have shown that while all things "Catholic" may retain some of their original meaning, the objects and images are mostly imbued with Vodou spiritual values. For example, with respect to the quote above, in Haitian Vodou there is a song for Atibon Legba, who, like St. Peter with his keys in Catholicism, facilitates contact between people and the spirit system in Vodou. The song says, "Louvri bayè pou mwen," or "Open the gates for me." The testimony above provides evidence of a practice in nineteenth-century New Orleanian Voudou similar to that of Haiti.[15] Catholic imagery, symbols, and tools such as crosses and rosaries were suffused with symbolic meaning for Voudou practitioners in subversive acts of empowerment.

THE VOUDOU ALTAR

Little is known of Marie Laveau's Voudou practice beyond her emphasis on gris-gris, spirits, and offerings or layouts; however, descriptions of the interior of her house can serve as a form of self-representation and offer insights similar to that of portraiture.[16] Some informants from the LWP interviews recall Laveau's altars and the figures she placed upon them. Marie Dédé told of a memory from her childhood growing up in the St. Ann Street neighborhood, where Marie Laveau's house once stood. She remembered peeping into the front room of the house, which was reserved for priestess services: "[Marie Laveau] had so many candles burning. . . . I don't see how that house never caught on fire. . . . She had all kinds of saints' pictures and flowers on the altar. [She] had a big [statue of] St. Anthony . . . and she would turn him upside down on his head in her yard when she had 'work' to perform" (Long, 2006, 108–9). Another informant identified the altar in the front room of the house as one for "good work," or "benevolent conjurations," and "an altar for bad work" in the back of her house: "It was surmounted by statues of a bear, a lion, a tiger, and a wolf. In her incantations she called upon the spirit of the snake, who represented

Lucifer, the chief devil. This is what led to the belief that she had a snake in a box" (Raphael Villère, interview by Hazel Breaux, LWP folder 25).

This and other testimonies identify Laveau's back room as a location where she created charms for ill. In reality the spaces were probably divided between "cool" spirits in front and "hot" in the back in a possible Rada and Petwo division (Hebblethwaite, personal communication, 2020). Nevertheless, the New Orleanian perception grew that Marie Laveau in particular, and Voudou practices in general, could not only help but also harm people by way of trickery, creating fear as the turn toward racism and segregation intensifed in the city, especially after the Civil War.[17] However, when one considers the items on her altar—representations of animal spirits and flowers—a congruence arises between those objects and Native American spirituality. Scholars have suggested, with the support of oral histories, that Native Americans taught Laveau their spiritual traditions and how to employ medicinal plants in healing practices, given that she was also a known member of the Native American community (Raphael Villère, interview by Hazel Breaux, LWP folder 25; Fandrich 2005, 192; Long 2006, 34–36). Likewise, the association of the snake with the devil is incorrect in its interpretation and based on a Eurocentric perspective. In Haitian Vodou the snake is associated with Danmbala Wèdo, Rada spirit of fertility, as well as *dyab*, a fierce spirit of protection that is not always negative (Valdman et al. 2007, 231).

As we consider facets of Marie Laveau's power, we must recall her alliance with the Catholic Church. Baptized by Père Antoine a few months after her birth, as an adult Laveau remained a regular churchgoer and formed a close friendship with the priest (Fandrich 2005, 153; Long 2005, 270; Ward 2004, 23–24). Oral histories indicate that, when her treatments were successful, she insisted that her clients thank God, the Virgin Mary, and the saints for their help. She made it clear that she was not performing the deed of mercy, but, rather, that the heavenly spirits were the actors. This technique protected her practice from being labeled satanic by the Catholic community. Thus her transcultural approach is evident not only in the items on her altars but also in her prescriptions (Fandrich 2005, 201).

A description of a Voudou ceremony by Charles Dudley Warner published in *Harper's Weekly Magazine* shows how African and Catholic images and objects were used in combination during the nineteenth century, but it contrasts with what we know of Laveau's practice:

> On one side of the middle room where we sat was constructed a sort of buffet or bureau, used as an altar. On it stood an image of the Virgin Mary in painted plaster, about two feet high, flanked by lighted candles and a couple of cruets, with some other small objects. On a shelf below were two other candles, and on this shelf and the floor in front were various offerings to be used in the rites—plates of apples, grapes, bananas, oranges; dishes of sugar, of sugar-plums; a dish of powdered orris root, packages of candles, bottles of brandy and of water.
>
> The doctor squatted on one side of the altar, and his wife, a stout woman of darker hue, on the other. "Commençons," said the woman, in a low voice. . . . The doctor nodded, bent over, and gave three sharp raps on the floor with a bit of wood. (This is the usual opening of Voudoo rites). All the others rapped three times on the floor with their knuckles. Any one coming in to join the circle afterward, stooped and rapped three times. After a moment's silence, all kneeled and repeated together in French the Apostles' Creed, and still on their knees, they said two prayers to the Virgin Mary. (1887, 454–55)[18]

Warner goes on to describe an infectious chant, the Dansé Calinda, a flame ignited with poured brandy that permeated the room, and additional dancing, after which the faithful approached the Voudou priest with a lit candle. The priest extinguished the candle with his mouth. At regular intervals he would fill his mouth with a liquid (called *foula* in Haitian Vodou) and spray it back out as a mist over the heads of the participants in order to heat up the ritual and bring down the spirits. He then placed his hands into the bowl with the liquid recently in flames and scooped out liquid, using it to vigorously "shampoo" the clients' faces and heads. Finally, the priest took the person by the right hand and spun him in circles numerous times, finally released him to whirl into the room (Warner 1887, 455). The author explains that this was the basic process for each of the believers, with slight modifications that were apparently case dependent, according to the needs or wishes of the client.

F3. John Durkin, *A Voudoo Dance*. From Charles Dudley Warner, "A Voudoo Dance," *Harper's Weekly Magazine*, June 25, 1887.

Although Warner's description contains racial epithets characteristic of the time, the excerpt above is less sensationalized than most material of the period and therefore gives the reader a relatively objective glimpse into a nineteenth-century Voudou ritual in New Orleans beyond the charms, altar work, and layouts offered by Laveau. The accompanying illustration (fig. 3) portrays the excitement of the ceremony and provides a good visual example of the altar, which resembles that described in Laveau's front room.

Before the mid-nineteenth century, Voudou practices did not raise concern in a manner that required police intervention. However, during the decade prior to the Civil War, there were numerous arrests in a somewhat sanctioned social attack on "Voudous." The proceedings were detailed in the press and the public interest in Voudou grew (Fandrich 2005, 136). Warner's article marks a period after the Civil War when Voudouists were somewhat less persecuted, but their events, such as the celebrations surrounding St. John's Eve on June 21, were of great interest to the media. The popular press vilified St. John's Voudou ceremonies, likening them to sexual orgies while instigating fear, awe, and disparaging judgment among readers with racial prejudice. The impetus for this oppressive perspective was the turn toward further segregation and the rise of Jim Crow laws.

CENTURY MAGAZINE'S DEPICTION OF MARIE LAVEAU

Some of this sensational interest and racial prejudice surrounding Voudou practices from an outside perspective is evident in an 1886 article called "Creole Slave Songs," which included a section about Voudou in which a portrait of Marie Laveau and her daughter appeared (fig. 4). The white author claimed to have met the two women before the elder's death. After introducing Voudou as a form of worship "as dark and horrid as bestialized savagery could make the worship of a snake," the author describes the scene upon his meeting of Marie Laveau:

> In the center of a small room whose ancient cypress floor was worn with scrubbing and sprinkled with crumbs of soft brick—a Creole affectation of superior cleanliness—sat quaking with feebleness in an ill-looking old rocking-chair, her body bowed, and her wild, gray witch's tresses hanging about her shriveled, yellow neck, the queen of the Voodoos. . . . They said she was over a hundred years old, and there was nothing to cast doubt upon the statement. She had shrunken away from her skin; it was like a turtle's. Yet withal one could hardly help but see that the face, now so withered, had once been handsome and commanding. There was still a faint shadow of departed beauty on the forehead, the spark of an old fire in the sunken, glistening eyes, and a vestige of imperiousness in the fine, slightly aquiline nose, and even about her silent, woe-begone mouth. . . . her daughter, was also present, a woman of some seventy years, and a most striking and majestic figure. In features, stature, and bearing, she was regal. One had to but look on her, impute her brilliancies—too untamable and severe to be called charms or graces—to her mother, and remember what New Orleans was long years ago, to understand how the name of Marie Laveau should have driven itself inextricably into the traditions of the town and the times. Had this visit been postponed a few months it would have been too late. Marie Laveau is dead; Malvina Latour is queen. (Cable 1886, 817–18)

In this passage, George Washington Cable describes an aging woman in a sharply critical tone. He refers to her hair as unkept, as "wild, gray witch's tresses." He continues to draw upon the stereotypical haggard appearance of an aging witch in successive sentences: "She had shrunken away from her skin"; "the face, now so withered"; and "the spark of an old fire in the sunken, glistening eyes." The choice of the word "witch," and the harsh adjectives used to describe her physical features, reveals a commonly held misconception originally rooted in racism and Christian dogma that Voudou is related to witchcraft. In the 1960s Lucy Mair conducted a study on witchcraft and its perceptions. When nine out of ten participants in her study were asked their first word association with witchcraft, they replied, "Voodoo." Even in a contemporary setting, "Voodoo" is often thought to be a more heinous form of witchcraft (Mair 1969, 234; Fandrich 2005, 257). Marie Laveau was not a witch, nor did she elicit the work of a Christian devil in her practice as many may have accused. Rather, she may have been calling upon *dyab*, or *diab*, which can be synonymous with a "hot spirit," and not the Christian devil per se, although Vodouists often recast Christian ideas. Above all, in her work Laveau was a priestess, like her Western or Central African predecessors, who performed rites of healing, blessing, and counseling to her people (Fandrich 2005, 11–12). Cable's racist and fictitious description of Laveau as a witch, due to her practice of Voudou and her old, wrinkled appearance, causes readers to be skeptical of her as a person of influence in the African American community of New Orleans. While the author lays claim to Laveau's reign as "queen" of the Voudouists, he simultaneously undermines her perceived power by drawing the reader's mind to associations with witchcraft. In fact Marie Laveau was influential primarily because she practiced African diaspora traditions, thereby preserving and holding dear that which provided her community with a meaningful sense of identity and continuity.

Likewise, the author makes several racist references to Laveau's mixed heritage through the features he assigns to her body. He describes her level of cleanliness as a "Creole affectation," mentions her "shriveled yellow neck," and finds "a vestige of imperiousness in the fine, slightly aquiline nose." With the combination of physical features—yellow skin, aquiline nose—and his direct statement of her "Creole" status, he draws attention

F4. E. W. Kemble, *Marie Laveau*. From George Washington Cable, "Creole Slave Songs," *Century Magazine* 31 (April 1886).

to what are stereotypically features of a person with mixed African and European heritage, utilizing racial terms of the white community to identify Creoles and Blacks with darker skin as inferior groups.

The printed illustration also depicts Laveau as decrepit and witch-like. Laveau and her daughter occupy the space at the center of the image, the elder slouched in a chair—a figure whose stature is minimized not only by the daughter's height but also that of the chair. With clenched fists the elder Laveau glances off to the side, as if muttering some unintelligible phrase. In their features both figures more closely resemble men than women. Their noses and eyebrows have a masculine prominence; the physical stature of Laveau's daughter, with her broad shoulders and thick arms, also looks manly. By describing and depicting the daughter as "severe" and without "grace" or "charms," Cable seeks to disempower the second Marie Laveau by using language that creates a mental image of a woman incompatible with the gendered and genteel expectations of ladies in elite society, thus branding her as inferior.

The caricature of Marie Laveau and her daughter in *Century Magazine* reveals a perspective taken by some members of the dominant culture in New Orleans that Voudou was evil. In this image Lavau's power as priestess is questioned through her implied intention to create ill in society, a perception likely held by numerous segments of the population of New Orleans and abroad. However, it was also this fear of Laveau's retribution among some members of the white elite that caused them to avoid the realities of Voudou, giving Laveau and her daughter the space and freedom in which to carry out their community work, which consisted primarily of counseling, consoling, and healing members of their community by dealing with spirits to address people's problems.

THE SPIRIT OF MARIE LAVEAU

The last portrait I offer for analysis is a recent one created by Sallie Ann Glassman, an ordained priestess of Haitian Vodou who is the owner of the Island of Salvation Botanica (a Vodou supply store), an artist, and the author of *Vodou Visions: An Encounter with Divine Mystery* (2014), as well as the *New Orleans Voodoo Tarot Book and Card Set* (1992). One of her tarot cards features a portrait of Marie Laveau (fig. 5). Here Laveau stands in

F5. Sallie Ann Glassman, *Marie Laveau*. From *New Orleans Voodoo Tarot/Book and Card Set* (Rochester VT: Destiny, aka Inner Traditions, 1992). Courtesy Sallie Ann Glassman.

her sovereignty in her salon. She gazes at the viewer in a direct but kind manner, inviting the viewer into her space. Her left hand reaches back to pull open the curtain made of cowrie shells, a mode of Atlantic currency until the mid-nineteenth century and a form of Vodun initiate costume in the twentieth century. She is a priestess who is both self-assured and welcoming to those who come to her for assistance as they navigate the mysteries of their lives.

Tarot cards and playing cards are used in divination ceremonies or counseling sessions to aid in communication with higher powers. The cards have symbols through which the spirits speak. By creating a tarot card with an image of Marie Laveau, Glassman is acknowledging Laveau's legend and consciously shifting her power from that of a priestess to that of a spirit (lwa) to be called upon for strength and guidance.

As mentioned, Laveau has a strong presence in the historical memory of the city of New Orleans. For many outside New Orleans, hers is the face that represents a broad, more generic understanding of a "Voodoo" that does not recognize nuances of the practice, especially historic nuances. From inside New Orleans, where Glassman lives, practices, and organizes a ceremony for Laveau every year, Laveau is a predecessor to present-day priestesses who, like Laveau, negotiate their contemporary opportunities and engage those that serve their communities best. Finally, by adding Laveau to the pantheon of ancestral spirits, Glassman is further transforming the pantheon through renegotiation and reorganization.

CONCLUSION

Marie Laveau and her representations offer a window to the context of her life in New Orleans and the practice of Voudou in the nineteenth century. An investigation of an early portrait of Laveau wearing a tignon unwrapped the history of the Senegambian forced settlement in New Orleans and the influence of their foundational culture, which valued women's agency with the example of the signares as well as priestesses.

Descriptions of Laveau's altar and of a nineteenth-century Voudou ritual in New Orleans grant insight to her practice while raising questions about the role of saints in this context. Of course, Catholicism was originally imposed by French and Spanish colonists, causing enslaved people and free Blacks who practiced Voudou to either mask or create hybrid spirit forms with Catholic names and attributes. LWP oral testimonies reveal the roles of colonialism and transculturation in the veneration of saints as well as the integration of several Voudou practices and spirits into Catholic ceremonies and spaces. Thus we can see that, although colonial administrations forced the practice of Catholicism in New Orleans, in the process changing the face of Voudou, Voudouists negotiated public and Catholic spaces where their hybrid expressions were accepted and in turn changed the face of Catholicism—and visual culture—in New Orleans.

A sensationalized illustration of Laveau and her daughter built upon the dominant culture's fear of Voudou in post–Civil War New Orleans. By portraying Laveau and her daughter as haggard and witch-like, the author employs a racist agenda that calls attention to those physical attributes not in keeping with white ideals of beauty and femininity in order to mark the Voudouists as inferior and demonize their beliefs, rituals, and heritage.

Finally, a recent representation of Laveau by an American artist who practices Haitian Vodou reveals an assured and caring figure, which was likely the plain truth all along. Together these portraits and altar descriptions paint a picture of the priestess that is nuanced and complex, revealing perceptions from within and outside the practice of Voudou historically. Laveau's social role as a free woman of color, while not unusual in nineteenth century New Orleans, is more remarkable than the fearsome legends surrounding her, because her steady actions inspired large groups of people to carry forth transcultural versions of their ancestral faith and rituals despite the odds.

NOTES

1. "Voudou" is the nineteenth-century spelling of a form of African diaspora religious practice with many connections throughout the Atlantic World, including New Orleans. In its contemporary spelling, "Voodoo" is a term that applies generally to African American magical belief in the United States. This term has been highly commercialized, commodified, and vilified in popular media. "Hoodoo" is a historic derivation of "Voodoo" used by Anglophone African Americans. "Vodou" is the term applied to the African-based religion practiced in Haiti.
2. In my research I utilized interviews from the Works Progress Administration's Louisiana Writers' Project (LWP), which were conducted from 1935 to 1941 and

recorded many oral histories about folk traditions in Louisiana, including Voudou. I want to thank the Cammie G. Henry Research Center, Eugene P. Watson Library, Northwestern State University of Louisiana, Natchitoches, for maintaining these archival documents and making them accessible.

3. Although it is certain that there was a second Marie Laveau, scholars are unsure whether one of Laveau's daughters, half-sister, or an outsider filled that role (Fandrich 2005, 170–71, 176–80; Long 2006, 190–207).
4. Brown (2003, 30–32) points out that the possibility of manumission created networks within subalternized communities aspiring to freedom and often helping one another obtain that goal.
5. At the time this chapter was researched and written, the Louisiana State Museum Registrar provided a photographic copy of the original painting to verify its existence (Elizabeth Sherwood, personal communication, February 2018). While this chapter was in press, the original portrait attributed to George Catlin resurfaced in a private collection through its sale. Since the Catlin painting's reappearance, scholars who have examined the work disagree as to the identities of both the painter and the sitter (Tom Strider, personal communication, August 12, 2022).
6. See the undated "Tourist Guide of the City of New Orleans," at Tulane University, 297; and Fandrich 2005, 177.
7. Long (2006, 238n31) notes that she spoke with William Truettner, scholar and curator at the American Art Museum, Smithsonian Institution on January 3, 2001, to verify that the portrait is typical of Catlin's style.
8. These laws were known throughout the Spanish Caribbean at the same time.
9. The fact that people of color could blur their status sartorially suggests an internal market system, likely connected to larger regional and transatlantic networks circulating a range of raw to luxury items (Brown 2003, 30).
10. "Creole" is a complex term in Louisiana. In use here it refers to the spoken language derived from French, sometimes called "Gumbo French." In the nineteenth century, Louisiana residents of French and Spanish descent, regardless of skin color, began to refer to themselves as "Creole" when Anglo-Americans arrived after the Louisiana Purchase. Today "Creole" often refers to people of mixed race with generations of heritage in Louisiana.
11. The Code noir was a French governmental decree that regulated the life, death, purchase, and treatment of slaves within the French colonial empire. For example, the code specified that slaves must be baptized in the Roman Catholic Church, prohibited any public exercise of religion other than Roman Catholicism, and issued rules and punishments governing sexual and marital relationships both between slaves and among interracial relations, as well as other matters (such as banning Jews from the colonies). Variations of the Code noir were in effect officially from 1685, with the original edict issued by Louis XIV, until 1848. After

the colonial period in New Orleans, some of the rules were upheld by the Catholic Church, in name if not in practice.
12. A derivation of "quadroon," a nineteenth- and early twentieth-century racial term for a person with one-quarter Black heritage.
13. Addressing the ritual arts of the Lucumí of Cuba, Brown (2003, 22) argues that the local material culture combined with European imports and West African trade goods created "marvelous hybrids" that "reflected the processes of creolization and re-Africanization."
14. I'm using the term "transculturation" to indicate the "different phases of the process of transition from one culture to another because this does not consist merely in acquiring another culture . . . , but the process also necessarily involves the loss or uprooting of a previous culture. . . . In addition, it carries the idea of the consequent creation of new cultural phenomena, which could be called neoculturation" (Ortiz [1947] 1995, 102–3).
15. In fieldwork conducted on May 4–5, 2018, in Little Haiti, Miami, Florida, I observed a Haitian Vodou ceremony utilizing this song to open a portion of the ceremony.
16. Layouts, or parterres, are arrangements of offerings, usually including herbs, food, liquor, flowers, and candles laid upon a white ground cloth (personal fieldwork, Little Haiti, Miami, May 4–5, 2018; Long 2006, 110–11).
17. See Robert McKinney's interview with Laveau's student Mary Washington, LWP folder 25; and Long 2006, 118.
18. The ceremony I witnessed did not include the Catholic prayers mentioned herein (personal fieldwork, May 4–5, Little Haiti, Miami, 2018).

REFERENCES

Bell, Caryn Cossé. 1997. *Revolution, Romanticism, and the Afro-Creole Protest Tradition in Louisiana, 1718–1868*. Baton Rouge: Louisiana State University Press.

Bennett, James B. 2005. *Religion and the Rise of Jim Crow in New Orleans*. Princeton NJ: Princeton University Press.

Brooks, George E. 1976. "The Signares of St. Louis and Gorée: Women Entrepreneurs in Eighteenth-Century Senegal." In *Women in Africa*, edited by Nancy J. Hafkin and Edna G. Bay, 19–44. Stanford CA: Stanford University Press.

Brown, David H. 2003. *Santería Enthroned*. Chicago: University of Chicago Press.

Cable, George Washington. 1886. "Creole Slave Songs." *Century Magazine* 31, no. 6: 807–28.

Donaldson, Thomas. 1886. "The George Catlin Indian Gallery in the U.S. National Museum (Smithsonian Institution): With Memoir and Statistics." *Annual 1885* 24: n.p.

Fandrich, Ina J. 2005. *The Mysterious Voodoo Queen, Marie Laveaux: A Study of Powerful Female Leadership in Nineteenth-Century New Orleans*. New York: Routledge.

———. 2007. "Yorùbá Influences on Haitain Vodou and New Orleans Voodoo." *Journal of Black Studies* 37, no. 5: 775–91.

Glassman, Sallie A. 2014. *Vodou Visions: An Encounter with Divine Mystery*. New York: Villard.

Glassman, Sallie A., and Louis Martinié. 1992. *New Orleans Voodoo Tarot Book and Card Set*. Merrimac MA: Destiny.

Gurney, George, and Therese Thau Heyman, eds. 2002. *George Catlin and His Indian Gallery*. Washington DC: Smithsonian.

Hall, Gwendolyn. 1992. *Africans in Colonial Louisiana: The Development of Afro-Creole Culture in the Eighteenth Century*. Baton Rouge: Louisiana State University Press.

Hurston, Zora Neale. 1931. "Hoodoo in America." *Journal of American Folklore* 44, no. 174: 317–417.

Latrobe, Benjamin Henry Boneval. 1951. *Impressions Respecting New Orleans: Diary and Sketches, 1818–1820*. New York: Columbia University Press.

Long, Carolyn M. 2002. "Perceptions of New Orleans Voodoo: Sin, Fraud, Entertainment, and Religion." *Nova Religio* 6, no. 1: 86–101.

———. 2005. "Marie Laveau: A Nineteenth-Century Voudou Priestess." *Louisiana History* 46, no. 5: 262–92.

———. 2006. *A New Orleans Voudou Priestess: The Legend and Reality of Marie Laveau*. Gainesville: University Press of Florida.

Louisiana Writer's Project. 1935–43. Federal Writers' Collection, Cammie G. Henry Research Center, Watson Memorial Library, Northwestern State University, Natchitoches LA.

Mair, Lucy. 1969. *Witchcraft*. New York: McGraw-Hill.

Ortiz, Fernando. [1947] 1995. *Cuban Counterpoint, Tobacco, and Sugar*. Durham NC: Duke University Press.

Shaw, Gwendolyn D. B., and Emily K. Shubert. 2006. *Portraits of a People: Picturing African Americans in the Nineteenth Century*. Andover MA: Addison Gallery of American Art, Phillips Academy.

Tallant, Robert. [1946] 1974. *Voodoo in New Orleans*. Gretna LA: Pelican.

"Tignon of Colonial Louisiana." 2013. Media Nola, Tulane University. Accessed February 28, 2018. http://medianola.org/discover/place/945/Tignon-of-Colonial-Louisiana-#reference_4.

"The Tignon and Women of Color in Old New Orleans." 2005. African American Resource Center, New Orleans Public Library. Accessed February 28, 2018. http://archive.is/ya2d.

Truettner, William H. 1979. *The Natural Man Observed: A Study of Catlin's Indian Gallery*. Washington DC: Smithsonian.

Valdman, Albert, Iskra Iskrova, and Benjamin Hebblethwaite. 2007. *Haitian Creole-English Bilingual Dictionary*. Bloomington: Indiana University Press.

Ward, Martha. 2004. *Voodoo Queen: The Spirited Lives of Marie Laveau.* Jackson: University Press of Mississippi.

Warner, Charles Dudley. 1997. "A Voudoo Dance." *Harper's Weekly Magazine* (June 25): 454–55.

Wehmeyer, Stephen C. 2000. "Indian Altars of the Spiritual Church: Kongo Echos in New Orleans." *African Arts* 33, no. 4: 62–69, 95–96.

3 Shamanic Healing, Initiation, and Ritual Technique in a Kwak'wala Narrative from the Boas-Hunt Corpus

Daniel J. Frim

The Kwakwaka'wakw are a confederation of First Nation groups from northern Vancouver Island, smaller neighboring islands, and nearby areas of mainland British Columbia, who traditionally speak dialects of the Kwak'wala language.[1] Beginning in 1886 (Cole 1999, 100), Franz Boas conducted ethnographic and linguistic research with members of Kwakwaka'wakw communities and oversaw the documentation of a large body of Kwak'wala oral narratives. Most of these texts were collected and written down by George Hunt, Boas's half-English, half-Tlingit, Kwak'wala-speaking consultant and ethnographic coworker (Berman 1994). In the present chapter, I analyze a Kwak'wala narrative from this corpus. My analysis focuses on how the text portrays shamanism: a complex of healing rituals and other practices performed by specialist shamans (sing. *paχəla*). Kwakwaka'wakw shamanism has generated a small body of anthropological literature, most of which focuses on the sleight-of-hand techniques that Boas and Hunt describe in their writings on shamanic ritual. These techniques play a role in the narrative that I will analyze, and I aim to elucidate the status that the text ascribes to them. Although I begin by reviewing previous analyses of Kwakwaka'wakw shamanism, most of which use terms like "fraud" or "trickery" to characterize it, I strive to address the topic in a more respectful tone, and I arrive at conclusions quite different from these earlier characterizations.

In a posthumously published discussion of Kwakwaka'wakw shamanism, Boas (1966, 120–48) suggests that Kwakwaka'wakw attitudes toward shamanic ritual involved an ambiguous interplay between skepticism and faith. He writes: "It is perfectly well known by all concerned that a great part of the shamanistic procedure is based on fraud; still, it is believed in by the shaman as well as by his patients and friends. Exposures do not weaken the belief in the 'true' power of shamanism. Owing to this peculiar state of mind, the shaman himself is doubtful in regard to his powers and is always ready to bolster them up by fraud" (121). Boas's assessment is based, in part, on information provided by George Hunt, who grew up in the Hudson's Bay Company trading post of Fort Rupert surrounded by the Kwakwa̱ka'wakw village of Tsa̱xis. Although he was of non-Kwakwa̱ka'wakw descent on both his European father's and Indigenous mother's sides, "Hunt was steeped in Kwakwa̱ka'wakw culture and social life from a young age" (Berman 1994, 485), and he underwent shamanic initiation in a Kwakwa̱ka'wakw framework as a young adult.

Hunt reported his initiatory experiences to Boas on multiple occasions, both orally and in writing (Berman forthcoming), resulting in the publication of three accounts. The earliest of these (Boas 1966, 121–23) originated in "a very confidential conversation" that took place between Hunt and Boas in 1900 (121). In it Hunt recalls suffering from periodic fits of fainting and mania after experiencing an injury at age thirteen. These fits leave Hunt feeling as if he has "been in another world," and one of his relatives interprets them to mean "that the supernatural powers were certainly trying to get" Hunt (121). At a later point, the spirit of a killer whale visits Hunt in a dream.[2] The spirit informs him that a particular boy has fallen ill and provides instructions on how to heal him: "His disease is in the right side of his chest. Suck it four times and show to the people the disease that you are going to find [i.e., that will be sucked out]" (121–22). The next morning the boy's grandfather approaches Hunt and tells him that the boy has dreamed that Hunt will cure him. Hunt agrees to perform a healing rite, but he warns the man that he has yet to learn a "shaman's song" to sing during the procedure.[3] In the evening, Hunt enters the boy's house, where shamans and a large group of villagers have gathered. Hunt is suddenly overtaken by a trance, and he runs "back into the woods" before reentering the house singing a "sacred song" (122). After regaining normal consciousness, Hunt sucks on the boy's chest, just as the whale instructed. Hunt recalls, "Every time I sucked I found something in my mouth, and I put it away" (122). The boy recovers soon after the procedure. The killer whale visits Hunt again in a second dream and tells him how to heal another sick person. The next day Hunt follows the spirit's instructions and performs another successful shamanic cure. As is the case in other shamans' initiation stories documented by Hunt and Boas, Hunt's healing powers are attributed to a guardian spirit, with whom he forms a relationship after experiencing health difficulties of his own (125–35).

By contrast, in the two later accounts of Hunt's initiation, almost "all the supernatural elements" that appear in the 1900 account are "eliminated" (Boas 1966, 125). One of these later narratives (Boas 1930a, 1–40; 1930b, 1–41) was written by Hunt in 1922 (Berman forthcoming).[4] In the other published rendition (Boas 1966, 123–24), which is told from Boas's third-person perspective, Boas (123) indicates that he is summarizing an account he received from Hunt in 1925. (In truth, while the summary does derive in part from a 1925 manuscript written by Hunt, some of its content must have originated in other recollections [Berman forthcoming and personal communication]. Nevertheless, for convenience, I refer to it simply as the "1925 account.") In both the 1922 and 1925 versions of Hunt's experiences, instead of receiving shamanic power from a killer whale, Hunt is inducted by the members of a shamanic guild. He gains the assistance of a "spy" or "dreamer," who is responsible for identifying prospective patients and for gathering information about their symptoms, which the shamans claim to have learned in dreams.[5] In Kwakwa̱ka'wakw society, shamans (Boas 1966, 135) and other ritual practitioners bear special names in the context of their work; shamans' "spies," likewise, had spy names. According to the 1925 account, the spy who assists Hunt is known as "Killer Whale," so Hunt is to claim that his shamanic guardian spirit is a killer whale (124; see also below for further discussion of this detail).

In his 1922 account, Hunt emphasizes that he "was the principal one who does not believe in all the ways of the shamans," and that when a group of shamans offer to initiate him, he accepts their invitation only so "that I should really learn whether they were real or whether they only pretended to be shamans" (Boas 1930b, 5).[6] Among other skills, they teach him how to generate the appearance of sucking pathogenic objects out of patients' bodies. This involves hiding eagle down between one's gums and upper lip, biting the tip of one's tongue or sucking blood out of one's gums to redden the down, and then spitting the down into one's hand, by which point it has the appearance of a bloody worm.[7] Using this technique Hunt performs successful cures in several different villages; he attributes the first of these successes to the fact that his patient, the boy who dreamt that Hunt would heal him, "believed strongly in his dream about me" (13). Some of the patients Hunt cures have eluded the best efforts of local shamans, whose healing performances are not as impressive as Hunt's. On several occasions these shamans try to persuade Hunt to reveal his technique, but he refuses. A shaman named ʔaʔixagidalagəlis is particularly adamant, imploring Hunt "to have mercy and tell me what stuck on the palm of your hand last night. Was it the true sickness or was it only made up? for I beg you to have mercy and tell me about the way you did it so that I can imitate you" (31). ʔaʔixagidalagəlis reveals his own sleight-of-hand techniques (e.g., he holds his ceremonial rattle between his fingers in such a manner that the raven figure carved on the rattle appears to be "biting" the palm of his hand), and, as Hunt notes in his summary of the conversation, "he [ʔaʔixagidalagəlis] said that there was not one true shaman among the shamans in this our world here" (32). Hunt later reflects that, over the course of his travels, "only one shaman was seen by me, who sucked at a sick man and I never found out whether he was a real shaman or only made up. Only for this reason I believe that he is a shaman; he does not allow those who are made well to pay him" (40–41). Hunt's efforts to test or debunk shamans' claims and his mostly skeptical assessments of their abilities drastically distinguish his 1922 narrative from the account he gave in 1900.

Boas does not establish a clear picture of how Hunt's varying recollections related to more widespread Kwakwa̲ka̲'wakw attitudes toward shamanism.[8] On the one hand, Boas suggests that Hunt's skeptical accounts reflect "the relation between Indian and white. The Indian likes to appear rational and knows that shamanistic practices are disbelieved by the whites." The tendency to disavow belief in shamanism is further reinforced "by the attitude of the Canadian government and the missionaries, who relentlessly persecute most of the Indian practices," and this tendency is most pronounced among Indigenous people whose "contacts with the whites" are close. Boas implies that such colonial pressures had less of an influence on Hunt when Hunt told Boas about his shamanic initiation during their "very confidential conversation" in 1900 than when he narrated the two other published accounts (Boas 1966, 121); Boas does not state why this shift occurred.[9] The implication, in any event, is that Hunt's skepticism is disingenuous, and that individuals whose "contacts with the whites" are less substantial than Hunt's would be less likely to voice similar attitudes.

On the other hand, as noted above, Boas asserts that "knowledge of fraud" was a widespread element in Kwakwaka'wakw perceptions of shamanism and that "a deep-seated belief in the supernatural power of shamanism persists" *in spite* of it (1966, 125), both among shamans and among their "patients and friends" (121). Boas suggests that, "owing to sickness, to fasting, and other forms of castigation of the body" that take place during the initiation process, shamans imbue their memories of the "imaginary experiences of this period" with "a reality which in the beginning was quite absent" (121), without fully dislodging more skeptical feelings.[10] This proposal is an attempt to characterize and explain individual shamans' attitudes toward their craft, but it does not clarify the cultural dimensions of how shamanism was perceived by its practitioners. When shamans transmitted their techniques to new initiates, how did they communicate regarding the procedures that Boas describes as "fraud"? Did they, in fact, consider these methods to be fraudulent? Or, were sleight-of-hand techniques integrated into the shamanic belief system alongside guardian spirits and the extraction of diseases from patients' bodies? Just as importantly, how did non-shamans reconcile awareness of shamanic sleight of hand with "a deep-seated belief in the supernatural power of shamanism"? Did they consider sleight-of-hand methods antithetical to genuine shamanic power, and did they express anger and disappointment upon discovering such techniques (as Hunt does in his 1922 account)? Or, did patients accept these methods as part and parcel of shamanic practice while maintaining confidence in shamans' abilities to effect healing?

Several anthropologists have addressed these or related questions while revisiting Boas and Hunt's materials on Kwakwaka'wakw shamanism. Claude Lévi-Strauss ([1949] 1963) analyzes Hunt's shamanic initiation story from

1922 alongside ethnographic accounts of shamanism and sorcery in other Indigenous societies of the Americas. He argues that, over the course of Hunt's experiences, Hunt develops a sense of "pride in his achievements" as a shaman (Lévi-Strauss 1963, 178) and a perception of his own shamanic technique as "less false than others" (176). Meanwhile, ʔaʔixagidalagəlis exposes his own procedures and expresses skeptical attitudes toward shamanism more broadly as soon as he loses the "social consensus"—that is, the faith and interest—of his community, which has turned its attention to Hunt's more impressive ritual displays (180). Lévi-Strauss argues that shamanic healing owes its believability to communal performances during which shamans and their audiences collaboratively assimilate the chaotic realities of disease into conventional narratives about illness and recovery. The "social consensus" that forms around shamanic performances helps conceal the sleight-of-hand techniques that shamans may use to communicate with their audiences, making it possible even for the practitioners themselves to trust in the efficacy of their methods. Sleight of hand, accordingly, is only visible in the absence of "social consensus," and it has no place in traditional beliefs regarding shamanism.

Several other scholars accord sleight-of-hand techniques a more explicit status in Kwakwa̱ka'wakw shamanic ideology. Irving Goldman (1975, 98–106) argues that sleight of hand is necessary owing to humanity's state of spiritual "decadence"—in other words, to "an increasing separation between an original mythical state of being and a contemporary reality.... What was real then is simulated now" (103). Stanley Walens, along similar lines, suggests that "the shamans themselves, and the rest of the Kwakiutl [i.e., Kwakwa̱ka'wakw] as well, seem well aware of the artificiality of the tricks" used in shamanic performances (1981, 24). He proposes that these techniques were believed to exert a sympathetic influence on spirits: "Once a shaman . . . begins sucking on the body of the sick person, the spirit powers to whom he is related will also begin to suck" (23). Walens does not identify specific textual or ethnographic evidence supporting this proposal, and I am not aware of any such evidence, but his hypothesis is related to Goldman's: both authors suggest that in Kwakwa̱ka'wakw religious thought, "tricks" are acknowledged as a legitimate part of shamanic ritual but are seen as secondary to or imitative of genuine healing power.

Michael Taussig (1998), who analyzes Hunt's 1922 initiation account in a broad comparative framework, arrives at somewhat different conclusions. He argues that the "tension" between Hunt's self-avowed skepticism and his desire to be initiated "seems so crucial, so carefully highlighted, that it is surely fair to venture the hypothesis that *learning shamanism means doubting it at the same time*, and that the development of such a split consciousness involving belief and nonbelief is what this learning process is all about" (232, emphasis in the original). According to Taussig shamanic sleight of hand "seems [to be] common knowledge" and a "public secret" in the Kwakwaka'wakw communities of Hunt's time (250). Shamans elicit confidence and awe by exposing their impressive "tricks" while also maintaining some of the secrecy that surrounds these methods (Taussig 1998, 250). Furthermore, Taussig, adapting Walens's hypothesis, asks whether a Kwakwaka'wakw shaman's "trick 'tricks' (calls, encourages, seduces?) first and foremost the spirit so as to become a fluidly efficacious technique," and whether "imitation in being fraudulent ensures realness and works its wonderful magic" (238). This proposal partly resembles the interpretation I will develop in my analysis, insofar as Taussig suggests that what he refers to as "tricks" were thought to play an essential role in supernaturally efficacious shamanic rituals.

The scholars whose work I have summarized investigate shamanic sleight of hand either in detailed analyses of Hunt's first-person account from 1922 (Lévi-Strauss 1963; Taussig 1998) or in brief attempts to contextualize shamanism within Kwakwaka'wakw religious thinking (Goldman 1975; Walens 1981). In the present chapter, I approach this topic differently, analyzing a Kwak'wala narrative that depicts shamanic initiation in a mythological framework. The human protagonist of this text, titled "Qateṅac and Qatemo," descends into the undersea world, where he encounters an injured spirit-being.[11] The protagonist inaccurately claims to be a shaman, and he heals the spirit-being by surreptitiously performing a nonsupernatural cure while enacting a shamanic ritual. The spirit-being then grants supernatural power to the protagonist, making him "a very great shaman" (Boas and Hunt 1906, 25). Finally, the protagonist returns to his village, where he has a career as a shamanic healer. In its depiction of the protagonist's behavior as he heals the spirit beneath the sea, the narrative projects shamanic sleight-of-hand techniques into the mythological past, providing evidence that such methods held an important status in beliefs about shamanism. Accordingly, in Kwakwa̱ka'wakw communities around the turn of the twentieth century, at least some groups thought that sleight-of-hand techniques had a role to play in shamanic ritual and made attempts to define or to explain this role; the text of "Qateṅac and Qatemo" represents one such attempt. Contrary to Hunt's skeptical 1922 account, in which methods of illusion stand in opposition to genuine shamanic power, "Qateṅac and Qatemo" asserts that *both* sleight of hand *and* supernatural power are intrinsic to shamanism. Shamanic sleight-of-hand techniques, according to the narrative, are not fraudulent. Rather, they are legitimate ritual procedures, and they do not preclude the operation of supernatural power in shamanic healing.

Before launching into my examination of "Qateṅac and Qatemo," I must call attention to an unproven axiom of my analysis: that the sleight-of-hand procedures described by Boas and Hunt were, in fact, practiced by Kwakwa̱ka'wakw shamans in the second half of the nineteenth century. While I make this assumption about *what* shamans did, the aim of my investigation is to understand what their actions *meant*, especially in their own eyes, but also from the perspectives of their patients and other Kwakwa̱ka'wakw audiences in that period.[12] In keeping with this goal, I avoid value-laden words such as "fraud" or "trickery" when referring to shamanic practices. As a more neutral, but still imperfect alternative, I use the term "sleight of hand" to refer to methods of creating or controlling appearances, as this term need not bear connotations of fraud in English usage.[13]

THE STORY OF "QATEṄAC AND QATEMO"

"Qateṅac and Qatemo" was written down by Hunt, who typically documented Kwak'wala narratives "in his own words" after hearing them performed orally (Berman 1994, 491). The story is part of the oral-literary repertoire of the LiGʷiłdaʔχʷ (now also known as the Laich-Kwil-Tach), the southernmost group of Kwakwa̱ka'wakw tribes, whose neighbors to the south spoke Comox, a Coast Salish language. "Qateṅac" and "Qatemo" are the only two human personal names in the text, and, while neither one seems to be analyzable in Kwak'wala, similar names are attested in Comox stories, including a narrative paralleling "Qateṅac and Qatemo" (Boas 2002, 231–33).[14] It is likely, therefore, that "Qateṅac and Qatemo" developed via one or more LiG^wiłda?χ^w storytellers adapting a preexisting Coast Salish story (Boas 1935b, 147).[15] The narrative is one of many from the Pacific Northwest in which a human wounds a spirit-being with a projectile, discovers that the spirit is unable to see the projectile, and then removes it, thereby healing the spirit and gaining a reward (Boas [1916, 820–21] labels this formula "The Invisible Arrow" and cites twenty-four examples from Alaska, British Columbia, and Oregon). I provide a summary of the story below:

> The narrative is set among the "first" (presumably meaning "ancient" or "primordial") ancestors of the LiGwiłda?χ^w. A man named Qatemo is a skilled shaman, and another individual, Qateṅac, is jealous of him. Qateṅac begins performing ablutions in a river every morning and every evening in the company of his unnamed younger brother (such ablutions are a common practice for people hoping to encounter a spirit-being and to gain supernatural power). After repeating this procedure for four days, Qateṅac hears a rustling sound from some nearby bushes while performing an additional ablution. Frightened, he throws a piece of bark into the bushes, and the rustling stops. Before dawn the next morning, for reasons that the text does not explain, Qateṅac wakes his younger brother, and the two of them travel by canoe toward an island. When they are halfway to the island, they pass a stalk of kelp in the water. Qateṅac tells his brother, "I will climb down this kelp and see the world beneath us" (Boas and Hunt 1906, 24). He instructs his brother to search for him along the beach each morning.
>
> Qateṅac descends the stalk of kelp until he arrives at the roof of a house, through which the stalk is growing. He hears someone in the house say, "Go, see what makes the sound of falling on our roof" (my translation). A man approaches Qateṅac and says, "Come, Qateṅac, I am sent by the chief to invite you in" (Boas and Hunt 1906, 24). Qateṅac enters the house and sees a crowd of people standing around a sick man. They are attempting to cure him, but "none of the shamans could get

[i.e., find and extract] the sickness of the sick person" (24). A man asks Qateṅac whether he is a shaman capable of healing the patient, and Qateṅac replies that he is "a great shaman" (25). Qateṅac is instructed to examine the sick man, whereupon Qateṅac approaches him and discovers a piece of bark stuck in his side. Qateṅac realizes that it is the piece of bark he threw into the bushes while bathing the previous evening; the shamans in the house have been unable to see it. Qateṅac also realizes that the man is, in fact, the *Sisiuł* (a supernatural being with two serpentine heads and a human head in between). Qateṅac touches the bark, causing the man to scream in pain, and "Qateṅac pretended (-*buła*) that there was difficulty in sucking out [the sickness] from his side. Three times he tried in vain to suck it out. Then the fourth time he took the bark and hid it, and the man [i.e., the *Sisiuł*] got well at once" (25). The *Sisiuł* says, "Oh, my dear Qateṅac! You will be a very great shaman. You shall see now what supernatural gift you will receive from me" (25). At the time of the *Sisiuł*'s utterance, "supernatural power (*nawalak*^{w}) came to Qateṅac," and "as soon as the supernatural power came into the house, a pond appeared in the house, and reed matting was growing in the pond. A petrel came soaring over it; and as soon as Qateṅac came to his senses, the pond and the reed matting and the petrel disappeared" (25).

Qateṅac is dismissed by the *Sisiuł*, whereupon he travels underwater to shore. Four days have passed since he descended the stalk of kelp, and his brother finds him on the beach, "lying dead at the high-water mark" (26). Qateṅac awakes, bathes in the river, and shows his new supernatural power (i.e., his ability to make the pond, reed matting, and petrel appear) to his brother. In the evening, Qateṅac displays his power before a gathering of his tribespeople, and he cures those who are ill. Qatemo (the shaman of whom Qateṅac was jealous at the beginning of the story) "did not believe that Qateṅac was a real shaman" (26). Qatemo feigns illness and begs Qateṅac to cure him. Qateṅac, recognizing Qatemo's ruse, kills Qatemo by crushing his innards and extracting them through his anus. Qateṅac "always now healed the sick ones among his fellow villagers.[16] And the pond and the reed matting and the petrel always appeared when he was healing" (27).

QATEṄAC'S SHAMANIC INITIATION AND CAREER

In this section, I will make three arguments: (1) that the scene in which Qateṅac heals the *Sisiuɬ* alludes to shamanic sleight of hand; (2) that after Qateṅac returns to his village, he uses supernatural power to effect shamanic cures; and (3) that the narrative depicts Qateṅac's performance in the house beneath the sea and his subsequent acts of healing as separate stages of his initiation and career as a shaman (see also Wright in this volume). This last observation justifies treating sleight of hand and supernatural power as distinct concepts. A priori, one might suspect that any such distinction imposes Western categories on the text. I argue, on the contrary, that sleight of hand and supernatural power are separate concepts in the shamanic ideology that the narrative espouses (although, as I propose in the next section, the text begins to erode this distinction in the process of asserting that both are inherent to shamanism).

Qateṅac's actions in healing the *Sisiuɬ* correspond to the sleight-of-hand techniques that Hunt describes in his 1922 initiation narrative. Those techniques generate visible signs of the supernatural mechanisms traditionally believed to underlie shamanic healing, such as the removal of pathogenic objects from patients' bodies. Qateṅac, correspondingly, suppresses signs of the nonsupernatural mechanism underlying his cure of the *Sisiuɬ* (i.e., his dislodging of a piece of bark from the *Sisiuɬ*'s side). The text indicates this in two ways. Most straightforwardly, it reports that after removing the bark from the *Sisiuɬ*, Qateṅac "hid it." In addition, throughout the curing process, Qateṅac strives to create the appearance that he is a shaman capable of healing his patient solely via ritual means. After Qateṅac enters the house beneath the sea, he states that he is "a great shaman," and, as a result, he is invited to examine the *Sisiuɬ*. Qateṅac discovers that the source of the *Sisiuɬ*'s suffering is a piece of bark stuck in his side. Qateṅac touches the bark, causing the *Sisiuɬ* to scream in pain. Then "Qateṅac pretended that there was difficulty in sucking out [the sickness] from his side. Three times he tried in vain to suck it out. Then the fourth time he took the bark and hid it. Then the man [i.e., the *Sisiuɬ*] got well" (Boas and Hunt 1906, 25).[17] In the word *bəlxʷəmalabuɬa*, which Boas and Hunt translate as "pretended that there was difficulty," the morpheme -*buɬa* 'to pretend' (Boas 1947, 337; or, perhaps more precisely, 'to seem as though performing an action, being in a state, having an identity, or acting with expected intentions' [my gloss]) indicates that the appearance of Qateṅac's actions corresponds to a situation different from reality.[18] In order to make sense of Qateṅac's behavior, it is useful to point out that, in Hunt's 1922 account, shamans are said to perform either one or four bouts of sucking during healing rites: "When they do not get the sickness when they suck the first time, then they only get the sickness when they have sucked four times" (Boas 1930b, 3). Regardless of which version of the sucking ritual was more common, four is "the number of ritual efficacy" in Kwakwa̱ka'wakw ceremonialism (Berman 1991, 391), with many rites comprising four parts or involving fourfold repetitions of particular acts. By sucking four times on the *Sisiuł*'s body, therefore, Qateṅac enacts a dramatic and convincing shamanic ritual. In this way, and by hiding the piece of bark that he extracts from the *Sisiuł*'s body, Qateṅac generates the appearance that his success in curing the *Sisiuł* stems from shamanic prowess. I interpret this behavior as a narrative icon representing shamanic sleight of hand more broadly.

By contrast Qateṅac subsequently acquires supernatural power as a shaman and uses it to heal those who are ill in his village. After Qateṅac cures the *Sisiuł*, the *Sisiuł* tells him, "You will be a very great shaman. You shall see now what supernatural gift you will receive from me" (Boas and Hunt 1906, 25).[19] Then "the supernatural power (*nawalak^w*) came to Qateṅac," and, "as soon as the supernatural power came into the house (*nawalak^{w}əmgal'iłəχs*)" (25), a pond, reed matting, and a flying petrel appear. The term translated here as "supernatural power" (occurring in the first instance as a noun and in the second as the root of a verbal form) is *nawalak^w*, "the general term for the supernatural, the wonderful" (Boas 1966, 165).[20] The arrival of *nawalak^w* coincides with the spontaneous appearance of the pond, the matting, and the bird. I do not know the significance of these apparitions, but they are evidently associated with the *nawalak^w* that "came into the house." Their connection to shamanism seems less apparent,[21] but from this point forward, they show up whenever Qateṅac engages in shamanic healing, and they are later described as Qateṅac's *pəχala?ina?e*—literally his "shamanhood," or "way of being a shaman."[22] These apparitions mark his subsequent shamanic cures as supernatural. Qateṅac's shamanic power receives further confirmation from the episode in which he kills Qatemo, the shaman whom he envied at the beginning of the narrative. When Qateṅac returns home with his new abilities and begins healing sick villagers, "Qatemo did not believe that Qateṅac was a real shaman: therefore he lied and said that he was sick" (Boas and Hunt 1906, 26). Qateṅac immediately recognizes the ruse and kills Qatemo by tearing apart his organs and removing them through his anus. Qateṅac's victory over a skeptic emphasizes that there is nothing illusory about his power. Just as Qateṅac's performance in the house beneath the sea stands in for shamans' sleight-of-hand techniques, his feats as a shaman after he returns to his village represent the supernatural dimensions of shamanic healing.

Significantly, the narrative separates its depiction of shamanic sleight of hand from its portrayal of shamanic power, locating each within a different stage of Qateṅac's career as a shaman. In order to clarify this observation, it is necessary to point out that "Qateṅac and Qatemo" fits within a widespread category of Kwak'wala narratives Judith Berman (1991) has identified as "the adolescent-hero plot-type." In stories of this sort, the protagonist (who is often an adolescent) leaves home, travels to an otherworldly realm, enters the house of a donor spirit, receives a gift from the spirit, and brings the gift back to his or her village (433–35). In many adolescent-hero tales, the gift that the protagonist receives from the donor spirit is initiation as a ritualist. Typically this involves the protagonist acquiring the right to perform a masked dance (dances were and remain a strictly guarded form of intellectual property in Kwakwa̱ka'wakw communities). Along related lines, in "Qateṅac and Qatemo," Qateṅac is initiated as a shaman during his encounter with the *Sisiuł*. A turning point in this process occurs when the *Sisiuł* declares, "Oh, my dear Qateṅac! You will be a very great shaman. You shall see now what supernatural gift you will receive from me" (Boas and Hunt 1906, 25). This pronouncement by the *Sisiuł* corresponds to statements that donor spirits often make, in which they declare the passage of sacred property, including dances and associated names and ritual paraphernalia, into the possession of the protagonist or the protagonist's family.[23] Comparably, the *Sisiuł*'s announcement marks Qateṅac's endowment with supernatural power as a shaman, separating Qateṅac's prior sleight-of-hand performance from his subsequent, supernatural feats of shamanic healing. This separation suggests that sleight of hand and supernatural power were distinct concepts in the ideological system to which the narrative gives voice. The fact that the story projects both concepts into the mythological past indicates that both had an important status in Kwakwa̱ka'wakw shamanism, at least as it was understood in some circles. In the following section, I aim to elucidate this status.

SLEIGHT OF HAND AND SUPERNATURAL POWER
QATEṅAC'S PERFORMANCE

Although "Qateṅac and Qatem̓o" distinguishes between sleight of hand and supernatural power, it asserts that both are essential to shamanism and that there is no tension between the two. The text legitimates Qateṅac's sleight-of-hand performance by highlighting its integral role in his initiation as a shaman. The sentences preceding the performance frame it as a climactic juncture in the narrative, at which point two previously disconnected threads of the plot dramatically converge. The first two of these sentences report, "As soon as (gəl?əml'awis) Qateṅac went to him [the sick man], he saw the piece of bark lying flat on the side of the man who was lying down. As soon as (gəl?əml'e) Qateṅac had discovered the piece of bark, he recognized it as the same that he had thrown at the river where he had been purifying in the evening" (Boas and Hunt 1906, 25). Twice, forms of a sentence-initial auxiliary meaning "as soon as" are used to introduce cognitive events—specifically, a pair of related inferences that Qateṅac makes. The division of these events between two separate sentences, despite the rapidity with which one event triggers the next, marks a dramatic decrease in the speed of narration, which I interpret as a stylistic shift pointing toward an upcoming climax.[24] The narrative then reports, "The shamans did not see the piece of bark lying there" (25), and it appends a pair of declarations to the end of this sentence. The first declaration begins with the pronominal element yəχa, which stands in apposition to the preceding phrase ("the piece of bark lying there"). This first declaration means, literally, "which, behold! was the cause of the man's lying down on his side in the house." In Kwak'wala, the final word in this syntactic unit is $bax^wəsi$, "the man." The next declaration begins with yəχa in apposition to $bax^wəsi$. This second declaration means, literally, "who, behold! was the Sisiuɫ."[25] I believe that the pair of declarations, each of which is marked with the morpheme -χuλ, "behold!," and each of which is appended to the preceding syntactic unit with *yəχa*, affect breathless excitement over the developments they report.

In these declarations Qateṅac and the audience discover for the first time that the sick man in the house beneath the sea is the *Sisiuɫ* (until this point, the *Sisiuɫ* has been identified as a "sick person," as a "man," and possibly also as Q'umugʷa, a well known spirit-being associated with the undersea world).[26] This discovery reintroduces and clarifies a previously abandoned and as yet unresolved thread of the plot. Earlier in the narrative, while Qateṅac was performing ablutions in a river, he heard a rustling sound coming from some nearby bushes, and he reacted by throwing bark toward the source of the noise. At that point it was evident that the event bore significance of some sort, because it occurred after Qateṅac had been performing ablutions for four days. The number four plays a nearly pervasive role in the structuring of Kwak'wala narratives and rituals, and in three other stories from the Boas-Hunt corpus, human protagonists encounter spirit-beings after four days of bathing.[27] Therefore, when Qateṅac hears a mysterious rustling sound and throws a piece of bark in its direction, the audience suspects that something important has occurred, but the significance of this event is left unspecified. This dangling ambiguity is resolved when Qateṅac discovers that the rustling sound was caused by the *Sisiuɫ*, and that when he threw a piece of bark into the bushes, the bark hit the *Sisiuɫ*.

It now becomes evident that the events of the narrative have, with preternatural consistency, brought Qateṅac steadily closer to being reunited with this spirit-being. The morning after his unknowing first encounter with the *Sisiuɫ* by the river, Qateṅac arises before dawn and departs with his brother on a canoe trip for reasons that neither he nor the narrator indicates. He chances upon a stalk of kelp floating in the water, and by climbing it down to the bottom of the sea, Qateṅac reencounters the spirit-being that he injured. Now, finally, he proceeds to heal this spirit, earning himself the reward of being initiated as a shaman. His sleight-of-hand performance completes the sequence of events that, the audience now senses, has led determinedly to his acquisition of supernatural power. By highlighting Qateṅac's performance as a culminating step in his progress toward gaining supernatural abilities as a shaman, the narrative endorses sleight of hand while also asserting the supernatural basis of shamanic healing.

Qateṅac's Performance: A Model for His Shamanic Career

The narrative may go further in its efforts to assert that shamanic ritual is both supernaturally efficacious and rooted in sleight of hand. As noted above, "Qateṅac and Qatemo" generally adheres to the "adolescent-hero plot-type." Characters in adolescent-hero tales do not often undergo *shamanic* initiation, but they are frequently initiated as performers of masked dances. In many of these stories, after arriving at the donor spirit's house, the protagonist watches as spirit-beings perform dance rituals. Then "the spirit dances seen by the hero are 'imitated' by him (*nanaxċo, hayigi?*) when he returns [to the human world], thus providing for the origin of the dances among humans" (Berman 1991, 259). In other words, ritual performances that the protagonist witnesses in the house of the donor spirit serve as paradigmatic models for rituals that he or she will later perform and transmit to others (cf. Berman 1991, 691). By analogy, in "Qateṅac and Qatemo," when the *Sisiuł* displays power after announcing that Qateṅac "will be a very great shaman" (Boas and Hunt 1906, 25), this display clearly functions as a model for Qateṅac's subsequent shamanic healing rites. What is essential to note, for the purposes of my argument, is that Qateṅac's sleight-of-hand performance may *also* serve as a paradigmatic model for his later career. A specific detail in the narrative supports this interpretation:

After Qateṅac climbs down a stalk of kelp to the roof of the house beneath the sea, someone in the house says, "Go, see what makes the sound of falling on our roof" (my translation). Immediately, "a man came to the place where Qateṅac was standing. The man said, 'Come, Qateṅac, I am sent by the chief to invite you in'" (Boas and Hunt 1906, 24). It is striking that, whereas the voice in the house seems to know nothing about Qateṅac, the individual who obeys the voice's command addresses Qateṅac by name and invites him inside. This contrast is reminiscent of a motif attested in a pair of Kwak'wala narratives belonging to the Dzawada̱'enux̱w (Dᶻawadə?enuχʷ) tribe. In one of these stories, a primordial ancestor named Qawadiliqala travels inland from his village, eventually arriving at a house that belongs to a pack of wolves. The wolves are performing dances from the Winter Ceremonial (a body of rituals traditionally practiced by Kwakwa̱ka'wakw communities in early winter). When Qawadiliqala watches the wolves through a knothole in the side of the house, they err in their performance.

Someone in the house orders a being named Mouse-Woman to go outside and determine the cause of the difficulty.[28] Qawadiliqala hides, but Mouse-Woman "came right just to the place where he was hiding, and said, 'Oh, my dear Qawadiliqala! Come! Why do you hide yourself? Come into your house, chief!'" (38). Qawadiliqala follows Mouse-Woman inside. At first the wolves "did not look up at all" (38), probably in a gesture of shame. Soon, however, they welcome Qawadiliqala and display a series of Winter Ceremonial dances to him, thereby initiating him as a ritualist and giving him the right to perform and transmit these dances.

In a separate Dzawada'enuxw narrative, a mountain-goat hunter named Təwixil'ak^w enters a passageway that leads him deep into a mountain, where he discovers a house belonging to a herd of mountain goats. He hears them singing songs of the Winter Ceremonial. Then someone in the house says, "O friends! what has happened to our house [to disturb our proceedings]?–Come, Mouse-Woman, go and look about outside of our winter-dance house" (Boas and Hunt 1905, 11–12).[29] Mouse-Woman exits the house and proceeds immediately to the place where Təwixil'ak^w has been hiding. She tells him, "O friend Təwixil'ak^w! do not hide from me. I have already seen you. Take care! I shall come four times, and then you shall enter the house" (12). Mouse-Woman goes back inside and tells the mountain goats that she has not found anyone. The mountain goats resume their ritual performance, but they again sense a disturbance and send Mouse-Woman out to determine the cause of the problem. After several iterations of these events, Təwixil'ak^w rushes into the house. The mountain goats are performing a ritual in which they dance bearing a magic feather. During the dance the goats sing, "Come, Unable-to-Climb-up-to-Take-Hold-of-End!" (15). They are apparently preparing to initiate a dancer from among their ranks.[30] Təwixil'ak^w, following instructions provided by Mouse-Woman, grabs the feather and declares that he is the one named Unable-to-Climb-up-to-Take-Hold-of-End.[31]

At this time the mountain goats are in human form; animals are believed to wear skins or "masks" that give them their animal forms, and, when they are not wearing their masks, they look like humans (Berman 2000, 63). It is possible that the mountain goats have assumed human form specifically as part of their Winter Ceremonial activities (73–74), but the implication could simply be that they remove their skins whenever they are at home. When Təwixil'akʷ enters their ritual proceedings, the mountain goats rush to reassume animal form:

> Some of the mountain goats got dressed in time, and some failed to get in[to their clothes, i.e., their mountain-goat skins]. Only their right hands were in their clothes, for that was what they put into their clothing first, their right hands. That is why Winter Ceremonial dancers do in that way, extending first their right hands into the grizzly bear mask [i.e., dance regalia], and the thunderbird mask, and the raven mask, and the *hoxʷhokʷ* [avian spirit-being] mask, and all the [dance regalia] that they don. (original text from Boas and Hunt 1905, 15–16; my translation)

After failing to hide their human forms from Təwixil'akʷ, "the mountain goats all hung their heads" (16).[32] A conversation ensues in which Təwixil'akʷ again asserts that he is the one named Unable-to-Climb-up-to-Take-Hold-of-End (whom the mountain goats invoked in their song) and again expresses his desire for the magic feather that was displayed in the mountain goats' dance. One of the chiefs of the mountain goats instructs his followers to "look up" and not to "be ashamed on account of our friend [i.e., Təwixil'akʷ]," for "indeed, he does not wish for anything very great" (17). Təwixil'akʷ is given the feather, which is a powerful hunting implement and weapon. He also receives the name Dabənd to transmit within his family (*dabənd*, which means "to take hold of end," is the final element of the sequence "Unable-to-Climb-up-to-Take-Hold-of-End").

In both of the scenes I have summarized, the protagonist arrives outside a house belonging to spirit-beings and spies on them performing Winter Ceremonial dances. One of the spirits suspects that someone is outside and sends Mouse-Woman to investigate. Mouse-Woman finds the protagonist, addresses him by name, and leads him into the house, where he receives gifts from the spirits. I propose that the scene preceding Qateṅac's entry into the house beneath the sea alludes to this sequence of events.[33] The voice in the house that says, "Go, see what makes the sound of falling on our roof," corresponds to the wolf or mountain goat who dispatches Mouse-Woman to inspect the area outside the house in each of the two

Dzawada̱'enux̱w narratives I have cited. The man who obeys the voice's command, who addresses Qateṅac by name, and who invites him into the house corresponds to Mouse-Woman.

What is the significance of this plot sequence in the stories of Qawadiliqala and Təwixil'akʷ, and why does "Qateṅac and Qateṁo" allude to it? In each of these Dzawada̱'enux̱w narratives, Mouse-Woman helps the protagonist enter or intrude upon a group of spirits who are performing Winter Ceremonial dances, and, as a result, the protagonist gains heritable intellectual property associated with these rituals.[34] Qawadiliqala acquires the right to perform the wolves' dances, while Təwixil'akʷ acquires the name Dabənd, which the mountain goats mention in their ceremonial song. This turn of events is the mythological equivalent of a traditional procedure in the Winter Ceremonial: if a noninitiate "penetrated the initiates' secrets," he or she would be forced to undergo initiation (Berman 1991, 264–66).[35] By entering the animals' ceremonial proceedings, Qawadiliqala and Təwixil'akʷ each assume the role of such an interloper. The gifts they subsequently receive (which, in Qawadiliqala's case, are explicitly said to include ritual initiation) correspond to the prescribed initiation of someone who discovers the secrets of a human Winter Ceremonial.

It must be noted, at this point, that Winter Ceremonial rites often involve simulating the behavior and appearance of spirit-beings by donning masks and other forms of disguise (see, e.g., Berman 2000, 81-82, and 1991, 691–92), as well as via elaborate sleight-of-hand techniques. As Berman (1991, 264–65) explains,

> "Illusions" used in the performances [of the Winter Ceremonial] included bodiless voices produced by whistles hidden in the initiates' clothing, or by kelp tubes that conducted human speech to various empty spots on the dance-house floor; initiates disappearing into the earth by means of hidden trenches; novices flying on invisible lines hung from the rafters, or from trees outside; and decapitated dancers carrying their own severed heads in the form of grisly and strikingly realistic portrait-heads carved of wood. Initiates also became masters of mime and mimicry, "throwing" and "catching" invisible substances. In such fashion did initiates enact the presence and powers of spirits.

Crucially, Berman suggests that mimetic acts such as these are not, as Goldman would have it, merely due to "an increasing separation between an original mythical state of being and a contemporary reality," or to the idea that "what was real then is simulated now" (Goldman 1975, 103).[36] Instead they are fundamental to the Winter Ceremonial, and they are equivalent to acts of mimesis performed by spirit-beings as part of *their* ceremonial rites. When the primordial "myth people" or "history people" (a community believed to have inhabited beachside villages in the era before humans became firmly distinct from animals) first acquire and perform the Winter Ceremonial, their performance involves either putting on or taking off the furs, masks, and facial paints that effect their metamorphosis into animal form (see Berman 2000, 73–74 for a list of narratives describing this event).[37] Berman proposes that this motif "is echoed in several stories," including the story of Təwixil'akʷ, in which "a human hero surprises animals holding the winter dances in human form" (73–74).[38] In these narratives, animals' acts of masking and unmasking provide a paradigmatic model for the manipulation of appearances, via both masking and sleight of hand, that plays such an important role in human Winter Ceremonials (Berman 1991, 265). This is made explicit in the story of Təwixil'akʷ, which states that the contemporary procedure for putting on Winter Ceremonial vestments (literally referred to as "masks") memorializes the mountain goats' frantic attempt to don their animal skins in the face of a human intruder.

By alluding to narrative episodes in which Mouse-Woman helps humans intrude on animals' Winter Ceremonial performances, "Qateṅac and Qatemo" encourages its audience to interpret Qateṅac's shamanic initiation in light of these episodes. Təwixil'akʷ (and perhaps, by implication, Qawadiliqala as well) receives gifts from a group of animal ritualists after he discovers their ability to manipulate appearances with their masks. Qateṅac, by analogy, becomes a shaman when he discovers and successfully uses sleight of hand. Just as the animals' ability to put on and take off their masks provides a paradigmatic model for masking and sleight of hand in the Winter Ceremonial, so, too, does Qateṅac's sleight-of-hand performance in the house beneath the sea provide a paradigmatic model for his subsequent career as a supernaturally endowed shaman.

Reexamining Qateṅac's Performance

My analysis thus far has focused on the relationship between Qateṅac's healing rite beneath the sea and his subsequent career as a shaman. I have argued that this relationship signals the shared legitimacy of shamanic sleight of hand and supernatural shamanic power. It is worthwhile, at this point, to reexamine Qateṅac's healing of the *Sisiuł* and to observe that the undersea scene, considered in its own right, already hints at this shared legitimacy. In this scene Qateṅac conceals the nonsupernatural mechanism underlying his cure of the *Sisiuł* (i.e., his extraction of a piece of bark from the patient's side). Qateṅac's behavior corresponds to, but also differs from, the sleight-of-hand techniques that Hunt describes in his 1922 initiation narrative. Rather than concealing nonsupernatural healing mechanisms, those techniques generate visible signs of the supernatural mechanisms believed to underlie shamanic healing. This distinction reflects the fact that, unlike the shamans in Hunt's first-person account, Qateṅac is tasked with healing a spirit-being, whose injury requires the nonsupernatural ministrations of a human. The spirit shamans who attempted to aid the *Sisiuł* prior to Qateṅac's procedure "did not see the piece of bark [lying there] that was the cause of the man's lying sick in the house" (Boas and Hunt 1906, 25). This plot element has parallels in "Invisible Arrow" narratives from across the Pacific Northwest. In his motif-index of Kwak'wala oral literature, Boas (1935b, 104) remarks, "There is a mutual relation between human and supernatural beings. In some cases they are mutually invisible. As human beings hurt by supernaturals can be cured only by supernatural help, so supernaturals hurt by man can be helped by man only."[39] Qateṅac, accordingly, is able to heal the *Sisiuł* precisely by virtue of the fact that he is a human. This gives him the ability to extract the piece of bark stuck in the *Sisiuł*'s side, which spirit-beings cannot see.

I do not know Qateṅac's motives for concealing the nonsupernatural basis of his cure, and I cannot explain why he actively hides the bark, given that spirit-beings are, apparently, unable to see it. What is crucial to note, though, is that Qateṅac's cure involves *both* the careful manipulation of appearances (i.e., sleight of hand) *and* the efficacious use of a nonsupernatural healing mechanism invisible to spirit-beings. The text implies, correspondingly, that when shamans treat human patients, they use both sleight of hand and genuine supernatural power invisible to humans.

ATTITUDES TOWARD SHAMANISM IN NARRATIVE AND IN REALITY

"Qateṅac and Qatem̓o" provides an answer to the questions that anthropologists have pondered regarding the relationship between what Boas (1966, 125) describes as "knowledge of [shamans'] fraud" and "a deep-seated belief in the supernatural power of shamanism" in Kwakwaka̲'wakw communities around the turn of the twentieth century. It asserts that sleight-of-hand techniques are an essential part of shamanic ritual, alongside supernatural power. According to the narrative, therefore, there is nothing fraudulent about these techniques.

How widespread was this attitude toward shamanic sleight of hand outside the world of the narrative? Independent evidence suggests that similar views played a role in shamans' understanding of their craft. In the 1925 account of Hunt's shamanic initiation, the shamans guiding Hunt's training instruct him to sleep naked in a graveyard. One of the shamans, whose name is Kasnomahlas (Qasnumalas), "addressed the dead. 'O friends, ghosts, you see that we brought our friend to sleep among you tonight. Now, help him, and give him a good dream'" (Boas 1966, 124). After the shamans leave, Hunt dresses and departs as well, contrary to the shamans' instructions. Then,

> the following evening Kasnomahlas asked him [Hunt] what he had dreamed. He replied, "Nothing, only that I slept among the dead." This satisfied Kasnomahlas, who asked the novice to meet the shamans again that night. When he went there he found the two shamans and their spies Tsopala (*Cup̓ale*) and Hanyos (*χanəyus*). He was asked to sit down between the two shamans, and Kasnomahlas said, "Now, I know that the favorable supernatural power of the ground (*ʔaʔikamenoGa naxnawalak̓ʷəs*) has entered the body of our friend. Now we will tell him the secrets of the shamans."[40] Then he told him that the shamans had spies who informed them in regard to sickness among the people; also that they receive one quarter of the amount paid to the shaman. Hanyos lived in Fort Rupert. . . . His name as a spy was Killer-whale.

Tsopale's name as a spy was Wolf. This meant that the novice [i.e., Hunt] should say that the killer whale was his protector, while the protector of Kasnomahlas was said to be the wolf. The spy of a shaman whose protector was the toad had the name Toad-Voice (*Xʷakiwala*). The shamans always claimed to have dreamed what their spies told them. In regard to the call by the killer whale previously reported [in Hunt's initiation account from 1900], my informant told me in the present report, that in reality Hanyos had told him that Calumniated [the name of Hunt's second patient] was sick. (124)

In this episode the entry of "the supernatural power of the ground" into Hunt's body provides the occasion for Kasnomahlas to inform Hunt regarding shamans' communications with "spies." Spies aid shamans in simulating supernatural accomplishments (namely, clairvoyant dreams about patients' ailments), yet this method of simulation is only revealed to Hunt once he is endowed with genuine supernatural power. For Kasnomahlas, therefore, the simulation of supernatural power goes hand in hand with the genuine presence of such power. Furthermore, this passage gives the impression that the particular animal a shaman claims as his or her guardian spirit corresponds to the secret title of his or her "spy." I do not know whether this practice was widespread; it is not made explicit in Hunt's 1922 account, and I am not aware of any other attestations. It is striking, however, because matching the name of one's shamanic guardian spirit to the secret title of one's "spy" does not make the claim that one *has* a guardian spirit any more or less convincing. This practice suggests a respect for simulation as something other than a mode of deception. It is, therefore, reminiscent of the symbiotic relationship between supernatural power and sleight of hand that "Qateṅac and Qatemo" depicts. In light of the evidence I have cited from the 1925 account of Hunt's initiation, the ideology espoused by "Qateṅac and Qatemo" likely held salience among professional shamans.

If shamanic practitioners regarded sleight of hand as an important part of the healing process, to what extent were patients and audiences "in on" this aspect of shamanism? Was it, as Taussig (1998, 250) suggests, "common knowledge" and a "public secret," such that patients willingly accepted it as a part of shamanic treatment? In Hunt's 1922 initiation narrative, he recalls having set out to determine whether shamans "were real" or whether they "merely pretended" (Boas 1930b, 5). A similar trope appears in the initiation account of a shaman named Fool, who asserts, "Formerly I did not believe in shamans, for I used to tell them aloud that they were lying when they were curing the sick" (41), until he acquires shamanic power from a wolf, which enables him to effect supernatural cures. In these narratives Hunt and Fool evidently believe that shamans' techniques are *either* supernatural *or* fraudulent, leaving little room for sleight of hand as a legitimate aspect of shamanic practice. Other individuals in their communities who were not initiated as shamans may have held similar views (for reports by Hunt involving nonshamans' reactions to accusations or evidence of shamanic sleight-of-hand, see Boas 1921, 730–31 and 1930b, 277–78). It is noteworthy, in this regard, that the text of "Qateṅac and Qatemo" places Qateṅac's sleight-of-hand performance at a separate, earlier stage in his career than his supernatural cures. This could be interpreted as the text's concession to or acknowledgment of less tolerant attitudes toward sleight of hand.

On the other hand, the text may depict patients' and audiences' tacit awareness of shamanic sleight-of-hand techniques and their willing suspension of disbelief. It seems odd that the *Sisiuł* rewards Qateṅac's ostensible display of shamanic power by granting him shamanic power. This apparent ambiguity in the logic of the narrative may indicate that the *Sisiuł* recognizes Qateṅac's sleight of hand.[41] If so, the *Sisiuł*'s tacit awareness may represent a similar mindset among human patients and audiences to shamanic performances.

CONCLUSION

The text of "Qatenac and Qatemo" uses successive stages in the initiation and career of a shaman to represent sleight of hand and supernatural power and to suggest that both are essential, legitimate aspects of shamanism. It remains unclear, though, how this understanding might have manifested in different social circles outside of the narrative, or how it might have coexisted with other perceptions of shamanism. The explicit ethnographic documentation of Kwakwaka'wakw attitudes toward shamanism around the turn of the twentieth century is limited. Nevertheless, as I have attempted to demonstrate, texts like "Qateṅac and Qatemo" can help clarify Kwakwa̱ka'wakw religious concepts from that period. Hopefully, future analyses of Kwak'wala narratives, along with continued work aimed at understanding Hunt's ethnographic writings, will shed light on multiple late nineteenth- and early twentieth-century versions of Kwakwa̱ka'wakw religious ideology and on the negotiations that took place among their proponents.[42]

Future research should also situate Kwakwa̱ka'wakw ideologies concerning shamanic sleight of hand within broader comparative frameworks. It would be valuable, for example, to compare these ideologies with understandings of icons and sacramental objects in other religious traditions. Worshippers' veneration of these objects as sacred signs of, but not replacements for, the presence of spiritual beings may bear interesting similarities to the ideology that I have attempted to excavate from "Qateṅac and Qatemo," which regards supernatural power and its simulation through sleight of hand as coexistent aspects of shamanic ritual.

In addition, future work should evaluate the degree to which this ideology fits (or does not fit) within "Amerindian perspectivism" (Viveiros de Castro 2012, 45), an ideological system that Eduardo Viveiros de Castro has "abstract[ed]" from a variety of Indigenous American cosmologies, and which, he posits, underlies some of the commonalities among them (see 63–64). According to Viveiros de Castro, perspectivist cosmologies commonly hold that animals and spirits view themselves as humans and that they perceive their lifestyles and habitats in terms of human culture—for example, "Where we see a muddy salt-lick on a river bank, tapirs see their big ceremonial house" (2004, 6; see also the introduction and Wright in this volume). Viveiros de Castro emphasizes that these distinct perspectival visions are not "subjective and partial representations, each striving to grasp an external and unified nature [i.e., reality], which remains perfectly indifferent to those representations" (2012, 112). Instead perspectivism presupposes "a universe that is a hundred percent relational" (111), in which creatures and things possess identities only in relation to the perspectives from which they can be viewed. This presupposition, along with other aspects of perspectivism, means that "appearance" and "essence," "the visible and the invisible," are interchangeable (140–41). It is possible that perspectivist ideas like these, which Viveiros de Castro has "generaliz[ed]" (64) on the basis of many different cultural traditions, can help clarify more specific Kwakwaka'wakw attitudes toward shamanic rituals involving the alteration of appearances. These attitudes may, in turn, help refine understandings of perspectivism.

NOTES

1. I thank Professor Michael D. Jackson for his guidance on this project. I am also grateful to Professor Judith Berman and Professor Sergei Kan for their helpful comments on an earlier draft.
2. In this version of Hunt's narrative, it is not clear how much time passes between Hunt's injury at age thirteen and his initiation as a shaman, but, in his more detailed 1922 account, it can be inferred that he was at least eighteen or nineteen years old when he was initiated (I thank Judith Berman for pointing this out to me). I do not know to what extent one can assume that the accounts from 1900 and 1922 follow the same chronology.
3. Shamans typically sang during their procedures. It was believed that shamans learned their songs from their guardian spirits (Boas 1966, 135). Some shamans claimed this explicitly in their initiation accounts (130–31).
4. Boas rearranged the components of this text prior to publication (Berman forthcoming).
5. The term "spies" appears in the 1925 account. I do not know whether this word translates a particular Kwak'wala term. According to Boas (1966, 125), "These same persons were called the dreamers (*mimχala*)" in Hunt's 1922 account (which Boas published in Kwak'wala [1930a, 1–40] along with an English translation [1930b, 1–41]; the 1925 narrative, by contrast, appears only in the form of an English-language summary, and the Hunt manuscript from which it draws was written mostly in English [Berman forthcoming]). See Boas 1930a, 8–9, 13–14; and 1930b, 9, 14 for Hunt's descriptions of the role of "dreamer." In another context Hunt discusses the role of "dreamer shaman" (Boas 1930b, 274), *mimχala pəχəla* (Boas 1930a, 270); I do not know whether or to what extent this role is distinct from that of "dreamer." According to Hunt a "dreamer shaman" may have "good dreams" (Boas 1930b, 275) about patients and then describe these dreams to the patients themselves. Alternatively, if the "dreamer shaman" has "a bad dream" about an individual, a shamanic ritualist is summoned to diagnose and treat the patient.
6. Except when noted otherwise, translations of Kwak'wala texts are borrowed from Boas and Hunt.
7. This is how Boas (1966, 144) summarizes the technique.

8. My comments on Boas's analysis of Hunt's accounts and of Kwakwa̱ka̱'wakw shamanism more broadly are influenced by Michael Taussig's (1998, 231) similar critique.
9. At a later point in his discussion, after providing the 1925 account, Boas records the following statement that Hunt made "at the end of this report": "When I told you about the shaman in 1897 and 1900, I thought it best not to tell you everything, on account of my promise to Kasnomahlas and Life-Maker [the two shamans who oversaw the initiation] not to divulge their secrets. On account of this I was reluctant to tell you." Boas notes, "My informant and Kasnomahlas were very intimate. After the death of his first wife, he married the sister of Kasnomahlas" (Boas 1966, 124).
10. For example, according to the 1925 account of Hunt's initiation, after Hunt performed purifying ablutions in the sea, the shamans guiding his training told him not to dress and instructed him to sleep unclothed in a graveyard (Boas 1966, 123).
11. Here and throughout this chapter, I transfer Boas's transcriptions from his orthography into the orthography of the North American Phonetic Association. For most of the special characters in my transcriptions, I have used the First Nations Unicode Font developed under the supervision of Professor Patricia Shaw at the University of British Columbia.
12. Hunt's initiation took place in the 1870s (Boas 1966, 125), but my analysis of "Qateṅac and Qatem̓o" is probably most relevant to shamanic ideology around the turn of the twentieth century, when this text was documented.
13. For example, it is the recognized duty of a modern stage magician to generate illusions using sleight-of-hand techniques.
14. A name transcribed as "K·ātē′natc" appears in Boas 1895 (89–90), and the name of the protagonist in the Comox narrative paralleling "Qateṅac and Qatem̓o" (94–95) is transcribed as "K·atē′mot" (in the Kwak'wala story of "Qateṅac and Qatem̓o," Qateṅac is the protagonist, and Qatem̓o is his rival). Although Boas would later use "k·" and "q" to represent voiceless palato-velar and uvular stops, respectively, he is not consistent in his use of "k·" in Boas 1895.
15. The differences between the extant Comox version and "Qateṅac and Qatem̓o" are sufficient to justify using the textual details that are highlighted in my analysis of "Qateṅac and Qatem̓o" as windows onto the shamanic beliefs of the storytellers who gave this text its present form. I assume that these raconteurs were Kwakwa̱ka̱'wakw, instead of positing additional Comox narratives bearing closer similarities to the Kwak'wala text.
16. Up to this point, the translation of this excerpt is my own. The next sentence is borrowed from Boas and Hunt's translation.
17. I have modified Boas and Hunt's translation of the final sentence in this excerpt so as to represent the sentence divisions in the Kwak'wala text more accurately.

18. In order to gain a clearer understanding of this morpheme's usage, I conducted a computerized search through the English translations in Boas and Hunt 1905, Boas and Hunt 1906, and Boas 1910 for the word "pretend." The search led me to twenty-five Kwak'wala words that include the morpheme -buła. These words may be classified in the following categories of usage:

(1) Deceptive simulation of physical acts (eight unequivocal cases). For example, in one narrative in the sample, a human protagonist gets lost at sea and arrives in the land of a malevolent spirit-being. A helper being warns the man not to eat the food that the spirit-being gives him. Instead, he should "only pretend to eat (hamapbułaq); but it would be best for you to take of your (own) provisions, and just drop into your lap his food" (Boas and Hunt 1905, 257). In another interesting example, a group of black bear cubs attempt to hide the fact that they have killed a litter of grizzly bear cubs. They arrange the corpses of the grizzly bears so that the corpses look as though they are busily extracting plant resources from boxes. One of the black bear cubs proposes this ruse by saying, "Come, let [us make] this one [the eldest of the grizzly bear cubs] stretch out (his arm) into this box of cinquefoil roots, so that the dead eldest one [of the grizzly bear cubs] seems to be opening (xawabułe[?]sa) [the box]" (my translation, using glosses from Boas n.d.; text from Boas and Hunt 1906, 17).

(2) Deceptive simulation of emotional or other states (seven unequivocal cases). For example, in the story of the bears cited in the previous category, the grizzly bear cubs' mother kills the black bear cubs' mother (this is what prompts the black bear cubs to kill the grizzly bear cubs in revenge). The eldest black bear cub says to his brothers, "O brothers! let us pretend not to miss our (kiʔsbuła q̓aʔsəlax̌əns) dead mother, so that the children of Grisly-Bear-woman may not suspect that we are going to kill them when they come" (Boas and Hunt 1906, 16–17).

(3) Deceptive or nondeceptive assumption of identity (three cases). In one example a helper spirit named Mouse-Woman teaches a man how to perform a ritual that involves climbing a ceremonial pole; they use a spruce tree as a substitute for the pole. Mouse-Woman tells the man, "Well, the reason why I want us to come to this spruce tree standing on the beach is because it seems as though it were (yubułamaʔe) the ceremonial pole of this Baxʷbakʷalanuxʷsiweʔ [the spirit-being whose ceremony the man is learning]" (my translation; text from Boas 1910, 424). Here, -buła denotes resemblance or simulated identity by attaching to the copula yu- (I borrow this analysis of yu- from Littell 2016; for examples and discussions involving copulas with -buła attached, see Littell 2016, 117, 490, 550–51). In another example a man disguises himself as a particular woman as part of a plot to kill that woman's husband. The man in disguise is described as "the man who pretended to be a woman (c̓ədaqbuła bəgʷanəma)" (Boas 1910, 409). Here, instead of attaching to a copula, -buła attaches to c̓ədaq 'woman'.

(4) Actions performed under false pretenses (one case). In the previously cited narrative, after the man puts on his disguise as a woman, his older brother (who is a party to the ruse) instructs him, "go and sit down on the ground behind the house of our former brother-in-law [the man whom the brothers hope to kill], and pretend to look for lice (ƛaxabuɬaʔusaχʷa) on your apron" (Boas 1910, 409). After the disguised man arrives behind his former brother-in-law's house, the text reports, "He [the disguised man] had not been sitting there long, looking for lice on his apron" (409). The precise meaning of the older brother's advice is not, I believe, that the disguised younger brother should merely *pretend* to delouse his apron without truly doing so. Instead the older brother's advice seems to be that the disguised younger brother should, in fact, delouse his apron, but that he should do so under false pretenses as part of the ruse.

Of the remaining six examples (including the one from "Qateṅac and Qatem̓o"), I have left three unclassified because they seem to fit within more than one of the categories identified above. For instance, in one story, a man "pretended to cry (q̓ʷasabuɬi)" (Boas and Hunt 1906, 204) as part of an attempt to hide his murderous intentions toward his son-in-law. This usage probably best fits within the first category, but it is also relevant to the second category, insofar as it involves the simulation of an emotional gesture. Likewise, I am unsure whether Qateṅac's pretense "that there was difficulty in sucking out [the sickness] from" the *Sisiuɬ* (25) involves the simulation of a physical act or the simulation of a state. Two of the other unclassified examples approach but do not fully fit within any of the categories established above. For example, in the above-cited story of a castaway who arrives in the domain of a malevolent spirit-being, a helper being warns the man that a group of land otters "will come in the shape of your brother-in-law and of your father-in-law and of your elder brother and of your father and of your two younger brothers. In the morning they will come and pretend to find you (ʔalebuɬaƛuƛ), my dear! Just take care! It is they who come. They will make you foolish if you get into their canoe" (Boas and Hunt 1905, 264). This usage may fit within the fourth category, insofar as the land otters are predicted to "find" the man under the false pretense that they are his relatives; however, the fit is not perfect, insofar as the land otters would not, in fact, be "finding" the man. Along similar lines, I have not classified an example in which Mouse-Woman "pretend[s] to be able to hear (huλaq̓əsbuɬaʔən)" (Boas 1910, 431) a human character's thoughts. In this example, -*buɬa* attaches to a word meaning "one who listens (to thoughts of people)" (Boas 1947, 362), but I do not know enough about the usage of this word to determine whether the example fully fits within the third category. Finally I have refrained from classifying one example, in which a group of people cry but then claim "that they only pretended to cry (q̓ʷasabuɬa)" (Boas and Hunt 1905, 155), because I do not fully understand the intentions underlying this act.

19. The term that Boas and Hunt translate as "supernatural gift" is $\lambda ug^we?$. As Boas notes elsewhere (1966, 169), this word encompasses a wide variety of "gifts which human beings receive from spirits," not all of which are supernatural.
20. *Nawalak^w* typically refers either to "the attribute or the abstract idea of supernatural power" or to objects or beings endowed with this quality. In some cases, though, it refers to ritually sacred objects or people, such as "the whistles which are used in sacred ceremonies" or "the initiated participants in religious ceremonies" (Boas 1966, 166–67). In the present context, it evidently bears supernatural connotations, given that the arrival of *nawalak^w* in the house coincides with marvelous apparitions.
21. For partial parallels, see Boas 2002 (232–33); and 1921 (1143).
22. This word is derived by adding *-ine?*, a suffix that forms "abstract noun[s], denoting quality or condition" (Boas 1947, 325), to *pəχala*, "shaman."
23. See, for example, Boas and Hunt 1905 (51).
24. My observation here is based on Theodore M. Andersson's (1967, 40–41, 54–55) descriptions of "staging" and "retardation" techniques commonly used in Old Icelandic family sagas.
25. I have slightly adapted Boas and Hunt's (1906, 25) translations of these two declarations in order to represent them more literally.
26. Q'umug^{w}a is portrayed as the chief of the house beneath the sea. He may be equated with the sick *Sisiuɬ*, but it is not clear whether this is so.
27. Boas and Hunt 1905 (437–40), Boas 1910 (467), and Boas 1935a (124) (these examples are listed in Boas 1935b, 113).
28. In this text, as well as in the other narrative I will discuss, the mouse is referred to using the name *Hɛl'aṁolaGa*. Boas renders this name as "Mouse-Woman" in his translation of the story of Qawadiliqala, and I follow him in using this designation. It should be noted, however, that *Hɛl'aṁolaGa* does not mean "Mouse-Woman." Its derivation is not clear to me, but Boas (1935b, 162) glosses it elsewhere as "Quick-Woman."
29. Although Boas renders *Hɛl'aṁolaGa*, in this instance, as "Mouse," I substitute "Mouse-Woman" in order to maintain consistency with the previous example.
30. The first time the mountain goats resume their dance, one of them says, "Let us try again on behalf of our friend here" (Boas and Hunt 1905, 12). The "friend" is not identified but may be someone whom the ritual is meant to initiate.
31. I do not know to whom this name refers or the significance of the mountain goats' song.
32. I have added "all" to Boas and Hunt's translation, corresponding to *ṅax^{w}a* in the Kwak'wala text. I have also changed "mountain-goats" to "mountain goats," in line with the spelling used elsewhere in the present chapter.
33. It is possible that the text alludes specifically to the stories of Qawadiliqala and Təwixil'ak^w, but it is more likely that the sequence of events I have identified in

these two stories existed in other narratives, and that "Qateṅac and Qatemo" alludes to this conventional sequence, rather than to any specific story in which it occurs.

34. It should be acknowledged that in another, similar episode, Mouse-Woman again helps a human protagonist intrude on the ritual activities of spirit-beings, but with a very different outcome than in the stories of Qawadiliqala and Təwixil'ak^w. In a narrative that is attested in both Da'naxda'x̱w (Dənaxda?χ^w) and A̱'wa̱'etła̱la (ʔəẃəʔiƛəla) multiforms, a bereaved father spies on ghosts performing a ritual in which they make music to which the man's son is supposed to dance. Mouse-Woman instructs the father that if he waits long enough before entering the proceedings, his son will be revived. However, when the man sees his son begin to dance, he cannot resist the urge to embrace him. The father's embrace causes his son to dissolve into foam (Boas and Hunt 1905, 106; Boas 1910, 447). In this narrative, instead of helping the protagonist acquire ceremonial privileges, Mouse-Woman tries (and fails) to assist the protagonist in bringing his son back from the dead.
35. In interpreting the stories of Qawadiliqala and Təwixil'ak^w in light of this practice, I follow Berman's analysis of a comparable episode from another narrative.
36. See Berman 1991 (265); 2000 (86); and possibly 1991 (692). Berman appears to take a different approach elsewhere (1991, 691).
37. On the "myth people" or "history people," see, for example, Berman 1991 (88–90).
38. The texts that Berman cites are Boas and Hunt 1905 (7–25), the story of Təwixil'ak^w; Boas 1935a (200–212); and Boas 1935a (140–43). In the last of these examples, I do not discern clear evidence that the animals are engaged in the Winter Ceremonial when the human protagonist views them with their furs removed. Furthermore, as I noted earlier, even when Təwixil'ak^w intrudes on the mountain goats performing a Winter Ceremonial dance with their masks off, it is unclear whether the mountain goats are in human form specifically as part of their ritual, or whether they always assume human form when they are in their house. In either case I follow Berman's (1991, 265) proposal that the illusions of the Winter Ceremonial are modeled on animals' practice of "masking themselves in flesh and fur."
39. Boas cites the undersea scene in "Qateṅac and Qatemo" as an example.
40. Boas renders the second word as nax·naualk!ŭs, which appears to be a typographic error for nax·naualaklŭs. My transcription into the orthography of the North American Phonetic Association follows the latter form.
41. In a Ḵwikwa̱sut'inux̱w (Q^{w}iq^{w}əsut'inuχ^w) version of the "Invisible Arrow" plot, the possibility that the spirit-beings are aware of the protagonist's manipulation of appearances is made almost explicit. After the protagonist, ʔɛxsuk^{w}il'ak^w, arrives in the house of a spirit chief, he is asked whether he is a shaman capable of healing the chief's "head slave." ʔɛxsuk^{w}il'ak^w thinks to himself, "I will say that I am a shaman." As often occurs in Kwak'wala narratives, one of the spirits

overhears the protagonist's thoughts and announces them, saying, "He thinks he will say that he is a shaman." After the spirit chief promises to give his canoe and spear in exchange for healing his slave, "ʔεxsukʷiḷ'akʷ" sat down by the side of the Sea-Lion [i.e., the injured spirit-being], and pretended to feel for the sickness. Now and then he would push in the spear-point [i.e., the projectile with which he had injured the sea-lion during an earlier encounter], and the sea-lion would groan from pain, and then he would pretend to suck the side in which the spear stuck. The fourth time he bit the spear-point, pushed it in, and then pulled it out. Then the Sea-Lion said, 'This is a true shaman, for I felt the sickness leave my body. Now my chief will give him the canoe'" (Boas 1921, 1254). Here, the protagonist's intentions of "say[ing] that he is a shaman" are exposed, yet the spirit-beings still believe in and reward his ministrations as a healer. I have not included this story in the core of my analysis, because it is published in English without an accompanying Kwak'wala text, and because, unlike the corresponding scene in "Qateṅac and Qatemo," ʔεxsukʷiḷ'akʷ's healing of the sea-lion is embedded within a larger narrative that does not thematize shamanism or sleight of hand.

42. My comment here is influenced by Berman 1991 (703–14).

REFERENCES

Andersson, Theodore M. 1967. *The Icelandic Family Saga: An Analytic Reading*. Cambridge MA: Harvard University Press.

Berman, Judith. 1991. "The Seals' Sleeping Cave: The Interpretation of Boas' Kwak'wala Texts." PhD diss., University of Pennsylvania.

———. 1994. "George Hunt and the Kwak'wala Texts." *Anthropological Linguistics* 36, no. 4: 482–514.

———. 2000. "Red Salmon and Red Cedar Bark: Another Look at the Nineteenth-Century Kwakwa̲ka'wakw Winter Ceremonial." *B.C. Studies* 125-26: 53–98.

———. Forthcoming. *"To Put It Down Right": Essays on the Franz Boas–George Hunt Collaboration*. Vancouver: University of British Columbia Press.

Boas, Franz. n.d. "Kwakiutl Dictionary." Edited by by Helene Boas Yampolsky. Unpublished manuscript. American Philosophical Society, Philadelphia.

———. 1895. *Indianische Sagen von der nord-pacifischen Küste Amerikas*. Berlin: A. Asher.

———. 1916. *Tsimshian Mythology*. Washington DC: U.S. Bureau of American Ethnology.

———. 1921. *Ethnology of the Kwakiutl*. Washington: Government Printing Office.

———. 1930a. *Religion of the Kwakiutl Indians, Part 1, Texts*. New York: Columbia University Press.

———. 1930b. *Religion of the Kwakiutl Indians, Part 2, Translations*. New York: Columbia University Press.

———. 1935a. *Kwakiutl Tales, New Series, Part 1—Translations*. New York: Columbia University Press.

———. 1935b. *Kwakiutl Culture as Reflected in Mythology*. New York: G. E. Stechert.

———. 1947. "Kwakiutl Grammar with a Glossary of the Suffixes." *Transactions of the American Philosophical Society* 37, no. 3: 203–337.

———. 1966. *Kwakiutl Ethnography*. Edited by Helen Codere. Chicago: University of Chicago Press.

———. 2002. *Indian Myths and Legends from the North Pacific Coast of America: A Translation of Franz Boas' 1895 Edition of* Indianische Sagen von der nord-pacifischen Küste Amerikas. Edited by by Randy Bouchard and Dorothy Kennedy. Translated by Dietrich Bertz. Vancouver: Talonbooks.

Boas, Franz, and George Hunt. 1905. *Kwakiutl Texts*. New York: G. E. Stechert.

———. 1906. *Kwakiutl Texts, Second Series*. New York: G. E. Stechert.

Cole, Douglas. 1999. *Franz Boas: The Early Years, 1858–1906*. Seattle: University of Washington Press.

Goldman, Irving. 1975. *The Mouth of Heaven: An Introduction to Kwakiutl Religious Thought*. New York: John Wiley.

Lévi-Strauss, Claude. 1963. "The Sorcerer and His Magic." In *Structural Anthropology*, 161–80. Garden City NY: Doubleday.

Littell, Patrick. 2016. *Focus, Predication, and Polarity in Kwak'wala*. PhD diss., University of British Columbia.

Taussig, Michael. 1998. "Viscerality, Faith, and Skepticism: Another Theory of Magic." In *In Near Ruins: Cultural Theory at the End of the Century*, edited by Nicholas B. Dirks, 221–56. Minneapolis: University of Minnesota Press.

Viveiros de Castro, Eduardo. 2004. "Perspectival Anthropology and the Method of Controlled Equivocation." *Tipití* 2, no. 1: 3–22.

———. 2012. *Cosmological Perspectivism in Amazonia and Elsewhere*. Manchester: HAU Network of Ethnographic Theory.

Walens, Stanley. 1981. *Feasting with Cannibals: An Essay on Kwakiutl Cosmology*. Princeton NJ: Princeton University Press.

4 Language and Rituals of the Brotherhood of the Holy Spirit of the Kongos of Villa Mella

José María Santos Rovira

The Brotherhood of the Holy Spirit of the Kongos of Villa Mella is one of the few surviving Black brotherhoods in the Dominican Republic. With their eclectic festivals and rituals, they represent the last remnant of the linguistic and religious African past. This cultural legacy was formerly widespread within the country, but nowadays is mostly lost, mainly because their specific history and society forced them to integrate into the broader Dominican society.

The aim of this chapter is to give a picture of the state of this brotherhood, its sociocultural development throughout the last centuries, and the challenges the members face in keeping their African linguistic and religious heritage. Religion is quintessential for this community, and it is in religious environments where they feel proud of their ethnic origins and distinct from the surrounding society. It is also in religious environments where they are more willing to preserve their non-Spanish linguistic heritage.

Much of the research for this chapter was conducted using a participant-observer methodology. Between 2013 and 2016, the author spent a significant amount of time over several trips to this villa, engaging with the community members in various domains. Informal interviews and conversations with open-ended questions were conducted with nearly twenty people. These interactions were documented via written notes and some audio recordings. A specifically designed questionnaire was also delivered via interview with a limited number of consultants. Also, the author analyzed the collected lyrics of some songs and prayers of this community.

Language and religion are the main vehicles of the culture, and, without them, a community cannot preserve an important part of its cultural heritages. The Brotherhood of the Holy Spirit of the Kongos of Villa Mella is a by-product of the hybridism that distinguished Caribbean societies since the early periods of their formation. It is a community that assimilated the different surrounding traditions, mostly from Africa, and that has kept them alive until the present. This is a distinctive feature in the Dominican Republic, where the African legacy has been denied because of the country's specific history. Accordingly I propose that it is in those lyrics where it is possible to find the key elements of the three main linguistic and religious traditions that contributed to form the brotherhood: Spanish and Catholicism, African languages and Vodun, and Haitian Creole and Vodou.

SYNCRETIC BELIEFS IN AFRICA AND AMERICA

It is impossible to reconstruct the formation and the development of a given community or society without addressing some fundamental geographical, historical, and theological facts.[1] In the particular case of the Brotherhood of the Holy Spirit of the Kongos of Villa Mella, an overview of the evolution of the African American syncretic beliefs, as well as the origins and expansion of brotherhoods in America, provides a framework.

Enslaved people arrived in the New World from the first years, brought by their masters to work on their homes. Nevertheless the slave trade in America was launched in 1510 under the guise of legality, when the Spanish Crown ordered that Black enslaved people be brought to work in the mines, because of the refusal and the decimation of the Indigenous peoples of the Americas. Afterward Seville and Lisbon became the most important slave markets on the Iberian Peninsula (García Fuentes 1982, 3; 2005, 18). Between 1510 and 1890, 12 million Black enslaved people crossed the Atlantic. Among them 2,419,000 enslaved people arrived in the British Caribbean; 1,110,000 in the French Caribbean; and 844,000 in the Spanish Caribbean—801,000 in Cuba; 20,000 in Puerto Rico; and 16,000 in Santo Domingo (Maríñez 1997, 88; Moya 2012, 324).

Most of the enslaved people arrived in the former Spanish colony of Santo Domingo in the seventeenth century. In a 1606 census, 10,817 people, of whom 1,169 were free citizens and 9,648 were enslaved people, inhabited the island. In 1681, after a smallpox epidemic that decimated the Africans, the population decreased to 6,312 people; noticeably, among the 3,835 Black and mixed race people, just 1,106 remained as enslaved people, while 2,729 were already free citizens. In 1739 Santo Domingo had 12,259 inhabitants: a dozen were white families, but the rest were free Black and mixed-race families, as there were only a few scattered enslaved people (Larrazábal Blanco 1967, 183).

Although African enslaved people were forced to convert to Catholicism, some of them had already acquired European cultural and religious patterns in Africa (Dewulf 2015, 19; Souza 2005, 83). Some Black enslaved people shipped to the New World had Portuguese or Spanish names, and they were familiar with Iberian foodways, clothing, religion, and even languages before leaving Africa (Heywood and Thornton 2009, 194). This fact was crucial in Santo Domingo, as, during the rule of Diego de Colón (1509–24), only enslaved people who were baptized could be sold on the island (Larrazábal Blanco 1967, 14).

The Portuguese were the first to bring Catholicism to Africa. In 1480 a Portuguese explorer named Diogo Cão returned to Lisbon, bringing a number of Kongolese people with him. In Portugal they were taught the Portuguese language, as well as the Catholic faith. Thus, when they returned to the Kingdom of Kongo, in 1484, they were already accustomed to the Portuguese way of life, in which Catholicism played a central role. As a result many curious Kongolese wanted to know more about the new religion. Portugal immediately sent a priest to teach them, with extraordinary results. In 1491 the Manikongo Nzinga a Nkuwu was baptized as King João I of Kongo; his wife, Ne Mbanda, as Queen Leonor; and his son, Nzinga Mvemba, as Prince Afonso, which led to the opening of the Kongolese society to a variety of mass conversion. Even the capital of the kingdom, Mbanza Kongo, was renamed as São Salvador (Levi 2009, 369). These new practices also expanded thanks to Kongolese rulers and noblemen, as they sent their children to Portugal to learn to read and write, and their children, upon their return to Kongo as bilingual and bicultural people, became the founders of a new culture. Such conversion was considered astonishing at its time, and during the next two centuries it was regarded as an example in all of Europe (Thornton 2013, 53).

Nevertheless, Kongolese Catholicism did not follow the traditional Church of Rome's practices. Instead it was a syncretic variant that blended both religious traditions: European Catholicism and spirit-based African traditional religions (Dewulf 2015, 23). In fact "the new faith was just the recipient of the old faith systems, now interwoven with Catholicism. In other words, Christianity provided the setting for the ancient African religions to live and continue, now inseparable from the host religion" (Levi 2009, 372). In essence this situation indicates "the emergence of a new culture which cannot be understood as a simple combination of European and African elements. It is, rather, a culture that started afresh, from the interpretations by Central Africans of European ethical and religious concepts, music, food, agricultural techniques, legal systems, and building styles, adapted then to their own interests and necessities" (Negrão and Viotti 2014, 142).

In this way the syncretic beliefs that became typical of the Caribbean (a combination of European and African elements), which reflect the "xenophile (inclusive) nature that seems natural to many Vodouists and Catholics" (Hebblethwaite 2015, 84), were not developed in the New World, but in the heart of central Africa. Significant groups of enslaved people, who had previously lived in the Iberian Peninsula or the Portuguese African enclaves of Cape Verde or São Tomé, brought to the Americas not only their syncretic beliefs but also their "syncretic traditions such as Afro-Iberian brotherhoods" (Dewulf 2015, 30).

BLACK BROTHERHOODS IN AFRICA AND AMERICA

The tradition of the Catholic Brotherhoods goes back to the Early Middle Ages, although it was in the thirteenth century, specifically at the Fourth Council of the Lateran, in 1215, when Pope Innocent III encouraged their creation in such a manner that at the end of the fifteenth century, dozens of them had been established in the Iberian Peninsula (Santos Rovira 2017, 165). In those associations members found not only religious guidance and support but also aid and assistance, if in need.

In Portugal the devotion to Our Lady of the Rosary (a cult founded in Cologne in the fifteenth century by Jakob Sprenger) contributed to the formation of several Black brotherhoods. The most important was the Brotherhood of Our Lady of the Rosary of the Black Men (Irmandade da Nossa Senhora do Rosario dos Homens Pretos), which was established in Lisbon in 1565 (Dewulf 2015, 21). One of the goals of those fraternities was to collect money to liberate their brothers, a fact which influenced their growth. In the Portuguese African enclaves, Black brotherhoods also flourished, again with devotion to Our Lady of the Rosary. The first was established on the Cape Verdean island of Santiago, in 1495, and the second on the island of São Tomé, in 1526. From there they disseminated their special vision of the African Iberian syncretic religion (22). This view reached not only Iberian America, but one traveler even founded a Black community in New Amsterdam in North America in the seventeenth century that "best resembled the confraternities or brotherhoods found among Kongolese and Angolan Blacks living in Brazil" (Hodges 1999, 28).

In the Caribbean Spanish colonies, brotherhoods appeared as early as 1503, with the establishment of the Fraternity of Our Lady of the Immaculate Conception (Cofradía de la Pura y Limpia Concepción de Nuestra Señora; Meier 2001, 32). The first Black brotherhood was founded in 1592 and named the Fraternity of the Miracles of Our Lady of Carmen and Jesus of Nazareth (Cofradía de Nuestra Señora de los Remedios del Carmen y Jesús Nazareno; Laviña Gómez 2000, 157). They grew to the extent that by 1612 five Black brotherhoods had been set up in the city of Santo Domingo. One of the particularities of those Black fraternities was that their members frequently shared the same ethnic origin. Hence, the Fraternity of Our Lady of Candelaria (Cofradía de Nuestra Señora de la Candelaria) was formed by Igbos and Mandinkas; the Fraternity of the Saints Cosme and Damian (Cofradía de los Santos Cosme y Damián), by the so-called Ararás, originally from the Bight of Benin; and the Fraternity of Saint Mary Magdalene (Cofradía de Santa María Magdalena), by Zapes, from Sierra Leone (Rodríguez Demorizi 1975, 155).[2]

But the central question, in this case, is: Did those Black brotherhoods perform Catholic prayers and rituals, like the "white" ones? The answer is not easy, as it involves several factors. As previously noted the syncretism

F6. A church in Villa Mella. Photo by author.

of the Caribbean religions was not fully created in the New World, but brought by the enslaved Africans of Congolese heritage, who were already familiar with it from their homelands (Dewulf 2015, 19; Souza 2005, 83). Nevertheless, the new environment, unknown to them, provoked a different variety of that syncretic Catholicism. As they felt the need for a link to their past and their ancestors, the aesthetics of African elements became quintessential for maintaining that link.

Enslaved Africans lacked proper places of worship. There were Catholic churches, but they were unavailable for them to perform their rituals. So they had to create different ones, adapted to their new living environment. They had to resemble Catholic churches, although they could include some "external" elements. As in their African homelands, the boundaries between sacred and profane places were vague. The central issue was not the appearance of the place, but the meaning the believers gave it.

Subsequently, enslaved people began to perform Catholic rituals and to pray to saints, but differently. They introduced Vodunist spirits and

F7. A house in Villa Mella. Photo by author.

rituals and built new forms of expression, in which Africa became a mark of identity—their new identity. From the fifteenth century onward, the Caribbean became a melting pot where influences from different origins mixed and were reinterpreted, and Black brotherhoods symbolized the new syncretic religion.

In their brotherhoods the members reinterpreted not only some elements of the traditional African religions but also African political systems and cultures. Their fraternities had a king and a captain, and queens were also nominated during festivals, recreating their homeland's hierarchies. Thanks to these structures, some enslaved or free Black citizens could gain prestige and authority in the eyes of their peers. Nowadays there are still some Black brotherhoods scattered throughout the Americas, in countries such as Argentina (Zubrzycki et al. 2008), Brazil (Figueiredo 1995; Kiddy 2001; Petter 2005; Rodrigues 2010); Colombia (Losonczy 2006; Triana 2011); Cuba (Fuentes Guerra and Schwegler 2005; Rivero Muñiz 2014; Schwegler and Rojas-Primus 2010; Thornton 2016); Jamaica (Bilby and

Bunseki 1983); Panama (Joly 1981; Lipski 2009); Peru (Sessarego 2015); and, of course, the Dominican Republic (Andrade 2009; Apodaca-Valdez 2012; Hernández Soto 2004; Hernández Soto and Sánchez 1997; Landies 2009; Santos Rovira 2017).

THE BROTHERHOOD OF THE HOLY SPIRIT

North of Santo Domingo, capital of the Dominican Republic, lies a village named Villa Mella, between the Isabela and the Ozama rivers, a place where the main sugarcane mills were located centuries ago. The villa was inhabited since the beginning of the sixteenth century, when some maroons ("escapees of enslavement") settled there, after the rebellion against Diego Colón in 1522. The villa increased its population in 1678, when a substantial number of Black maroons arrived, escaping from the French side of the island. Some of them settled in Villa Mella, while others founded a closer villa, San Lorenzo de los Mina, at the bank of the Ozama river (Deive 1989, 96; Larrazábal Blanco 1975, 166). Most of them had been shipped from the old Kingdom of Kongo, as well as from Dahomey and Angola, which is why they were collectively named "Kongos." In fact, between the sixteenth and nineteenth centuries, all the enslaved people embarked on ships in that region were referred to as "Kongos" (Santos Rovira 2017, 163).

Villa Mella got a second important increase in its population during the period of Haitian rule (1822–44), when a significant number of Haitians settled there.[3] From 1875 onward the villa has increased its population continuously, thanks to the regular arrival of Haitian workers to labor in the canebrakes (Hernández Soto 1996, 20). When the first national census was carried out between January 19 and December 24, 1920, as required by General Thomas Snowden, the governor of the Dominican Republic under the American occupation, Villa Mella was noted to be one of the municipalities with the highest percentage of Black citizens.

When I arrived there for the first time, it seemed to me as a place full of life. Despite their difficult living conditions, all the inhabitants performed their daily activities with smiles on the their faces and were very approachable and responsive, with dozens of children and youngsters playing freely in the surroundings.

F8. Arriving at Villa Mella. Photo by author.

The Villa Mella community is tight knit, and most socialization happens within the community, and even the young people usually marry within it. That is one of the main explanations for why they have been able to preserve their African and Haitian ethnic and cultural identity, instead of blending it, as commonly happened to most of the Dominican population. Most of them lack any kind of full-time job, barely surviving while working in the primary sector seasonally, while others are self-employed, selling low-cost products. Despite their poverty the people in the community are kind, friendly, and welcoming. The author of this paper appreciated this characteristic and had the opportunity to share with them different activities and social events.

The religious and social center of the community is the meeting place of the Brotherhood of the Holy Spirit of the Kongos of Villa Mella. This is the most famous fraternity in the country and well known internationally, as it was proclaimed a UNESCO Masterpiece of the Oral and Intangible Heritage of Humanity on May 18, 2001. This is the community's most distinguishing characteristic, and they are extremely proud of it.

The history of the brotherhood is obscure, as myths frequently adulterate history. In fieldwork carried out in October-November 2016, the author of

F9. The author talking with some *villamelleros*. Photo by author.

this paper witnessed the mythological starting point of the brotherhood, in the words of Casimiro Minier, its king at the time. He explained that the Holy Spirit appeared to his great-grandmother, Feliciana Brazobán, and gave her the musical instruments that they still play, as well as the command to build a church and to pray and to sing to Him every year on His day. Correspondingly the role of the brotherhood is to celebrate the day of the Holy Spirit (Pentecost), and the day of Our Lady of the Rosary, as well as the funerals for all the members of the brotherhood and their relatives.[4] They can also celebrate funerals for other people, even if they were not members of the brotherhood, "if the deceased had expressed this will before death or *mounted* on any relative" (Hernández Soto 1996, 29).

Funerals are becoming the only activities this brotherhood performs regularly (the celebrations of the Holy Spirit and Our Lady of the Rosary take place just once a year), providing an idea of how important those rituals are for the members of this community. Indeed the afterlife is remarkably important in the traditional Dominican culture, as it is claimed that there is no gap between life and death, between the living and the deceased (Davis 1987, 118). Moreover, there is a connection between both, and, as also happens in the African traditional religions and Vodou, the soul of the dead relative will become an ancestor and, after an unknown time, could become a recognized spirit. If someone can communicate with those

F10. The meeting place of the Brotherhood of the Holy Spirit of the Kongos of Villa Mella. Photo by author.

souls, ancestors, or spirits, he or she will benefit from their wisdom (Ossa Martínez 2011, 48).

In the same manner with African traditional religions and Vodou, the ceremonies for the dead include three different moments:

> Rites of separation: from the moment the person is declared dead to the closure of the tomb.
> Rites of margin: from the closure of the tomb to the celebration of the *banko*.[5] This is the time when the deceased remains away from both life and the afterlife.
> Rites of integration: the celebration of the *banko*.

It is clear that the funerals celebrated by the Brotherhood of the Holy Spirit of the Kongos of Villa Mella do not follow traditional European Catholic practices, but the African Vodunist ones. We can easily figure out why Black brotherhoods were not fully accepted by the clergy in the past, and why they were always suspected of carrying out heterodox practices, along with spiritism (Laviña Gómez 2000, 159). The rituals practiced by Black enslaved people mentioned in the Caroline Code of 1789 are the same ones displayed these days by this brotherhood (Hernández Soto 1996, 19). On the contrary, as a by-product of a diaspora community, this fraternity integrates the three key elements of their beliefs: Spanish and Catholicism, Fon and Vodun, and Haitian Creole and Vodou.

PRAYERS AND RITUALS OF THE BROTHERHOOD

Language and religion are the essential matrices of a nation and the basis of its conception of the world (Latino de Genoud 2002, 97). Villa Mella roots are firmly tied to their African and Haitian linguistic and religious heritage. Besides, they are one of the few Dominican communities that has been able to preserve both legacies, in a sometimes anti-African and anti-Haitian environment, as they represent the essence of their beliefs. The Brotherhood of the Holy Spirit of the Kongos of Villa Mella employs three languages in its prayers and rituals: Spanish (the official and main language), African languages (mainly Fon and Kikongo), and Haitian Creole. Three are also rooted in the religions the brotherhood integrates: Catholicism (the official and main religion), African Vodun, and Haitian Vodou.

Spanish is the main language of the community of Villa Mella, and all the members of the Brotherhood of the Holy Spirit of the Kongos of Villa Mella speak it natively. Therefore, Spanish becomes the main language of the prayers and rituals of this fraternity, although frequently mixed with terms from other languages. So the form of the language produced is a variety of code-switching between those elements, producing what one may call a liturgical language. Officially all of them are Catholics, which is the way they define themselves and their religious beliefs. However, it must be noted that, even though most of their prayers and songs are properly Catholic, there are also an important number of heterogeneous practices.

African languages were present in the community since its foundation. Nowadays, although they are not natively spoken by anyone, they persist in the religious level because of the strong belief that they are part of a former holy language. Nevertheless, while all the senior members of the brotherhood can follow the general semantics of these prayers and lyrics, it is doubtful they can follow the complex theological nuances. Prayers

F11. A ceremonial dance the author attended in Villa Mella. Photo by author.

and songs have never been written down, and they were transmitted orally from generation to generation, which caused them to be extremely flexible by nature; accordingly, the singers are free to change words or sentences and to add new terms. Unfortunately, although the older members of the Brotherhood of the Holy Spirit of the Kongos of Villa Mella themselves do foster the preservation of African languages in prayers and songs, the broader Dominican society does not. Thus, the younger generations are generally forsaking the language they are unfamiliar with and replacing its words and strophes with Spanish, the language of which they are native speakers. One may think, then, that the last remains of the African languages are severely endangered, as the young members are less likely to learn them. But my perception is that, since religion is so central to this community, it is likely that African words and phrases will persist in the domain of religious practices. Also they constitute the most suitable speech for the African music sung in their rituals and they are repeated due to the "cyclical and repetitive nature, with very short musical sentences" of songs (Hernández Soto 1996, 136).

The main African languages still present in the prayers and songs of the Brotherhood of the Holy Spirit of the Kongos of Villa Mella are Fon, the language of the old Kingdom of Dahomey, alongside Kikongo, the language of the old Kingdom of Kongo. It must be noted that both were also the main languages used in eighteenth-century Haitian Vodou (Geggus 1991). I have found several possible terms from Fon: *banko* (going to afterlife to become a spirit), *khokho* (ancestor), *kumandé* (there is no death, or command), as well as possible terms from Kikongo, such as *Kalunga* (name of spirit), *bembe* (funeral song; drum dance), *kumbá* (make noise; party) in various songs of the brotherhood, as follows:[6]

> Ya cantan los gallos,
> *kumandé*,
> al amanecer,
> *kumandé*.

> *Bembe khokho,*
> *Bembe khokho,*
> *Bembe khokho.*

> ¡*Kalunga* eh!
> ¡Eh *Kalunga*!
> Adiós que me voy.
> ¡*Kalunga* eh!
> ¡Ay!, para nunca más.
> ¡Ay!, que no vuelvo yo.
> ¡*Kalunga* eh!
> Voy a desandar.
> ¡*Kalunga* eh!

English translation:

> Roosters are singing
> There is no death / Command

at dawn
There is no death / Command

funeral dance for ancestors
funeral dance for ancestors
funeral dance for ancestors

Kalunga hey!
Hey *Kalunga*!
Goodbye I am leaving.
Kalunga hey!
Oh! for ever again.
Oh! I am not coming back.
Kalunga hey!
I am going to retrace
Kalunga hey!

The prayer to Kalunga is the most important at any ritual, and the most representative of the connection with the African past. In the Kongo region, Kalunga is worshipped as the goddess of the sea, as well as the goddess of death (Díaz Fabelo 2000, 71; Escalante 1989, 17; Hernández Soto 2009, 145; Landies 2009, 112; Ochoa 2007, 473; Usanna 2010, 109). In this community Kalunga is easily assimilated in the Holy Spirit and prayed to accordingly. The prayer to Kalunga is always the first and the last to be sung at the beginning and the end—a reflection of life and death. At funerals a doll with eyes, nose, and mouth, made of a bottle filled with sand and covered with colored paper, holds a double meaning: the deceased and Kalunga (Hernández Soto 1996, 115). Next to this bottle, relatives place different images of the venerated saints of the dead in addition to images of his or her favored Dominican Vodou spirits.

While all the members of the community share the same basic religion—Catholicism—they vary in the degree of importance that Dominican Vodou holds in their lives. For most of them, there is no border between both beliefs, as they assume religion as inclusive, instead of exclusive. Here is where the strongest connection with African traditional religions lies. African Vodun and Caribbean Vodou are expansive religions, without written canonical or sacred texts until recently, transforming and adapting themselves to the environment, with the music, the songs, the prayers, and the dances gradually evolving (Hebblethwaite 2012, 5). In the same way, the ritual practices of the Brotherhood of the Holy Spirit of the Kongos of Villa Mella blend European Catholic, African Vodunist, and Haitian Vodouist elements (Apodaca-Valdez 2012; Davis 1987, 67). Of course the African practices are not identically reproduced "but rather reconstructed, and in some cases invented" (McGee 2008, 31). Nevertheless, there is no agreement among Dominicans on how to name these non-Catholic religious practices, so it might be described in different ways: "popular religion"; "to believe in the saints"; "to believe in the 21 Divisions"; and also "Dominican Vodou," although the word *Vodou* is usually avoided because it is reminiscent of a putative "black magic and the religion which come from Haiti" (Apodaca-Valdez 2012; Hernández Soto 1996).

The third language used in the lyrics of this fraternity is Haitian Creole, a language still spoken in the sugarcane *bateyes* (Jansen 2013, 77), as well as in some communities with Haitian immigrants. Specifically, "in Villa Mella, considered one of the most African villages in the Dominican Republic, Haitian words have been recorded as part of the core vocabulary" (Lipski 1994). Words like *malé* ("I am going"); *pambué*, from Haitian Creole *pa mwen* ("mine"); or *ki mandé* ("who asks") occur in the main songs:

Oy bembe yagua,
malé,
bembe yagua,
malé.

En el nombre de Juana,
pambué,
en el nombre de Juana,
pambué.

Traigan la botella,
ki mandé,

traigan la botella,
ki mandé,
para beber.

English translation:

Oy bembe yagua,
I'm leaving,
bembe yagua,
I'm leaving.

In the name of Juana who's mine
pambué,
in the name of Juana who's mine
Pambué.

Bring the bottle
ki mandé,

bring the bottle
ki mandé,
to drink.

Because of the traditional association of Haitian Creole with negative magic, there is a strong opposition to using it openly, but at the same time it is considered a kind of holy language in the eyes of firm Vodou believers. There is a double consciousness in which the members of this brotherhood construct their identity as dependent on, yet simultaneously distinct from, Haitian Vodou, which is considered the closest religion in the Caribbean to the African source traditions (Moya 2012, 334). Accordingly I found a significant number of elements that refer to it. Frequently at funerals some relatives of the deceased fall into a trance (Hernández Soto 1996, 139). Indeed African Caribbean religious systems have in common the trance of possession, along with the hope that the ancestors and spirits have the power to heal and to change the daily life of the ones who pray to them (Sánchez-Carretero 2009, 393). To celebrate the rite called Cabo de Año, one year after the funeral, the relatives of the deceased build, adjacent to their home, a type of shelter, covered with palm leaves and with a supporting central pylon, which is reminiscent of the Haitian *poto mitan* ("centerpost").

On the other hand, there are some elements that make a difference between the Dominican and the Haitian Vodouist practices: more flexibility in the liturgy; no regulations for priests, ritual, and ceremonial spontaneity; and the lack of places for the practices that used to be held inside homes (Andújar Persinal 1999, 191). Although there are 21 Divisions, like in Haitian Vodou, in Dominican Vodou they are also organized into three ethnic groups, which make up the putative foundation of the human race: "Caucasoids, Negroids, and Mongoloids" (Nei and Roychoudhury 1974, 421).[7] They form the three main groups: División Blanca, División Negra, and División India, the last also named the "Water Division," which encompasses all Amerindian mysteries (Apodaca-Valdez 2012). It is named the Water Division because all its *lua* (spirits) ask for water when they mount their "horse." In this division all the mysteries come from Amerindian heroes and *caciques*. They are the Taino lua, which include the five caciques who ruled the island at the time of the arrival of the Spanish: Bohechío, Caonabo, Guacanagarix, Guarionex, and Higuanamá (Cassá 1995, 124), and the princess Anacaona, sister of Bohechío. Another spirit also found in this division is Enriquillo (a historical Taino warrior).

The recorded lyrics in this chapter are a hybrid linguistic construction in which several languages mix. In addition to sentences and strophes where Spanish sentences include Fon (Ya cantan los gallos / *kumandé* / al amanecer / *kumandé*), Kikongo (¡*Kalunga* eh! / ¡eh *Kalunga*! / Adiós que me voy / ¡*Kalunga* eh!) and Haitian Creole (En el nombre de Juana / *pambué* / en el nombre de Juana / *pambué*) words, those "foreign" languages can be mixed, too. I found sentences where Fon and Kikongo words are adjacent (*Bembe khokho*), as well as strophes where Kikongo and Haitian Creole meld (Oy *bembe* yagua / *malé* / *bembe* yagua / *malé*).

This mélange is not restricted to language, but is reflected in religion. The hybridization of the rituals of the Brotherhood of the Holy Spirit of the Kongos of Villa Mella is shown in the following song, in which the Catholic Virgen de la Altagracia is prayed to alongside with the Vodou lua Ogun Balenyó:

Pero bueno mami *ombe*
Ogun Balenyó
Pero bueno mami eeeeee
Ogun Balenyó

> Virgencita de Altagracia
> *Ogun Balenyó*
> Yo te lo dije morena
> *Ogun Balenyó*

English translation:

> But hey sweetie *ombe*
> *Ogun Balenyó*
> But hey sweetie eeeeee
> *Ogun Balenyó*

> Virgin of Altagracia
> *Ogun Balenyó*
> I told you, honey
> *Ogun Balenyó*

The same religious syncretism appears at the beginning of the ritual named *banko*, the most important for this brotherhood. In this case, traditional Catholic prayer is used to introduce a traditional African ceremony:

> [Nombre de pila],
> ven a recibir tu banko.
> En el nombre del Padre, del Hijo y del Espíritu Santo.
> Amén.

English translation:

> [Given name],
> come to get your banko.
> In the name of the Father, and of the Son, and of the Holy Spirit.
> Amen.

CONCLUSION: HYBRID BUT DISTINCT

The Brotherhood of the Holy Spirit of the Kongos of Villa Mella is unique among African American communities. Although there are some Black fraternities and brotherhoods in countries such as Argentina, Brazil, Colombia, Cuba, Dominican Republic, Jamaica, Panama, or Peru that perform syncretic festivals and rituals and utilize some kind of hybrid languages with clear traces of African origins, the Brotherhood of the Holy Spirit of the Kongos of Villa Mella is distinct.

Historically there has been a long-standing social conflict between Dominicans and Haitians. As a result African-related matters were systematically denied. Accordingly any trace of the remaining African linguistic heritage in Dominican Spanish was rejected. One of the best examples was written by the Dominican linguist Pedro Henríquez Ureña, in a letter sent to his friend, Alfonso Reyes, in 1919, and reproduced in Lebrón Saviñón (1992, 133): "Cuba is the only place where African linguistic elements remain, in some low-class groups, studied by Fernando Ortiz; the Blacks of Santo Domingo and Puerto Rico may have come too long ago, and in Santo Domingo, nothing remains of their languages." I agree that the African cultural presence is more significant in countries such as Brazil and Cuba, due to the fact that they received most of their enslaved people during the five decades before abolition in 1886, a reality that helped maintain linguistic, musical and religious practices (Moya 2012, 334). But Black communities in the Dominican Republic also preserved some key African elements in different domains. Consequently the African linguistic heritage in the country has been researched throughout the last decades (Granda Gutiérrez and Pérez Guerra 1989; Gutiérrez Maté 2010; Lipski 1994, 2005; Megenney 1982, 1990; Núñez Cedeño 1982; Pérez Guerra 1989, 1999; Santos Rovira 2015a, 2015b, 2017).

However, religion did not receive the same attention as other sociolinguistic variables, since there is no agreement about whether religion qualifies as one. For us it is clear that religion does affect language, since "it is through the various forms of language that the living vitality of a community's religious beliefs is passed down from generation to generation" (Mukherjee 2013, 1). Therefore, a deep analysis of a given community of speakers must take their religious affiliations and preferences into account. There is evidence that the degree of self-identification with a certain religion (or its multiple subcommunities), will impact the speaker's linguistic choices, as has been demonstrated in previous studies.[8] So, for an accurate appraisal of a given linguistic community, the study of the religious affiliations of its members becomes a necessity. The fact that the most distinguishing characteristic of the community of Villa Mella is the Brotherhood of the Holy Spirit of the Kongos provides solid evidence that this given community is characterized in terms of religion. In this way religion has become a major component in defining their ethnicity.

Religion is, for this community, quintessential. Through religion the members of the Brotherhood of the Holy Spirit of the Kongos of Villa Mella feel proud of their ethnic origins and different from the surrounding society, at least partially. Other African American communities like the Colombian Palenqueros also share this feeling (Schwegler 1996, 70). Thanks to religion this community metaphorically breaks the static conceptions of nation, culture, society, and identity, as they do not consider identity to be passive, but rather a dynamic and cognitive construct (Gruson 2006, 22).

In conclusion, religion is key in preserving the last remnant of their African linguistic heritage, which must resist tremendous outside pressures. An especially strong countenance is needed to succeed in this task. As "positive prestige is associated with Spanish, which is at the same time an essential prerequisite for social and economic advancement" (Jansen 2013, 95), it is hard to keep African language fragments or Haitian Creole alive in the Dominican society. Nevertheless, since religion is so central to this community, I think this domain will continue playing its role as the pillar of their African legacy and so preserve, at least in part, language fragments inherited from their ancestors. In the same way, religion becomes essential for preserving their Haitian linguistic heritage, as religious contexts are the only ones in which Haitian Creole keeps its prestige in the Dominican Republic.

NOTES

1. The term "syncretism" comes from Greek, where *syn* means "with," and *krasis* means "mixture." In the last decades, some anthropologists came to replace it with the term "creolization." However, I rather prefer to use the traditional term, as I consider it to reflect much better the idea of mixture.
2. The term *Arará* is also spelled as *Arida*, *Arda*, *Ardra*, *Arada*, and *Allada*, and it refers to enslaved people taken from the Bight of Benin (Pinto and Law 2019, 38). Although it is frequent to refer to them as originally from Dahomey, this term is not accurate, as it does not refer to the historical Kingdom of Dahomey at the time, but to the broader geographical area of the Bight of Benin.

3. Some of the most influential families in Villa Mella have surnames such as Ferrand or Minier—clearly Haitians. In fact the last two kings of the Brotherhood of the Holy Spirit of the Kongos of Villa Mella hold that surname: Sixto Minier and Casimiro Minier.
4. Note that the first Black brotherhoods were dedicated also to Our Lady of the Rosary, as explained earlier.
5. *Banko* is the name of the most important ritual of this Brotherhood, the moment when the deceased goes to the afterlife and becomes an ancestor.
6. Several sources identified *kumandé* as originally coming from the Fon language (Hernández Soto and Sánchez 1997; Hernández Soto 2009). In Fon, the word *ku* (also spelled as *kou*) means "to die" or "death," *ma* is a negative particle, and *de* an adverb meaning "here" or "close" (Höftmann and Ahohounkpanzon 2003). In addition Fon native speakers consulted by the author of this chapter recognized the full expression *kumandé* as a Fon sentence meaning "There is no death." Nevertheless, the author of this chapter acknowledge that it is extremely difficult to assure the exact etymology of this word, and that it could also be related to the Haitian Creole verb *koumande* ("to command").
7. "Caucasoids, Negroids, and Mongoloids" were the terms used to refer to the three foundational human races in the scientific literature for decades, and it is possible to find academic articles using these terms until the 1980s. Even so, with the rise of modern genetics, the concept of distinct human races in a biological sense has become obsolete.
8. Gumperz and Wilson (1971) have observed that, in the small Indian village of Kupwar, some groups preserved their heritage language in private domains, while using the state language in public ones, but others preferred a wider use of the state language, according to their religious choices. Spolsky and Walters (1980) note that Jews varied the phonemes of Hebrew according to their religious affiliation. Samant (2010) shows that Muslims in the United States with a deeper religious faith are less likely to adopt local phonetic features. For the Caribbean context, Pollard (1994) discusses how the Rastafarian movement defied the society by changes in language ("dread talk").

REFERENCES

Andrade, Manuel José. 2009. *Folklore de la República Dominicana*. Santo Domingo: Editora Búho.

Andújar Persinal, Carlos. 1999. *Identidad cultural y religiosidad popular*. Santo Domingo: Cole.

Apodaca-Valdez, Manuel. 2012. "El vudú dominicano: religiosidad, magia y cultura." *Delaware Review of Latin American Studies* 13, no. 2: 1–14.

Bilby, Kenneth M., and Fu-Kiau Kia Bunseki. 1983. "Kumina: A Kongo-Based Tradition in the New World." *Cahiers Du CEDAF* 8, no. 4: 1–114.

Cassá, Roberto. 1995. *Los indios de las Antillas*. Madrid: Mapfre.
Davis, Martha Ellen. 1987. *La otra ciencia: El vodú dominicano como religión y medicina popular*. Santo Domingo: Editora UASD.
Deive, Carlos Esteban. 1989. *Los guerrilleros negros*. Santo Domingo: Fundación Cultural Dominicana.
Dewulf, Jeroen. 2015. "Black Brotherhoods in North America: Afro-Iberian and West-Central African Influences." *African Studies Quarterly* 15, no. 3: 19–38.
Díaz Fabelo, Teodoro. 2000. *Diccionario de la lengua conga residual en Cuba*. Santiago de Cuba: Casa del Caribe.
Escalante, Aquiles. 1989. "Siginificado del Lumbalú, ritual funerario del Palenque de San Basilio." *Huellas* 26: 11–24.
Figueiredo, Aldrin Moura de. 1995. "Um Natal de negros: Esboço etnográfico sobre um ritual religioso num quilombo amazônico." *Revista de Antropologia* 38, no. 2: 207–38.
Fuentes Guerra, Jesús, and Armin Schwegler. 2005. *Lengua y ritos del Palo Monte Mayombe: dioses cubanos y sus fuentes africanas*. Madrid: Iberoamericana Vervuert.
García Fuentes, Lutgardo. 1982. "Licencias para la introduccion de esclavos en indias y envios desde Sevilla en el siglo XVI." *Jahrbuch Für Geschichte Lateinamerikas— Anuario de Historia de America Latina* 19: 1–46.
———. 2005. *El tráfico de negros hacia América*. Madrid: Tavera-Digibis.
Geggus, David. 1991. "Haitian Voodoo in the Eighteenth Century: Language, Culture, Resistance." *Jahrbuch für Geschichte Lateinamerikas* 28, no. 1: 21–51.
Granda Gutiérrez, Germán de, and Irene Pérez Guerra. 1989. "Sobre los componentes canario y africano del léxico del español dominicano. A propósito de *me(s)turado* y *toto*." *Anuario de Letras* 27: 281–94.
Gruson, Alberto. 2006. "Cultura e identidad." *Socioscopio: Revista Del Centro de Investigación Social CISOR* 4: 5–32.
Gumperz, John, and Robert Wilson. 1971. "Convergence and Creolization: A Case from the Indo-Aryan/Dravidian Border in India." In *Pidginization and Creolization of Languages*, edited by Dell Hymes, 153–69. Cambridge: Cambridge University Press.
Gutiérrez Maté, Miguel. 2010. "Génesis de los pronombres sujetos obligatorios del español del Caribe: la hipótesis del contacto afro-hispánico sometida a revisión." In *Ars longa: Diez años de AJIHLE*, edited by M. T. Encinas Manterola, M. González Manzano, M. Gutiérrez Maté, M. Á. López Vallejo, C. Martín Gallego, L. Romero Aguilera, and I. Vicente Miguel, 853–78. Buenos Aires: Voces del Sur.
Hebblethwaite, Benjamin. 2012. *Vodou songs in Haitian Creole and English*. Philadelphia: Temple University Press.
———. 2015. "Historical Linguistic Approaches to Haitian Creole: Vodou Rites, Spirit Names, and Songs: The Founders' Contributions to Asogwe Vodou." In *La Española-Isla de Encuentros*, edited by J. S. Barzen, S. Jansen, and H. L. Geiger, 65–86. Tübingen: Verlag.

Hernández Soto, Carlos. 1996. *Morir en Villa Mella: Ritos funerarios afrodominicanos.* Santo Domingo: CIASCA, 1996.

——. 2004. *¡Kalunga eh! Los Congos de Villa Mella.* Santo Domingo: Letra Gráfica.

——. 2009. "El banko, gran fiesta ritual de vivos y difuntos en la Sabana del Espíritu Santo, República Dominicana." In *Fiestas y rituales,* edited by J. Galán Casanova, 142–57. Lima: Corporación para la Promoción y Difusión de la Cultura.

Hernández Soto, Carlos, and Edis Sánchez. 1997. "Los Congos de Villa Mella, República Dominicana." *Latin American Music Review / Revista de Música Latinoamericana* 18, no. 2: 297–316.

Heywood, Linda, and John K. Thornton. 2009. "Intercultural Relations between Europeans and Blacks in New Netherland." In *Four Centuries of Dutch-American Relations, 1609–2009,* edited by H. Krabeendam, 192–203. Albany: State University of New York Press.

Hodges, Graham Russell. 1999. *Root and Branch: African Americans in New York and East Jersey, 1613–1863.* Chapel Hill: University of North Carolina Press, 1999.

Höftmann, Hildegard, and Michel Ahohounkpanzon. 2003. *Dictionnaire Fon-Français avec une esquisse grammaticale.* Köln: Rüdiger Köppe Verlag.

Jansen, Silke. 2013. "Language Maintenance and Language Loss in Marginalized Communities: The Case of the Bateyes in the Dominican Republic." *International Journal of the Sociology of Language* 221: 77–100.

Joly, Luz Graciela. 1981. "The Ritual Play of the Congos of North-Central Panama: Its Sociolinguistic Implications." Sociolinguistic Working Papers No. 85., University of Texas at Austin.

Kiddy, Elizabeth W. 2001. "Who Is the King of Congo? A New Look at African and Afro-Brazilian Kings in Brazil." In *Central Africans and Cultural Transformations in the American Diaspora,* edited by L. M. Heywood, 153–82. Cambridge: Cambridge University Press.

Laman, K. E. 1936. *Dictionnaire Kikongo-Français avec une étude phonétique décrivant les dialectes les plus importants de la langue dite Kikongo.* Bruxelles: Librairie Falk Fils.

Landies, Maurea E. 2009. "The Band Carries Medicine: Music, Healing and Community in Haitian/Dominican Rara/Gaga." PhD diss., Columbia University.

Larrazábal Blanco, Carlos. 1967. *Los negros esclavos y la esclavitud en Santo Domingo.* Santo Domingo: Julio D. Postigo e Hijos Editores.

Latino de Genoud, Rosa. 2002. "Algunas reflexiones sobre el vudú y la cultura haitiana." *CUYO: Anuario de Filosofía Argentina y Americana* 18–19: 98–121.

Laviña Gómez, Javier. 2000. "Sin sujeción a justicia: Iglesia, cofradías e identidad afroamericana." In *Estrategias de poder en América Latina,* edited by P. García Jordán, J. Gussinyer, and M. Izard, 151–64. Barcelona: Universidad de Barcelona.

Lebrón Saviñón, Mariano. 1992. "Del español en las Antillas." In *El español de América hacia el siglo XXI,* 125–40. Bogotá: Instituto Caro y Cuervo.

Levi, Joseph Abraham. 2009. "Portuguese and Other European Missionaries in Africa: A Look at Their Linguistic Production and Attitudes (1415–1885)." *Historiographia linguistica* 36, nos. 2–3: 363–392.

Lipski, John M. 1994. *A New Perspective on Afro-Dominican Spanish: The Haitian Contribution*. Albuquerque: University of New Mexico Press.

———. 2005. *A History of Afro-Hispanic Language: Five Centuries, Five Continents*. Cambridge: Cambridge University Press.

———. 2009. "Tracing the Origins of Panamanian *Congo* Speech: The Pathways of Regional Variation." *Diachronica* 26, no. 3: 380–407.

Losonczy, Anne-Marie. 2006. *La trama interétnica: ritual, sociedad y figuras de intercambio entre los grupos negros y emberá del Chocó*. Bogotá: Instituto Colombiano de Antropología e Historia.

Maríñez, Pablo. 1997. "Esclavitud y economía de plantación en el Caribe." *Sotavento* 1, no. 2: 83–102.

McGee, Adam. 2008. "Constructing Africa: Authenticity and Ginen in Haitian Vodou." *Journal of Haitian Studies* 14, no. 2: 30–51.

Megenney, William W. 1982. "Elementos subsaháricos en el español dominicano." In *El español del Caribe*, edited by O. Alba, 183–201. Santiago: Universidad Católica Madre y Maestra.

———. 1990. *África en Santo Domingo: su herencia lingüística*. Santo Domingo: Editorial Tiempo.

Meier, Johannes. 2001. "The Beginnings of the Catholic Church in the Caribbean." In *Christianity in the Caribbean: Essays on Church History*, edited by A. Lampe, 1–85. Kingston: University of the West Indies Press.

Moya, José C. 2012. "Migración africana y formación social en las Américas, 1500–2000." *Revista de Indias* 72, no. 255: 321–48.

Mukherjee, Sipra. 2013. "Reading Language and Religion Together." *International Journal of the Sociology of Language* 220: 1–6.

Negrão, Esmeralda V., and Evani Viotti. 2014. "Brazilian Portuguese as a Transatlantic Language: Agents of Linguistic Contact." *Interdisciplinary Journal of Portuguese Diaspora Studies* 3, no. 1: 135–54.

Nei, M., and A. K. Roychoudhury. 1974. "Genic Variation within and between the Three Major Races of Man, Caucasoids, Negroids, and Mongoloids." *American Journal of Human Genetics* 26: 421–43.

Núñez Cedeño, Rafael. 1982. "El español de Villa Mella: en desafío a las teorías fonológicas modernas." In *El español del Caribe*, edited by O. Alba, 221–36. Santiago: Universidad Católica Madre y Maestra.

Ochoa, Todd Ramón. 2007. "Versions of the Dead: Kalunga, Cuban-Kongo Materiality, and Ethnography." *Cultural Anthropology* 22, no. 4: 473–500.

Ossa Martínez, Marco Antonio de la. 2011. "El Gagá: confluencia, ritmo y sincretismo en los bateyes de la República Dominicana." *Cuadernos de Etnomusicología* 1: 29–51.

Pérez Guerra, Irene. 1989. "Africanismos lingüísticos en la República Dominicana." In *Estudios sobre el español de América y lingüística afroamericana*, 354–68. Bogotá: Instituto Caro y Cuervo.

———. 1999. "Contacto lingüístico domínico-haitiano en República Dominicana: datos para su estudio." In *El Caribe hispánico: perspectivas lingüísticas actuales*, edited by L. A. Ortiz López, 317–31. Madrid: Iberoamericana Vervuert.

Petter, Margarida Maria Taddoni. 2005. "Línguas Africanas no Brasil." *Niterói* 19: 193–217.

Pollard, V. 1994. *Dread Talk: The Language of the Rastafari*. Kingston: Canoe Press University of the West Indies.

Rivero Muñiz, Gilberto. 2014. "Las religiones afrocubanas. Presencia y desempeño en Cuba." *Islas* 56, no. 176: 146–64.

Rodrigues, Raymundo Nina. 2010. *Os africanos no Brasil*. Rio de Janeiro: Centro Edelstein de Pesquisas Sociais.

Rodríguez Demorizi, Emilio. 1975. *Sociedades, cofradías, escuelas, gremios y otras corporaciones dominicanas*. Santo Domingo: Editora Educativa Dominicana.

Samant, Sai. 2010. "Arab Americans and Sound Change in Southeastern Michigan." *English Today* 26: 27–33.

Sánchez-Carretero, Cristina. 2009. "'Con Dios y lo que me acompaña, me voy donde me da la gana': el impacto de la migración en las prácticas religiosas afrodominicanas." In *Migración y creencias: pensar las religiones en tiempos de movilidad*, edited by O. Odgers Ortiz, and J. C. Guadalajara Ruiz, 391–415. México: El Colegio de San Luis.

Santos Rovira, José María. 2015a. "Huellas africanas en el español caribeño. Estudio comparativo en una comunidad afrodominicana." In *Armonía y contrastes: Estudios sobre variación dialectal, histórica y sociolingüística del español*, edited by J. M. Santos Rovira, 99–106. Lugo: Axac.

———. 2015b. "Nuevos datos sobre la herencia africana del español caribeño. Estudio de campo en República Dominicana." *Anuario de Letras: Lingüística Y Filología* 3, no. 2: 237–71.

———. 2017. "La lengua de los congos dominicanos. Variación e identidad en Santo Domingo." *RILI (Revista Internacional de Lingüística Iberoamericana)* 15, no. 30: 161–77.

Schwegler, Armin. 1996. *Chi ma Kongo: Lengua y rito ancestrales en El Palenque de San Basilio (Colombia)*. Frankfurt: Vervuert Verlag.

Schwegler, Armin, and Constanza Rojas-Primus. 2010. "La lengua ritual del Palo Monte (Cuba): estudio comparativo (Holguín/Cienfuegos)." *RILI (Revista Internacional de Lingüística Iberoamericana)* 15, no. 1: 187–244.

Sessarego, Sandro. 2015. *Afro-Peruvian Spanish: Spanish Slavery and the Legacy of Spanish Creoles*. Amsterdam: John Benjamins.

Souza, Marina de Mello. 2005. "Reis do Congo no Brasil, séculos XVIII e XIX." *Revista de História* 152, no. 1: 79–98.

Spolsky, Bernard, and Joel Walters. 1985. "Jewish Styles of Worship: A Conversational Analysis." *International Journal of the Sociology of Language* 56: 51–65.

Thornton, John K. 2013. "Afro-Christian Syncretism in the Kingdom of Kongo." *Journal of African History* 54, no. 1: 53–77.

———. 2016. "The Kingdom of Kongo and Palo Mayombe: Reflections on an African-American Religion." *Slavery & Abolition: A Journal of Slave and Post-Slave Studies* 37, no. 1: 1–22.

Triana, Gloria. 2011. "Reflexiones sobre el lumbalú como ritual de memoria e identidad." *Aguaita* 22: 96–100.

Usanna, Karin Weyland. 2010. "The Absence of an African Presence in Argentina and the Dominican Republic: Caught between National Folklore and Myth." *Caribbean Studies* 38, no. 1: 107–27.

Zubrzycki, Bernarda, Ana Cristina Ottenheimer, Silvina Agnelli, and Gisele Kleidermacher. 2008. "Nuevas presencias africanas en la provincia de Buenos Aires." In *IX Congreso Argentino de Antropología Social*, 1–14. Misiones: Universidad Nacional de Misiones.

5

A Joyful Place

BANIWA JAGUAR SHAMANS' SONGS
AND HISTORICAL CHANGE

Robin M. Wright

For the Baniwa people of the Northwest Amazon, shamans' songs create a path over which the shamans' souls travel to the "Other World" of the powerful spirits who, for their part, interact and exchange with the shamans for the lost souls of the sick in "This World" of humans.[1] Songs open the way to the primordial world as the shamans bring its reality into the present and thus can potentially shape and even transform historical situations into a desired outcome. This chapter will reflect on the songs of Hohodene Baniwa shamans, or *pajés*, as they are known in the Northwest Amazon, *maliiri* in their own northern Arawakan language. The most powerful of the shamans are believed to attain the highest level of the cosmos, a place called "the joyful place" (*kathimakwe*), and to acquire the powers necessary to "heal the world" (*pamatchiatsa hekwapi*), as they say, from sorcery. In their long history of relations with non-Indigenous and colonial society, this power has been of vital importance to Baniwa survival and well-being.

My approach follows along the lines of Brabec de Mori and Seeger (2013, 283) in "analyzing the capacities and agencies of music and the sonic to bridge the gap" between humans of This World, and the powerful great spirits of the Other World. Shamans resort to the higher powers in the cosmos that are accessible through dreams, altered states of consciousness, and their songs in order to advise, counsel, and heal people of This World. Through their capacity to experience multitemporal and spatial worlds of the cosmos, the shamans bring the primordial into the present, and, in so doing, they "heal the world," overcoming the agents of disorder in the contemporary world as the Creator beings did in the primordial past.

What I shall do, first, is discuss the Hohodene animistic cosmos, its constituent parts and their interrelations; the "peoples" that comprise the cosmos, their interrelations and modes of communication, particularly through sounds and song; and the meanings attributed to these songs.[2] Then I focus on the sacred narratives that recount the primordial search for shamans' powers and the forms they take; the primordial sounds (e.g., thunder) that expansively transformed the world; and the vertical axis over which shamanic songs transit between the primordial Other World and This World.[3] I discuss next how, in contemporary shamanic practice, song mediation is understood to be the way for the primordial peoples to counsel humans as to the future courses of human action. This is the historicizing dimension in shamanic translations of primordial perspectives, bringing the Other World (*Apakwa Hekwapi*) into the present, and it is the way that the most advanced of the pajés, the jaguar shamans and seers, have to assume the perspective of the great spirits and even the Creator in order to protect humanity from harm. Finally, I discuss the stories of the Baniwa prophets in history in which powerful shaman seer-savants have transmitted the messages of divinity to the people, seeking to save communities from being overwhelmed by enemy others. These seer-savants have resorted to a higher power to reform their society from within.

My approach to shamanism is as a system of beliefs and practices that integrates cosmology into lived experience. I look at the cosmological meanings of shamanic symbols and the way shamans articulate those meanings in their performances. The shaman's songs, accompanied by his sacred rattle, enables him to engage the primordial world with the present, historicizing cosmology, in order to realize desired transformations. Cosmology—as understood through the sacred narratives (see also Frim in this volume)—provides a framework through which the shamans can transform actual events, through healing rituals for example, in which individuals are cured and protected from sickness (or other forms of disordering events), or whole communities from potential predatory threats, especially sorcery from outsiders or even those considered marginal within the communities. As Dereck Daschke (in this volume) has demonstrated for Santo Daime ayahuasca cures, "it's the song that cures," emphasizing the paramount importance of music in the healing process. Shamans can utilize this power to transform by mediating contact with non-Indigenous people, through political relations between the Indigenous communities and larger systems, such as the state, that seek to control, repress or manipulate local communities.

Shamans seek harmony within their communities, yet they themselves can represent a source of ambiguity and disharmony in their struggles for power. It has generally been recognized that shamans in Amazonia have an ambiguous role in their communities because they are both healers and sorcerers (Whitehead and Wright 2004). It has often happened that outbreaks of sickness have been interpreted as attacks by sorcerers. In those contexts communities have sought the help of trusted, powerful shamans to protect and heal them.

The pajés' principal function is that of curing through the extraction of pathogenic objects from the bodies of the sick. There are other specialists in the Indigenous communities that complement the shamans. The "owners of incantations," *iyapakethe iminali,* or *benzedores* in Portuguese, specialize in the performance of healing incantations of which there is an enormous variety often associated with knowledge of medicinal plants. There are priestly chanters who have vital roles of performing the pepper chants, or *kalidzamai* (*kariama* among the related Baré people) at rites of passage (birth, initiation, and death). The priestly chanters invoke spirits and spirit-categories that have to do with fundamental processes of creation that sustain the universe.

COSMOLOGY AND INTERRELATIONALITY

Baniwa cosmovision is deeply animistic, in the sense that the category of people is extended to all living beings: animals, birds, insects, stones, and all other kinds of being are believed to be distinct tribes of people. Animistic cosmologies acknowledge that "the world is full of persons, only some of whom are human, and that life is always lived in relationships with others" (Harvey 2006, xi). These "other peoples" include, for the Baniwa, the ancient spirit peoples called *Yoopinai*: invisible entities that occupy spaces everywhere in the environment (the earth, water, and air) within this world and with whom humans have constant exchanges. Relations with these other peoples are defined by spiritual protocol, including a deep respect for their spaces.

Failure to observe this protocol brings on sickness believed to be inflicted by these ancient spirit-peoples on humans. Then specialists are called in to remove the sickness and spiritually protect the patient. As Ernst Halbmayer (2012, 119) has described, the interactions of humans and nonhumans are constituted by complex and contingent relations that have to be permanently negotiated, processes that involve "politics of fragile inter-species and multi-world border management."

In Hohodene Baniwa belief, the cosmos consists of—from bottom to top—the underworld (called "Place of Our Bones"); This World of humans and all invisible spirit-peoples; and the upper, "Other World" of the sky inhabited by the most important spirits and the Creator. The different levels are illustrated in figure 12; the original drawing was done by Manuel "Mandu" da Silva, a highly respected and knowledgeable Hohodene pajé with whom I worked during various periods of research from 1976 to 2017.[4]

Each world is a circular disc, representing places that are connected by the "world-way" at the center, understood by the pajés to be a "stairway" or "sky umbilical cord" that connects the great spirits and the "sky womb" with their descendants in This World (the earth and all peoples). The predominant metaphor for the cosmos in Hohodene thought is that of an enormous tree, like the *samauma* (*Ceiba samauma*), and the diverse "peoples" inhabiting distinct levels of the tree correspond to what ecologists understand as different species (e.g., birds, sloths, humans) and their habitats.

Above this earth are the places in the sky of various female bird-spirit people called the "daughters of Dzuliferi," the primal shaman and elder brother of the Creator. In his training a shaman makes a "marriage" with one or more of these female bird-spirits, and, with them, the shaman will have spirit-children to serve as his helpers. Beyond those places is the Other World of the primordial "universe peoples," or "peoples of the day" (Hekwapinai), peoples of the beginning times, the very first ancestors.[5] To enter the Other World, the pajé "dies" in trance after snuffing the psychoactive powder known as *pariká*.[6] Once the shaman is there, he enters the places of the great spirits of sickness and of power, Kuwai and Dzuliferi,

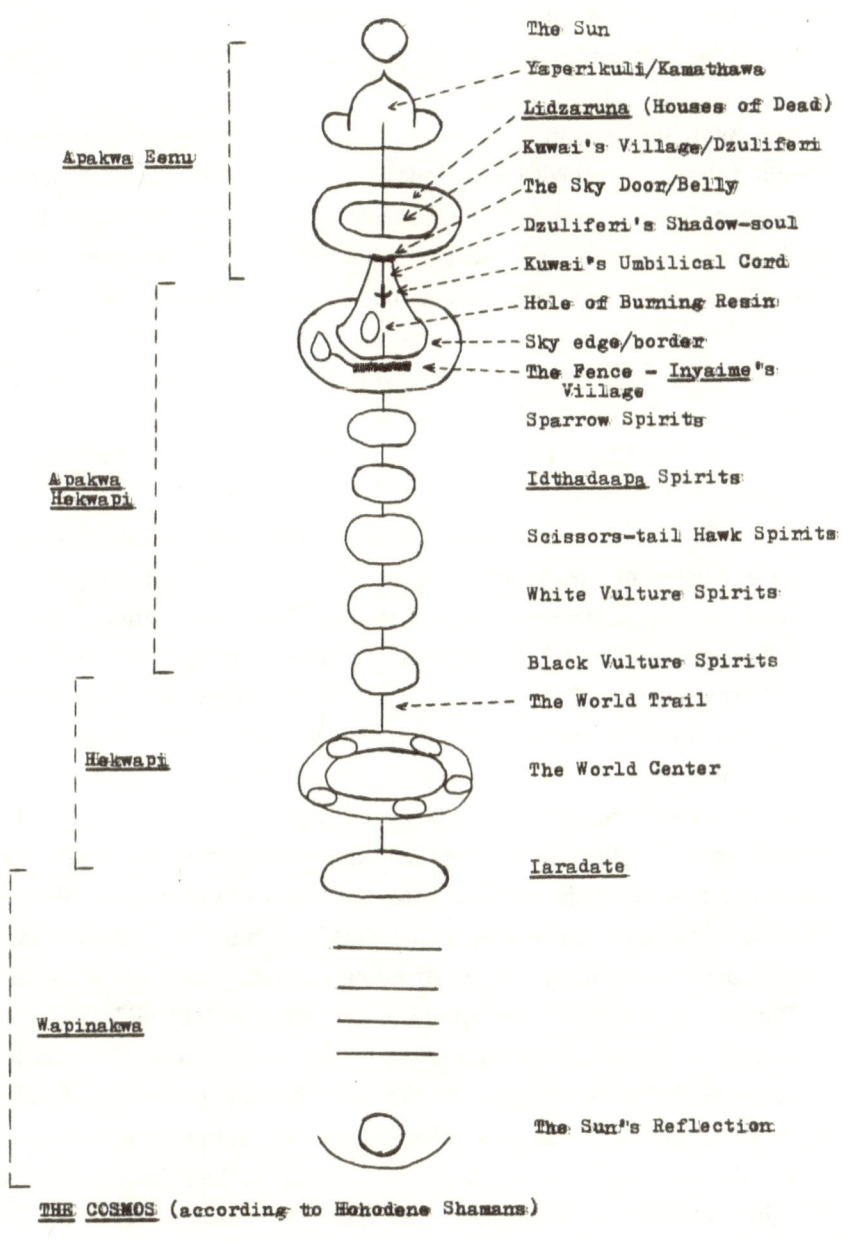

F12. The Cosmos (*Hekwapi*) according to Manuel da Silva, Hohodene jaguar shaman.

respectively. Kuwai is the source of all sicknesses that exist in the world and the one to whom shamans must appeal in their cures. Dzuliferi is known as the "spirit of power" and is the source of all healing, who gives the pajé songs, snuff, and tobacco.

From shamans' accounts the "body" of Kuwai is conceptualized as that of a giant sloth covered with poisonous fur; his "blood," on the other hand, is the sacred shamans' snuff called pariká, which the pajés use in their healing procedures. Dzuliferi is the most ancient of all the spirits and is primarily associated with healing; he gave tobacco to humanity, and some say that his body is covered with tobacco plants. Together with the powerful jaguar shaman spirits of the Other World, Kuwai and Dzuliferi control the comings and goings of human souls into the Other World; the shamans of This World exchange and negotiate with them throughout their professional lives.

Above the levels of the great spirits is the place of the Creator Nhiãperikuli, whose body is the Sun and who was responsible for bringing all creation into being. The stories that recount his deeds fill a book of narratives (Cornelio et al. 1999). At the Creator's House lives his "pet," the great spirit harpy eagle named Kamathawa who guards a box of the Creator's most infallible remedies. Few pajés reach this level, though at the end of their ten-year-long training, they should be able to reach a place near it. Yet there have been several very powerful pajés who have seen closely the brilliant light of the Creator's place. Nhiãperikuli does converse with these very powerful pajés and authorize them to act in his name, offering advice and counsel to the people in This World in times of extreme distress.

In common with many other Indigenous cosmologies of the Amazon, the Baniwa categories of other-than-human beings include all living species found in all habitats of the earthly environment. Prominent among these are the Yoopinai spirits that have their "houses" (-*pana*) in specific places along the riverbanks. It is said that they were born from the ashes of the fire that consumed the great spirit of sickness in the primordial times (Wright 1998, 2013, 2005). Today, they inflict sicknesses particularly on humans who transgress norms regarding bodily hygiene, food consumption, and environmental resources. These Yoopinai include, among others, the spirits of the forest called *awakarunanai* that can predate on humans who

F13. Yoopinai spirits of the forest. Drawn by Tiago Aguilar, shaman's apprentice, Aiary River.

venture deep into the tropical forest without having spoken the appropriate incantations. They include the river spirits, *umawalinai*, that can inflict sickness on human families that have not performed correct prophylactic postbirth incantations. The Yoopinai dwell in the air, the earth, and the rivers and can inflict various kinds of diseases, including—it is believed—the pandemic of COVID-19.

Birds, fish, animals are all "people" with "souls" (*ikaale*, s.; *nakaale*, pl.); the animals and fish have their houses, guarded by the Masters of Animals and Fish. The Masters allow these souls to leave their houses and transform into game animals or fish for humans. It is the pajé who requests of the Masters to open the doors and allow them to leave and become prey for humans. Each time the pajé does so, he must spiritually enter their house and dance with the Master, as in an exchange festival.

In the following section, I consider the story of the primordial search for shamans' powers in the Other World. The story focuses on the theme of mediation across borders between worlds through powerful sounds. The primordial sound of thunder, the felling of the primordial tree of sustenance, and the songs of the primordial shamans in their ascent to the sky are all ways of crossing boundaries between worlds that underlie the foundations for shamanic practice today.

THE SOUND OF THUNDER AND SHAMANIC POWER

In Baniwa cosmogony sounds produced along the vertical dimension of the Baniwa cosmos are as important for understanding communication with powerful spirits as seeing them. "Sniffing" (inhaling) elements like the sacred pariká provided by powerful, otherworldly beings triggers radical alterations of perception that are the hallmark of Baniwa shamanic experience. The story of how the pajés originally obtained their powers from the great harpy eagle spirit Kamathawa is exemplary in defining their practice.[7] For its importance to Baniwa shamanism, I shall now focus my attention to understanding its meaning.

According to the narrative "Nhiãperikuli Looks for Shamans' Powers, *Malikai*," as told by elder ritual specialist Keramunhe (Ricardo Fontes) of the village of Ukuki Cachoeira (in Cornelio et al., 1999, 42–51), in the primordial times, prior to the creation of the earth and This World, Nhiãperikuli's younger brother went to the forest to look for shamans' powers. The first power he looked for was to make the sound of thunder (*eenu*). He tried kicking a hollow tree but failed to make the sound. Nhiãperikuli told him to go back to look for an ibacaba fruit tree (*Oenocarpus bacaba*) and wait. He set a trap for the harpy eagle Kamathawa on a branch and waited at the foot of the tree until midnight, and, at that time, he heard a loud crashing sound of something falling through the branches to the ground. He lit torchwood but saw nothing. So he waited until dawn, and then he climbed up the ibacaba tree. There he saw on the branch where the trap was laid an eagle feather, which he picked up and sniffed. Suddenly he felt struck, and his eyes began to see things differently. He saw all four directions at once, like the eagle does. He looked down and saw a white eagle on the ground, but it was a person. He descended the tree and slowly approached the white eagle. They greeted each other, and the eagle asked, "Were you looking for me?"

The young man replied, "Yes." The eagle person said, "Ah, good," and approached. The eagle plucked out one of its crest feathers, gave it to the young man, and told him to sniff it. When the young man did, he was struck by an even greater force and made the powerful sound of thunder, "Khuk'kulululululu!" The man then went home and greeted his brother, Nhiãperikuli, who looked around but saw no one, because his younger brother had become invisible. Thus Nhiãperikuli's younger brother first obtained the powers of the pajés.

In this first episode, ecological time (the ripening of the ibacaba fruit, thunderstorms that are frequent in August) and seasonal activities (hunting in the forest) are intertwined in the encounter between worlds. The ibacaba tree represents the vertical divide between worldly planes, upper and lower. Whenever, in Baniwa shamans' stories, a person looks for and meets an entity of superior power, there is first a vertical displacement (down to up, or up to down), followed by a horizontal displacement (from there to here, or here to there), and the first question the powerful entity of the Other World asks the person of the story, "You were looking for me?," which is answered by "Yes, I was looking for you," and the reply "Ah, yes, it is good." This spiritual protocol establishes common ground for exchange to take place between the two entities, the meeting of two subjectivities, one of whom is looking for a power that the other has on its body (e.g., feathers, fur), and the other is a spirit-person who gives the pajé power, in the form of its feather, through which he is able to see the world in a radically different way.[8]

The transformations in perspective occur when the young man ascends to the branch where the eagle was and sniffs its feather, which abruptly "opens" his eyes, revealing the world in all four directions at once. It allows him to see the great eagle spirit as a "person," white in color (indicating the spirit world), on the ground. He descends and approaches the eagle-person on the same plane. The eagle-person gives him a crest feather, which is likewise transformative, and another radical alteration of perceptions occurs: the impact is so forceful as to produce the sound of thunder, the most powerful sound from the sky realm (sky and thunder are the same word, *eenu*), and one among various powerful sounds associated with cosmic creation. All of these events occurred in the world before the present one of humans. Yet they provide a model for the pajés practice itself: a pajé's apprentice must reach a certain level in his knowledge of the world before powers can be granted to him that will enable him to produce powerful cosmic sounds.

The next episode relates the felling of the Great Tree of Sustenance (most likely the samauma tree) belonging to Kaali, the primordial master of gardens, at the place called Uaracapory on the upper Uaupés River, Northwest Amazon. This tree, called *Kaali ka thadapani*, is an axis mundi containing shaman's powers, *malikai*, located inside a hole at the top of the tree. Specifically, these powers include a jaguar-tooth collar with which the pajé transforms into the jaguar, and a type of pariká snuff produced from berries located in a hole at the top of the tree. The felling of the Great Tree will bring these powers to earth, where Nhiãperikuli will then prepare the pariká to later bestow it for humans. The Tapir was eager to have those powers for himself, but Nhiãperikuli instructs the Tapir to go catch fish while he and his fellow shamans chop down the Great Tree. The cutting and felling is anticipated by the song of the ground-dwelling *inambu* bird (the tinamou), who sings three times before the Great Tree comes crashing down to earth. Then Nhiãperikuli tries to get the shaman's powers—malikai—but swarms of bees prevent him from doing so. The gluttonous Tapir, who had anticipated the felling of the Great Tree with great anxiety, runs to its top, impervious to the bees, and steals the desired shamanic powers from its rightful owner, Nhiãperikuli. Later Tapir sniffs the pariká and shares it with several other companions. Tapir then transforms into a killer-jaguar who roars that he wants to eat people, a potentially catastrophic situation until Nhiãperikuli reclaims the shamanic powers and sends the Tapir away. Pajés of various domains (rivers and forest) came into being at that time; the spirit Master of Game Animals became the pajé of the forest.

This episode aligns several temporal phenomena and seasonal subsistence activities (fishing, cutting down trees to make new gardens, the appearance of certain constellations, the appearance of ant and fish species) together, as the primordial beings bring the shaman's powers down from their place high up on the axis mundi to the ground. The felling of the Great Tree coincides with the appearance of swarms of bees that prevented

Nhiãperikuli from getting the desired powers. Swarms of bees are usually associated with the Pleiades constellation in South American mythology, and, in this context, the constellation is very low on the horizon, which corresponds to a time of year when people begin to make their gardens. Later the vertical axis of the Great Tree was substituted for a ceremonial rattle-lance by the spirit Master of Gardens Kaali; elders today use such a lance to pray for abundance at the center of newly planted gardens. This episode of the story signals the beginning of the agricultural calendar, correlated with fishing and hunting cycles, and the appearance or disappearance of constellations. A pajé's power is thus deeply connected with all such cycles; it is said, for example, that a pajé can intervene if the rains or the dry season are unusually long or behind schedule.

The third and final episode brings the story around full circle with the ascension of the primal shamans (*wakaawenai*) as they sing their way up to the Other World, completing a connection with the primordial healer shaman and great "Spirit of Power" Dzuliferi. The primal shamans left the world to be at the side of Dzuliferi, who helps the pajé heal the sick in This World. Through the shamans' songs today, they will always return. It is as though the shaman's path is made in this episode. The song, as it is sung by the elder narrator of the story, is as follows:

Heee . . . oopi ka waakawa
(Song of the jaguar) . . . we have already gone away

Heee . . . oopi ka waakawa
(Song of the jaguar) we have already gone away

Heee . . . oopi wapadama linako
(Song of the jaguar) we have already transformed on it

wapadamakapiidzo oopi . . . Heee
We have already transformed on it . . . (song of the jaguar)

oopi ka waakawa linako . . . wapadamakapidzo.
We have already gone away on it . . . we have transformed

Piuka piadeta wapidzawaaa
You will ask us to return

Piuka karumita piadeta liapidza uata
You will always ask him to return

Padzu Padzuuu Dzuliferi
Father father Dzuliferi

This episode describes a moment of transformation and ascent of the primordial shamans (*wakaawenai*) to the Other World. Following this moment pajés in their cures will have to connect with and request of the primordial shamans and the Spirit of Power, Dzuliferi, to return the souls of sick people. A great many if not all of the pajés' songs begin by invoking "our father, Dzuliferi." In the next section, I shall describe in more detail the pajé's sung journey to heal.

The radical alteration of the pajés' perceptions occurs, in short, along the vertical dimension of the cosmos over which higher powers are brought down and into diverse communities, while shamanic song is the transformative mode of ascension to, and travels in, the Other World. Through song the soul of the pajé frees itself from its body and flies to other planes.

SHAMANS' SONGS

Shamans' songs are the clearest way for them to reveal the primordial world in the present. The shaman healers are directly connected not only with Dzuliferi, who, it is believed, gives them their songs and advises them on the whereabouts of lost souls, but also with Kuwai, the source of sicknesses caused by sorcery, whose body consists of all the sicknesses there are and who demonstrates to the shaman apprentices how to cure. These two great spirits complement each other in the curing process, in the training of new pajés, and in enacting the stories of creation. Dzuliferi is the elder brother of the principal Creator Nhiãperikuli; besides bestowing on humanity the gifts of tobacco and pepper (essential to all meals), he bestowed all incantations, healing chants and prayers, words that are empowered by the blowing of tobacco smoke over both the patient and the remedy (see figs. 14–15).

The pajés' songs narrate their journeys in the Other World, and pajés say the songs are the voice of the Spirit of Power, Dzuliferi. After snuffing pariká at the beginning of a cure, pajés align themselves to the sun by

F14. The Spirit of Sickness, Kuwai. Drawn by Tiago Aguilar.

F15. The Spirit of Power, Dzuliferi. Drawn by Tiago Aguilar.

using their rattles. They "open the way" that reveals the shaman's "ladder" to the Other World. The shamans arise from their seated position and begin to dance and sing in a circle around a designated space. It is said that, although we see them moving inside the dance space, they are really in the Other World, and their souls are moving in the space-time of that World. Simultaneously the primordial World is revealed to the pajés. Their journeys are always sung, step-by-step, through a poetic and lyric reconstruction of all places they walk through in the Other World. Above all a question constantly motivates their search: "Is it here that I will find the soul of my sick friend?" Mandu explained that pajés can only perform cures when they have received the songs from Dzuliferi about the sickness of a person and when the great spirits "authorize" them to communicate their messages to humans. This illustrates the importance of spiritual protocol for the pajés' quest.

Through a synesthetic construction of hearing-seeing-singing-body choreography, the pajés communicate images and information about the cosmos to the patients and observers who are listening and watching, reflecting on the pajés' voyage and confiding in his powers. It is also in this way that Dzuliferi informs humans about their future and important events to come.

The song I have chosen to discuss is considered by the pajés to be a powerful one that is sung when the world has reached a state of serious imbalance—that is, when there are a great many sicknesses among people, as in epidemics of sorcery or witchcraft. In such a state, the kind of treatment that a pajé must give requires an appeal to the highest powers of the cosmos, from the very sources of universal healing. Mandu stated (interview 2010) that, by the time they are accomplished pajés, they transform into pure spirit and can "see all that is happening in This World." He explained that they assume the place in the cosmos of the great spirit Dzuliferi, and some can actually see the House of the Creator demiurge Nhiãperikuli.[9] At that point they have gained the powers to "make everything" in this world, "in their thought." They are able "to do miracles" in the Other World, for example, and "remove the evils of This World from people." It is said they can "make the world better" through their song. Mandu described this song in the following way:

The pajé looks for the ancient, hidden world *(lidawanikwa oopi)* of Nhiãperikuli. In his thought, he sits where Nhiãperikuli sits and seeks to open the ancient hidden world. He uses the wood and crest feathers of the harpy eagle Kamathawa, Nhiãperikuli's pet, to open the hidden world. He blows away the clouds to open the sky and make a beautiful sky. The pajé thinks: "There are others who don't want to know, to become as in the beginning, but they cannot open the ancient, hidden world as the pajé does."[10] The hidden world is the place of joy *(kathimakwe)*, the world of Jaguar [an epithet] Nhiãperikuli. When the Other World opens for the pajé, he ascends to it. He sits in the place of Dzuliferi and opens the world again in the sky above. The pajé is then near Nhiãperikuli and sees the entire world.[11] He can make everything as Nhiãperikuli did in the beginning. He gets what Nhiãperikuli had in the beginning: how Nhiãperikuli saw the world in the beginning in his thought *(Nhiãperikuli ikenyuakarumi likapa kwameka hekwapi)*. He then can remake the world. The pajé is near the sun, *Heire*, the body *(idaki)* of Nhiãperikuli. He has arisen and has requested from the sun Heire to open the ancient hidden world of Nhiãperikuli. He sees that the world becomes joyful, that all people become joyful, as in the beginning. Thus the pajé makes the world better, healing the world, not letting it end. The pajé knows when the world will end. He advises Nhiãperikuli who does not let it come to an end.[12]

The "happiness place" or "place of joy" *(kathimakwe)* is, Mandu (who has seen this place) explained, "a beautiful place" in a beautiful green forest of the Other World where, it is said, there is a huge longhouse as big as "a city," in which bird-peoples of all kinds live, constantly singing their joyful songs. They greet and welcome the visits of the pajés, who must ascend, singing, as they proceed step-by-step over the long staircase to get there. In this beautiful green forest, there is never any sadness; the bird-peoples are always together and joyful. From this place, I presume, the pajé receives the powers that will "make the world better," referring to this plane, which can become overridden by sickness or sorcery. The following is a transcription and translation of the song that Mandu da Silva shared:

Heey Heey /
Heey, heey

Kahlie da uatsa, lidia lianhiaka wapidzaaa /
Where will it be, it comes back to stay with us

Hekwapi tepemi, Dzuliferi /
His world, *Dzuliferi*

Kahlie da uatsa, lidia lianhiaka wapidzaaa, lidawanikwa oopi /
Where will it be, it will come back to stay with us, his hidden place of long ago

Nuhfe, nuhfe Dzuliferi /
My grandfather, grandfather *Dzuliferi*

Neeni na uatsa nuka numheluu, lidawanikwa oopi
For now I come and open his hidden place of long ago

Nuhfe, Nuhfe /
My grandfather, grandfather

Kununu, kununu /
Sweep away, sweep away

Ithamanahle /
Its smoke (= the clouds)

Dzaui malinyai /
The jaguar-shamans

Neeni uatsa nuka na uatsa numhelu liemakaruitami /
Thus, will I open his dwelling place

Padzu Dzuliferi, Heee /
Father *Dzuliferi, Heee*

Neeni uatsa nuka hnuhra nuhra likudafiami, Yawi Kamathawa /
Thus, will I raise the wood of Jaguar *Kamathawa*[13]

Neeni uatsa nuka hnura runapekuru Yawi Kamathawa /
Thus, will I raise his crest feather, Jaguar *Kamathawa*

Li uatsa nuka nupiyu piyu nayeema ithamanahle /
Thus will I sweep away their tobacco smoke

Dzaui malinyai, nuka numhelu /
Of the jaguar-shamans, I come and open

Hekwapi tepemi /
The other world

Hade mita waamaka lidzarhi madzekali iukaka /
We never seek those who do not want to know how

Imhelu lidawakwami oopi, Nuhfe /
He opens the ancient, hidden world, my grandfather

Ikatsa uatsa nuuma numhelu lihriu hekwapi tepemi, Dzaui Nhiãperikuli /
Thus will I open, I open his world, Jaguar Nhiãperikuli

Ikatsa uatsa nuumaka awatsahi teku tekuhu likurumhethe nuwaka numhelu lihriuhu /
Thus will I look for medicine to open his world

Hade mita waamaka lidzahri madzeka liukaka imhelu, lhekwapi tepemi, midzaka thayri
Never do we seek those who do not want to know how to open his world, Eternal Master.[14]

Heee Likapa menawaka wamhelu lidawanikwami oopi /
He sees that we open his ancient world

Nuhfe, nuhfe Hee /
My grandfather, grandfather, *Heee*

Ikatsa uatsa liaruhfiami kathimakwemi hekwapi hekwapi tepemi Dzaui Nhiãperikuli, Heee /
Behold his medicine box in the place of happiness, his world of Jaguar Nhiãperikuli, *Heee*

Ikatsa lidawanikwami oopi nuhfe nuhfe Midzaka thayri /
Behold his ancient, hidden place, my grandfather, my grandfather, the Eternal Master

Ikatsa uatsa nuka numhelu liapidzaha, Heiri ienipe /
Behold I shall open it with him, the sun's children[15]

Hee nuka numhelu hekwapi tepemi Midzaka thayri /
Heee, I open his world, the Eternal Master

Neeni ikapa nuka nupiyu piyuhu nuka numhelu /
Thus you see I brush away and open

Wapidzawa nuka numhelu lidawanikwa oopi nuhfe nuhfe /
With us I open his ancient, hidden world, my grandfather, grandfather

Ikatsa uatsa liaruhfiami Dzaui Nhiãperkuli likathimakwe, Dzaui Nhiãperikuli Hee /
Behold his medicine box, Jaguar Nhiãperikuli, his place of joy, Jaguar Nhiãperikuli, *Heee.*

Ikatsa uatsa kathimakwe lihriu Dzaui Nhiãperikuli /
Behold his place of joy, Jaguar Nhiãperikuli

Neeni ikapa nuka numhelu liukakarumi limheluwa Hee /
Thus, I open it, he comes and opens it, *Heee*

Ikatsa uatsa liuka limhelu lidawanikwa oopi nuhfe nuhfe /
Behold he comes and opens his ancient, hidden world, my grandfather, grandfather

Imali uatsa nukaka numhelu awatsa hli teko, teko Maliweko-iakalekuthe /
For so will I open it with this *teko, teko* [medicine][16] in the village of Maliweko-ikuthe[17]

Nuka hnura likudahfiami Yawi Kamathawa /
I will raise the wood of Jaguar Kamathawa

Ikatsa uatsa nu uatsa liemakaruitami Dzuliferi /
Behold I am in his dwelling place, Dzuliferi

Liemakaruitami, Dzuliferi /
His dwelling place, Dzuliferi

Ikatsa lidiaka liema, limhelu hlekwapi tepe /
Behold he comes back and opens his world

Ikatsa liukaka limhelu lhekwapi tepe Dzuliferi /
Behold he comes to open his world, Dzuliferi

Kathimakwe lihriu /
His joyful place

Ikatsa uatsa Kathimakwe lihriu Midzaka thayri /
Behold his joyful place, the Eternal Master

Ikatsa uatsa lidawanikwami oopi /
Behold his ancient, hidden place

Imali uatsa nukaka numhelu idawanikwami oopi nuhfe nuhfe /
For I shall open his ancient, hidden place, my grandfather, my grandfather

*Ikatsa uatsa hademita uatsa waamaka lidzarhi lidawanikwami
    Dzaui Nhiãperikuli /*
Behold those who do not want to know will not open his ancient, hidden place,
    Jaguar Nhiãperikuli

Kadzu karumita liukaka limhelu wapedza Wapedzakiri /
Thus, he comes and opens it with us, our ancestor

Wapedzakiri, Midzaka thayri Wapedzakiri Dzuliferi /
Our ancestor, the Eternal Master, our ancestor Dzuliferi,

Wapedzakiri Dzaui Nhiãperikuli /
Our ancestor Jaguar Nhiãperikuli

*Ikatsa uatsa hliekwapitepemi, lhiekwapitepemi Dzaui Nhiãperikuli, nuka
    numhelu wapidzawa /*
Behold his world, his world Jaguar Nhiãperikuli, I open it for us

Apakwa lheenu, apakwa lheenu, waaka weema Dzaui Nhiãperikuli /
The other sky, the other sky, we go to stay with Jaguar Nhiãperikuli

Weemakawa Dzaui Nhiãperikuli weemakawa Pakwa lheenu /
We are with Jaguar Nhiãperikuli, we are in the Other sky

Lidaleepa nuhfe, nuhfe Heire daleepa /
His companion my grandfather, my grandfather, the primal sun Heire,

Lidaleepa nuhfe Heire /
His companion, my grandfather *Heire*

Lidaleepa Heire, Heire /
His companion Heire, Heire,

Lidaleepa waferikiri Dzaui Nhiãperikuli /
His companion, our grandfather Jaguar Nhiãperikuli

Nuka numhelu naapidza /
I open it with them

Ikatsa uatsa lidawanikwami oopi /
Behold his ancient, hidden world

Nufe Dzaui Nhiãperikuli /
My grandfather, Jaguar Nhiãperikuli

Ikatsa uatsa numhelu /
Behold I open it

Ikatsa Kathimakwe /
Behold the joyful place

Kathimakwe nahliu /
Their joyful place

Ikatsa nuka numhelu napidza /
Behold I open it with them

Midzakanai /
The Eternal ones

Kadzukarumita likenyuwa /
So will it be as in the beginning

Limhelu /
He opened it

Liarufiami /
His medicine-box

Midzakanai /
The Eternal ones

Lhiekwapi /
His world

Lidawanikwami oopi /
His ancient, hidden world

Nuhfe, nuhfe Dzaui Nhiãperikuli /
My grandfather, my grandfather Jaguar Nhiãperikuli

Haaaaaw ! Haaaaawff ! /
(At the conclusion of every shaman's song, the shaman sweeps his arms in front of him while exhaling his breath)

The song shared by Mandu takes the shaman to the highest level of the cosmos, where he sits by the side of the primal sun, understood to be the "companion" body of the Creator, and looks over the entire world. The "wood" of the harpy eagle Kamathawa refers to the vertical dimension of the cosmos, the axis mundi, at the top of which the harpy eagle sits. Once the shaman arrives at the top of the Other World, he opens the "joyful place," the "city" of birds, and the Creator's "medicine-box," guarded by the most powerful harpy Kamathawa and containing infallible remedies. These are then applied to the entire world. Where before there was only sadness, consumed by sickness, the world now receives the powers of the joyful place. Such a song would be entirely appropriate for great shamans to sing, those who go beyond the highest jaguar shamans to become seer-savants, for which there is a long tradition in the Baniwa historical past.

SONGS OF THE SEER-SAVANTS

Although it is impossible to say with any certainty, the traditions of the great seer-savants may have existed in some form prior to any written historical records about them. Stories of clan ancestors are remembered with great pride, for example, because they recount how the ancestors saved the clans from extinction in the early history of contacts with non-Indigenous societies. From the mid-nineteenth century to the present day, however, there has been an unbroken and documentable line of powerful jaguar shamans, seer-savants who emerged in the context of increasing contact with non-Indigenous intruders—powerful representatives of the state military, missionaries, and commercial interests. In the early 1850s the Brazilian nation-state stepped up its program of "civilizing" (*civilizar*) the Indigenous peoples of this frontier region by imposing repressive forms of colonial governmental authority that the Baniwa had not experienced prior to this time in their history (Wright 2005, chaps. 3–4; see Cruz and Chapinal in this volume).

The oral traditions about these seer-savants constitute a distinct body of Indigenous histories in which there is a confrontation between the powers of the jaguar shamans and the force of the state to subdue and dominate that power. These stories universally assert that the jaguar shamans' powerful knowledge is far superior to the threat presented by the outsiders; however, they consistently point to internal conflicts generated by sorcery. As seems likely from the historical documents, the increase in sorcery was generated by a series of conditions: unknown, but lethal, sicknesses against which the Indigenous people had no immunity; disruptions provoked by government forced-labor programs; commercial exploitation by river merchants; and the limitations of the pajés' powers to overcome the new sicknesses. In the oral narratives about the great pajés of the past, these limitations are given as the main incentive for a kind of spiritual vision quest in which pajés then have had direct experience of their deceased kin, the primordial Spirit of Power, and the Creator. A deep loss or setback, such as the death of their children, in some cases forced the shamans to seek this greater knowledge (Wright, in Whitehead and Wright 2004, 82–105; Wright 2005, chaps. 3–5).

One of the most widely known of these seer-savants was named Kamiko, whose career spanned the second half of the nineteenth century. His fame as a visionary was widespread among Indigenous and mestizo communities of the frontier border region between Brazil, Venezuela, and Colombia (Wright 1981, 2005). The oral traditions about Kamiko state that his principal message had to do with the elimination of sorcery and the installation of a society based on harmonious conviviality through a healing of the community. After having various entheogen-induced visionary experiences in which he claimed to have visited with God, who granted him special powers of prophecy, he began a tradition called the "Song of the Cross," in which people would dance with crosses or around a cross, and the prophet would instruct people to rid themselves of whatever sorcery material they had hidden.[18] As his fame grew, the local military government heard that he claimed to be a saint, and that he had a great following. According to the oral narratives, eventually the government in Caracas, Venezuela, sent emissaries, or *doutores* (learned men) to test his power and take him prisoner. Summarizing from the stories (Wright and Hill 1986, 46; Wright 2016):

> They prepared a coffin for him and ordered Kamiko to get inside the coffin. They nailed it shut, bound it with rope, and then threw it into the Orinoco River. They did this several times, but every time they submerged the coffin, after an hour or two, when they pulled it up, he was still alive. Then, they threw it into the river for one whole night. Next day, they pulled the coffin up, opened it, and in his place was a poisonous snake. During the night, his soul had left his body [some people say they could see him dancing on the other side of the river with his rattle]. Then they believed that Kamiko really was a saint.

In shamans' cures today, it is said that after they take pariká, their bodies lie prostrate "as though dead, inside a coffin" and that "they see their body turn into a skeleton of white bones." (Manuel da Silva, in Cornelio et al. 1999, 185). Their souls then journey throughout the Other World. High-ranking Baniwa jaguar shamans, however, go beyond this in their capacity to converse with deceased ancestors and to serve as emissaries of the Creator. Once they have received authorization from Nhiãperikuli, they become recognized as seer-savants, or prophets. Generally, heroic quantities of entheogens potentiate their visits to the House of the Sun, the House of Nhiãperikuli.[19] After obtaining an authorization from Nhiãperikuli to heal, they serve as his emissary to the people. Obtaining authorization is not unusual for pajés, who must regularly obtain this in their cure from Dzuliferi, who authorizes for individual cures. Obtaining it from Nhiãperikuli, however, is altogether different, since Nhiãperikuli is considered to be "God," the highest power in the cosmos, and the authorization would be for a collective healing.

According to the sources, Kamiko was raised by a popular Afro-Venezuelan, Catholic folk saint named Father Arnaoud (Wright 1981). Both Kamiko and Uetsu, Kamiko's spiritual grandson, in fact expressed Christian beliefs; Uetsu, it is said, sang "praises to God" as he dreamt in his hammock (Wright 2005, chaps. 3–5; Wright 2016, 179). Both were influenced by the folk Catholic traditions that had cross-fertilized with Baniwa shamanism since the end of the eighteenth Century.

Both Kamiko and Uetsu are described by the Baniva of Maroa (upper Guainia River) as "dreamers," or *talisri* (Wright 2005, chaps. 3–5). Dreams are one way these seer-savants experienced and conversed with the Creator deity.[20] Through dreaming the Baniwa seer-savants gained miraculous powers to overcome and thwart all attempts by the military to kill them, and Kamiko even foresaw the territorial government's own destruction by rebellion, which actually did occur in the 1920s. Although they appealed to the highest power in the vertical cosmos to overcome the aggression of the military outsiders, it is said nevertheless that "they refused the status of high priest, president, or great chief of the people" (Wright 2005, chaps. 3–5.) on the earthly plane. In other words, they refused to accept the hierarchical distinctions imposed upon them by the emerging Brazilian nation-state.

When Baniwa visionaries have spoken of their utopian visions, they have referred to a variety of highly anticipated situations: "when there will be no more sickness" (Wright 2005, chap. 5), the elimination of debt to the White merchants, the eradication of sorcery. They have encouraged social harmony (what some Christian Baniwa today call *buen vivir*), prosperity, abundance of food, and faithfulness to ancestral traditions. The utopian time refers both to the primordial world of happiness (*kathimakwe* 'the joyful place'), when the great spirits walked in their knowledge in the world, but it could also refer to an imminent future. Past, present, and future times collapse in these liminal moments.

Evidently the prophets earned their fame through their miraculous cures, through the resonance of their message with peoples' struggles, desires and hopes, and also through their knowledge and direct experience of all levels of the cosmos. They survived sorcerer attacks and surpassed all expectations in renewing their spiritual strength. They not only understand

and explain the sacred stories with depth and firsthand knowledge but they also demonstrate their abilities to divine, to foresee with an extraordinary clairvoyance, and, with this knowledge and power, to secure the future of their people against the destructive elements of this world. The Baniwa seer-savants have transcended the jaguar shamans in the sense that they downplayed the warrior ethos intrinsic to the jaguar shamans' power struggles. Nevertheless, the warrior ethos was vital to their rejecting the imposition of an external nation-state and its hierarchical structure of power.

Seer-savants in history have added a layer of spiritual power by combining songs with images from shamanic ascension to the highest level of the vertical cosmos, aimed at preventing and healing the divisions produced in Baniwa society by sorcery. The latter includes the disruptions (sicknesses, conflicts, violence) provoked by historical contact with the non-Indigenous world. Stories of the seer-savants clearly state that their powers to overcome the death trap of the military parallel those of the healer shamans to reverse the attacks of enemy sorcerers.

CONCLUSION

In Baniwa animistic cosmology, as we have seen, spirit-peoples permeate the universe from top to bottom, with several important spirits having great powers as primordial sources of sickness and healing. Cosmogonic narratives of the acquisition of shamanic power highlight the importance of the vertical axis connecting higher, celestial powers, with earthly subsistence cycles, and the song-path created between the earthly shamans and the higher realms. It is a sonic bridge that is created between the primordial world and the present-day world over which the shaman transits strictly following spiritual protocol.

During his cures today, the pajé must obtain authorization from the great spirits before he can heal in this world. The more experienced and accomplished pajés have acquired ever greater knowledge and power from the spirits during their careers. Among Northern Arawak peoples, the pajés considered highest in the existing hierarchy—the wise people, seer-savants, and dreamers—combine the characteristics of healer and priestly chanter; their charisma derives from their ability to "die" by consuming heroic doses of pariká mixed with the psychoactive *Banisteriopsis caapi* entheogens, to converse with deceased ancestors, and to act as emissaries of the Creator. While there does exist a distinction between two kinds of specialists and two kinds of knowledge, similar to eastern Tukanoans (Hugh-Jones 1994) it is not as clear cut. Among the Baniwa the pajé's career, as described in the traditions, includes a final phase in which they gain access to the highest realms of the cosmos as part of their healing mission. These highest realms are the source of the creative powers of the universe (Wright 2013). The priestly specialists have a protective function as well, complementing the healer shamans rather than being opposed to them.

It is true that these more powerful pajés are plagued by the aggressive attacks of rival shamans and sorcerers in This World and in the Other World against whom they must learn to protect themselves by locating or constructing spiritual sanctuaries and by deceiving their enemies and successfully destroying them. Their foreknowledge of imminent enemy attacks comes from the superior vision they have through their mirrors, their spirit allies, and the long-distance gaze of the harpy eagle.

Finally, through their song, the pajés may reach the highest levels of the cosmos to obtain powers to make the world better. It requires that they open in their vision and song the "hidden place" (*lidawanikwa oopi*), the joyful place (*kathimakwe*) from which vantage point they see as the Creator saw, purifying the entire world of the evils that threaten it with collapse. The seer-savants in Baniwa history have used this power to preserve the autonomy of their followers from the imposition of an external order—the nation-state and its representatives. In this way Baniwa shamans utilize the powers acquired from the primordial past to shape the events of contemporary history.

ACKNOWLEDGMENTS

My sincere thanks to Ercilia Lima da Silva, Hohodene, who has served as interpreter for Mandu, her father, since 2009. I would also like to thank Alexandra "Sasha" Aikhenvald, renowned specialist in Arawakan languages, and the anonymous reviewers of this chapter for their helpful comments and suggestions. Finally, I'd like to thank the students in my Contemporary Shamanisms course for their stimulating discussions.

NOTES

1. The Baniwa are a northern Arawak-speaking people with a population of approximately 12,000, living in the frontier region of northwestern Brazil, southeastern Colombia, and southwestern Venezuela. They are a horticultural society, divided into several clans, such as the Hohodene ("Children of the Tinamou"), consisting of a number of agnatically related, multifamily communities along the Içana River and its tributaries. Their language is very similar to Kuripako and Wakuenai, two other northern Arawak-speaking people of southwestern Venezuela and southeastern Colombia (populations approximately 3,000 and 1,500, respectively). Baniwa and Kuripako languages differ from that of the Baniva, a small population of approximately 600 speakers living along the upper Guainia River in southeastern Venezuela, and whose language is endangered. I have done research among the Baniwa of the Aiary River since 1976 (see Wright 1998, 2005, 2013); Hill (1993, 2009) has done research among the Wakuenai in southern Venezuela since the 1980s (1993, 2009); and Journet (1995) among the Kuripako in southeastern Colombia.
2. "Peoples" refer to all human and other-than-human beings that populate the world as the Baniwa know it.
3. These narratives may be found in a collection I co-organized with Baniwa narrators in 1999 (Cornelio et al. 1999), published in the *Narradores Indigenas do Alto Rio Negro* series, and can be found in the archives of the AILLA (Archive of the Indigenous Languages of Latin America, ailla.utexas.org). Collections of Wakuenai, or Kuripako, dance songs and song-texts, organized by Jonathan Hill, are likewise found in the AILLA archives.
4. Figure 1 is a reproduction of a hand drawing and was originally published in my dissertation (Wright 1981).
5. The words for "day" and "universe," or "world," are the same, *Hekwapi*.
6. Pariká snuff is derived from the dark red exudate of the inner bark of the *Virola* tree that the shamans snuff every time they realize a cure.
7. It is said that the great eagle lives at the top of the cosmos (as, in fact, harpy eagles make their nests on the tops of the tallest trees of the forest) and guards the house and medicine box of its master, the Creator Nhiãperikuli. Extraordinary powers are attributed to the harpy's strength, penetrating vision and clairvoyance, and the piercing sounds it can produce. The shamans utilize harpy eagle feathers in order to "brush away" the skies of clouds and bring on the summer season. Shamans themselves can transform into the powerful harpy eagle by putting on the "eagle's shirt" (*kamathawa iyamakana*) when they search for lost souls of the sick.
8. The young man of the story is a hunter, and, like hunting, shamanic activity is governed by spiritual protocol.

9. As did the shaman prophets to be discussed later in this chapter.
10. "To become as in the beginning" refers to the shaman's transformation and entry into the primordial world.
11. The sun that we see in the sky is the body (*idaki*) of Nhiãperikuli. The primal sun of the narratives, called Heire, is considered the bodily "companion" to the Creator Nhiãperikuli. In some stories they are interchangeable. Nhiãperikuli is not limited to any shape or form and is said to be a spirit that permeates the universe.
12. The Baniwa tell stories of when the primordial world did come to an end; at that time animals and monstrous beings, Yoopinai, roamed over the earth killing and devouring people "with poison" (sorcery). The world was in darkness and all people were sad. Then Nhiãperikuli made the sun return and the world became joyful again.
13. When Jaguar is used before the names of Nhiãperikuli and Kamathawa, it is an epithet for a shaman of great power.
14. *Midzaka* also means "not made by man," but the translation of "eternal" is also accepted. For example, at Hipana, the Baniwa rapids of creation on the Aiary River, there are several large holes at the middle of the rapids from which the first ancestors emerged at the beginning of time. Nhiãperikuli is the "Eternal Master" of these holes, just as Kaali is the spirit "Master" of gardens: all things which grow in gardens are produced by Kaali.
15. "The sun's children" is the ceremonial name for the Hohodene clan.
16. I was informed that this is the stem of a plant, but I was not able to determine which plant.
17. An ancient spirit of thunder and lightning.
18. The specific entheogen consists of a highly potent mixture of *caapi* (*Banisteriopsis caapi*) and *yumpa* (*Anadenanthera peregrina*).
19. The psychoactive experience resulting from the mixture of the two DMT (dimethyltryptamine) alkaloids, besides interactions with the souls of the deceased and dead ancestors, is one of intense "light."
20. Dreams can be a way in which people have experiences with the great spirits, such as Dzuliferi, or with the ancestors.

REFERENCES

Bacigalupo, Ana Mariela. 2016. *Thunder Shaman*. Austin: University of Texas Press.

Brabec de Mori, Bernd, and Anthony Seeger. 2013. "Introduction: Considering Music, Humans, and Non-humans." *Ethnomusicology Forum* 22, no. 3: 269–86.

Cornelio, J., and Robin M. Wright. 1999. *Waferinaipe Ianheke: A Sabedoria dos Nossos Antepassados*. São Gabriel da Cachoeira: ACIRA/FOIRN.

Halbmayer, Ernst. 2012. "Debating Animism, Perspectivism, and the Construction of Ontologies." *Indiana* 29: 9–23.

Hill, Jonathan. 1993. *Keepers of the Sacred Chants: The Poetics of Ritual Power in an Amazonian Society*. Tucson: University of Arizona Press.

———. 2009. *Made from Bone: Trickster Myths, Music, and History from the Amazon*. Urbana: University of Illinois Press.

Hill, Jonathan, and Robin M. Wright. 1988. "Time, Narrative, and Ritual: Historical Interpretations from an Amazonian Society." In *Rethinking History and Myth*, edited by Jonathan Hill, 78–105. Urbana: University of Illinois Press.

Hugh-Jones, S. 1994. "Shamans, Prophets, Priests and Pastors." In *Shamanism, History, and the State*, edited by N. Thomas and C. Humphrey, 32–75. Ann Arbor: University of Michigan Press.

Journet, N. 1995. *Le paix des jardins: structures sociales des indiens Curripaco du haut rio Negro (Colombie)*. Paris: Institut D'Ethnologie, Musée de L'Homme.

Wright, Robin M. 1981. "The History and Religion of the Baniwa Peoples of the Upper Rio Negro Valley." PhD diss., Stanford University.

———. 1998. *Cosmos, Self, and History in Baniwa Religion: For Those Unborn*. Austin: University of Texas Press.

———. 2004. "The Wicked and the Wise Men." In *In Darkness and Secrecy: The Anthropology of Assault Sorcery in Amazonia*. Durham NC: Duke University Press.

———. 2005. *História indígena e do indigenismo do Alto Rio Negro*. Campinas: Mercado de Letras.

———. 2014. *Mysteries of the Jaguar Shamans of the Northwest Amazon*. Lincoln: University of Nebraska Press.

———. 2016. "Wise People of Great Power." *Journal of the International Society for the Study of Religion, Nature, and Culture* 10, no. 2: 170–88.

Wright, Robin M., O. Gonzalez-Ñanez, and C. Xavier Leal. 2017. "Multi-centric Mythscapes." In *Pilgrimage and Ambiguity: Sharing the Sacred*, edited by Angela Hobart and Thierry Zarcone, 201–32. Canon Pyon: Sean Kingston.

Wright, Robin, and J. Hill. 1986. "History, Ritual and Myth: Nineteenth-Century Millenarian Movements in the Northwest Amazon." *Ethnohistory* 33, no. 1: 31–54.

6

Embodying, Reshaping, and Combining the Past and the Future

A MAPUCHE SHAMAN'S HISTORICAL AGENCY IN CHILE

Ana Mariella Bacigalupo

Francisca pulled her headscarf over her eyes and increased the tempo of her drumming in her home in the Mapuche community of Millali, in the Araucanian region of southern Chile.[1] Her head rolled loosely as she entered into trance, while I spat water over her head to enable a spirit to take hold of Francisca's body. Music and song create a path over which the shaman's souls travel to the world of spirits who interact and exchange with shamans for the lost souls of the sick in this world (see Wright in this volume), effect healing and grant knowledge.

Francisca's head bowed with the weight of the past that possessed her as she spoke of the present and the future: "The ancient shamans, the ancient leaders from the earth above are speaking. . . . Settlers will bring more suffering for Mapuche. There will be tears, a lot of tears, a lot of sadness. There will be raiding and war. Many spirit owners of the forests will die. There are people of another blood, of another thought—the wingka (non-Mapuche)—who don't want our tranquility." Francisca appealed to Mapuche chiefs, shamans, and warriors of the past to defeat the evil spirits of the present—the sources of her patients' illnesses and of local conflicts over wealth and prestige. She predicted that if Mapuche enacted their communal, egalitarian ideals, a new world order would ensue.

The past is never dead (Sartre 2004). Rather, it is contained by, reshaped by, and ultimately fused with the present (Benjamin 1999, 462; Lambek 2003, 12; Shaw 2002, 265; Overing 1990, 611). Like other spiritual practitioners around the world who produce history by embodying beings from different historical periods (Bacigalupo 2013), Francisca drew from the "before time," the past, and the future to take control of the present.[2] But *machi* (shamans) like Francisca are unique in that they both embody and collapse these temporalities—experiencing multiple times at once—to transform the future.

Because machi share personhood with ancestor machi, spirits, animals, and forces of nature from different times and places, the stories they tell are always larger narratives about Mapuche experiences, perceptions, and morals that resonate with the people who listen to them. Machi are masters at weaving dramatic personal histories into larger webs of meaning through deeply emotional performances that envision how the world ought to be.[3]

The conventional view of shamanism highlights shamans' altered states of consciousness—dreams, visions, possessions, and ritual engagements with texts—as well as their ability to heal illnesses brought on by sorcery. Many scholars have reduced these experiences to discourses of social affliction that may then be analyzed as social texts. Yet the experiences of machi are better understood through scholarship on altered states of consciousness—as sensory practices linked to alternative modes of historicization (Hirsch and Stewart 2005). In this work the body of the possessed mediates the past and brings it into the present (Lambek 2003; Stoller 1995; Stewart 2012). "Every memory carried forward as the 'spirit' or 'soul' of the past is, as a matter of fact physically present, albeit invisible, in the living bodies of descendants: bone, muscle, blood, nerve. . . . Memories take place, take time" (Benson, this volume).

Dreams, visions, and ecstatic states such as possession are both perceptual and imaginative experiences. Altered states of consciousness "express individual and collective imaginations that represent the habits of the past, offer solutions for the present, and suggestions for the future" (Stewart 2012, 15, 211). But they also do something more: provide the sensory means by which machi and spirits transform temporality.

For machi multitemporality is a historical process linking the "before time" with "today time." The effectiveness of machi in ritual depends neither on their closeness to the events narrated nor on rational formulations based on archival documents or other written representations. Instead, it depends on their ability to embody and transform the suffering of the spirits from the before time and the historical past of today time to gain power in the present and create a better future for the collectivity.[4] By reordering the simultaneous temporalities of Mapuche cosmogony in ritual, the machi is able to effect change in the current world—transform illness into healing—and produce a more promising future.

A machi's ability to embody and transform temporalities resides in history, but this ability also makes history: machi create collective Mapuche histories as well as their own, producing a complex layering of multiple forms of knowledge from different people and times. Memory can express the politics of the past, as well as the ongoing struggles over ritual reformulations of history (Shaw 2002, 84, 104). Francisca remembered the pasts of her machi thunder spirit, of patients, and of the Mapuche collectivity through her embodied practices. She "evoked the past, manipulated the present and provoked the future" (Stoller 1995, 37). Through possessions, visions, and dreams, Francisca connected with past shamans and locations in Patagonia and attempted to gain mastery over the Indigenous and colonial past and to change the Mapuche's history—and ongoing experience—of power inequalities. The narratives about the past that emerged in rituals also became part of the community's oral history, told around the hearth in the cold of winter.

I discuss Francisca's perception of illness and healing as the history of ethnic conflict in Millali and analyze how her complex healing strategies were propelled by three ritual modes: divinations in which she embodied the past to see the future; sacrifices through which she effected healing in the present to construct a better future; and multitemporality by which she departed from the ideal cultural role of "machi from the past."

ILLNESS AND HEALING AS HISTORY

Mapuche use illness to conceptualize a history of intra- and interethnic conflict. They experience factional conflicts and encounters with whites as painful, unwanted transformations in personhood that threaten ethnic identity.[5] Intra- and interethnic conflicts in the present can also create illness, death, and chaos in the primordial world. A machi's diagnosis and healing are simultaneously historical explanations and unique creative acts that transform illness into health and chaos into order, ritually remaking the world and changing everyday life.[6]

While illness can serve as a forum for articulating social conflict and negotiating meaning, it can at the same time provide a frame for understanding how misfortune is inherited. Explaining misfortune through conflict and inheritance can create anxiety and strain social relations, but this explanation also links it to illness, makes suffering meaningful, allows patients to cope (Kleinman 1988), and gives them a way to heal with the help of machi. Mapuche people hire machi such as Francisca to heal them from many forms of illness, both natural and spiritual.

In her construction of *wekufü* (spirits) as evil *wingka* or gringos (white people from the United States or Europe), Francisca actively combated settlers' power and values from within a Mapuche shamanic logic and reduced Mapuche factionalism. But even though Francisca and other people in Millali attempted to break away from non-Mapuche values, they inevitably reproduced wingka systems of domination. At the same time, by holding non-Mapuche wekufü responsible for these illnesses and for *awingkamiento* (becoming like wingka or non-Mapuche), people in Millali have been able to re-create their identity as a moral, spiritual culture. Mapuche there continue to use accusations of sorcery and awingkamiento to define what it means to be Mapuche and as a tool to police those who espouse non-Mapuche ideologies.[7]

Francisca advocated for older Mapuche practices, histories, rituals, spiritual systems, and ideals of collective well-being, and she accused those who did not hold these values of being sorcerers and awingkados (like wingka). Francisca's patients needed to know at least some Mapudungun (the Mapuche language) to participate in her rituals. She hurled the terms *wingka* (non-Mapuche) and *gringo* at Mapuche participants who did not repeat her phrases in Mapudungun during healing rituals: "Speak, you idiots. I'm going to hit all of you. Why don't you speak? Are you gringos? What's wrong with you? You wingka shitasses are not helping. She [Mariella] is not Mapuche, and she is cooperating."

Francisca conducted all-night *datun* (complex healing rituals) to cure patients of a variety of illnesses. The rituals have ancient roots, but machi today heal illnesses related to the management and consequences of modernity: soul loss, evil spirit possession, spiritual punishment for transgression, stress, insomnia, alienation, depression, and bad luck. In the process, machi also legitimate Mapuche histories and political struggles for land and sovereignty. Francisca prayed, gave her patients massages and enemas, performed smoke exorcisms, prescribed medicinal plants for patients to drink or use as poultices, prescribed pharmaceutical remedies, shared advice about social relationships, and showed patients how to regain control over their lives and their health by contributing to the collective good.

As a machi Francisca gained prestige for treating a large number of Mapuche and wingka patients, for combining empathetic and authoritarian healing techniques and for speaking both Mapudungun and Spanish. Before seeing patients Francisca usually dreamed about the required remedy and often about their family situation and the route to their house. She drew on older Mapuche healing therapies that reinforce the connections between thought, emotion, and the body. She made her patients take responsibility for their actions and participate actively in the healing process, adapting her rituals to their needs. But she also practiced countersorcery against those who hexed her clients and friends, and she chastised her patients for transgressing Mapuche norms and for being greedy, stingy, and unfaithful.

Taussig (1987, 237) has argued that shamans in Colombia seek to appropriate the other's power by becoming the "shock absorbers of history." The ways in which machi appropriate and resist this power are complex and often contradictory. Francisca and other machi sometimes brought foreign powers, objects, and images into their local epistemologies and ontologies while rejecting the underlying systems of knowledge. Francisca used Catholic bibles as ritual objects, equated the Virgin Mary with the moon, considered Jesus a machi, and killed evil spirits with antibiotics. Some elements of these foreign systems do seep into machi practice and transform it. Catholic morality, alphabetic literacy, and the existence of "natural illnesses," for example, became part of Francisca's practice.

It was Francisca's multivalent approach to shamanism that allowed her to envision her power taking the shape of a bible. "Shamanism is the mirror image of alienation," writes Taylor (2007, 159). "It is the ability to control the polarity of the process of identification and to suck foreign beings into one's selfhood instead of the other way round." Francisca linked distinct, unequal, but mutually transforming Mapuche and non-Mapuche relationships, practices, and discourses and incorporated these into her complex healing strategies, which allowed her to embody three different modes of historicization. I turn first to Francisca's divination rituals in which she embodied the past to foretell the future through dreams, psychic sight, the power of her body, and experiences of possession.

DIVINATION: EMBODYING THE PAST TO SEE PRESENT AND FUTURE

"I dreamed that this place is charged with sorcery. The evil wekufü spirits are trapped between the mountains, which makes people envious. There are sorcerers everywhere," Francisca whispered, her voice barely audible above the clamor of stones hitting the bottom of my truck. We had driven past the tourist town of Pucon, where the paved road ended, and through the lush, hilly countryside on our way to the community of Longkofilu to heal Segundo and his family. "The old *kalku* [sorcerer] from the top of the hill hexed Segundo and his family because she wants them all to die so that she can get the land."

I stopped suddenly as we reached a river flowing over the dirt road. "A *cuero* [manta ray, an evil wekufü]," Francisca said, as she pointed to a small dark triangular shape floating downstream. The river looked too deep to cross. I wanted to turn back. "We will get stuck," I said. "What if the wekufü drown us?" Francisca glared at me. "You will not believe in wekufü," she argued. "You go straight. I pray. Go." Francisca invoked the Mapuche deity Ngünechen and the warriors of the four skies and squeezed my hand. I pressed on the accelerator, and we made it across. The river was shallower than it had seemed. Francisca laughed as she slapped my knee: "It is good that you trusted me."

"How did you know it was shallow?" I blurted out. "I am a *pewütun* machi [omniscient diviner shaman]," replied Francisca matter-of-factly. "Ngünechen gave me all the intelligence and power. He taught me everything from above. When something is going to happen, I dream, my right arm twitches, and the *filew* [collective ancestral spirit of all machi] tell me. And then I tell people."

I persisted. "You say you are a *kuyfi* machi [from the past]. So how does the machi from the past know the *ka antü* [the future]? Mapuche say this is a different time." Francisca squinted at me. "The machi is from the past," she said. "The past takes hold of the machi and lights up the future behind her. So the machi advises what will happen."

"Memories are the prism through which the present is configured even as present experience reconfigures these memories," writes Shaw (2002, 265). "Memory works backwards and forwards." While Western people imagine the past behind them and the future in front, Mapuche reverse this imagined positioning of the body in time. According to Mapuche poet Leonel Lienlaf, the past is "always in front of us; it is what we see, hear, and know. [We view] the present as beside us, and the future as behind us because we don't see it and we haven't known or experienced it."

Francisca had performed several divination rituals for Segundo and Anita (his younger daughter) at Francisca's home prior to our trip to Lonkofilu. She had used gestures, movements, and sounds to divine the present and future of Segundo's family in what Connerton (1989, 72) would call the "primacy of ritual as a bodily habit" in the construction of memory. Francisca used a holistic and practical approach to discover the natural and spiritual causes of the illness in Segundo's household, analyze its social context, and determine the cure.

Francisca had looked at the family's urine samples, which were "dark yellow and thick with evil." She stared into their eyes with her *vista* (psychic sight) and saw that Segundo's children were hexed: Anita "runs to the woods like an animal and rubs her hands together.[8] No one will marry her. Carmen [the elder daughter] cannot think because the evil has possessed her head. Joaquin [the youngest son] . . . wants to be like a wingka, and he is ill." Francisca diagnosed their misfortunes by drumming over Segundo's used undershirt: "Segundo's house creaks and the dogs bark because of the sorcery. They have bad luck. Segundo's wife died. The witch made Segundo deaf. He cries all the time. . . . The kalku threw putrid dogs' legs on the wheat fields to make them barren. The *añchimalleñ* and wekufü spirits have been busy doing harm." Segundo told Francisca that his family had been attacked by evil spirits, which confirmed Francisca's divination.

Divination rituals are therapeutic because they reconnect a client's individual and social bodies with the physical world, the moral order (Kapferer 1997; Graw 2009; Holbraad 2012; Werbner 2015), and the world of spirits in which their life may be reinterpreted and reinvigorated. Francisca could change people's bad luck and illness, but when a patient's problems recurred over time despite her healing practices, she explained this failure as the patient's destiny or as an evil spirit attacking their family. For Mapuche evil is an external force that threatens to destroy the temporal and moral order established by the cyclical rebirth of spirits of the past and by endorsement of ancestral ways. When people are hexed, they cease to act in socially appropriate ways and therefore lose their personhood and connection with the cosmic order. Anita ran to the woods like an animal. Joaquin wanted to become a wingka. Segundo cried and became deaf. Machi like Francisca heal disruptions in the temporal and moral order caused by sorcery, which often manifest as illnesses and social conflicts.

Segundo's family welcomed us into their small wooden house and served us chicha made from fresh apples. After three gulps Francisca slammed her glass down on the table and asked for the sacks of medicinal plants she had brought for the ritual. A neighbor who would serve as Francisca's *dungumachife* (ritual translator) arrived. We all sat in the shade of a large boldo tree, pulled leaves from the different plants, and put them in various bowls as indicated by Francisca.

She repeatedly demonstrated her knowledge by holding up a leaf, identifying it, and explaining how the spirits had told her to use it to heal Segundo's family. Many names of medicinal plants rolled off Francisca's tongue: *linco, triwe, boldo, rauli, quila, llankalawen, pulli-pulli, foye*. After she said each one, she exclaimed, "Juy!," to stress the power of the plant's medicine. Finally Francisca held up a leaf of *alwe lawen* and turned to Segundo: "This is to refresh the heart and the bone so that the sadness leaves. I dreamed I should give this to you to make you feel encouraged, happy, and forget the finished one [Segundo's deceased wife]."

That night in Longko Filu, Francisca used spirit possession to divine the social and moral causes of the suffering experienced by Segundo and his family, which complemented what she had learned through dreaming, psychic sight, visions, and the power of her right arm. Since the ritual creation and manipulation of history is accomplished through the body of the shaman, the spirits and deities that mimic Mapuche realities play a central role.[9]

Francisca sat on a low stool next to Segundo, who was lying on the floor of his living room with potted foye and triwe trees at his head and feet. Even on this dark night, she tied her headscarf over her eyes so that she would not be distracted from seeing the present and the future. Spirits both duplicate human society and transform it (Lambek 1996, 28–29), and to bring them forth is to gain control over their mirror image of physical reality, which then transforms the power of the shaman. Francisca's power to diagnose and cure depended on "out-doubling the doubling of the spirit image" (Taussig 1993, 127–28). She soon entered into a trance, and the spirit of Rosa, her shamanic predecessor, took over her body and speech:

> The old people from above feed me wisdom from all times. Today I can see everything. A sorcerer is trying to manipulate you and cause you harm.... She has sent her messengers [evil wekufü spirits].... They have tried to transform your being.... I see people wandering in the forest without any destination, like animals without an owner.... There are people taking chalky stones from the cemetery to do you harm.... There will be suffering, bitterness, and crying in this family.... [Speaking to the family:] The sorcery makes you fight among yourselves like dogs. You insult and hurt each other. You feel headaches and heartaches. You feel weak, dizzy, forgetful, and desperate. You don't know what to do. You are afraid.... [To Ngünechen:] My patient's body itches.... Who can be happy with pain in the stomach, back, hip, knee, and cramps in the feet? ... Sometimes he feels a lot of heat. He is weak. His heart is sad. He is confused with this illness. He believes that his heart and his head grow big. Sometimes he sees a dog [a symbol of sorcery].... He doesn't remember his dreams. [To the family:] You should be strong, united, to be healthy. Confront things as a family.... The sorcerer will not be successful because we have more strength and better spirits.... I am praying for you, my children, so that you will be well.... Now we shall clean these bodies and do good remedies so that the sorcery leaves.

Divination trances provide clues to the underlying pathologies of the social world. Francisca divined that the suffering and fighting experienced by Segundo's family were caused by a sorcerer and her evil wekufü spirit helpers, and she told the family to remain united and to have faith in her so that they would be healed. She linked sorcery to the loss of Mapuche morality, spirituality, and history, to the dispossession and conflict that had created an imbalance in the relationships among Mapuche families and communities and led to envy and jealousy among neighbors. In addition to insights gained from divination, Francisca's ability to heal in the present and create a better future depended on the efficacy of her sacrifices, her second mode of ritual historicization.

SACRIFICE AND HEALING: REORDERING THE COSMOS

Machi sacrifice their lives, bodies, and spirits to reorder the moral cosmos, effect healing, and create a better future for others. Mapuche refer to this huge sacrifice as *rume kutrankawün*: a great illness suffered to obtain something for the collective good (Juan Nanculef, personal communication, July 22, 2014). The moral validity of sacrifice is tied to the perceived efficacy of ritual acts and the validity of the possible future worlds the acts of sacrifice seek to effect (Mayblin and Course 2014).

A machi's sacrifice is a form of remembering, but in order for the sacrifice to be efficacious, spirits must consider the machi worthy of the knowledge and power they give her. Like Maya katun cycles (Farriss 1987), Mapuche shamanic histories combine linear and cyclical time to provide guidelines for interpreting events in the present and in the past, help shape events as they unfold, and describe the human ritual agency required to keep time and the cosmos in orderly motion. While a machi's sacrifice creates social order, sorcery disrupts it. Sorcerers sacrifice their victims' lives and well-being to gain wealth and power for themselves in the present. Machi combat the chaos provoked by sorcery, renew the power of the spirits, and reorder the cosmos through a very different type of sacrifice: through the offering of their own labor, spirit, and personhood.

The performance of shamanic sacrifice and healing is also a political act. Although the explicit goal of Francisca's ritual in Segundo's house was to produce healing, her ritual narratives pointed to a larger Mapuche history that was not an "incidental memory" (Cole 2001, 133), secondary to the primary goal. Francisca voiced the suffering experienced by Segundo and his family, but the family's suffering was also part of the collective reality of Mapuche people. Francisco Chureo (2001), the director of the Makewe-Pelales Mapuche hospital, has argued that Mapuche depression originates in their lack of land and the breakdown of their families due to migration (Menard 2003) and to the hegemonic imposition of Chilean knowledge. Machi try to heal holistically the suffering, alienation, and chaos of colonialism and growing social and economic inequalities by manipulating invisible forces that affect physical bodies, communities, and land (Bacigalupo 2001, 2007).

I assisted Francisca in two all-night rituals during which she invoked the deity Ngünechen, the stars, and the spirit masters of the ecosystem to heal Segundo's family and change their future. The family had already taken several measures to protect themselves against evil spirits. For four consecutive days before our arrival, they had drunk Francisca's emetic medicine to expel the sorcery. As counterhexes they had tied red yarn around their wrists, painted white crosses on their doors, and drawn a circle of ashes around the temporary rewe (axis mundi) they had fashioned so that Francisca could connect with other spiritual realms.

During those rituals the idiom of sacrifice was applied broadly to all participants in the healing process, not just in relation to the work of the machi and the sacrifice of her spirit. Francisca highlighted the family's sacrifice of their labor and money to ensure that the healing would be effective. Segundo lay on a sheepskin on the floor, with a potted foye tree at his head and a laurel tree at his feet, which pointed toward the door on the east. Francisca placed the 40,000 pesos that Segundo had given her for the datun beside his head and prayed, "Segundo made a great sacrifice to get money for healing. He is paying for his recovery with money. So please help me heal him, strengthen his spirit and his heart. We will bring order back to this land." Patients' payments help machi to recover the money they spend on initiation and assure them that their knowledge, powers, and services are valued.

Francisca also used the idiom of sacrifice to describe my participation: "Mariella sacrifices herself a lot for me. I told her, 'We are going far.' 'Yes, mamita,' she said. She will play *wada* [gourd rattles] and *kaskawilla* [sleigh bells]. And she will rub medicinal plants on the sick person." Segundo nodded. The dungumachife turned to me: "My God sees that you are helping a machi. He is grateful for your sacrifice and is going to help you." Francisca pulled her headscarf over her eyes and prayed:

> Old Man of the Sky, Old Woman of the Sky, of the rainbows, of the stars. Through my sacrifice and prayer, I give you these people who have come to ask for help. They have been humiliated. They are suffering . . . I have come to cleanse and purify your children. We ask to be respected. We are praying with force and making sacrifices so that you listen to us and give us what we are asking for . . . Help them be healed and united as a family . . . I am sacrificing the best plants. My ancient ones have sent me here to sacrifice myself to return you to health and happiness. Then, you will have a future.

The dungumachife engaged in a highly stylized conversation with Francisca. I alternated between playing sleigh bells and massaging the patient's body with a mixture of crushed laurel leaves, other soothing herbs, and water. Segundo's children took their own turns at being the patient while the others shook short branches of laurel leaves (*iaf-iaf*) to induce healing. Then Francisca drummed loudly and signaled for me to rub all the patients' arms with another potion made of aguardiente and crushed bitter foye leaves, while she prayed to expel the evil spirits. The family shook foye branches to exorcise the evil wekufü spirits. Francisca then had a vision of an evil *añchimalleñ* spirit in the shape of a wingka woman.

Then Francisca circled inside and outside the house, drumming loudly to chase the evil spirits away. I followed, sprinkling a mixture of ammonia, aguardiente, and chili peppers in the corners of the house. The men followed me, thumping knives and axes on the floor and walls to cleanse them of evil spirits. Francisca threw a kitchen knife toward the door four times to test the wekufü's power. Twice the knife fell pointing toward the door—a sign that Francisca was defeating the spirits. Twice it fell pointing toward the family, indicating that the sorcery was still affecting them.

Francisca took a break while Anita heated the *kultrung* (drum). Sweat dripped down Francisca's nose. Outside Carmen and Anita prepared a *sahumerio* (smoke exorcism) made from *wilkawe*, foye, *ruda, ajenjo,* chili peppers, salt, aguardiente, vinegar, and sulfur, and Joaquin fired a gun from the roof. The smoke snaked down the path, back to the alleged witch's house, which Francisca interpreted as proof of the witch's culpability. During the night we heard the patter of footsteps and a dog barking outside the house. Anita shot the revolver through the window to kill evil spirits, and the noise subsided. Since dreaming is an important part of the ritual, at midnight all participants took a nap in order to dream. A few hours later I had a nightmare about a huge dog that barked at the head of my bed. I screamed. Anita shot through the window again. Segundo dreamed that the witch said, "I am screwed now. They all know who I am," and left. Francisca saw this dream as a sign that healing had begun.

Francisca completed the ritual with a prayer, reminding the spirits of the sacrifices made and asking them to ensure the family a good future: "I have sacrificed my words, my knowledge, my strength, and my remedies for this family. . . . I have completed my work with your help, Old Father, Old Mother Hawk, old people of the skies and mountains. . . . This family has sacrificed their money and work to ask for your help. Take care of this family and protect them from evil."[10]

The more power and wealth a machi gains, the more she is subject to accusations of sorcery—the other side of sacrifice. Those machi (like Francisca) who are labeled as sorcerers can become scapegoats for a community. The sorcerer then becomes the sacrifice—"an efficacious act of casting out by destroying the person rather than an act of exchange with the divine" (Rio 2014)—which allows community members to regain control over their lives and future. Francisca made others aware of her self-sacrifice to prove that she was not a sorcerer: "I sacrificed myself to heal my patients. But the money I got is to pay for my *pürun* to renew my powers, not for me."

To be recognized as a machi as opposed to a sorcerer one must be recognized as a machi "from the past." But Francisca had not always performed the ideal role of a machi from the past, and as a result she became ill and almost died. Machi Angela thus had to heal Francisca in a ritual requiring that Francisca embody multitemporality—her third mode of ritual historicization. She then became a "true machi" of the past and was able to reinsert herself back into her present.

EMBODYING MULTITEMPORALITY: RESHAPING THE PAST

The ritual language of machi prayers and other forms of ordained speech depict the real source of divine power as existing on a multitemporal plane. If a Mapuche shaman can access this plane, where distinct times become simultaneous, then she can be several different people at once.[11] The "machi from old times" must fulfill their destiny as machi by embodying the spirits from the past to see the past, present, and future simultaneously and shape the cosmic reordering of the world.

Machi view possessions as multilayered ecstatic experiences in which the machi and the filew go into *küymi* (trance), the filew acts as an intermediary between humans and Ngünechen, and the filew "speaks the words of Ngünechen through the machi's mouth" (Bacigalupo 2007, 101–2).[12] Machi, like Panamanian Kuna chanters (Taussig 1993, 109), are always retelling or reinterpreting something that was said before. Machi hear the message of Ngünechen through the words of the filew (generic machi spirit) and the *püllü* (individual machi spirit). The machi then repeats and interprets the words of the filew and the püllü in her ecstatic discourse. The machi's words are in turn repeated and interpreted by the dungumachife, who makes the machi's words intelligible to the ritual participants. Francisca elaborated, "My head gets drunk, and the filew comes down and gets inside the stomach. It heats and compresses it. . . . Then the voice comes out and repeats what Ngünechen tells it."

But Francisca did not always live up to her machi destiny, nor her community's expectations of a machi from the old times. Some believed that her wisdom and her ability to see the past, present, and future were diminished because of awingkamiento, which made her vulnerable to sorcery and suspected of being a sorcerer herself. Machi Juana's husband observed,

> Before few people got the machi spirit. Now everyone wants to be a powerful machi. . . . It is the same ancient machi püllu that returns [in the body of new machi], but with less potency, with less *kimün* [wisdom] . . . because Mapuche are too awingkados. Mapuche now have another mind [they think like wingka], and machi have their tongues in a wingka context. We think of ourselves in Chilean history. People change, the Mapuche change, the wisdom changes, the destiny of the

wingka changes. . . . These young machi are spoiled, arrogant . . . and they don't know shit. . . . The role of the machi is to heal and service the community.

Because of these accusations of sorcery, the breakdown in Francisca's social and spiritual networks and the death of her son, she experienced an illness that was a result of awingkamiento called called *nervios* (embodied distress), which had physical, emotional, and spiritual components.[13]

In addition Francisca experienced *wenukutran* (spiritual illness) and *kastikukutran* (punishment illness) because she had transgressed her role as machi of the past: she had neglected to make sacrifices for others, and she had not performed rituals to renew her powers. Furthermore, Francisca had sacrificed her spirit horse to feed the mourners at her son's funeral and to ensure that her son would travel to the Wenu Mapu (Mapuche sky). Francisca's premature slaughter of her own spirit horse, with whom she shared personhood, was a form of spiritual suicide that transgressed the shamanic temporal cycles of death and rebirth. Although most machi are punished by their spirits because they watch television or allow themselves to be photographed or filmed, few commit the major transgressions against machi being and temporality that Francisca did. Through her illness Francisca learned that the spirits and deities would not tolerate her temporal misbehavior. If she wanted to live, she had to erase her previous transgressions, live as her ancestors did, locate her being and spirit in the ancestral past, and embrace multitemporality. Only then would she regain her agency, the gift of healing, and the knowledge to ensure a better future for others.

This juxtaposition of the old and the new, machi from the old times and modernized Mapuche awingkado-sorcerers who transgress machi norms, made necessary a resurgence of the past. Machi Angela therefore performed a healing ritual to reshape Francisca's past and reconnect her with the spirits and deities by helping her to embody multitemporality.

At midnight on January 28, 1995, Francisca lay on the floor while Angela played her drum loudly over her, imploring Ngünechen to forgive Francisca for transgressing her role as machi of the past and to let her live. I had arrived at Francisca's house early that morning to find two of her daughters sobbing, and Francisca lying on a mattress in the living room, dressed in her best black woolen wrap and wearing the heavy silver pin she used to protect herself from evil spirits. Her eyes were closed, her face was white and clammy, her hands were cold. I could feel no pulse. Francisca was so ill that her daughters thought she was dead. They had washed her and changed her clothes in preparation for the funeral. Francisca's daughters had sent me and her brother-in-law José to fetch Angela, who belonged to the same school of machi practice.

That night Angela treated Francisca in a datun, a complex healing ritual that involved bringing Francisca back in line with Mapuche expectations for a machi from old times by helping her to experience multitemporality and by renewing her powers and her relationships with ancient machi, deities, spirits, and her spirit animals. When machi are initiated, they exchange spiritual essences, personhood, and bodily substances such as breath, blood, and saliva with a specific sheep and horse, which become their "spirit animals." Machi relationships with these spirit animals reflect a complex understanding of personal consciousness in which machi are separate agents but at the same time share selves with their spirit animals. Francisca told me, "I dreamed they gave me a horse. My power is riding on a horse. Now I am strong and will jump like a horse."

Francisca had decided that I should record the first half of her datun (before midnight, when her illness would be diagnosed) but not the second half (when her future would be decided), lest it offend Ngünechen. Since the structure of this ritual was similar to the one Francisca performed for Segundo, in what follows I focus exclusively on the healing of Francisca's temporal transgressions.

José and I arrived at Francisca's house with Angela, her brother (who was also her dungumachife), and her niece (who served as her ritual helper). Angela inquired about Francisca's health. Francisca's grandson Cesar sacrificed a sheep for the machi. He slit its throat, and Francisca and Angela drank the warm blood mixed with chili to gain strength. The two of them bragged competitively about their shamanic powers and the patients they had healed. Meanwhile, José, Cesar, and I prepared the remedies for the ritual. José planted two bamboo canes as a temporary rewe outside the kitchen door on the east and tied triwe and foye branches to them. I placed soothing medicinal plants (triwe, nulawen, *limpia plata*) in one wooden bowl and the remedies meant to exorcise evil (*llanten, fulcon,* foye) in another. Francisca's daughter Aurora heated the skin of machi Angela's kultrung to make its sound deeper.

Francisca lay face up on a sheepskin on the floor, bare-breasted but wearing a petticoat, with her head toward the kitchen door. Cesar placed pots with foye, triwe, and külon branches at her feet and head. Angela sat on a low stool beside Francisca, smoking a cigarette to help her concentrate. She donned her silver breastplate and headdress for protection against evil spirits and placed two crossed kitchen knives behind Francisca's head. She played the sleigh bells and kultrung softly as she invoked the spirits of the past and narrated in four phases the history of her calling, powers, and initiation, as well as Francisca's. Her kultrung was heated after each phase. She described Francisca as her "sister" and as a "daughter" of the deities who was destined to become a machi but ignored her destiny for many years:

> Old Woman who created machi, Old Man who created machi, you have destined us to exist and gave us wisdom and strength, this is why we are standing here before the filew. . . . We did not choose to become a machi. You told us we must be machi to help, to save the children [patients]. . . . When she was in her mother's womb, this daughter [Francisca] was destined to become an orator, a machi. . . . My sister [Francisca] is the descendant from a lineage of sacred singing women machi that does not end. . . . But she waited too long to become a machi.

Machi are not singular subjects; they also embody the spirits and deities whom they mimic and about whom they chant.[14] They see the world through different "modalities of personhood" (Bem 1993), temporalities, genders, and points of view (Bacigalupo 2007, 77).[15] Angela named a variety of nature spirits and ancestors (the deity Ngünechen, the Virgin Mary, and Jesus), all of whom duplicate the human world in terms of family relationships and social and spiritual hierarchies. By calling them forth into the ritual space and embodying them, Angela became simultaneously human and spirit and sought to gain control of the world they represent.

During the healing ritual, Angela also embodied the different dimensions of the deity Ngünechen (Bacigalupo 1997), each associated with a specific time: Üllcha Domo Ngünechen, a young servant and daughter of Ngünechen from the present who has the power of unbound female fertility, childbirth, and the stars; Weche Wentru Ngünechen, a young servant and son of Ngünechen from the present who has the power of Chilean military officers, masculinity, and lightning and who kills evil spirits; Fücha Wentru Ngünechen, or Chau Dios, the old Father God from the past who has the wisdom and power of the Christian God, Jesus, the apostles, the sun, and ancient *longko* (community head who leads collective rituals); Kuse Domo Ngünechen, or Ñuke Dios, the old Mother God from the past who has the power of fertility and the wisdom of the Virgin Mary, the moon, and ancient machi; the multigendered and multitemporal Ngünechen, who links worldly and spiritual realities; and a young sister, equal to Francisca, in the present to embody and implement these different qualities and times.

Angela wiped the sweat from her brow, and her niece pulled Angela's headscarf over her face as she proceeded with the faster drumbeat—*trekan kawellu kultruntun* (the traveling horse)—on which machi gallop to other worlds and gain knowledge. Six young men from the community were also present, and they clashed rüngi above her head and screamed, "Ya ya ya ya!" Angela's head shook, and she entered küymi. Angela played a forceful beat often referred to as *tropümkultruniin* (Ñanculef and Gumucio 1991, 5) as she began the *pewütun* (divination). The dungumachife spoke about good machi from the past and the damage wrought by awingkamiento. Angela spoke about Francisca's transgressions:

> *Dungumachife*: In the beginning, the Ancient Father created good machi, good filew, and that's why we lived on the breasts of the mountains.... But now that the land has become awingkado, it is different... Mapuche thought has been tossed aside. People use wingka tricks. Some machi do, too.
>
> *Machi Angela*: The daughter machi [Francisca] is ill, and the filew asked us to come ... Filew is kneeling and crying because her heart has declined.... This daughter left the language of the old machi leader, who is like a *choyke* [Patagonian ostrich].... She doesn't have her

machi animals; she hasn't performed her renewal ritual. . . . She has no strength. . . . She is wounded even in the place where she prays. . . . They sent her *witranalwe*. . . . It makes her ill and competes with her filew. . . . They [bad spirits] filled her heart with evil and left shadows in her eyes. . . . Now she lost consciousness and has a fever. . . . She doesn't have muscles in her hands, she doesn't have blood of service [to the machi profession] . . . she walks crooked, she has melancholy.

Bernardita (Francisca's granddaughter): On the day of the Ascension of the Virgin Mary [December 8], Francisca was going to renew her rewe. But none of her helpers showed up . . . [and] her heart declined. Her own family harmed her.

Mapuche believe that challenges to the past and the amorality of sorcery trap and weaken people, tying them up, agitating them, contaminating them, knotting their life paths, and confusing them. Healing takes place as the machi exorcises the evil spirits lodged in the bodies, souls, hearts, and households of her patients, by shooting or stabbing these manifestations and by purging and otherwise cleansing the patient. Angela rubbed Francisca's arms and legs with the blunt side of a knife to unravel the knots caused by Francisca's temporal transgressions and sorcery. She sought to purify and strengthen Francisca's spirit and lift it so that she would be influenced by the healing powers of Ngünechen.[16] Healing transforms a patient from knotted to unraveled, contaminated to purified, weak to strong, and agitated to calm. The goal was for Francisca to regain her role as machi of the past (Bacigalupo 2007, 75–76).

Angela sang and massaged Francisca with medicinal plants while her niece-helper played the kultrung. Then the helper and I rubbed Francisca's body with "soft" medicinal plants while Angela played her kultrung face down for maximum therapeutic effect. Francisca's daughters and I also shook iaf-iaf to induce healing.

Shamanic songs are both a way for spirits to counsel humans as to the future courses of their action (see Wright in this volume), and a way for shamans to intercede for their patients before the spirits. Music can also effect personal transformation, collective bonding, bodily healing (see Daschke in this volume). Machi Angela and the dungumachife asked

Ngünechen to forgive Francisca for her transgressions and to help her so that she would be integrated back into her machi practice, family, and community:

> *Dungumachife:* Give her guidance and strength. . . . Your daughter machi [Francisca] is paying money to complete her designation. . . . Untie her tongue. Awaken her bones and spirit for service so that she can have her prayer, her discourse, her song [*tayül*].
>
> *Machi Angela:* I am calming her illness. I am returning her elasticity. . . . Help me stretch and purify your children . . . reorganize the middle of her body, blow on her, . . . revitalize her heart, blood, bones to become servants to the machi ancestor leaders. . . . Give her back her breath, infinity of ancestor machi, help the daughter machi. . . . If God allows, this machi shall recover. Defend her, encourage her. Don't let her be defeated. Bring her back to life, unravel her like a thread. . . . Give her a clear vision. Illuminate her on this dawn. Give her back her good machi dreams. May she do good prayers with a sincere heart, with a clean mind. Let her produce well-being. . . . Let her have her saddled spirit horse again. . . . You [Francisca] will go to many places singing your tayül, your sacred song. . . . Old Woman visionary, Old Man visionary told me this.

Then Francisca herself unexpectedly went into trance. She sat up and swayed, holding on to her breasts and playing sleigh bells as she faced east. Her body trembled. Cesar brought in her chosen shamanic spirit sheep and moved its front legs, making it dance to the music. By recovering her spirit sheep, who shared personhood with her, she regained her strength, protecting her from sorcery attacks.

Indigenous broad notions of territory include both geography and cosmology, and specific landscapes are linked to an Indigenous peoples' past (see Benítez de la Cruz and García Chapinal in this volume). By strengthening her ties to her rewe (axis mundi), Francisca reestablished her role as mediator between this world and that of spirits and her place in a larger cosmology. By strengthening her ties, to the landscapes of Millali and its forces, Francisca reinforced her relationship to the past and its spirits, and her identity as machi of the past. She also renewed her marriage to her spirit, her ties of affinity to the family of her deceased husband, and her position of subservience as a machi bride to her machi spirit and to Ngünechen, who granted her power and knowledge. Machi Angela had Francisca exchange saliva and *neyen* (breath and life) with her spirit sheep to reestablish her shared personhood with it. Francisca breathed on the sheep's nose and spat into her hand. The sheep licked the saliva, a sign that it had accepted her spirit. She prayed:

> They gave me my sheep from above and I put it in my heart. Then I forgot my ways and my heart raced. I became ill. . . . My tongue was small and blocked. Now I have recovered my sheep, my heart, again and I can scream louder. Have compassion for me, Old Man from the sky, Old Woman from the sky. With my mentality and bones of service, heal me. We are doing the necessary things for my machi being. . . . Now you are supporting me again . . . I have been revitalized. I have recovered my strength. . . . I am fulfilling my destiny. I will do my duty and perform the renewal ceremony. I believe in my heart again.

A machi's songs have a performative function: they bring about the healing and transformation that she requests. By singing about herself as a machi who must transform herself to become like a machi of the past, Francisca made it so. At the same time, the prescribed speech of prayers limited her range of responses and stressed her public position (as a machi) along with a sense of social distance from and respect for the established spiritual, political, and social order (see also Bloch 1998; Irvine 1979). The deity Ngünechen would have machi from the old times channel the past to order the cosmos and heal the present and future, not intervene in the particular circumstances of Francisca's or Angela's lives.

Anthropologists often distinguish between the shaman, who controls the alteration of her own consciousness, serves as a conduit for the spirit, truly sees, and interprets the healing images, and the patient, who gains awareness of her inner being, talks but does not truly see, and experiences trances and visions that are controlled by the shaman (Laderman 1994, 192; Taussig 1987, 198). Machi Francisca was exceptional in being both patient and shaman. She was made ill by her transgressions, but she also altered her own consciousness to access her own healing images and therapies.

Along with Angela, Francisca, too, became a conduit for the spirits, who demanded that she be a machi from the past.

The body is always invested with relations of power and domination, argued Foucault (1979, 25–26), but it "becomes a useful force only if it is both a productive body and a subjected body." Through her illness Francisca learned that the spirits and deities would not tolerate her temporal misbehavior. If she wanted to live, she had to erase her previous transgressions, live as her ancestors did, locate her being and spirit in the ancestral past, and embrace multitemporality. Only then would she regain her agency, the gift of healing, and the knowledge to ensure a better future for others.

CONCLUSION: EMBODIED SHAMANIC HISTORIES

Machi care for the knowledge and power of the past, which they embody to pass on to future generations.[17] But machi like Francisca also fuse past, present, and future, and they ritually embody, reproduce, and reshape time to forge a better future for all Mapuche. Like the Colombian Nasa (Rappaport 1998, 9–10), Mapuche understand their present to be morally linked with their past, which they activate to achieve their political goals. Through her divinations, healing rituals, and the ritual that restored her as a machi of the past, Francisca located her own body in a state of multitemporality to gain knowledge and power from the spirits. She linked her body, her personal history, and the experiences of her patients to Mapuche collective histories and sought to restore the cosmic order, as well as her own reputation as a good machi, through self-sacrifice.

Healing rituals allow people to reshape the world by "regimenting present activity and by invoking futures and pasts that set the present in perspective" (Stewart 2012, 212–13). Mapuche rituals transform the past into narratives about "what should have happened" (Morphy and Morphy 1985, 462), "condensing the experience of the conquest and creating analogies with the hopes and tribulations of the present" (Taussig 1984, 88). The present, replete with its own interests and preoccupations, appropriates and revises the past (Jackson 2007, 80). Like Australian Aborigines (Goodall 2002, 12; Attwood 2005, 248, 249), Mapuche see different time frames blurring into one another, each incorporating experiences and ideas into a new form.

Buryat shamans in Mongolia distinguish between personalizing knowledge of the past through memory and dispersing the knowledge of individuals to larger groups, or making history (Buyandelger 2013). Mapuche call both processes "history" because living shamans are never just individuals, and their narratives and performances are never just personalized knowledge of the past. Machi are always multiple persons who experience multiple times at once.

Machi use multitemporality to reorder the world and then return to the present. They transform "unconscious temporalization to everyday historical consciousness" and "internal temporality to articulated history" (Stewart 2012, 215). Jean-Paul Sartre (2004) argued that imagination allows people to think beyond perception, which enables them to think about changing current circumstances. But Francisca experienced the spirits and people of the past as real, not imagined, which allowed her to transcend the present through ritual action. Machi and their patients express their agency through dreams, visions, and spirit possessions: they look into the future and into the past to find ways of acting in the present.

NOTES

1. This article is a revised version of a chapter which was published in *Thunder Shaman: Making History with Mapuche Spirits in Chile and Patagonia* (Austin: University of Texas Press, 2016).
2. See Stoller (1995); Steedly (1993); Lambek (2002); Nielssen (2011); Kendall (1999); Shaw (2002); and Buyandelger (2013).
3. Cole (2001, 281) finds a similar phenomenon among the Betsimisaraka of Madagascar.
4. Lambek (2002, 17) argues that "historical consciousness entails the continuous, creative bringing into being and crafting of the past in the present and the present in respect to the past (poesis), and judicious interventions in the present that are thickly informed dispositions cultivated in, and with respect to the past, including understandings of temporal passage and human agency (phronesis)."
5. See Kristensen (2010) and Pandolfi (2007) for addition perspectives on illness as history.
6. Overing (1990) noted a similar process in Piaroa healing chants.
7. Likewise, Taylor (2007) notes that Shuar do not imitate whites but compete with them.
8. Similarly, the Amazonian Baniwa whom are hexed temporarily lose their humanity and go the forest to become like tree animals for a few days (Wright 2013, 124).

9. Some of the typical cultural logics of spirit possession played out: the "paradox of agency," whereby mediums gain a voice by giving their own up to the spirits (Jackson and Karp 1990), the embodied political metaphor of a spirit "mounting" a subordinate human (Matory 1994), and the machi as a bride of the spirit and also a masculine mounted warrior, which also reflects gendered and colonial hierarchical relations (Bacigalupo 2007).
10. Both the individual sacrifice of machi in healing rituals and the collective sacrifices of ngillatun rituals are expected to ensure a better future, but they have different focuses. In healing rituals machi sacrifice their present lives, the knowledge and power of the spirits who possess them, and their bodies in order to create a better future for their patients. Mapuche sacrifice their animals and work during collective ngillatun rituals for the benefit of the entire community; the goal is to integrate the ritual community and to maintain a reciprocal relationship with other people, spirits, and the deity Ngenechen in the present. Mapuche pray to give thanks for abundance and well-being and to request the same on behalf of the entire ritual congregation (Bacigalupo 1995, 2001). Their interactions with friends, relatives, spirits, and deities always involve a greeting (*chalintun*), asking about the health of relatives (*pentukun*), and the sacrifice (*langümün*) of an animal who represents the human and is collectively consumed. Gifts of wine can also replace animal meat (Foerster 1993, 112; Course 2011). The assumption is that these collective sacrificial acts will be reciprocated.
11. See Freud (1976, 399) and Stewart (2012, 212–13) for other examples of how those who access a multitemporal plane become different people.
12. Some *ngenpin* (ritual orators) and *werken* (messengers) believe that ancestral knowledge comes from outside of them—from spirits and ancestors—and that they acquire authority by virtue of being able to channel this knowledge of the past although they do not possess authorship over it. They argue that the knowledge that they wield is true because it is not a personal product but is collective ancestral knowledge that emerges from the anonymous force of machi and longko who sustain it. Similarly, the werken transmit Mapuche political messages as independent from those of Chilean political parties. The authority of the werken resides in their capacity to transmit the teachings of an anonymous and invisible mass (Menard 2003, 22).
13. As Low (1994, 141–42) describes it, "Nervios is constructed by local discourses and institutions, then expressed and acted upon as a metaphor of social, psychological, political or economic distress. The relationships between nervios and embodied distress, therefore is culturally mediated, both in terms of what forms of distress cause suffering and in terms of its metaphorical expression." Francisca experienced disorientation, dizziness, and fainting, fits of crying or anger, insomnia and headaches, sensations of hot and cold, and body aches.

14. Taussig (1993, 2, 19) argues that the image affects the thing it represents, that the representation shares in or takes power from the represented, and that the ability to mime is the capacity to make "other."
15. The anthropologist Mischa Titiev (1968, 303) argues that "there is often an element of bisexualism in a machi's dealings with the other world," and Métraux (1942, 333) states that when machi are healing, "they may address various supernatural beings, one of whom is likely to be a female-male personage." What these authors fail to notice is that the machi actually becomes these different gendered beings in healing, and that these ritual gendered performances do not necessarily translate into bisexualism in the machi's everyday life.
16. Peruvian *curanderos* use similar categories for illness and healing (Glass-Coffin 1998; Joralemon and Sharon 1993).
17. Likewise, the goal of West African Dogon Sigui rituals and those of Songhay healers is to pass on the knowledge to the next generation (Stoller 1980).

REFERENCES

Attwood Bain. 2005. *Telling the Truth About Aboriginal History*. Sydney: Allen & Unwin.

Bacigalupo, Ana Mariella. 1995. "El Rol Sacerdotal de la Machi en los Valles Centrales de la Araucanía." In *Modernización o Sabiduría en Tierra Mapuche?*, edited by Ricardo Salas, Ramón Curivil, Cristián Parker, Ana Mariella Bacigalupo, Alejandro Saavedra, and Armando Marileo Armando, 51–98. Santiago: Ediciones San Pablo.

———. 1997. "Las múltiples máscaras de Ngünechen: las batallas ontológicas y semánticas del ser supremo Mapuche en Chile." *Journal of Latin American Lore* 20: 173–204.

———. 2001. *La voz del kultrun en la modernidad: Tradición y cambio en la terapeútica de siete machi*. Santiago: Editorial Universidad Católica.

———. 2007. *Shamans of the Foye Tree: Gender, Power, and Healing among Chilean Mapuche*. Austin: University of Texas Press.

———. 2013. "Mapuche Struggles to Obliterate Dominant History: Mythohistory, Spiritual Agency, and Shamanic Historical Consciousness in Southern Chile." *Identities: Global Studies in Culture and Power* 20, no. 1: 77–95.

———. 2016. *Thunder Shaman: Making History with Mapuche Spirits in Chile and Patagonia*. Austin: University of Texas Press.

Bem, Sandra. 1993. *The Lenses of Gender: Transforming the Debate on Sexual Inequality*. New Haven CT: Yale University Press.

Benjamin, Walter. 1999. *The Arcades Project*. Cambridge MA: Harvard University Press.

Bloch, Maurice. 1998. "Time, Narratives, and the Multiplicity of Representations of the Past." In *How We Think They Think*, edited by Maurice Bloch, 100–113. Boulder CO: Westview.

Brown, Michael Forbes. 1996. "On Resisting Resistance." *American Anthropologist* 98, no. 4: 729–49.

Bourdieu, Pierre. 1984. *Distinction*. New York: Routledge.

Buyandelger, Manduhai. 2013. *Tragic Spirits: Shamanism, Memory and Gender in Contemporary Mongolia*. Chicago: University of Chicago Press.

Cole, Jennifer. 2001. *Forget Colonialism? Sacrifice and the Art of Memory in Madagascar*. Berkeley: University of California Press.

Comaroff, Jean. 1985. *Body of Power, Spirit of Resistance*. Chicago: University of Chicago Press.

Connerton, Paul. 1989. *How Societies Remember*. Cambridge: Cambridge University Press.

Course, Magnus. 2011. *Becoming Mapuche: Person and Ritual in Indigenous Chile*. Champaign: University of Illinois Press.

De Boeck, Filip. 1999. "Domesticating Diamonds and Dollars: Identity, Expenditure, and Sharing in Southwestern Zaire (1984–1997)." In *Globalization and Identity: Dialectics of Flow and Culture*, edited by B. Meyer and Paul Geschiere, 177–209. Oxford: Blackwell.

De Martinao, Ernesto. 2012. "Crisis of Presence and Religious Reintegration. Prefaced and Translated by Tobia Farnetti and Charles Stewart HAU." *Journal of Ethnographic Theory* 12, no. 2: 431–50.

Derrida, Jacques. 2007. *Psyche: Inventions of the Other*. Vol. 1. Stanford CA: Stanford University Press.

Durkheim, Émile. [1912] 2001. *Elementary Forms of Religious Life*. Oxford: Oxford University Press.

Evans-Pritchard. E. 1956. *Nuer Religion*. Oxford: Clarendon.

Farriss, Nancy M. 1987. "Remembering the Future, Anticipating the Past: History, Time, and Cosmology among the Maya of Yucatan." *Comparative Studies in Society and History* 29, no. 3: 566–93.

Foerster, Rolf. 1983. *Martín Painemal: Vida de un dirigente mapuche*. Santiago: Grupo de Investigaciones Agrarias (GIA).

Foucault, Michel. 1979. *Discipline and Punishment: The Birth of the Prison*. New York: Vintage.

Freud, Sigmund. [1900] 1976. *The Interpretation of Dreams*. London: Penguin.

Glass-Coffin, Bonnie. 1998. *The Gift of Life: Female Spirituality and Healing in Northern Peru*. Albuquerque: University of New Mexico Press.

Goodall, Heather. 2002. "Too Early Yet or Not Soon Enough? Reflections on Sharing Histories as Process." *Australian Historical Studies* 33, no. 118: 7–24.

Gordillo, Gaston. 2003. "Shamanic Forms of Resistance in the Argentine Chaco: A Political Economy." *Journal of Latin American Anthropology* 8, no. 3: 104–26.

Graw, Knut. 2009. "Beyond Expertise: Reflections on Specialist Agency and the Autonomy of the Divinatory Ritual Process." *Africa* 79, no. 1: 92–109.

Hale, Charles. 2002. "Does Multiculturalism Menace? Governance, Cultural Rights, and the Politics of Identity in Guatemala." *Journal of Latin American Studies* 34: 485–524.

Hirsch, Eric, and Charles Stewart. 2005. "Introduction: Ethnographies of Historicity." *History and Anthropology* 16: 261–74.

Holbraad, Martin. 2012. *Truth in Motion: The Recursive Anthropology of Cuban Divination*. Chicago: University of Chicago Press.

Hubert, Henri, and Marcel Mauss. 1981. *Sacrifice: Its Nature and Functions*. Chicago: University of Chicago Press.

Irvine, Judith T. 1979. "Formality and Informality in Communicative Events." *American Anthropologist* 81, no. 4: 773–90.

Jackson, Michael. 2007. *Excursions*. Durham NC: Duke University Press.

Joralemon, Don, and Sharon Douglas. 1993. *Sorcery and Shamanism: Curanderos and Clients in Northern Peru*. Salt Lake City: University of Utah Press.

Kapferer, Bruce. 1997. *The Feast of the Sorcerer*. Chicago: University of Chicago Press.

Keenan, Dennis King. 2005. *The Question of Sacrifice*. Bloomington: Indiana University Press.

Kendall, Laurel. 1999. "Shamans." In *Encyclopedia of Women and World Religions*, edited by Serenity Young, 892–95. New York: Macmillan.

Kleinman, Arthur. 1988. *The Illness Narratives: Suffering, Healing and the Human Condition*. New York: Basic Books.

Kristensen, Dorthe. 2010. "Uncanny Memories, Violence, and Indigenous Medicine in Southern Chile." In *Remembering Violence: Anthropological Perspectives on Intergenerational Transmission*, edited by Nicolas Argenti and Katharina Schramm, 63–80. New York: Berghahn.

Kuramochi, Yosuke, and Rosendo Huisca. 1990. "Contribuciones etnográficas al estudio del machitun." *Actas de Lengua y Literatura Mapuche* 4 (December): 237–56.

Laderman, Carol. 1994. "The Embodiment of Symbols and the Acculturation of the Anthropologist." In *Embodiment and Experience: The Existential Ground of Culture and Self*, edited by Thomas Csordas, 183–97. Cambridge: Cambridge University Press.

Lambek, Michael. 1996. "The Past Imperfect: Remembering as Moral Practice." In *Tense Past: Cultural Essays in Trauma and Memory*, edited by Antze Paul and Lambek Michael, 235–54. New York: Routledge.

———. 2003. *The Weight of the Past: Living with History in Mahajanga, Madagascar*. Basingstoke: Palgrave Macmillan.

Low, Setha M. 1994. "Embodied Metaphors: Nerves as Lived Experience." In *Embodiment and Experience: The Existential Ground of Culture and Self*, edited by Csordas Thomas, 139–62. Cambridge: Cambridge University Press.

Matory, Lorand. 1994. "Rival Empires: Islam and the Religions of Spirit Possession among the Ọyọ-Yoruba." *American Ethnologist* 21, no. 3: 495–515.

Mayblin, Maya, and Magnus Course. 2014. "The Other Side of Sacrifice: Introduction." *Ethnos* 79, no. 3: 307–19.

Menard, André. 2003. "Manuel Aburto Panguilef: de la República Indigena al sionismo mapuche." Nuke Mapu Working Papers.

Métraux, Alfred. 1942. "Le shamanisme araucan." *Revista del Instituto de Antropología de la Universidad Nacional de Tucumán* 20, no. 10: 309–62.

Morphy, Howard, and Frances Morphy. 1985. "The Myths of Ngalakan History: Ideology and Images of the Past in Northern Australia." *Man* 19: 459–78.

Nielssen, Hilde. 2011. *Ritual Imagination: A Study of Tromba Possession among the Betsimisaraka in Eastern Madagascar*. Leiden: Brill.

Ñanculef, Juan, and Gumucio Juan Carlos. 1991. "El trabajo de la machi: Contenido y expresividad." *Nütram* 25: 2–12.

Overing, Joanna. 1990. "The Shaman as a Maker of Worlds: Nelson Goodman in the Amazon." *Man* 25: 601–19.

Pandolfi, Mariella. 2007. "Memory within the Body: Women's Narrative and Identity in a Southern Italian Village." In *Beyond the Body Proper: Reading the Anthropology of Material Life*, edited by M. Lock and J. Faquhar, 451–58. Durham NC: Duke University Press.

Rappaport, Joanne. 1998. *The Politics of Memory: Native Historical Interpretation in the Colombian Andes*. Durham NC: Duke University Press.

Rio, Knut. 2014. "A Shared Intentional Space of Witch-Hunt and Sacrifice." *Ethnos* 79, no. 3: 320–41.

Sartre, Jean-Paul. [1940] 2004. *The Imaginary: A Phenomenological Psychology of the Imagination*. Translated by J. Webber. London: Routledge.

Schindler, Helmut. 1988. "Con Reverencia Nombreys al Pillan y Huecuvoe (Sermón IV, Luis de Valdivia, 1621)." *Revista Indigena Latinoamericana* 1: 15–27.

Schindler, Helmut, and Minerva Schindler-Yáñez. 2006. "La Piedra Santa del río Lumaco." In *Acerca de la Espiritualidad Mapuche*, edited by Helmut Schindler, 1–68. München: Martin Meidenbauer Verlagsbuchhandlung.

Shaw, Rosalind. 2002. *Memories of the Slave Trade: Ritual and the Historical Imagination in Sierra Leone*. Chicago: University of Chicago Press.

Stewart, Charles. 2012. *Dreaming and Historical Consciousness in Island Greece*. Cambridge MA: Harvard University Press.

Stoller, Paul. 1980. "The Epistemology of Sorkotarey: Language, Metaphor, and Healing among the Songhay." *Ethos* 8, no. 2: 117–31.

———. 1995. *Embodying Colonial Memories: Spirit Possession, Power, and the Hauka in West Africa*. New York: Routledge.

Taussig, Michael. 1984. "History as Sorcery." *Representations* 7: 87–109.

———. 1987. *Shamanism, Colonialism, and the Wild Man: A Study in Terror and Healing*. Chicago: University of Chicago Press.

———. 1993. *Mimesis and Alterity: A Particular History of the Senses*. New York: Routledge.

Taylor, Anne-Christine. 2007. "Sick of History: Contrasting Regimes of Historicity in the Upper Amazon." In *Time and Memory in Indigenous Amazonia: Anthropological Perspectives*, edited by Carlos Fausto and Michael Heckenberger, 133–68. Gainesville: University Press of Florida.

Titiev, Mischa. 1968. "Araucanian Shamanism." *Boletín del Museo Nacional de Historia Natural* 30: 299–213.

Werbner, Richard. 2015. *Divination Graps: African Encounters with the Almost Said*. Bloomington: Indiana University Press.

Wright, Robin M. 2013. *Mysteries of the Jaguar Shamans of the Northwest Amazon*. Lincoln: University of Nebraska Press.

7 Other Knowledges

TENSIONS AND NEGOTIATION BETWEEN RELIGION, KNOWLEDGES, AND SCHOOL IN A WIXÁRIKA COMMUNITY

Iritamei Francisco Benítez de la Cruz and Itxaso García Chapinal

The division between religion and knowledge-science is a characteristic of the Western knowledge system. However, in other epistemic systems, religious practices are frequently a common method to (re)produce and preserve knowledges. Therefore, the regular educational system implemented by national authorities, which has become representative of the Western knowledge system in rural areas of the Global South, often conflicts not only with local religion but also with local epistemic systems.

An example of this situation can be seen in Wixárika communities, an Indigenous group in western Mexico. This article aims to analyze the debate around public primary school in the Wixárika community of Miwaxieti, in the north of Jalisco. Due to the legacy of colonialism, as represented by the public primary school, tensions arise with the local religious and knowledge system, as well as controversies over the loss of local practices and knowledge, especially among younger generations. At the same time, the primary school has become an influential actor in community social life.

In order to have a broader understanding of the situation, it is necessary to analyze coloniality and its epistemological system. It is also important to introduce the history and evolution of Wixárika communities, as well as the public school system, to comprehend the present-day context of Miwaxieti, and the legal frame of education in Mexico. In addition, the opinion of different members of the community regarding communication and negotiation with the school system will be heard and examined.

The analysis of Miwaxieti is based on fieldwork. The two authors carried out two stays during which they interviewed different actors of the community, as well as lived with a local family and took part in everyday activities in and out of the primary school. Moreover, one of authors comes from a Wixárika community and has worked as a teacher for more than fifteen years. This facilitated the authors' access to more diverse sources of information and their integration into Miwaxieti community.

EPISTEMOLOGICAL DIVERSITY

Since the historical colonization of the Americas, a global pattern has been imposed based on the hierarchical distinction between supposed races. This pattern, also known as the modern colonial system, continues today, adapted to the current socioeconomic situation (Quijano and Wallerstein 1992, 550–51). Part of this imposition is colonial Western epistemology, the main characteristics of which are the centrality of European experiences; the aspirations of universality and objectivity; the use of imperial languages (Spanish, Portuguese, French, English, German, Italian); the written word; and the division between religion and knowledge-science (Mignolo 2009, 6; Garcés 2007, 226).

Despite the marginalization of other practices and knowledges, other epistemic systems have resisted. These resistances have (re)produced epistemologies different from Western science based on their previous knowledges, methods of organization, and experiences (Sousa Santos 2018, 2). The Wixárika epistemic system is an example of this resistance. It is important to emphasize that, in this system, division between religion and knowledge does not exist. Mythological stories explain natural phenomena and rationalize social behavior and economic activities. Geography and the preservation of traditions are not only proof of that cosmological past but also a way to revive them and connect the past to the present. New knowledge is generated by the experience of elderly people and their communication with gods through dreams, and the consumption of peyote, a cactus with hallucinogenic effects. In addition, religious festivities and practices are a way of transmitting knowledge to younger generations. Thus religion can be considered a central part of the epistemic system.

Given this situation it is necessary to identify other knowledges, values, and methods and promote dialogue among them (Sousa Santos 2014, 297). For this purpose the universality and objectivity of colonial epistemology should be questioned. However, the querying of occidental universality and acknowledging epistemic diversity do not mean cultural or epistemic relativism; they imply a more complex analysis of different worldviews and entanglements between them (Sousa Santos and Meneses 2014, 10).

HISTORY AND TERRITORY OF THE WIXÁRIKA COMMUNITY

The Wixárika community lives in the Sierra Wixárika, in the region of the Gran Nayar. The State of Mexico recognizes as Wixárika territory approximately 4.000 km² (Ramírez de la Cruz 2002, 73). Due to its natural resources, such as wood and minerals, this territory has been invaded by neighbor *ejidatarios*, or non-Indigenous common land holders, as well as by multinational corporations (Liffman 2012, 71).

However, the Wixárika communities consider their *kiekari*, or territory, an area of approximately 90.000 km² that reaches several states. The kiekari is defined by the main sacred centers: Xapawiyeme (Isla de los Alacranes, Jalisco) in the south, where Watari the goddess of water lives; Hauxamanaka (Cerro Gordo, Durango) in the north, home of the first sower Watakame; Haramara (San Blas, Nayarit) in the west, where the goddess of the corn Tatei Niwetsika lives; and Pariya Tekia (Cerro Quemado, Wirikuta, San Luis Potosí) in the east, home of the sun god Tau. From the five main Wixárika sacred places, only Teekata (Santa Catarina, Jalisco), where the fire god Tatewari lives, is in the region recognized as Wixárika by the State of Mexico, and it marks the center of their geography (Bernal Guzmán 2018, 86).

Wixárika territory has a significant religious and cultural meaning. Geography is part of the Wixárika cosmology, and landscape offers evidence of Wixárika people's past, like a "conceptual written document" (Liffman 2012, 104).[1] Pilgrimages to sacred places are processes to read, perform, and revive that history, while Wixárika people reclaim that territory as theirs, by using religious events as political tools (50, 116).

The large area of the kiekari has been interpreted as a sign of a nomadic or seminomadic past, and pilgrimages are part of that preserved past

(Iturrioz Leza 2004, 216). Within the framework of occidental knowledge, the origin of the Wixárika people is not clear, due to the lack of archaeological excavations and references in colonial documents. Historians believe that small chiefdoms with a common culture populated the Sierra Wixárika and the coast of the current State of Nayarit in the fifteenth century (Neurath 2002, 66).

Linguistic investigations show that Wixárika language comes from the Yutoaztecan family, one of the largest and most extended linguistic families in the Americas. However, the linguistic and cultural relation to Nahuatl is not so near (Iturrioz Leza 2004, 17). The closest member of their family language is Cora, spoken by the Cora people, who also are territorial neighbors (15).

The toponymy of the Wixárika territory shows a complex relationship between the Aztecan and the Wixárika cultures. The villages with Nahuatl names, like Ocotán, Colotlán, or Mezquitic, are only at the border of the territory where Wixárika people live. Other toponyms of Nahuatl origin in the region are "surnames" for Spanish names, such as San Andrés "Cohamiata" or San Sebastián "Teponahuastlán." These facts have been interpreted as a sign of a simultaneous arrival of Nahuatl and Spanish population to the area. The former settlements may have been part of a military defense ring that also had administrative and missionary functions, partly composed by Nahuatl workers. The latter establishments might have been founded as Indian villages, to gather the Indigenous population and impose on them administrative and religious changes (Iturrioz Leza 2004, 207).

The contact between Wixárika and Aztecan people before the conquest has not been clarified. Nowadays a Nahuatl dialect, Mexicanero, is spoken in the region. Some linguists have thus concluded that Nahuatl speakers lived in the region before the conquest; others contend that the Mexicanero people are a regional evolution of the Nahuatl population that arrived with the Spanish administration (Iturrioz Leza 2004, 209). Nevertheless, studies on this topic are not conclusive, and we can only talk about different hypotheses.

Despite the arrival of the first Spaniards in the decade of 1530 under the leadership of Nuño de Guzmán, the Sierra Wixárika was not conquered until the eighteenth century. After the first violent actions of the conquerors, the population fled to the mountains and maintained some degree of autonomy (Liffman 2012, 72). After the Mixton War (in the 1540s), in which the Wixárika and other Indigenous populations revolted against the colonial powers, a Cora kingdom was established (Neurath 2002, 79).

Taking advantage of their position between two opposed political entities, Wixáritari authorities developed an opportunistic policy and a changeable alliance system to preserve their autonomy (Neurath 2002, 74). In exchange for their sporadic support to control northern regions, the Wixáritari were granted a high level of independence regarding religion and land (N72). However, this situation did not prevent Indigenous uprisings against the colonial institutions, and the Sierra Wixárika was finally conquered in 1722 (74).

However, the Crown could not exercise total control over the territory and population. This allowed the Wixáritari to maintain a high level of independence from Spanish rule and control over the entrance to their territory. Hence they were able to preserve their religion and culture with little Catholic and occidental influence, but they could adopt new practices and tools, such as musical instruments and animal husbandry (Neurath 2002, 21). Thus, it must be said that the Wixáritari have preserved many cultural, social, and religious aspects of their identity due to the control over their territory and their resistance to the entrance of foreigners, which opposes the widespread idea that the Wixáritari have lived isolated from colonial and Mexican society.

Together with the military intervention, the Catholic Church was the most important representative of colonial authorities in the Sierra Wixárika. They aimed to evangelize Indigenous inhabitants and teach them Spanish through education (Tanck Estrada 1997, 39). Numerous missionary expeditions were organized and convents founded in villages, in order to gather the dispersed Indigenous population (Torres Contreras 2000, 203). However, the result was the creation of villages along the routes that went through the region, but never the conversion of the population (Neurath 2002, 57). The Franciscans did not leave the Sierra Wixárika after the first colonial times, but their presence was interrupted during different violent conflicts, such as the War of Independence (1810–21) or the Lozada rebellion (1853–73). Nowadays Franciscans have a boarding school in Teekata and maintain some convents, like in Tsikwaita.

CUSTOMS, RELIGION, AND TRADITIONAL EDUCATION

How the Wixárika people use the land is closely related to their religion and epistemic system. The social and religious calendar is organized around the cultivation of the *milpa*, a crop-growing system characterized by the production of maize, beans, and calabash. The entire community takes part in it. The main cultivated product is corn in five regional varieties. The fact that Wixáritari consider themselves "the guardians of the corn colors" shows the importance of this cereal in their culture (Anaya Corona and Guzmán Mejía 2007, 179).[2]

Wixárika temporality is organized around the agricultural cycle of corn. The period of the most work is between June and September, in the rainy season, from the preparation of the field to the gathering of the harvest. Each important moment is marked by a festivity, where gods and ancestors are honored (Durin and Rojas Cortés 2005, 156). During the dry season, pilgrimages and political activities, such as assemblies and the change of traditional authorities, take place (159).

In the Wixárika religious system, the rainy season is related to the darkness and night, which represent the period before the creation of the current world (Neurath, 2001, 505). Generally, female goddesses are related to this period, such as Tatei Uteanaka, the mother of corn; Takutsi, the main fertility goddess; or Ni'ariwame, who creates lightning and violent rains in summer (Saumade 2013, 49). On the contrary, the dry season is related to light and the sun, both elements of the current world. The divinities related to this period are usually masculine—for example, Tatutsi Maxakwaxi, the main deer god; Tatewari, the fire god; and Tayau, the sun god (Neurath 2002, 150).

The central role of corn is shown in Wixárika narratives. According to their oral tradition, the Wixárika people are descendants of the first sower, Watakame, and the five corn-women, the Niwetsika goddesses, who represent at the same time other important plants, such as beans and zucchini (Miranda 2013, 182). Despite the local variations, compiled narratives share key elements that demonstrate the consistency of the myth. In the dark period, Watakame was searching for food, since he had nothing to cultivate. Guided by some ants, he met Tatei Uteanaka, the mother of the Niwetsika corn-women, who gave him some corn grain. After that one of the Niwetsika women went with Watakame back to his home with the promise that she would not work. However, Watakame's mother did not agree with this decision and made her work. In some narratives the women had to cook the corn; in others they have to mill the grain. However, the consequence is always the same: her destruction because she is cooking or milling herself, as she herself represents the corn (71). The myth continues explaining the relation of Watakame with the other four Niwetsika goddesses, the mistakes they made to lose their corn condition, and the reasons why planting has become more laborious. This type of narrative is usually recounted in regular familiar gatherings around the fire. As we will see, the fire is an element regularly linked to knowledge.

Regarding the social role of cultivation, all family members actively take part in cultivation according to their age and gender—for example, women are excluded from the planting, due to the narrative above (Neurath 2002, 139). It is an important moment for knowledge transmission to younger generations, which not only involves cultivation methods but also religious and epistemic sources (Anaya Corona and Guzmán Mejía 2007, 175).

In addition, at the beginning and at the end of the cultivation, different ceremonies are carried out. These events are important social mechanisms to reaffirm ethnic identity of the Wixárika people, as well as to transmit and (re)produce their religious and epistemic system (Neurath 2001, 517). Among the festivities, *Tateí neixa* after the first harvest stands out. It is an initiation ritual for children, who are introduced together with the first grains to gods. The *mara'akame,* or shaman, teaches younger generations local contents so that they will be able to maintain their traditions.

In this festivity the first pilgrimage of divinities to Wirikuta is remembered and represented. Narratives explain that, in the creation of the world, gods and goddesses were born in the Pacific Ocean and guided by Tatutsi Maxakwaxi, the deer god, to Wirikuta, where the sun came out for the first time (Medina Miranda 2012, 330). The birth of the sun was the result of the self-sacrifice of a child who threw himself into the fire. By doing so he became Tayau, the father-sun god and the most important divinity in the Wixárika religious system (Neurath 2000, 73). During the journey many deities turned into rocks, peaks, caves, lakes, or rivers. These geographical features are evidence of the first pilgrimage, as well as signs to read in the landscape (65). In Wirikuta the deer sacrificed himself and became peyote for the first hunters and pilgrims. The peyote is also considered corn, a blue corn that has lost its original characteristic (Medina Miranda 2013, 168). This relation between the deer, the peyote, and the corn shows the complexity of Wixárika deities, who change their personalities and appearances depending on the context, and who represent multiple elements, like the Niwetsika goddesses (Neurath 2000, 169).

In reference to the peyote, this cactus with psychotropic effects is hunted by pilgrims in Wirikuta and brought to their home communities for ritual uses (see also Daschke in this volume). It is considered an ancestor with special wisdom that enables communication with deities; the group normally consumes it in rituals where abstinence, fasting, and prolonged singing are important elements for communication (Bonfiglioli and Gutierrez del Ángel 2012, 200–201). In the festivity of Hikuri Neixa, celebrated in May at the end of the dry season, all participants consume peyote in some parts of the ritual in different ways (dry or dispersed in water) and perform complex dances representing the arrival of rain (Neurath 2002, 259). These collective festivities are important mechanisms for the (re-)production and transmission of knowledge. Through songs, dances, and performances, mythological narratives as well as values are reinforced and transmitted to young generations, such as the importance of water or the relation between humans and other natural elements.

The mara'akame is a very important social actor in the Wixárika communities. He plays different social roles, from religious leader to adviser and healer. He completes a special long training, which makes him an expert in local knowledge. His tutelary god is Tatewari, the grandfather fire, who represents wisdom and old age. These two concepts are closely related in the Wixárika epistemology (Iturrioz Leza 2004, 165). He has the knowledge and power to communicate with gods through dreams, *jicaras* or small bowls made from the fruit of the squash, and the consumption of peyote. Due to his position as a cultural expert, he is partly in charge of children's education (Anaya Corona and Guzmán Mejía 2007, 137). Mara'akate (pl.) are usually connected at regional and national levels with other actors with the same or similar functions in Indigenous communities. They regularly participate in exchange and political meetings representing their community, and their participation in such events give them access to experiences, languages, and linguistic registers unusual for other members of the Wixárika communities.

It is important to mention that the relationship between gods and humans is considered equal to family relationships. This is shown in the names, such as the grandfather fire (Tatewari), the brother deer (Tamátsimáxakwaxí), or the mother earth (Yurienaka). The sharing of these relationships is what makes them Wixárika, a member of the family (Iturrioz Leza 2004, 167).

Besides corn cultivation everyday activities and interactions are also moments for teaching. Wixáritari children learn techniques in everyday interactions for resolving daily problems. Adult family members are responsible for transmitting information to younger generations, who assimilate it through repetition and an increase in their responsibilities in those activities (Anaya Corona and Guzmán Mejía 2007, 137).

The main characteristics of traditional education are orality and experience. Knowledge is acquired through songs, talks, and participation in activities. Furthermore, elderly people and parents oversee teaching. Elderly people are a cornerstone in this process, since they are considered the link between the past and the present; the continuity of the group depends on the transmission of their wisdom (Iturrioz Leza 2004, 169).

PUBLIC EDUCATION

The school has an important role in the expansion of the Western knowledge system, since it introduces new values, content, and sources of information. Even though the legal distinction of castes disappeared after the independence wars, ethnic and racial origin is still a factor for social categorization, which also influences the public education system (Staples 1997, 56). Consequently, in Mexico there are two subsystems under the Secretaría de Educación Pública (SEP, Ministry of Education): primary school, for non-Indigenous populations in rural and urban areas, and Educación Intercultural Bilingüe (EIB, Intercultural Bilingual Education), primary education in Indigenous communities.

The first public schools in the Sierra Wixárika were built in the 1960s. The Wixárika communities regained approximately four thousand hectares, while accepting the construction of primary schools in the head villages (Liffman 2012, 77). This educational effort of the authorities was again propelled in the 1980s, with the creation of the Departamento de Educación Indígena (Indigenous Education Department) in Jalisco (Durin and Rojas Cortés 2005, 167).

Important political changes were made in the 1990s related to Indigenous groups such as the recognition of multiculturality and multiethnicity in the Mexican constitution (Ramírez Castañeda 2006, 70). Further steps were taken in the same direction in the early 2000s, with the approval of the Ley General de Derechos Lingüísticos de los Pueblos Indígenas (Law of Linguistic Rights of Indigenous People, 2003). This law recognizes and aims to protect linguistic rights for individuals, as well as groups (Fernández Castro 2014, 9). Moreover, it affirms that every person has the right to communicate in his or her native tongue in the private or public sphere, as well as in the media (10). Regarding this last point, Universidad de Guadalajara (UdG, Guadalajara University) acquired a license to open a radio station in June 2017 whose programs are mostly in Wixárika (Pérez Márquez 2017). The radio started transmitting in June 2018 under the name of XHPBUG-FM. In addition, some books in Wixárika and Spanish have been published that are characterized by the merger of oral tradition and new forms of literature (Poffenberger 2007, 46), such as the 2007 book of Iritemai Gabriel Pacheco Salvador, *Los Dones del Wiexu* (Wiexu's talents).

The law of 2003 also refers to the obligation of educational authorities to guarantee access to bilingual and intercultural education, which should respect the dignity and identity of Indigenous people (Fernández Castro 2014, 10–11). Along with this law, the Educación Intercultural Bilingüe (EIB, Intercultural Bilingual Education) program was established. Authorities tried to implement an educational program adapted to the cultural and linguistic reality of Indigenous communities. Despite their efforts the result has been a curriculum with folkloric aspects that reinforce the exotic image of the Indigenous peoples in the dominant society (Dietz and Mateos Cortés 2012, 240).

Even though laws and discourse have changed, they have not been translated into reality. First, the IEB is only applied in primary school; thus, Hispanicization is still the main goal, since students need to master the Spanish language to continue with their schooling. Additionally, the school does not consider local knowledges, sources of information, teaching methods, or values, and the IBE is only applied in Indigenous communities. This lack of intercultural programs in non-Indigenous regions entails that ethnic groups must learn from the "national society" but have nothing to contribute to it in return.

CASE STUDY: MIWAXIETI AND ITS SCHOOL

Miwaxieti is a Wixárika community in the north of Jalisco that belongs to the head village of Tateikie (San André Coahmiata). The sources of information about its history, evolution, and changes drawn upon here are the interviews and informal conversations with its inhabitants. Miwaxieti was founded at the beginning of the twentieth century by a group of families that escaped from the violence of the different revolutionary groups. This fact explains why the community is especially hard to access: until 1996 it was only accessible on foot. The members of the elders' council report that the first important acts of the community were to obtain the baton and the stamp so that it could be considered a community.

Another important element in constituting a Wixárika community is the *tukipa*, or religious center. In addition to being a place for religious ceremonies, it is considered a site for learning and a source of information. Its structure and orientation reflect the image of the Wixárika universe, with a circular floor plan and beams pointing toward the main sacred places. These characteristics make the tukipa an important place for knowledge and identity formation, as a member of the elders' council explains: "We have a ceremonial center, it's from us, where we have our roots, our identity is there."[3] The references to "roots" shows the interesting relationship between the Wixárika people and nature, since they consider themselves relatives to natural elements, animals or plants, as shown by the names of the gods (see Wright and Frim in this volume). An approximately eighty-year-old woman adds that "we have here the house of gods [*tukipa*], you [talking to her grandson] should be there with your bodies and spirits, to be strengthened for life."[4] Therefore, apart from wisdom, the tukipa is also a source of physical and spiritual strength.

An event highlighted by all the inhabitants of Miwaxieti who were interviewed is the arrival of the primary public school, commonly known as "the school," in the 1980s. This event created a big debate in the community, since not all the *comuneros*, or family members with the right to take part in assemblies, agreed with its establishment. Some of them perceived the school as a threat, such as the old mara'akame: "If we hand our children over to the school, they will someday lose the culture. . . . That is why we don't want the school in Chalate [Miwaxieti]."[5] In this statement "the culture" refers to the Wixárika traditions and values. It is also important to note the anxiety in the utterance of "hand our children over to the school." It seems that even though children still live with their families, the school is an element of estrangement between them. Another argument against the school was the loss of workforce. Due to the socioeconomic system based on subsistence agriculture, the involvement of all family members in the cultivation process is necessary. Moreover, it is important to remember that sowing is also an important moment for local knowledge transmission.

On the other hand, other comuneros did not want their children to go to school far away from home. They argued that the school would be beneficial for the whole community, as a member of the elders' council involved in the process explained: "[Paraphrasing a conversation] from this moment on they will have their school, so that children are not lacking their studies, so that after studying they can support their community and save the people."[6] This statement shows that an improvement in the lives of students as well as in the lives of all members of the community was expected from the arrival of the school, which reflects the importance of group solidarity. They hoped that the school would provide the necessary tools or information for the protection of the community. However, the man of the elders' council did not explain what or who threatens the lives of the Miwaxieti.

SOURCES OF INFORMATION

Three decades after the opening of the primary school, Miwaxieti also has a preschool (ages three to five), a complete primary school (ages six to twelve) and a secondary school (ages twelve to fifteen). Some changes can be seen, such as the increase of the rate of students who finish school, and rates of bilingualism (Wixárika and Spanish). Some members of the community have also gone to university.

However, expectations for the school have not been fulfilled. The elder comunero who defended the school in the 1980s looked disappointed: "I haven't heard anybody saying, 'Don't worry, we are taking care of land ownership problems, we are solving the missing documents issue, we are watching over what is to come.'"[7] Despite learning Spanish younger generations have not applied their new knowledge to protect their community. The comunero adds: "Now at school these things [hunting, corn cultivation, offerings to ancestors] are not valued."[8] The lack of the school's interest in local knowledge and practices results, he says, in a loss of identity in younger generations.

Even former students criticized the curriculum of the school. A young mother in her twenties, with a son in primary school, affirmed that "it is important that the child learns all cultural [Wixáritari] bonds ... the school puts different ideas in their heads."[9] Another mother who attended until secondary school and has four children enrolled regretted that teachers explain "only what books say."[10] Both mothers agreed on the importance of learning local knowledge that is described as making offerings, embroidering, or weaving. The former added that "it is important for the kid to learn all the cultural bonds because he develops in it," by emphasizing the importance of local culture for personal development.[11]

The mara'akame makes a stronger statement against the school by assuring that "there is no one in charge of looking after children and teachers culturally, there is no cultural adviser. A traditional counselor is necessary, who knows our practices and traditions, who knows our history, identity, and cosmology."[12] This affirmation of a man with a key role in the traditional education shows the deficient connection between the two educational systems in Miwaxieti, as well as the lack of confidence in the school, which is considered a threat to their local history, knowledge system, religion, and identity. In this statement the dispute over authority can also be observed. Teachers, who belong to the Wixárika community in the primary school and are the school's authority figures, need, like children, the supervision of a "cultural adviser" or "traditional counselor"; from the point of view of the mara'akame, there is no person in the school who has mastered Wixárika epistemology. The lack of a proper formation for teachers is shared by other community members, such as a father in his forties with two children at the school who stated that "teachers aren't really prepared . . . their training is incomplete."[13] However, the mara'akame does not want to expel the school from the community, but to adapt it to their necessities, by creating the figure of a "traditional and cultural adviser."

Teachers partially share these interviewees' point of view. When the teacher of first and second grade in the primary school is asked about the curriculum, she asserts that local knowledge and values are being lost because the curriculum does not have any references to local concerns: "A lot of things are being lost because of that [lack of a program with local content]."[14] Her four coworkers agreed with her and added that books are tailored to an urban context, making it difficult to teach local knowledge. Through the analysis of textbooks, this statement is rapidly confirmed: Spanish textbooks are only addressed to native speakers, and history books do not mention cultures before the colonial times in the Sierra Wixárika nor explain social processes, such as the implantation of colonial institutions or social uprisings and their consequences. Instead they focus on actions of national heroes, such as Benito Juárez or Miguel Hidalgo. Furthermore, in subjects like "Jalisco, la entidad donde vivo" (Jalisco, the state where I live), which is centered on the history, geography, and culture of the State of Jalisco, and "Formación cívica y ética" (Civic and ethical education), which deals with social and political issues, the references to Indigenous populations are addressed from a non-Indigenous perspective or linked to the past—for example, the heritage of cultures before the colony. An example of the former can be found in the "Formación cívica y ética" book for sixth grade, where students are asked whether they know somebody who speaks an Indigenous language.

Despite being Wixáritari, teachers do not consider themselves qualified to transmit local knowledge and practices, as the first and second grade teacher recognizes: "Many times, even if I belong to this ethnic group, many times I don't know."[15] Books and teachers are not recognized as sources of information in the local epistemological system. Wixárika traditional education is based on the experiences and knowledges of elderly people and the mara'akame. This situation has created conflicts between teachers, parents, and the mara'akame, who strongly criticizes teachers: "[Paraphrasing a conversation with a teacher] you are Wixáritari people,

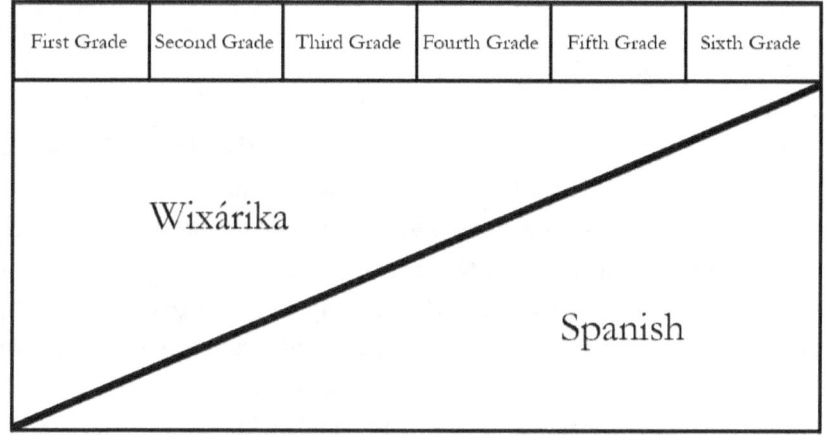

F16. Use of the Wixárika and Spanish language in the primary school as explained by the teachers in a meeting. Chart courtesy of the authors.

here you are in charge of the whole community, you come from abroad, . . . you have asked for our children, you must look after them."¹⁶ He adds that they do not appreciate Wixárika traditions and knowledges anymore, since they consider themselves *teiwarixi*, which literally means "neighbor," but is also the word to name the non-Indigenous population.

Therefore, teachers are identified as part of the problem, due to the lack of attention they pay to Wixárika epistemic content. They are also, to an extent, considered foreign (teachers "come from abroad"; they behave like "neighbors"), even if they are Wixáritari. This perception may have its origin in the lack of control over teachers' formation, which is controlled by Universidad Pedagógica Nacional (UPN, National Pedagogical University).

Languages in the school are a significant matter due to the importance of the native tongue among the Wixáritari for its role in maintaining the cohesion of the group and for transmitting knowledge, as one of the teachers explains: "We use the language [Wixárika] not to lose our identity because based on the language we transmit knowledges, values, everything."¹⁷ This perspective is shared not only by parents with children at school but also by the mara'akame. While Spanish is a useful tool to defend the community from Spanish-language institutions or foreign attacks as well as to participate in politics and social debates at the regional and national level, it is also considered a threat.

Teachers conduct lessons in Spanish and use the native language only to answer difficult questions. This practice of transitional bilingual education is more evident in the last grade, where Wixárika is barely used. Nevertheless, teachers argue that they use this method because children need to be fluent in Spanish by the end of the primary school, since in secondary school non-Indigenous teachers instruct completely in Spanish.

It must be emphasized that the fact of learning new languages is not questioned; rather, the problem originates from the value given to different languages by coloniality and the consequent subordination of the native speakers of nondominant languages. Spanish is also an important tool for political and social participation at the regional and national level, as well as for debate with other Indigenous communities about shared problems. However, this bilingualism (an Indigenous language plus Spanish) is not well valued and is considered dangerous for "national unity," which is represented by the imperial Spanish language (Dietz and Mateos Cortés 2012, 240).

TEMPORALITY AND NEW PERFORMANCES

Temporality is another determining element in the conflict. On the one hand, school is scheduled on the basis of the official calendar, which starts in August and finishes in June, with two vacations periods for Christmas and Easter. On the other hand, Wixárika social and religious life is organized around the agricultural cycle.

The significance of temporality is not only related to the overlapping of activities and obligations but also to different ways of socializing and bringing up children. This problem affects children as well as teachers, who, besides teaching hours, must attend meetings and training courses in different villages. During the rainy season it is estimated that 70 percent of the workforce is required for the cultivation of crops (Durin and Rojas Cortés 2005, 154); thus, all family members are necessary. Moreover, local knowledge is closely related to agricultural work, as children learn by participating in activities. If they are not part of them, their traditional education and local knowledge fall behind.

These overlapping commitments make children and teachers have to choose between attending school or fulfilling local activities. Due to the economic and social importance of cultivation, many parents prefer their children to work in the fields rather than attend school. Therefore, absenteeism rates in school increase during the rainy season.

Among all rituals related to corn cultivation, Tatei Neixa stands out due to its focus on children. It symbolizes the initiation of children under six years old in *el costumbre* (the custom), and they are introduced to gods through songs. The mara'akate sings the song that describes the first trip of gods to Wirikuta, accompanied by the rhythm of drums. The allegorical pilgrimage lasts all day and takes place outside the tukipa on an altar, with many symbolic objects especially built for the event. Through the song children learn the first journey of the gods to Wirikuta as well as the signs they left in the landscape. Therefore, this song registers a reading of the conceptual writing that geography is for the Wixáritari (see also the introduction to this volume). In order to assure the participation of all children, the event usually takes place on the weekend. On the one hand, this reflects how school alters religious festivities; on the other hand, it shows that there is also room for negotiation.

Other important variations in the community related to school are the introduction of new festivities, such as Children's Day (April 30) and Mother's Day (May 10). They are accepted in Miwaxieti as part of "school culture" and confirm the school's role in socialization. To celebrate Children's Day, teachers organize different activities for the children (e.g., playing football and board games), as well as for parents, who are invited to a special traditional lunch. After that the entire community gathers in the main square, and children together with parents and teachers play different games or little pieces of theater related to school.

At the same time, graduation from primary school has become a major event. However, this celebration does not share many characteristics with urban graduation parties. In Miwaxieti each year the sixth grade students ask a person—usually a man with standing in the community—to be their patron and take charge of organizing and paying for the festivity. The main points of the event are the sacrifice of an animal, which will be eaten later, and the giving of presents to the graduated children. The main ceremony takes place at the school, but decoration and performances are closely related to the symbols of the tukipa and to Wixárika cosmology. This celebration, which occurs during the rainy season, might be interpreted as a distinctly Indigenous acknowledgment of the school as a place to learn and a source of wisdom.

NEGOTIATION

Despite the tensions between the school and the Wixárika epistemic system, none of the members of Miwaxieti who were interviewed thought that the expulsion of the school was a solution. The school is considered useful because it is expected to compensate their well-known disadvantages in relation to the non-Indigenous society (Durin and Rojas Cortés 2005, 166). However, they want to adapt it to their necessities. In Miwaxieti the inhabitants, with their different perspectives and experiences, made some suggestions.

First, elderly members of the community underlined the importance of making offers to the gods in the tukipa and sacred places—a practice that, from their point of view, young generations have partly abandoned, as an eighty-year-old women affirmed: "Because of not offering, for not paying and making no offerings to gods, this has created [brought] them [parents] illnesses, because the Wixárika culture is to offer rituals to gods."[18] The mara'akame agreed with this statement but introduced a new practice: "It must be offered there at the school with the votive *jícaras* [traditional bowls] designed by mothers . . . so that there is more acquisition of wisdom."[19] Therefore, although school has been accepted as a place for learning and a source of information, it does not fulfill some requirements to ensure that the objective of acquiring new knowledge is actually accomplished. For that purpose it is necessary to adapt the school to the rituals and offerings of the Wixárika religious and epistemic system, where offerings play an important role in the transmission and (re)production of knowledge. In addition, the mara'akame defended the creation of a new figure for the school: a traditional counselor or cultural adviser. This person must have high competencies in Wixárika history and cosmology so that he or she makes sure that they are correctly preserved for better transmission.

For their part teachers proposed to include Wixárika knowledge in school materials. The fourth-grade teacher promoted the creation of books to learn to read in Wixárika, apart from the textbook. The first- and second-grade teacher suggested the creation of a new local school program: "A program in our language . . . our own program in accordance with the context, with characteristics from here, from the region."[20] For this purpose, she added, the implication of other social actors in the community is necessary: "First we must make inquiry, in each school, with parents, for example, what contents we should teach, they should tell us, support us on it, so that we have an integral education, with occidental knowledge and ours."[21]

These proposals might be interpreted as an act of empowerment and an attempt to appropriate the school, which, even though it is accepted, remains an external institution. The inclusion of local knowledge in school programs is an important step to reinforce them, which is essential to achieve a symmetric relation with other epistemic systems and to question the colonial hierarchy.

A successful example of appropriation of the school is the intercultural secondary school in Tsikwaita, another community under the head village of Taeikie. This school is supported by the Jesuits and their private university in Guadalajara (ITESO, Instituto Tecnológico y de Estudios Superiores de Occidente). The innovation of its program is that it is the result of assemblies and enquiries with the elders' council and parents (Liffman 2012, 192). The school curriculum includes subjects such as Human and Indigenous Rights and Wixárika History, where territory losses and similar educational projects in Mexico are analyzed (CGEIB 2007, 139). The school also has different workshops, where students learn carpentry or farming methods (141).

The community of Tsikwaita values very positively the intercultural secondary school, and the rate of dropping out has decreased (CGEIB 2007, 146). However, the introduction of local knowledge in the school curriculum decontextualizes practical knowledge (e.g., how to make a wood musical instrument) from Wixárika cosmology (e.g., the symbols of the instrument, its function). These types of activities usually tend to institutionalize and standardize cultural practices, which results in the loss of meaning and function. Additionally, it might be interpreted as a reinforcement of the colonial epistemic system, since its methods (school) seem to be the only way to give relevance to Wixárika knowledge, which has its own methods of transmission, including rituals, pilgrimages and participation in activities led by adults, elders, and mara'akate.

CONCLUSION

Findings from our fieldwork suggest that the division between religion and knowledge of the Western knowledge system does not apply to the Wixárika epistemology, where practices usually considered religious are sources of information, as well as methods for the transmission of local knowledge. Complex narratives, where gods transform and adapt different personalities, and explain and link environmental matters such as corn cultivation to social practices such as festivities. These subjects are transmitted to the younger generation in daily life as well as in significant religious events. This system, which is the result of experiences and adaptations to different circumstances of the Wixárika society, is in constant change, adding new contents and eliminating those that are not updated or useful anymore.

The Wixárika epistemic system and religion has been altered by the primary school—the main representative of Western knowledge in Miwaxieti. The school has been partly recognized as a place for knowledge, as the traditional tukipa and new festivities brought by the school are celebrated according to the Wixárika symbology and practices. Text modifications in traditional songs or stories are still not visible. Despite discrepancies between social actors and the authorities of the community and the school, there is a will in the Miwaxieti population to negotiate and adapt school to their necessities, without giving up their local knowledge and religion. Dialogue is enriched by the diversity of actors and perspectives contributing with solutions such as the mara'akame, teachers from the community who are trained in the Mexican Spanish language system, as well as elderly people. This negotiation process is a practical example of an intercultural dialogue between religious and knowledge systems that challenge the universality of Western epistemology, providing hope that Wixárika language, culture, and religion will persist.

NOTES

1. [The quotations in all of the endnotes for this chapter are the original in Spanish:] "Un escrito conceptual."
2. "Los guardianes de los colores del maíz."
3. "Tenemos un centro ceremonial, es de nosotros que nos enraizamos con eso, ahora nuestro identidad está ahí."
4. "Aquí tenemos la casa de dios [tukipa o centro ceremonial], ahí deben estar ustedes presenciando sus cuerpos, sus espíritus, a que sean fortalecidos para la vida."
5. "Si entregamos a nuestros hijos a la escuela, algún día esos niños van a perder la cultura ... por eso no queremos la escuela aquí cerca en Chalate."
6. "A partir de estos tiempos tendrán sus escuelas, que no les falte los estudios de los niños para que estudiados puedan apoyar a su comunidad y puedan salvar al pueblo."
7. "Nadie dice 'no se preocupen nosotros nos estamos encargándonos sobre las problemáticas de la tenencia de tierras, nosotros estamos arreglando los documentos que faltan, nosotros estamos vigilando lo que está por suceder.'"
8. "Ahora en la escuela como que ya no valoran todo eso."
9. "Es importante que el niño aprenda todos los lazos culturales [Wixáritari] ... la escuela les mete otras ideas [a los niños]."
10. "Nada más lo que dicen los libros."
11. "Es muy importante que el niño aprenda todo los lazos culturales porque en ella se desarolla."
12. "No hay quien se encargue a vigilar culturalmente a los niños y maestros, no hay un asesor cultural, hace falta un orientador tradicional ahí, que sepa los usos y tradiciones, que conozca nuestra historia, identidad y cosmovisión."
13. "Los maestros no están capacitados así realmente ... es una educación incompleta."
14. "Se están perdiendo muchas cosas a causa pues de eso."
15. "Muchas de las veces siendo yo, perteneciendo a esta etnia, muchas veces no sé."
16. "Ustedes son gente wixáritari, aquí se les ha encargado toda comunidad, vienen a trabajar desde afuera, ... nos han pedido nuestros hijos, ahora cuídenlo."
17. "El idioma lo utilizamos para que no se pierda nuestra identidad porque a base del idioma se transmite los conocimientos, los valores, todo."
18. "Por no ofrendar, por no pagar y ofrecer a los dioses les genera enfermedades porque la cultura Wixárika es ofrecer los ritos a los dioses."
19. "Se tiene que ofrendar ahí en la escuela con las jícaras votivas diseñadas por las madres de familia ... para que haya más adquisición de sabiduría."
20. "Un programa en nuestro idioma ... un programa propio pues de acuerdo al contexto, a las características pues de aquí de la zona."
21. "Primero debemos hacer una consulta, pues en cada escuela, con los padres de familia, por ejemplo, qué contenidos debemos de impartir, que ellos nos digan, nos apoyen en eso, pues para que tengamos una educación integral, pues, así como saber de lo occidental y lo de nosotros."

REFERENCES

Anaya Corona, María del Carmen and Rafael Guzmán Mejía. 2007. *Cultura de maíz-peyote-venado: sustentabilidad del pueblo wixárika*. Guadalajara: Universidad de Guadalajara.

Bernal Guzmán, Luis. G. 2018. "La cultura del peyote." *Horizonte Histórico-Revista Semestral De Los Estudiantes De La Licenciatura En Historia De La UAA* 15: 83–94.

Bonfiglioli, Carlo, and Arturo Gutiérrez del Ángel. 2012. "Peyote, enfermedad y regeneración de la vida entre huicholes y tarahumaras." *Cuicuilco* 19, no. 53 (January-April): 195–227.

Conde Flores, Silvia, and Laura Gabriela Conde Flores. 2016. *Formación cívica y ética: Sexto grado*. Mexico City: Secretaría de Educación Pública.

Coordinadora General de Educación Intercultural Bilingüe CGEIB. 2007. *Experiencias Innovadoras en Educación Intercultural*. Vol. 1. Mexico City: Secretaría de Educación Pública.

Dietz, Gunther, and Laura Selene Mateos Cortés. 2012. "Una década de educación intercultural: debates entre empoderamiento indígena y transversalización de la diversidad." In *¿A dónde chingados va México?: un análisis político y socio-económico de dos sexenios (2000–2012)*, edited by Salvador Martí i Puig, 229–49. Barcelona: Catarata.

Durin, Séverine, and Angélica Rojas Cortés. 2005. "El conflicto entre la escuela y la cultura huichola: traslape y negociación de tiempos." *Relaciones* 26, no. 101 (Winter): 148–90.

Fernández Castro, Luis. 2014. *Derechos Lingüísticos de los Pueblos Indígenas*. Mexico City: Comisión Nacional de los Derechos Humanos.

Garcés, Fernando. 2007. "Las políticas del conocimiento y la colonialidad lingüística y epistémica." In *El giro decolonial: reflexiones para una diversidad epistémica más allá del capitalismo global*, edited by Santiago Castro-Gómez and Ramón Grosfoguel, 217–42. Bogota: Siglo del Hombre Editores.

Iturrioz Leza, Jose Luis. 2004. *Lenguas y literaturas indígenas de Jalisco*. Guadalajara: Secretaría de Cultura.

Liffman, Paul M. 2012. *La territorialidad wixárika y el espacio nacional: reivindicación indígena en el occidente de México*. Zamora: Colegio de Michoacán.

Medina Miranda, Héctor M. 2012. "Desatando los caminos ancestrales. Notaciones con cuerdas y rutas de peregrinación huicholas." In *Hilando al norte: nudos, redes, vestidos, textiles*, edited by Arturo Gutiérrez, 321–39. San Luis Potosí: El Colegio de San Luis / El Colegio de la Frontera Norte.

———. 2013. "Las personalidades del maíz en la mitología wixárika o cómo las mazorcas de los ancestros se transformaron en peyotes." *Revista del Colegio de San Luis* 3, no. 5 (January-June): 164–83.

Mignolo, Walter D. 2009. "Epistemic Disobedience, Independent Thought and De-Colonial Freedom." *Theory, Culture & Society* 26, nos. 7-8: 1–23.

Neurath, Johannes. 2000. "El don de ver: El proceso de iniciación y sus implicaciones para la cosmovisión huichola." *Desacatos*, no. 5: 57–77.

———. 2001. "Lluvia en el desierto: el culto a los ancestros, los ritos agrícolas y la dinámica étnica de los huicholes tiapuritari." In *Cosmovisión, ritual e identidad de los pueblos indígenas de México*, edited by Felix Báez-Jorge and Broda, 485–526. Mexico City: Fondo de Cultura Económica.

———. 2002. *Las fiestas de la Casa Grande: procesos rituales, cosmovisión y estructura social en una comunidad huichola*. Mexico City.: CONALCUTA-INAH / Universidad de Guadalajara.

Pérez Márquez, Ramón Michelle. 2017. "Conquista histórica la concesión para operar Radio Wixárika." Tukari, accessed February 3, 2017. http://www.tukari.udg.mx/noticia/conquista-historica-la-concesion-para-operar-radio-wixarika.

Poffenberger, Abbey. 2007. "Iritemai Gabriel Pacheco Salvador: literatura huichol actual." *Graffylia: Revista de la Facultad de filosofía y Letras*, no. 7: 46–53.

Quijano, Anibal, and Wallerstein, Immanuel. 1992. "Americanity as a Concept, or the Americas in the Modern World-System." *International Social Science Journal* 134: 549–57.

Ramírez Castañeda, Elisa. 2006. *La educación indígena en México*. Mexico City: UNAM.

Ramírez de la Cruz, Xitakame Julio. 2002. "Nosotros los huicholes." In *Reflexiones sobre la identidad étnica*, edited by Jose Luis Iturrioz Leza, 71–78. Guadalajara: Universidad de Guadalajara.

Saumade, Fredéric. 2013. "Toro, venado, maíz, peyote. El cuadrante de la cultura wixarika." *Revista del Colegio de San Luis* 3, no. 5: 16–54.

Sousa Santos, Boaventura de. 2014. *Epistemologies of the South: Justice against epistemicide*. London: Paradigm.

———. 2018. *The End of the Cognitive Empire: The Coming of Age of Epistemologies of the South*. Durham NC: Duke University Press.

Sousa Santos, Boaventura de, and Maria Paula Meneses, eds. 2014. *Epistemologías del Sur (Perspectivas)*. Madrid: Ediciones Akal.

Staples, Anne. 1997. "Una falsa promesa: la educación indígena después de la independencia." In *Educación rural e indígena en Iberoamérica*, edited by Pilar Gonzalbo Aizpuru, 53–63. Mexico City: Colegio de México.

Tanck de Estrada, Dorothy. 1997. "Escuelas en los pueblos indios de la intendencia de México en 1808, según los reglamentos de los bienes de la comunidad." In *Educación rural e indígena en Iberoamérica*, edited by Pilar Gonzalbo Aizpuru, 39–52. Mexico City: Colegio de México.

Torres Contreras, José de Jesús. 2000. *El hostigamiento a "el costumbre" huichol: los procesos de hibridación social*. Guadalajara: Universidad de Guadalajara.

8 It's the Song That Cures

HEALING, MUSIC, AND AYAHUASCA IN
BRAZIL'S SANTO DAIME CHURCHES

Dereck Daschke

The first time I drank ayahuasca in Brazil, I experienced the deafening roar of the cosmic engine. This all-pervading din was generated by a single maraca played by my shamanic guide, an American musician and healer named Michael Bailot. This moment was a prelude to the many hours over the next five weeks that I would spend in a visionary state called *miração* that fed off of, and into, the liturgical music of the Church of Santo Daime. From my participant-observer position, I concluded that Santo Daime rituals were developed specifically to create this symbiotic relationship between the properties of the Amazonian tea and the music performed by the community—that is, the music shaped and colored the ayahuasca experience, and the ayahuasca enhanced and transformed the experience of the music. The result of my personal involvement with Santo Daime's central ritual, the *trabalho de cura* ("work of healing," often simply called a "work" or *trabalho*), was healing on psychological, social, and even spiritual levels.[1] Thus my own participation affirmed for me the paramount importance of the role of music in Santo Daime's central healing process, which Marcelo Mercante calls "the axis-mundi of the ritual and of the religious system itself" (2006, 209).[2] As my guide Michael once told me, "It's the song that cures."[3]

This chapter will present an overview of the role of music in the Santo Daime traditions and support a theory as to how and why their particular style of music can effect healing (see Wright in this volume). While my own experiences from 2015 in Central and Western Brazil allow me to convey some of the intangible and idiosyncratic qualities of the Santo Daime practitioner's experience, the foundations for the claims about the religion, its doctrines and practices, and its appeal to and effects on its members will be grounded in existing scholarship and ethnographies.

Santo Daime's strong ties to Amazonian shamanism and, in particular, the role of these specific songs or *hinos* (hymns) are key to understanding what healing means in this community. Santo Daime reflects specific processes common to shamanic healing—what anthropologist Michael Winkelman calls "*shamanistic* healing" (2010, 51, 55–56). In fact, Santo Daime has been identified as "collective shamanism" (Couto 1989, 221; MacRae 1992, 107–8) or a "shamanic collective trance" that is "responsible for individual healings" (Silva 1981; Mercante 2006, 333). The various aspects of healing that would traditionally be done by a shaman in a solitary role are functionally reproduced and enacted by an entire group.[4]

While there are many perspectives regarding shaman(ist)ic healing and how it functions, I will posit a very general model that identifies three essential aspects of the process:

1. Participants experience an *altered state of consciousness* (ASC)
2. Participants move through a *symbol-laden ritual process*
3. Participants are *received into a community*

To establish these three aspects in Santo Daime, I will start with the last part first, to delineate salient aspects of the history, structure, and meaning of the Santo Daime community. Second, I will describe critical elements of the ASC—namely, the particular qualities of ayahuasca and its effects on human consciousness. Finally, I will explore the ritual process, which here involves collective performance of music and song. Understanding the way music heals depends on fully understanding Daime and its effects, the nature of the Santo Daime community, and the particular ways that ritual interacts with both to effect personal transformation, collective bonding, and even bodily healing.

INCORPORATED INTO A COMMUNITY: SANTO DAIME CHURCHES

Santo Daime is a highly syncretic set of beliefs and practices, borrowing and combining four distinct religious traditions: Amazonian shamanism,

Portuguese Catholicism, Espiritismo (a Brazilian version of the European Spiritism developed by Allan Kardec), and Umbanda. Umbanda is itself a new Brazilian religion that unifies Espiritismo with various West African traditions brought to the country with the slave trade, especially Nigerian Yoruba, which provides Umbanda with the names of the orixás, its spirit pantheon (Hale 2009, x, 58). The official name of the church is Centro Eclético da Fluente Luz Universal Raimundo Irineu Serra (CEFLURIS), or the Church of the Universal Flowing Light.

A man of African slave descent, Raimundo Irineu Serra established the church in Acre, Brazil in the 1920s. A decade earlier, while working on a rubber plantation in Perú, Brazilian coworkers invited him to partake in ayahuasca ceremonies conducted by a local Indigenous community (MacRae 1992, 48–52). During one of these rituals he experienced a *miração* of Clara, the "Queen of the Forest," who also identified herself as the Virgin Mary. She offered herself as his "patroness, guide, and protector" and instructed him to "sing the first hymn of the doctrine presented to him at that moment" (Goldman 2010, xxii). From there Clara set him on his mission with the title "Chefe Imperio Juramidam" (Imperial Leader Juramidam), "identifying him with Inca spiritual entities, his predecessors in the use of ayahuasca" and reflecting his call to bring ayahuasca out of the forest and into the lives of contemporary Brazilians. For this reason he is revered as Mestre ("Master") Irineu (MacRae 2009, 53). "Mestre Irineu's mission is Juramidam's, a divine being that represents Christ, and reveals His doctrines and teachings, through hymns that correspond to the sacred Bible" (Fróes 1986, 25; in MacRae 2009, 53).

From the very inception of the Santo Daime church, then, the symbolic order of the religious system was the product of an ayahuasca experience and appeared as both a hino and the image of a spiritual entity that blended shamanic, spiritualized conceptions of the natural world with distinctively Christian images and concepts. Thus the song externalized a set of symbols and doctrines that laid the foundations for the Santo Daime church as a healing ministry. His successor, Padrinho ("Godfather") Sebastião de Moto, expanded the appeal and social reach of the church but fundamentally allowed it to develop within the same framework created by Mestre Irineu.

Today Santo Daime has a variety of churches established throughout Brazil. Many of these connect their lineage to the original communities of Mestre Irineu and Padrinho Sebastião; others are independent churches or offshoots of an alternative tradition, such as the Barquinha Santa Cruz (Beyer 2009, 290–91). These churches are heterodox to a degree; whereas they largely all operate under the same structures, rituals, and doctrines, a great deal of innovation and idiosyncrasies exists from church to church (Quinlan 2001, 135–36). I personally participated in works in the central state of Goiás, in the cities of Pirenópolis, Abadiânia, Goiânia, and Anápolis, as well as at Colônia 5000, founded by Padrinho Sebastião, and Centro Espírita Daniel Pereira de Matos of the Barquinha tradition, both in Rio Branco, Acre, the western state where Santo Daime was born. With the exception of Colônia 5000 on the outskirts of the city, my encounters with Santo Daime attested to a robust urban presence that attracted participants largely from the Brazilian professional class: lawyers, teachers, administrators, and the like. Even as an outsider, I encountered no identifiable barriers to participation, though this fact could partly be attributed to my association with Michael Bailot, who is a fairly well-known presence in the Daimista community.

Santo Daime doctrine envisions (sometimes quite literally) its community, known as Daimistas, as a strong family unit. Tellingly, this family is comprised not only of human fathers, mothers, sons, daughters, brothers, and sisters but also of the revered founders Irineu and Sebastião, and of divine beings, including Mary, Jesus, and various orixás.[5] It "also extend[s] to the elements of Nature and to spiritual beings of the forest and the rivers, as well as to the Sun, the Moon and the stars" (MacRae 1992, 54). Moreover, this communal spirit is recognized as a distinct, positive effect of ayahuasca (Winkelman 2014, 10). Santo Daime doctrine and the ayahuasca experience constantly reinforce a message of communal equality and spiritual democracy, making the group a safe and affirming environment in which to work through personal issues that emerge in course of the trabalho de cura (MacRae 1992, 78, 108). Significantly, each work I attended concluded with everyone calling out "Bom trabalho!" (Good work!), applauding, hugging, and then sitting down for a meal that breaks the fast required before ayahuasca use. Even as a novice, non-Brazilian, academic "outsider," I felt welcome throughout each ceremony; accepted, at least outwardly, as if I were a long-standing member of the group. Indeed, such is the communal effect of conducting difficult but rewarding "work" together with *meus irmãos*—"my brothers," as the Santo Daime community often refers to itself in the hinos.

ILLNESS AND HEALING IN SANTO DAIME

Alex Polyani de Alverga, who is at the same time a prominent elder in the Santo Daime church and a recognized scholar of it in his own right, explains throughout *The Religion of Ayahuasca* (2010, 13) that the fundamental goal of Santo Daime practice is to harmonize the experiences and realities of the external world, including spirit entities, with those of the inner worlds of mind and body. In Santo Daime health (*saúde*) is "a state of 'plentitude of life' in which a person is in harmony with life, vigor and all of the elements of nature" (Freire and Barsé 2000, 15; in Sulla 2005, 46). On the other hand, illnesses (*doença*), "considered to be a sign of transgression of the divine order, provide possibilities of atonement, and opportunities to regain spiritual equilibrium" (MacRae 1992, 55). Humans as a whole are regarded to be in a general state of malaise, imbalance, and disconnection from God.

In other words, "healing is a synonym of salvation, principally from drinking the 'Holy Light,' the Daime," because it purges blockages and opens up venues within one's mind, body, and soul to gain self-knowledge and spiritual revelation (Mercante 2006, 326–28). In fact, Daimistas understand this transformation to be the manifestation of "Christ Consciousness" in the individual. Mestre Irineu understood the Juramidã mission to be to "replant" the doctrine of Jesus Christ that had been removed from the Earth following his resurrection and assumption into heaven. Moreover, the Second Coming had already been fulfilled by Christ's incarnation in the *ayahuasca* vine itself (Beyer 2009, 290)—that is, Christ, understood by Christians to be the logos, the Living Word, had taken not a human form upon his return, but, rather, the form of a plant. Jesus Christ literally implanted his "Christ Consciousness" as a "conscious seed" in the vine and leaf that make the Daime. Thus, it is a "living matrix of consciousness" that conveys Christ's healing powers, for self and the world, through "the Doctrine," which, as discussed below, is conveyed in tandem by the Daime and the music of the hymns sung in the trabalho (Goldman 2010, xxiv). By consuming the plant in Daime, Daimistas literally take Christ into themselves, and his Christ Consciousness is incarnated in their *mirações* (the plural form of *miração*; Goldman 2010, xxiv; Larsen 2010, xiv). It is notable how clearly this concept of doctrine almost literally grafts traditional Christian belief onto the plant-based shamanism of the Amazon, with a nod to Spiritism in the concept of a manifesting supraconsciousness, synthesizing three major religious influences into one fundamental spiritual proposal.

This healing is meant to be a continuous process of self-transformation, even for those not overtly sick (Mercante 2006, 348). Daime, as Daimistas call the sacramental ayahuasca, effects healing and integration in all parts of the human being, but it works from the inside out, transforming the core of the person most immediately and curing the physical body at the end, "as it is the last one to get sick" (329). There may even be few or no visible results of the healing encounter, but Daimistas do not interpret this as a sign of failure. Rather, they recognize that the trabalhos bring about individual and collective well-being and transformation (MacRae 1992, 111–12). Even individual healing in Santo Daime affects the community and vice versa, in terms of relationships and reinforcement of "social and spiritual laws" (Groisman, 1999, 113; in Mercante 2006, 334). In short, this community conceives of health very much in psychological and spiritual ways, while recognizing the body and community as specific physical sites and symbolic contexts for sickness and recovery. Therefore, to integrate all of these different aspects of the person, this process of healing needs a different place, a spiritual space, in which to perform its work (35, 131). That space in Santo Daime is the miração.

AYAHUASCA AND THE MIRAÇÃO

McClenon (2001, 7–10) observes that effective healers "capture the imagination"—in other words, a key aspect of their performance as healers is to shock or surprise those who seek treatment. They will behave in a way that radically challenges ordinary expectations, sometimes even doing something that, to the rational mind, seems impossible. These performances induce a mental state akin to hypnosis or trance and render a person open to suggestion, which is provided in the form of cultural narratives, symbols, and signs (Rouget 1985, 285–91). Whereas "shamanic consciousness" can be induced in several different ways—drumming, breathing techniques, ecstatic dancing, or some combination thereof—many cultures incorporate one of the sacred "plant medicines," also known as hallucinogens, psychedelics, or entheogens (Winkelman 2010, 132–34). Ayahuasca is one of the most powerful of these sacred medicines, especially in its ability to invoke extraordinary visions in the drinker, very often of spirits, angels, figures from religious pantheons, Ascended Masters, and even space aliens (Beyer 2009, 252–66; Strassman 2001, 185–219).

The tradition of brewing and drinking the sacramental tea ayahuasca has played a central role in the shamanic work of the Amazonian peoples for centuries (Metzner 2005, 10–12). It is brewed from two components, the vine *Banisteriopsis caapi* and the leaf *Psychotria viridis*, more commonly called *jagube* and *chacruna* or *rainha* (queen), respectively. Simply put, in these ayahuasca shamanisms, the ingestion of the substance itself induces the ASC, which thoroughly captures the imaginations of its practitioners. Whereas other types of shamanism might necessitate a more ecstatic or theatrical display to draw a healer and his or her patients into the same altered reality, ayahuasca simply and quickly puts the drinker in a stable, if temporary, subjective space suitable for transformational inner work, lasting roughly three to four hours. Not only does ayahuasca make this space possible, it is also understood to fill that space with healing beings, images, and insights, provided in part by the culture of the people who conduct the ritual and in part by the person undergoing the experience (Mercante 2006, 36).

Daimistas call this state of mind the miração, "an inner perception combining insight and ecstasy" (Alverga 2010, 2). "The miração is the 'third vision,'" Alverga explains. "Its effect, deeply therapeutic and consciousness-expanding, is due to the abolition of conditioning and illusions that impede authentic spiritual insight" (56). The Daimista must interpret and understand the "spontaneous mental imagery" of the miração, linking this revelatory experience to the day-to-day aspects of one's own life. The miração integrates, aligns, and transforms the inner and outer worlds as well as the relationship between the mind and body. As Mercante (2006, 3) writes,

"The miração brings into consciousness the elements responsible for and capable of facilitating that integrative process."

The word we might use for a creative life process driven by spontaneous images is "imagination." Csordas (1996) notes the "efficacy" of imagination, in the sense that one cannot fail to imagine what one intends to imagine. The appearance of such images in our minds is instantaneous and effortless, and the contents of imagination are experienced as exactly what they appear to be. "As it turns out," he writes, "much to the enhancement of the performative force in ritual healing, *these are characteristics we expect of divine action.* . . . The imaginal world operates *empirically* as a convincingly efficacious spiritual world" (107; emphasis in original). In Santo Daime the spiritual world is not only overtly and constantly evoked in the culture, but, in the imaginal space created by the miração, it explicitly has a foothold inside one's own head. Therefore, the entities of that world could hardly be experienced as anything other than completely real, effective, and displaying the exact qualities the culture has led the participant to expect of them, including healing powers.

Yet spiritual images are not the only kind of ideation this type of healing ritual conjures. Personal memories constitute a great deal of the imaginal component of a ritual healing experience. Csordas states that "memory is a powerful symbol of the self," and so it follows that memories evoked in a healing process are indications where the self needs attention and repair (1996, 101, 105–11). Daime elicits both strong images and strong emotion in the miração, and inevitably among its most powerful contents are personal memories (Mercante 2006, 323–24). What happens with these memories in that space is highly unpredictable, but one very common effect is to allow the individual to engage with them in new and even relatively objective ways (Shanon 2014, 65). Within the ritual performance of Santo Daime, the interaction between the imagery of the wounded self, represented by memory, and the imagery of healing spirits, invoked by the surrounding culture, transforms one's battered self-image into a being blessed, loved, and healed by the spirits (Csordas 1996, 94).

The miração is the quintessence of Santo Daime as religious experience: it is the vehicle for revelation, the authenticator of doctrine, the originator of song, the medium for healing. It is also the means by which Mestre

Irineu received his call to build a new church around the sacrament of ayahuasca and thereby bring a new kind of perception, identified as Christ Consciousness, into the world.

THE SYMBOL-LADEN RITUAL PROCESS

The three key factors of shamanistic healing laid out at the beginning of this piece are all intimately and inextricably related to one another. Therefore, a healing ceremony requires a community of some sort, even if symbolic or implied, as in an invocation of spirits or ancestors. Of course, even this kind of symbolic community is constructed within a more tangible, earth-bound one and, in fact, expresses the latter's values and norms. Healing ceremonies, in a sense, are a moment when a society speaks its unspoken order out loud—loud enough to be heard and felt within the bodies of its members (Winkelman and Baker 2010, 225–26; Brody 1989, 153, 161–62).

While the key ritual is the *trabalho de cura*, there are a wide variety of works that aim to achieve certain outcomes, each with specific liturgies of prayers and songs (Mercante 2006, 211–58). Some of these are specifically healing works; others are quieter meditation works; some celebrate significant anniversaries and birthdays. Some works intentionally invite incorporation or mediumship of orixás, helpful spirits called *pretos velhos* (Afro-Brazilian slaves), or other entities. These entities are often individually identifiable by the Santo Daime community, even when incorporated within their *aparelho*, or "instrument" (i.e., the Daimista in whose body they are residing); they are named, have recognizable personalities, and appear regularly in ceremonies.

Given the doctrine of the church and its understanding of holistic wellness, even the works that are not "works of healing" are still, ultimately, healing works. In describing the therapeutic processes of healing rituals, Csordas (1996, 105) states that "revelatory images and imaginal performance are the experiential substance of the ritual relationship between healing and patient"—meaning that the images and activities that engage the recipient of the healing are, in fact, the reality that effects the cure. As ayahuasca invokes strong imagery and engages the imagination, both of these factors are essential to the healing work performed in ayahuasca rituals, as is the ceremony itself, symbolizing the community in toto. The images that manifest within the miração link the internal and external worlds (Mercante 2006, 360). As such they are the key materials in the process Winkelman (2010, 195-200) calls "psychointegration," which coordinates information across regions of the brain that are sealed off from one another in ordinary consciousness. Thus information from the body, emotions, memory, concepts of selfhood, and cultural identity are integrated in such a state.

It is crucial, then, to recognize that external, cultural symbols somehow *also* enter and exist within the body. Winkelman and Baker (2010, 225) call this phenomenon "symbolic penetration," which begins with a type of deep social conditioning called "entrainment":

> Entrainment occurs whenever we are exposed to a particular symbol at the same time that we are experiencing a specific physical and emotional state. Eventually, we can re-experience this state when we encounter the symbol.... The process by which an entire constellation of associated physiological and emotional responses comes to be evoked by a particular religious symbol is known as symbolic penetration. Symbolic penetration makes it possible for religious meanings to evoke a wide range of biological processes.

In this light it is instructive to recognize just how many of Santo Daime's symbols, ritual actions, and aspects of doctrine invoke something entering the human body and remaining there to do healing work—starting with, most obviously, the ingestion of the Daime (Alverga 2010, 24, 177). Once the cultural message of healing is embodied, it can then be transcribed into the language of specific bodily systems and effect a cure at the biological level, potentially even of the most resistant and aggressive types of diseases, such as cancer, as attested to by numerous Daimistas (Sulla 2005, 79-80).[6]

If an ASC is the vehicle by which cultural codes are rendered available for translation into other psychological and biological systems, the trabalho seems specifically cultivated to take advantage of the communication between culture and body in the forms of religious symbolism and music (Winkelman 2010, 134-35; 193-95). Notably, singing itself is produced from within the interior of the body, involving the diaphragm, lungs, vocal cords, sinuses, mouth, tongue, and lips. Even hearing music and song requires sound waves literally to enter the body—through the eardrum, to be sure, but the vibrations also register an effect on the organs and abdominal cavity (Stoller 1996, 178; Rouget 1985, 120). Quinlan (2001, 147) argues that in Santo Daime ceremonies, the hinos "translate" miração experience into a language more accessible to ordinary consciousness. Shanon (2014, 61) suggests that certain ayahuasca visions "could be regarded as music in the visual mode."[7]

Even the Santo Daime ritual for producing Daime, known as a *feitío*, involves a group of Daimistas removing the bark of the jagube vine while drinking ayahuasca, singing hinos, and swinging heavy mallets to a steady beat (MacRae 1992, 88–92). In other words, the feitío appears to physically infuse Daime at its creation with the church's sacred songs. Daimistas also understand that the public, outer work of transforming leaf and vine into Daime parallels the inner work of transformation and the development of spiritual gifts, qualities, and attributes and thereby "creates the force for healing" (Quinlan 2001, 146).

In the *hinos de cura* in particular, the musical element amplifies and solidifies this process and its effects, for music "brings about a transformation in the structure of consciousness, by effectuating a particular and exceptional type of relation of the self to the world" (Rouget 1985, 123). Rebel Araújo (2005, 137) refers to a moment when "the biographical unites itself with the collective through the hymns" (in Mercante 2006, 317). Music has its own ability, variously, to induce, sustain, and resolve ASCs (Rouget 1985, 316–20). In combination with ayahuasca, the capacity of music in a ritual setting to elicit emotion, alter consciousness, and transform the human experience of the world is powerful indeed. In the miração the symbols of the culture literally can take on a life of their own, in the mind and body.

Both in the hinos and in the religious environment surrounding the trabalho, numerous symbols are conspicuous to participants throughout the ceremony. These include the major symbols of Christianity, such as decorating the church space with images of Jesus and Mary (representing, as well, the king and queen of the cosmos and the male and female principles that are joined together in the Daime); angels and archangels, especially Michael; and depictions of the Umbandan orixás, who each represent their own set of qualities and values. The orixás are also doubly symbolized by the Catholic images of Jesus and saints; Jesus is a form of Oxolá, the creator of humankind and king of the orixás, and St. Sebastian, for example, signifies Oxóssi (Hale 2009, 113–19).

Several other symbols appear prominently: the six-pointed star, which symbolizes the joining of heaven and earth and the union of male and female divinity, is worn on official members' uniforms and is often the architectural shape of the ceremonial space. Similarly, the double-barred Caravaca cross "symbolizes the male and female principles of heaven and earth meeting in the place of androgyny: the heart" (Goldman 2010, xxv). Furthermore, the two crossbeams represent two distinct parts of the mission of Christ: the lower one, the ministry of his first incarnation, which was meant to call humanity to God by planting the seed of the divine through compassion, and the upper one, the Second Coming, "is the birth of that seed . . . in the hearts of all humanity" (xxv). The hummingbird, or *beija-flor*, is also frequently depicted in the ceremonial site, as it represents the "healing spirit" of Christ Consciousness, which manifests through the miração. The revered founders of Santo Daime, Mestre Irineu and Padrinho Sebastião, also take on symbolic significance in the religious ceremony, and they are present in photographs, artwork, and invoked by name in many hinos. Notably, Mestre Irineu and Padrinho Sebastião themselves composed many of the most adored hinos in their own miração states, so the hinários bear their names as authors before the hymns. Finally, Daime and its components, jagube and chacruna, are themselves among the most important symbols, representing the Doctrine conveyed by Christ Consciousness, the totality of the religious system in liquid form, and sometimes even the blood of Christ itself (Beyer 2009, 289; Alverga 2010, 135; Goldman 2010, xxiv).

THE HYMNS

The tradition of receiving healing revelations under the effects of ayahuasca and conveying this information through song relates directly to Santo Daime's shamanic heritage.[8] Shamans of the Amazonian regions of Perú, Bolivia, and Brazil receive songs known as *icaros*, from a Quechua word suggesting "to blow healing smoke" (MacRae 1992, 30). As Metzner (2005, 14) writes, "One significant element of virtually all shamanic curing ceremonies involving ayahuasca . . . is the shaman's singing, which is invariably considered essential to the success of the healing or divinatory process." Training shamans involves learning both the local plant pharmacopeia and the chants and songs that accompany their use (Winkelman, 2014, 7). The songs are taught to an apprentice while he is under the influence of the tea, but, in addition, the "spirits of the plants literally present themselves to the curandero and teach him healing and blessing songs, both the melody and the words" (Shoemaker 2014, 76). As such, "communication between the shaman and the plants is two-way" (Beyer 2009, 63).

Once learned the songs can be used to call the spirits for healing and protection and can even induce a trance in their own right, without the use of entheogens (MacRae 1992, 30–31). Like icaros, many hinos were revealed in mirações to Mestre Irineu, Padrinho Sebastião, and other significant figures of the church. Daimista communities collected them in liturgical hymnals (*hinários*) to be performed in ceremony, including the Hinário da Cura, "Hymnal of Healing," the liturgy for healing works. Many others are the product of the mirações of regular members of the church and may be collected in individual communities' hinários (MacRae 1992, 81). Simply put, at the core of Santo Daime is a dynamic relationship between the miração and the hino, both as lyric and music, which facilitates the health and well-being of the community and the individuals within it. While I will devote a considerable amount of space below to lyrics of hymns that make overt use of the major symbols of Santo Daime and expectations of healing itself, it is important to note that most hymns are much less obvious about facilitating the healing work through words per se. Therefore, I will take a moment here to discuss the effect of the hinos purely as music.

Few things are as effective in eliciting emotion as music (Rouget 1985, 123), and Santo Daime hinos evoke a wide range of emotions over the course of a service. Many are generally bright and upbeat, though some are slow and contemplative. Many suggest a particularly Portuguese emotion, well-attested in Brazil, known as *saudade*, a kind of wistful melancholy or national nostalgia that seems to capture something essential about the culture in much of its music (Garsd 2015). In my travels I witnessed a variety of musical accompaniment to the hinos. Acoustic guitars were by far the most common instrument; in the ceremony I attended in Rio Branco, the musicians played guitars exclusively (though at one informal gathering an accordion made an appearance). By contrast, in all the churches I attended in the state of Goiás, besides the guitar, congregants played maracas in a distinctive four-beat rhythm. Other instruments occasionally were employed, and the musical cadre at Céu de Sant'ana resembled an expansive jazz-rock band. Notably, all of these musicians also participate in the Daime ritual and so experience mirações as they play.

The musicians are among those seated at the *mesa branca* ("white table," a ceremonial altar reflecting Espiritismo influences), around which sit important members of the church, including the Padrinho or Madrinha ("Godfather" or "Godmother," church elder and leader), as well as key or lead vocalists. By far the most important instrument in Santo Daime is the human voice. I noted a significant difference in the way that congregants sang the hymns between churches in the two states I visited: in Goiás the singing was entirely collective, with all participants singing all parts of the hymns together, but in Acre many of the hymns were structured as a call-and-response between a solo vocalist, usually seated at the mesa branca, leading with a verse, and the rest of the participants responding in unison with a repetition of the verse or a chorus. It is understood that, as they perform the hymns, the members seated around the mesa branca generate *a corrente*, "the current" (sometimes called *a força*, "the force"), a type of mystical healing energy that flows from person to person with the music and brings the collective power of the Daime-infused community to bear on the participants (MacRae 1992, 101). Like the music, the current is comprised of the "spirit" of both the group as a whole and those who make it up individually—a kind of literalization of the expression "esprit de corps."

HYMN AS DOCTRINE

"Doctrine" has a specific meaning and unique nature in Santo Daime (MacRae 1992, 53–55). Quinlan (2001, 142) states, "Music and song is the life blood transmission of the teachings of the Santo Daime doctrine." Goldman (2010, xxiv–v) elaborates: "The Doctrine, which is the organizing principle of humanity's awakening, is seen within the Daime to possess an active intelligence of its own. . . . In one voice the whole community prays and praises God together musically." Moreover, several distinct aspects of these songs seem not only inherently designed to inculcate the doctrine in participants but also to condition visceral and psychological responses to the ideas and the symbols it contains. For example, Sulla (2005, 64) notes the line of one hino sung at healing works:

> "The sicknesses that appear/ Is discipline for those who work to deserve." Thus, it is generally seen that the symptoms of illness are experienced by a person so that he or she can see and understand the blockages and/or destructive patterns that he or she has, and the work that he or she needs to accomplish. At the same time, then, the song explains the meaning of the symptoms and the symptoms affirm the truth of the doctrine conveyed in the song.

The melodies, the doctrine as expressed in the lyrics, and the exceedingly repetitive structure of the hinos as a whole all work within the ASC of the *miração* to entrain the Santo Daime doctrine into each member of the church and to root the entire complex of its symbols in their bodies, priming them to be triggered in the rituals of the trabalho (Brody 1989, 163). The entire Santo Daime ceremony seems to be designed to elicit healing responses in its participants by invoking the central symbols of the community, all of which also come to signify healing itself through the promulgation of the doctrine.

While not every hino is explicitly about healing or divine instruction, a great many are, and undeniably the entire context of the trabalho focuses the individuals and the community on a healing intention during the ceremony. I will now introduce a small sample of these hymns that most clearly illustrate their active engagement with the Daimistas' well-being, instruction, healing, and transformation. The bar at the side of a verse indicates it is to be repeated, and choruses are repeated after each verse. Some songs and their reiterated verses and choruses are even repeated in their entirety once or twice, effectively reinforcing the ideas they express over and over again.

EU PEÇO CURA (LUCIANA)

Chorus:

> *Eu peço cura*
> *Eu peço cura*
> *Eu peço cura*
> *Pra mim e meus irmãos*
>
> *Reto pensar*
> *Reto agir*
> *É o ABC*
> *Pra na luz seguir*
>
> *Fácil é pecar*
> *Na tentação cair*
> *Difícil é*
> *Reto seguir*
>
> *Vamos nos transformer*
> *Sermos merecedores*
> *E nossas curas*
> *Podermos alcançar*
>> (Chorus repeated after each verse; repeat in entirety)

English translation:

> I ask for a cure
> I ask for a cure
> I ask for a cure
> For me and my brothers
>
> Think straight
> Act straight
> It's ABC
> In the light to follow
>
> It is easy to sin
> Into temptation to fall

It is difficult
To go straight

Let's transform ourselves
Being worthy
And our cures
We can reach

The repetitive structure entrains specific aspects of Santo Daime doctrine in this hymn. The title phrase, *Eu peço cura*, "I ask for a cure," is repeated three times as the first verse, which is also the chorus. The chorus is itself repeated after each verse, and then the whole song is repeated, which means that in this hino the congregants "ask for a cure" a total of *thirty* times. This request for healing is both personal and collective, as the chorus states it is for "for me and my brothers"—that is, the individual singer and the Daimista community (Mercante 2006, 37–38). The subsequent verses all provide moral instruction about acting and thinking correctly, so that the congregants will be worthy of transformation and healing.

DECLARAÇÃO (GOMES)

Chorus:
Ao Divino Pai eu pedi
E a Rainha para ordenar
Com Vosso Divino Poder
Para meu chefe me curar

Meu chefe veio me curar
Que a Rainha mandou
Com o poder do Pai Eterno
E as forças do Redentor

Eu recebi esta cura
Com muita satisfação
Me acho hoje curado
Junto com meus três irmãos

   (Chorus repeated after each verse; each verse repeated)

English translation:

> I asked the Divine Father
> And the Queen to order
> With Your Divine Power
> So that my Master heals me
> My Master came to cure me
> The Queen sent [him]
> With the power of the Eternal Father
> And the forces of the Redeemer
> I received this healing
> With much satisfaction
> I think today I am healed
> Along with my three brothers

This hymn introduces significant figures of the Santo Daime pantheon: God (Divine Father), Mary or Clara (the Queen [*rainha*]; also another word for the *chacruna* vine), Mestre Irineu (My Master), and Jesus (The Redeemer). It culminates with a declaration (*Declaração*) of healing received by the singer and the community (the three brothers). Again, the highly repetitive structure of this hymn conditions the singer to associate these symbolic figures with positive feelings, community, and, most importantly, an expectation of healing by participating in the Daime trabalho, facilitating the symbolic penetration of this complex of meaning, associations, and emotions. These divine symbols are effectively entrained not only by participants singing the song but also by hearing the song sung collectively by the Santo Daime community, receiving it simultaneously into mind and body, from within and without. This process can be similarly inferred from the structure and content of the hymns that follow below, as well. As noted, many hinos are sung about—and to—Daime itself, extolling its divine, healing, and instructive properties. For example:

O DAIME É NOSSO PAI (TETÉO)

Chorus
> *O Daime é o nosso pai*
> *É o nosso irmão e companheiro*

> *É ele é quem nos cura*
> *E nos livra de todo mal*
> *O Daime é o nosso irmão*
> *Não se escusando de tomar*
> *Dentro dele tem tudo*
> *Que o amigo procurar*
> *Vamos todos meus irmãos*
> *Trabalhar e se firmar*
> *Vamos crer em Jesus Cristo*
> *Nosso mestre ensinador*
>   (Chorus repeated after each verse; each verse repeated)

English translation:

> Daime is our father
> He is our brother and companion.
>
> It is he who heals us
> And delivers us from all evil
>
> Daime is our brother
> Do not refuse to take
>
> Inside it has everything
> Let the friend search
>
> Let's all my brothers
> Work and stand
>
> Let's believe in Jesus Christ
> Our master teacher

This hymn establishes critical symbolic relationships between the Daimista and the Daime. The repeated chorus states first that Daime is father, brother, and companion, representing it as both family and community, and then, critically, "it is he who heals us" and, like Christ, delivers the community from evil. The subsequent verses reinforce the doctrine of the chorus, implicitly tying "brother" Daime to the brothers of the community, and the teachings revealed by Daime to the teachings of Jesus Christ.

Other hinos adopt a central focus on the two founders of the church, Mestre Irineu and Padrinho Sebastião. Aside from the hinos and hinários revealed to and by these two men, many hymns articulate their significance in Daimistas' healing and educational processes. The hino "Cura" valorizes both: Irineu for giving Daime "to heal me of my sickness," with the phrase "to heal me" (*para me curar*) voiced four times prior to any repetitions of the verses, and Sebastião for commanding the community to "rise up."

CURA (BOAS)

(Chorus repeated after each verse; each verse repeated)

> *Mestre Irineu foi quem me deu*
> *Daime para me Curar*
>
> *Para me curar, para me curar*
> *Para me curar minhas doenças*
>
> *São Sebastião veio e ordenou*
> *Vamos todos levanter*
>
> *Vamos levantar, vamos levantar*
> *Vamos levantar nossos irmãos*

English translation:

> Mestre Irineu was the one who gave me
> Daime to heal me
>
> To heal me, to heal me
> To heal me of my sicknesses
>
> Saint Sebastião came and commanded
> All of us to rise up
>
> Let's rise up, let's rise up
> Let's rise up my brothers and sisters

CONCLUSION: HOW THE SONG CURES

Santo Daime doctrine affirms that its essential instruction and power manifests when it is consumed in the rituals of the trabalho. The hinos' lyrics reinforce healing, community, and the benevolence of the spirit world. The symbiotic manner in which the music enhances the Daime, and the Daime enhances the music, enacts and reflects the entrainment and penetration of the culture's symbols in these hymns and the ritual environment. The Daimista's subjective experience is continually responding to the song in imaginal, ideological, emotional, psychological, and bodily ways.

Returning to the three stages of shamanistic healing I introduced at the start of this chapter, it is clear that the Daime enters the body physiochemically and captures the Daimista's imagination in a miração, eliciting images, memories, and emotions in response to a new psychospiritual reality he or she has entered. Communal symbols of the ceremonies provide the Daimista's psyche both context and meaning. The music, esprit de corps, and effects of the ayahuasca all enhance the emotionality of the experience and deepen the ASC. The total psychic environment creates the conditions for psychointegration, resulting in a self transformed at its core, free of personal blockages and open to connections throughout the community, whether human, natural, or supernatural. The net effect is to be transformed, reintegrated, "made whole" inside and out, in mind, body, spirit, society, and planet. The perception of the outer world is brought in line with the expectations and requirements of the inner world, and vice versa.

It is the song that cures, indeed, because in Santo Daime the song is the entire spiritual system set to music, resonating in the psychic space of the miração and harmonizing the human body (where the miração originates by consuming the Daime and producing the song), the social body (where the rituals of consumption and performance are located), and cosmic body (as spiritual entities appear in the hymns and often the Daimista's mirações). The music is the bridge between the inner and outer worlds, and Daime is the key in which it is sung.

NOTES

1. As will be described below, Santo Daime has strong roots in another Brazilian spiritual tradition called Umbanda, in which, notes Gidal (2016, 143), "the word 'work' has additional meaning . . . as the healing work that spirits offer people. Spiritual work fulfills the obligation of charity (*cardidade*), the fundamental tenet and root ethic of Umbanda doctrine."
2. See Mercante (2006, 39–48) on the method of participant observation as it relates to studying Santo Daime communities.
3. The author gratefully acknowledges Michael Bailot's guidance through Santo Daime churches of Brazil and assistance in coming to understand the significance of the ayahuasca experience in these and other shamanic settings.
4. However, group shamanism is also attested to in premodern Amazonian culture (Andritzky 1989; in Winkelman 2014, 8).
5. Apparently Mestre Irineu originally tried to keep his new practices distinct from African diaspora traditions, such as Candomblé, which had taken hold in Brazil along the Northeast coast (McRae 1992, 86–87). The Barquinha tradition of Acre, which was founded outside of the direct Mestre Irineu-Padrinho Sebastião lineage, was perhaps the first to incorporate the Umbandan orixás and mediumship with *pretos velhos*, the spirits of African slaves (Beyer 2009, 290).
6. The specific mechanisms posited for such a translation between culture and body lie outside the scope of this study, but some that work in concert with the theoretical approaches laid out here are Greenfield (2008, 167–91); Beyer (2009, 148–57); and Winkelman (2010, 144–54). To an extent what is being posited here are the actual mechanisms of the placebo effect—what Brody (1989, 163) helpfully calls, instead, a "context effect" or "meaning response," and the ways in which the Santo Daime rituals, including the specific effects of the ingestion of ayahuasca, trigger this response.
7. Some of my own experiences illustrate exactly this thought. In one miração I witnessed a serpentine series of *jagube* vines wending their way across my field of (inner) vision, intersecting and forming a solid latticework of vegetation. They continued to grow and then sprout the leaves of the *chacruna*. Paying closer attention I understood that the rhythm of the maracas was producing the *jagube*, and that the melody of the hino being sung was producing the *chacruna*. This memorable example of synesthesia fixed in my mind the conviction that the music and the plant were inextricably bound together (see also Beyer 2009, 233–34).
8. Though, notably, Umbanda has its own traditions of spiritual healing through song that surely also contribute to the form and function of the work of music in Santo Daime. See Gidal (2016, 40–48).

REFERENCES

Alverga, Alex Polari de. 2010. *The Religion of Ayahuasca: The Teachings of the Church of Santo Daime*. Translated by Rosana Workman. Rochester VT: Park Street.

Andritzky, W. 1989. "Sociopsychotherapeutic Functions of Ayahuasca Healing in Amazonia." *Journal of Psychoactive Drugs* 21, no. 1 (January-March): 77-79.

Araújo, Maria Clara Rebel. 2005. "Santo Daime: Teoecologia e adaptação aos tempos modernos." Master's thesis, Universidade Estadual do Rio de Janeiro.

Beyer, Stephan B. 2009. *Singing to the Plants: A Guide to Mestizo Shamanism in the Upper Amazon*. Albuquerque: University of New Mexico Press.

Boas, Glauco Villas. "Cura." Accessed March 26, 2018. http://www.nossairmandade.com/hymn.php?hid=1641.

Brody, Howard. 2010. "Ritual, Medicine, and the Placebo Response." In *The Problem of Ritual Efficacy*, edited by William Sax, Johannes Quack, and Jan Weinhold, 151-67. New York: Oxford University Press.

Couto, F. L. R. 1989. "Sinais dos tempos: santos e xamãs." Master's thesis, Universidade de Brasilia.

Csordas, Thomas J. 1996. "Imaginal Performance and Memory in Ritual Healing." In *The Performance of Healing*, edited by Carol Laderman and Marina Roseman, 91-113. New York: Routledge.

Freire, M. A. C., and I. F. Barsé. 2000. *Florais da Amazônia: O renascimento da elementterapia*. Porto Alegre: Hercules.

Fróes, Vera. 1986. *História do povo Juramidam: A cultura do Santo Daime*. Manaus: Suframa.

Garsd, Jasmine. 2014. "Saudade: An Untranslatable, Undeniably Potent Word." NPR, February 28, 2014. https://www.npr.org/sections/altlatino/2014/02/28/282552613/saudade-an-untranslatable-undeniably-potent-word.

Gidal, Marc. 2016. *Spirit Song: Afro-Brazilian Religious Music and Boundaries*. New York: Oxford University Press.

Goldman, Jonathan. 2010. "Preface." In *The Religion of Ayahuasca: The Teachings of the Church of Santo Daime* by Alex Polari de Alverga, xx-xiii. Rochester VT: Park Street.

Gomes, Antônio. "Declaração." Accessed March 26, 2018. http://www.nossairmandade.com/hymn.php?hid=831.

Greenfield, Sidney M. 2008. *Spirits with Scalpels: The Culturalbiology of Religious Healing in Brazil*. Walnut Creek CA: Left Coast.

Groisman, Alberto. 1999. *Eu venho da floresta: Um estudo sobre o contexto simbólico do usodo Santo Daime*. Florianópolis: Editora da UFSC.

Hale, Lindsay. 2009. *Hearing the Mermaid's Song: The Umbanda Religion in Rio de Janeiro*. Albuquerque: University of New Mexico Press.

Larsen, Stephen. 2010. "Foreword." In *The Religion of Ayahuasca: The Teachings of the Church of Santo Daime* by Alex Polari de Alverga, ix-xix. Rochester VT: Park Street.

Luciana. n.d. "Eu Peço Cura." In *Trabalho de cura: Desenvolvimento mediúnico*. n.p.

MacRae, Edward. 1992. *Guided by the Moon: Shamanism and the Ritual Use of Ayahuasca in the Santo Daime Religion in Brazil*. Neip: International Group for Psychoactive Studies.

McClenon, James. 2001. *Wondrous Healing: Shamanism, Human Evolution, and the Origins of Religion*. DeKalb: Northern Illinois University Press.

Mercante, Marcelo S. 2006. "Images of Healing: Spontaneous Mental Imagery and Healing Process of the Barquinha, a Brazilian Ayahuasca Religious System." PhD diss., Saybrook Graduate School and Research Center.

Meta, Sebastião. n.d. *Hinário de Cura*. Accessed January 12, 2022. https://songfisher.org/book/cura.pdf.

Metzner, Ralph. 2005. "Introduction: Amazonian Vine of Visions." In *The Ayahuasca Experience: A Sourcebook on the Sacred Vine of Spirits* by Ralph Metzner, 1–39. Rochester VT: Park Street.

Quinlan, Maggi. 2001. "Healing from the Gods: Ayahuasca and the Curing of Disease States." PhD diss., California Institute of Integral Studies.

Rouget, Gilbert. 1985. *Music and Trance: A Theory of the Relations between Music and Possession*. Translated by Brunhilde Biebuyck and Gilbert Rouget. Chicago: University of Chicago Press.

Shanon, Benny. 2014. "Moments of Insight, Healing, and Transformation: A Cognitive Phenomenological Analysis." In *The Therapeutic Use of Ayahuasca*, edited by Beatriz Caiuby Labate and Clancy Cavnar, 59–75. Heidelberg: Springer.

Shoemaker, Alan. 2014. *Ayahuasca Medicine: The Shamanic World of Amazonian Sacred Plant Healing*. Rochester VT: Park Street.

Stoller, Paul. 1996. "Sounds and Things: Pulsations of Power in Songhay." In *The Performance of Healing*, edited by Carol Laderman and Marina Roseman, 165–84. New York: Routledge.

Strassman, Rick. 2001. *DMT: The Spirit Molecule*. Rochester VT: Park Street.

Sulla, P. Joseph, III. 2005. "The System of Healing Used in the Santo Daime Community Céu do Mapiá." Master's thesis, Saybrook Graduate School and Research Center.

Tetéo. "O Daime é Nosso Pai." Accessed March 26, 2018. http://www.nossairmandade.com/hymn.php?hid=1120.

Winkelman, Michael J. 2010. *Shamanism: A Biopsychosocial Paradigm of Consciousness and Healing*. 2nd ed. Santa Barbara CA: Praeger.

———. 2014. "Therapeutic Applications of Ayahuasca and Other Sacred Medicines." In *The Therapeutic Use of Ayahuasca*, edited by Beatriz Caiuby Labate and Clancy Cavnar, 1–21. Heidelberg: Springer.

Winkelman, Michael J., and Baker, John R. 2010. *Supernatural as Natural: A Biocultural Approach to Religion*. New York: Routledge.

9   Finding Orisha in New Places

Jeffery M. Gonzalez

This chapter offers a visual and narrative analysis of events, locations, ceremonies, and festivals of the Orisha religion in order to understand the adaptive strategies that West Africans and their descendants used to maintain their practices. The study examines multiple countries, creating a network for comparative analysis. This research project benefited from two visits to Nigeria in 2017. In early January I participated in the Obatala festival of Ile-Ife, and, in November I attended the Yemoja festival in the Molete subdivision of Ibadan. These research trips served as a basis for the comparative project that is reflected in this chapter. The research began as an analytical study focused on the development of sacred places in new locations but grew to include a photographic journal that charted the diversity of Orisha culture. These photographs indicate the agency of practitioners, the persistence of memory, and the strength of resistance necessary to continue their religious traditions. Spaces become sacred through the intervention of adherents who reimagine the divine in nature.

The chapter benefits from the previous work of scholars who studied the identification and development of profane and sacred spaces, the impact of transnational spaces, and the development of an African identity outside of continental Africa (see also Laughlin, Santos Rovira, and Benson in this volume). Moreover, this chapter identifies examples of numerous transformative processes within what I call the "Orisha diaspora."[1] I use the term to discuss and distinguish between the communities involved in

Orisha worship. Vincent (2006) develops a similar concept, coining the expression the "Orisha Atlantic" while juxtaposing it against the "Black Atlantic" developed by Thompson (1983) and Gilroy (1993). The term "Orisha diaspora" emphasizes distance from Africa and recognizes the adaptive process that religions undergo in new spaces and places. Additionally, it provides a space for dialogue for the integrative processes that occurred across the Caribbean and Latin America.

The terms "African slaves" ("enslaved people" elsewhere in this volume) and the "Orisha diaspora" highlight not only the human condition but also the presence of numerous Yoruba subgroups that helped maintain and develop Orisha worship across the Americas. The word "slaves" is laden with complexity, as many Africans purchased or were granted their freedom after they arrived on Caribbean islands.[2] It is impossible to talk about the Orisha diaspora without recognizing the continuous waves of transformation and dispersal that occurred during the transatlantic slave trade and into the present. In locations such as Brazil, Cuba, and Trinidad and Tobago, the first wave encompasses the period through the end of the transatlantic slave trade and the establishment of Orisha traditions by African slaves.[3] The second wave includes the dispersal of Lukumí practitioners after the Cuban Revolution of 1959 and the integration of African religious traditions within the American Black Nationalist movement by the early 1960s.[4] I posit that the third wave coincides with the expansion of the internet in the early 1990s and the ability to share information and establish global networks. While the exact dates and composition of these waves are open for discussion, the purpose of identifying these time bands is to frame the origins of Orisha expansion. In other words, the expansion of Orisha in the African diaspora is a process of waves circulating the relevant regions of the Americas. Not all countries in the diaspora had the same access to the expanding global network. Cuba was severally limited but was able to participate in this third wave with limited internet access due to the expanding religious tourism that brought secondhand access to global information.

However, this study does not discuss assimilation or acculturation among communities in the diaspora (see also Benson and Benítez de la Cruz; and García Chapinal in this volume). Neither does it focus on how syncretism served to address the challenges of survival, or seek to value one physical space of worship over another. Rather, this study looks at the actual practices, and the ways believers interact with nature and redefine the profane as sacred spaces, permanently or dynamically, to worship Orisha. Therefore, this study includes events across the globe, starting with the Yemọja festival in Ibadan, Nigeria, continuing through Cuba, Brazil, and Trinidad, and finalizing with events across the United States.

DEFINING THE SACRED: THEORY BUILDING

Defining, clarifying, and categorizing the religiosity of humanity dates back to the nineteenth century with the works of Tylor ([1871] 1958), Frazer ([1890] 1960), and Weber ([1885] 1993). However, it is the dichotomy of the sacred and the profane first proposed by Emile Durkheim ([1915] 2008, 37) in *The Elementary Forms of the Religious Life* that provides a foundational understanding: "This division of the world into two domains, the one containing all that is sacred, the other all that is profane, is the distinctive trait of religious thought; the beliefs, myths, dogmas and legends are either representations or systems of representations which express the nature of sacred things, the virtues and powers which are attributed to them, or their relations with each other and with profane things." These concepts continued to be developed by Eliade (1959) and serves as a foundation for the examination of sacred places in the Orisha diaspora. Pals (2006, 199) summarizes the dichotomy of sacred and profane proposed by Eliade, noting that "the profane is the realm of the everyday business—of things ordinary, random and largely unimportant. The sacred is just the opposite. It is the sphere of the supernatural, of things extraordinary, memorable, and momentous. While the profane is vanishing and fragile, full of shadows, the sacred is eternal, full of substance and reality."

The transformation suffered by African slaves upon their arrival in the diaspora was nothing short of dramatic and deadly. They were adjusting to the abhorrent conditions of slave labor on the farms and fields while trying to adjust to the trauma of cultural displacement. Life had changed for them, and, as human chattel, they needed to adapt or face death under the yoke of servitude. We can only imagine what the profane must have been like for those who survived the arduous conditions of enslavement.

The need to connect with the supernatural, extraordinary, and familiar must have been overwhelming.

Further analyzing the concept of sacred space, Jackson and Henrie (1983, 94) developed three categories to differentiate sacred from profane space. They write, "Sacred space is another category of space, defined as that portion of the earth's surface which is recognized by individuals or groups as worthy of devotion, loyalty or esteem." The three categories include mystico-religious, homeland, and historical space. I contend that sacred places in the Orisha diaspora carry more meaning that just a mystico-religious dimension. African slaves not only looked to recreate the mystical places of their homeland but also longed for and remembered profane spaces of towns, villages, and compounds. Their memory served to empower new places with familiar sacred meaning (see also Benson in this volume). The rivers dedicated to Ochún in the Lukumí tradition of Cuba both served to locate the divine in a new homeland as well as to remind them of the annual festivals and rituals they performed in their hometowns. The same is true for the relocation of numerous other Orishas across the diaspora. In her extensive research on the Yoruba in Trinidad during the 1970s, including interviews with many of the oldest surviving African descendants on the island, Warner Lewis (1994) documented several dirges and songs reflecting the feeling of separation and pain—songs that reinforce the duality of sacred places and yearning for homeland that permeates the selection of those places. Below is one song that reflects the imagery of flight, the idea of destination, and the yearning for an ancestral home (139):

Ògé, gbé me délé o	Plover (fast flying bird), carry me home
Ògé, gbé me dé	Plover carry me to my destination
O mò ràjò	(Just as) you go on a journey
O bà yúnlé o	(And) return home
Ogé gbè mi dé láàyè	Plover, carry me home alive
Ògé, gbé me délé o	Plover (fast flying bird), carry me home
Ògé, e gbé a dé	Plover, carry us to our destinations
Omo kò í ràjò	A child doesn't go on a journey
Kò baà délé o	Without reaching back home
Ogé o gbè mi dé	Plover, carry me safely to my haven

Studying the pilgrimage experiences of immigrants, Prorok (2003, 283) reflects that "the myths that tie specific supernatural entities to specific places at home may not be conducive to transplantation, and the collective conscious that produces a community of potential pilgrims may be so frayed by the migration experience that its original form cannot be recovered." If, as noted by Prorok, the transplantation of a mystico-religious place is difficult for migrants, the experience must have been exponentially more complex for Africans slaves across the diaspora. They suffered the separation of homeland and family, the afflictions of slavery, the difficulty of communication in a new language, and the imposition of European values, beliefs, religion, and customs. Moreover, the slave systems across the Caribbean and Latin America provided little opportunities for slaves to buy their freedom and return home.[5]

The nostalgia and pain of exile helped the African slaves find new ways of cultural resistance. They appropriated new spaces and redefined them as sacred places, giving them a location for a renewed sense of homeland (see also Benson in this volume). As Olupona (2011, 23) writes, "Sacred places occupy a significant category in the phenomenology of African religion because they are sites of origins and endings for individuals, peoples, customs, and traditions. They have metaphorical and ontological significance for both the individual and the collective." Yorubaland is a magical place where Orishas live among their communities. The landscape, peppered with shrines and sacred places, comes alive with festivals and annual rituals. The mountains, rivers, forests, lagoons, and mythical landmarks commemorate and validate daily life. The identity of towns, villages and compounds is interwoven with both historical and mythical stories of the Orishas.

As noted by Kunin (1998; quoted in Olupona 2011), "Dynamic sacred place is temporary and disassociated from physical space; it is 'fluid,' for any place can become contextually sacred." This was clearly the case when the first Orisha worshipers arrived in the diaspora. They no longer had access to the long historical and mystical places where the divine resided in Yorubaland; they needed the Orishas to be portable, to leave their affiliated homelands and find new abodes in the beachfronts, rivers, lakes, streams, and lagoons of their land of captivity. Along the way they developed new traditions and festivals, infusing the profane spaces of their captor's lands with familiar religious, social, and cultural beliefs.

THE BEAUTY OF PLACE: DIVERSITY IN YORUBALAND

Evening was quickly approaching as we made our way through the dirt roads toward the town of Idogo to visit the Yewa River and its associated shrine to the eponymous river deity Iyewa. It had been a long day traveling from Lagos, stopping in Ilaro, and finally reaching Idogo. This was my second fifteen-day trip to Nigeria, which focused on visiting numerous river shrines and participating in festivals dedicated to female Orishas. The area surrounding the shrine, cleared annually for the festival dedicated to the Orisha Yewa, was covered in brush and almost impossible to reach. The view of the sun setting on the river was stunning, and the local residents boarding canoes to return home added to the charm at the river's edge. While there were no rituals going on in the shrine area, the river is used for daily travel and fishing—a fitting example of how the sacred and the profane reside together in the mind of the Yoruba and their descendants of the Orisha diaspora.

The beauty of shrines, the diversity of locations, and the landscape identified as sacred were breathtaking. Photographs of sacred places in Yorubaland exemplify the diversity of locations and waterways used to identify and venerate Orisha. By no means do these photographs represent the totality of sacred places, but rather serve to highlight the types of places that exist in Yorubaland and the experiential memories African slaves had to reassess as they redefined the sacred in their new world.

F17. Yewa River, Idogo, Nigeria. Photo by author.

F18. Ogun River, Abeokuta, Nigeria. Photo by author.

F19. Olókun's Well, Ile-Ife. Photo by author.

F20. Sogidi River in Awe, Nigeria. Photo by author.

F21. Ogun Shrine, Ilaro, Nigeria. Photo by author.

F22. Arugba next to Ogunleki statue, Ibadan, Nigeria. Photo by author.

F23. Carrying offering to the Ogunpa River, Ibadan, Nigeria, 2017. Photo by author.

F24. Our Lady of the Regla, Regla, Cuba. Photo by author.

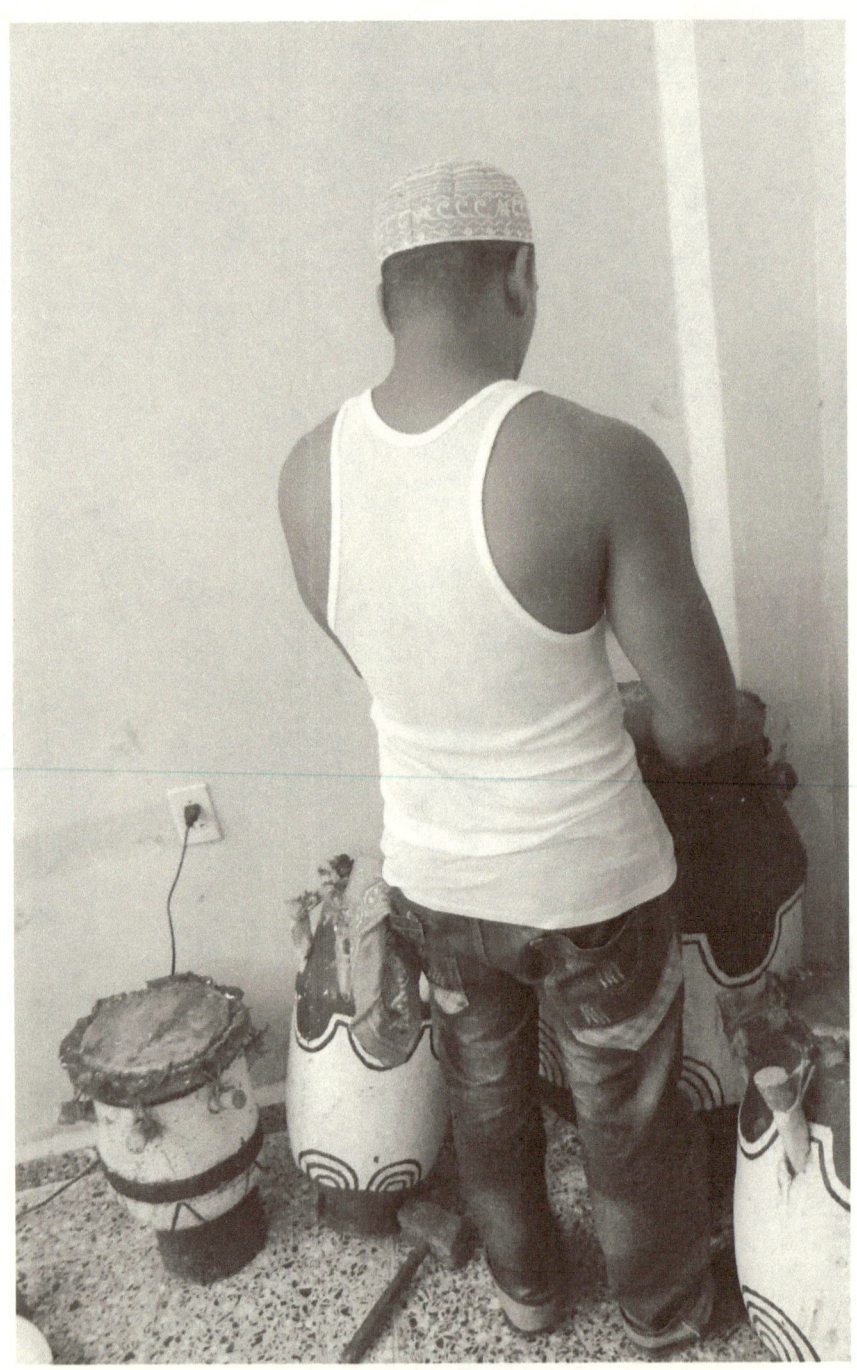

F25. Olókun drums, Matanzas, Cuba. Photo by author.

F26. Olókun offerings at the sea, Matanzas, Cuba. Photo by author.

F27. Festival in 1950. Photo provenance is uncertain, but photo may be part of the Marcel Gautherot and Maureen Bisilliat Collection. Instituto Moreira Salles, Rio de Janeiro.

F28. Bahia, 2012. Photo by Jan Sochor.

F29. Rio de Janeiro, 2019. Photo by Mídia Ninja. Courtesy Creative Commons.

F30. Worshipping at ocean, Miami, 2014. Photo by author.

F31. Drumming and singing at estuary of Oleta River State Park, 2017. Photo by author.

F32. Oloshas United, Miami, 2017. Photo by author.

F33. Cabrillo Beach, California, 2017. Oloshas United–Los Angeles, celebrating Oshun and Yemayá. Photo by Gloria Olegario.

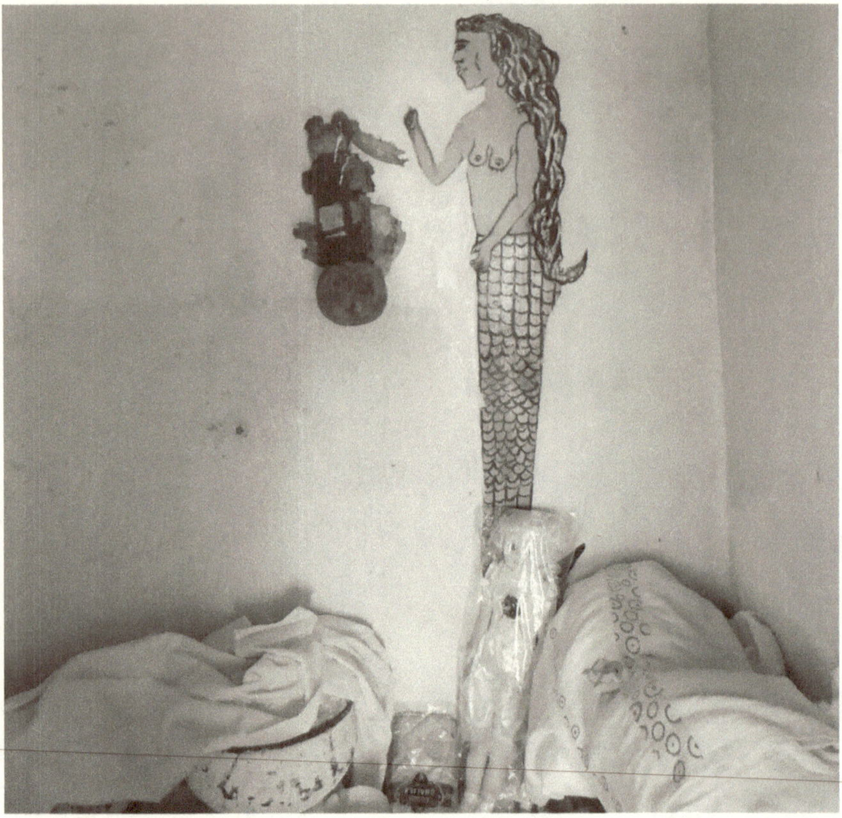

F34. Shrine of Yemọja, Ilaro, Nigeria. Photo by author.

F35. Casa Yemanja, Bahia, Brazil. Photo by Paul R. Burley. Wikimedia.

YEMỌJA FESTIVAL IN IBADAN

The Yemọja festival in Ibadan, which is hosted by Babalorisa Omikunmi Abiola Egbelade and lasts for seventeen days, is a communal festival that includes all the Orisha communities in Ibadan. Yemọja is known as the "mother of fish" whose home is with the Ogun River (Odò Ògùn). As with numerous female Orishas, she watches over women, childbirth, small children, and she contributes to the overall well-being of the community. Festivals dedicated to Yemọja are celebrated all over Yorubaland and in the Orisha diaspora. The last two days of the festival are the culminating ceremonies to Yemọja. In Ibadan they occur in the Ogunpa River in the Molete community. While the priests and priestesses of Ibadan acknowledge the Ogun River as the ancestral home of Yemọja, they are not able to travel the fifty miles to carry their offerings to it. Additionally, the Yemọja community in Ibadan has a long tradition of taking offerings to the Ogunpa River dating back to the nineteenth century.

On the evening of November 4, 2017, Babalorisa Omikunmi Abiola Egbelade, as the chief priest of the Yemọja shrine, led the first procession to the Ogunpa River, carrying part of the sacrificial offerings of a cleansing ritual. The faithful walk bear-footed along the road with their heads uncovered in a procession, chanting, singing, and playing drums. Believing it is a sign of respect and providing access to blessing from the earth and heavens. The energy was charged and dynamic, the mood sacred yet festive.

The next morning adherents carried offerings of animals, yams, *obi kola*, gin, and cloth to the Ogunpa River. The animals sacrificed to Yemọja, among other offerings, floated downstream as the faithful sang, chanted, and danced at the riverbank. Afterward the faithful returned to the shrine and prepared for the final procession of the Ogunleki carving, a symbolic representation of Yemọja carried by one of the oldest priestesses, the Arugba, who is always past childbearing age. The choice of Arugba varies among the numerous shrines in Yorubaland. In some cases, such as in Abeokuta, a young female initiate who has never had a boyfriend carries the sacred icons.

According to Solomon Omojie-mgbejume, the Amoja Yemọja of Ibadan, "Yemọja is known as Arugbo odo-ancient one of the river or old one of the river, so the Arugba must have passed childbearing age."[6] This perspective is different from other lineages where the Arugba must be a young girl who has not reached puberty. In both cases the Arugba must be a female who does not participate in the physical pleasures of the flesh; instead she must be dedicated to communing with the divine.

Solomon Omojie-mgbejume shared the following *oriki* (praise poetry) to Yemọja that speaks to her power and diversity as a water deity. While the references to the sea and the lagoon are allegorical in emphasizing Yemọja's expansive nature, the oriki hints at the diverse thinking about the nature of water and her power. Ayorinde (2004) notes that the characteristics and functions of the Orishas are adaptive and transferable in the Lukimi system of Cuba. Relying on the work of Barber (1990), Ayorinde believes that this adaptive process began in Yorubaland and continued in Cuba. Therefore, these adaptive ideas about water may have facilitated the association of Yemọja with the ocean in the Orisha diaspora. Solomon reported that Yemọja could be venerated in any body of water, as they are all interconnected.[7]

ORIKI YEMỌJA

Òkun rèé	This is the sea
ọsà rèé	This is the lagoon
Orò mi alé lódó bí òsùmàrè	The spirit of water is in the river like a rainbow

This concept survives in Cuba, where the renowned anthropologist Fernando Ortiz has described Yemayá as the "goddess of the streams and waterways" (1906, 34). Cabrera (1996, 20), whose fieldwork focused on the countryside outside of Havana in the 1940s and 1950s, calls Yemayá the Queen of the Universe because she is "the water, salt water or fresh, the ocean, the mother of everything that was created." In Trinidad, Houk (1995, 149) surveyed thirty-seven compounds and found fifteen stools dedicated to Emanje.[8] His research also revealed Emanje as a water goddess (187). Verger (1998, 293) opens his chapter on Yemọja with the statement that she is "the divinity of waters fresh and salty." Her association with all waterways is consistent across the Orisha diaspora, where all traditions acknowledge the interconnected nature of rivers and streams with the ocean.

LOST MY HOME

For the African slaves arriving on distant shores, the ancestral homes of the Orisha were lost in the long arduous journey to the Caribbean and the Americas. The Orisha traditions lost the physical locality of compound, town, and village critical to the established history and trajectory of sacred space. Additionally, the slave trade forced the cohabitation and mingling of numerous ethnic groups and subgroups. This occurred while the slaves were still in Lagos waiting to board the slave ships and continued into the cities and farmlands of the new world. As noted earlier, with the examples of the numerous river Orishas that exist in Yorubaland, the slaves needed to negotiate sacred ownership in their new lands. Was it possible to find a sacred place for Yemayá, Oyá, Ochún, Olosa, Yewa, Oba, and other river deities? How did the African slaves and their descendants retell and recreate mythical stories without access to the original sacred waters? There was urgency in finding each Orisha a home. This task, I contend, went hand in hand with their own desires to find a new place for themselves called "home." The Yoruba needed to reestablish both profane and sacred spaces. The Orisha and their sacred places had been part of their daily lives, and the African slaves desired to establish some type of order within the chaos of slavery. Survival meant they needed to make their world familiar; developing sacred places for the Orishas helped establish some familiarity. They needed to feel that the Orishas lived in their new world, to know that Ochún, Oyá, Yewa, and Yemayá had not abandoned them. Through stories, history, myths, and memories, the Orishas survived the journey and made themselves ready to permeate the rivers, streams and beaches of Cuba, Trinidad, and Brazil with their mythical and sacred powers. This was more than survival for the African slaves; it was resistance. Conferring sacredness to their new homes enabled agency, a unique way of refusing to integrate completely while remembering their homeland.

The land of the slave owners would never be the same as the slaves' homeland. However, they began the arduous task of reestablishing sacred places and developing religious relationships with the land. The African slaves created meaning throughout their landscape. They began to identify sacred places and to associate these locations with Orisha and the stories from their home. Yet the associations that occurred during this first wave were not uniform or identical, as numerous orishas shared similar characteristics and sacred places in Nigeria. Historians discuss the numerous wars that led up to the decimation of the Oyo Empire in 1830 as the primary reason for the significant presence of Oyo related subgroups in the Orisha diaspora. The influx of enslaved people from Oyo is clear in the universal presence and veneration of Sango worship across Cuba, Brazil and Trinidad. For example, Ile-Ife dominant Orishas such as Osara, Oranfe and Ijugbe are not present in the Orisha diaspora; however, Oyo deities—Sango, Oyá, Aganju, Yemoja, Oba, and Osun—predominate. Notably, not all Orishas needed new sacred places, or at least did not find themselves competing for sacred assignment in their new lands. Ogun, Orisha of iron and war, assimilated easily into the new landscape. The same occurred with Obatala, the Orisha charged with shaping human beings. The river deities seem to have received the greater redefinition in the diaspora.

In Trinidad both Ochún and Emanje are water goddesses. Warner-Lewis (1991) notes that Ochún is most often associated with the ocean. This may be due to the syncretic identification of Ochún with St. Philomena, whose image includes an anchor. Nonetheless, one of Warner-Lewis's (1991, 133) informants reported "Yemanja's habitation of 'the whirlpools and suckholes' at the confluence of the river and the sea and Ochún's domination of the free-flowing upper reaches of the river." Buhler (2006, 32) identifies Ochún as the Orishas of the rivers and lakes.

In Cuba Ochún became the owner of all rivers while Yemayá took authority over the ocean alongside the sea deity Olókun. To negotiate this dual ownership, the Lukumí of Cuba developed a story that relegated Olókun to the bottom, or depth, of the ocean, chained by Obatala because of Olókun's desire to control both land and sea. So terrible and powerful is Olókun that when Olorun (Sky Deity) separated himself from the earth and went to the highest heavens, and Olókun stayed on earth, Obatala had to chain him with seven chains, because in one moment of fury he could drown all of humanity and all animals (Cabrera 1996, 26).

The Lukumí developed myths that explained and rationalized their experiences across the ocean and in the land of their captives. The story about Olókun serves as an example of how the Lukumí reconstructed the memory of the long, arduous, and deadly voyage into a myth about the ocean. Olókun came to represent the most terrible and powerful force of nature: the final resting place of tens of thousands of African slaves, who died during the journey and were thrown overboard. Another Orisha was needed to mediate this deadly power while sharing the good that was associated with the ocean. Yemayá, the universal mother, became that mediator between Olókun and the inhabitants of the land. The strength of the ocean reimagined in the soft, flowing waves became an indicator of Yemayá's benevolence.

A similar transformation occurred among Orisha worshippers in Brazil where they conferred ownership of the ocean to Yemayá. As noted by Pares (2013, 228), "The male orixa Olokum, the Nago sea god in the Ijebu, Awori and Egbado area, like his Jeje counterparts, lost his standing in Bahia to the female Iemanjá, the goddess of the Ogun River, originally worshipped by the Egba of Abeokuta." Johnson (2002, 113) also discusses the role of Oxum as the freshwater goddess and Yemanjá the mother of fish and goddess of the sea.

CUBA AND BRAZIL

The traditions discussed in this section are examples of celebrations established by African slaves and their early descendants. These celebrations highlight the transformative and adaptive process African slaves used with agency to maintain their culture and veneration of Orisha.

Cuba

In Cuba the Lukumí found the religious festivals of the Catholic saints as an ideal disguise to continue—albeit in a different format—the festivals from Yorubaland. The annual procession in the Havana neighborhood of Regla on September 7 for the Catholic Marian image La Caridad Del Cobre (Our Lady of Charity) associated with Ochún, and La Virgen de Regla (Our Lady of the Rule) associated with Yemayá became the perfect vehicles. These traditions date back to the turn of the twentieth century, when Pepa Herrera (Eshu Bi) and Susana Cantero (Omi Toke) each led processions dedicated to Yemayá.[9] After offering Obi Agbon (coconut) to Yemayá on the shores of the harbor in front of the church dedicated to La Virgen de

Regla, they would proceed to visit the homes of the oldest priests and priestesses in a procession through the town. The religious descendants of these pioneering priestesses tell how the Catholic statues were prepared for the procession through ritual baths of herbs. The Lukumí icons would ride along, under the flowing capes of Catholic statues that are reminiscent of Yoruba processions. The Cuban processions continued through the early years of the revolution and then stopped due to the religious oppression of the communist regime. Recently, Juan Dionisio Lozano of the Museo Municipal de Regla rescued the tradition and reinitiated the annual processions in September 2015 to include chanting to the Orishas and the playing of bata drums. While Lukumí practitioners no longer make wooden icons to carry on their heads, they continue the festivals with processions through the town.

The festivals dedicated to water deities were not limited to the city of Havana but took place across the island. In Pedro Betancourt African slaves and their descendants would visit a local waterspout to honor Yemayá as part of a series of offerings before the annual harvest.[10] In 2015 the descendants revitalized the annual festival, albeit in a shorter form, visiting the waterspout to honor Yemayá.

In the city of Matanzas, the annual festival for Olókun, the deity of the ocean, is celebrated on the feast day of Our Lady of the Rule, when Yemayá is also celebrated.[11] The annual festival was dormant for many years due to the restrictions placed by the Cuban government, the death of many Orisha-serving elders, and the harsh economic conditions on the island. In September 2014, the descendants of the Cabildo Ewado revived the traditional ceremonies leading to a procession (today, by car) to the water's edge for the delivery of offerings and the closing prayers and chants to Yemayá and Olókun along the Bay of Matanzas.[12] When I attended this annual event in 2016, the house was standing room only, with representatives from all the cult houses of Matanzas, as well as practitioners from other parts of the island and a large group of international visitors, many of them practitioners from the United States. The atmosphere was ecstatic as the Orishas manifested themselves through their *hijos* (children) or mounts.[13] Elegba, the Orisha that owns the pathways and divine messenger of Olodumare, was the first to join the festivals; he danced, talked to the faithful, and provided divine advice as the ceremonies continued. Once the Olókun drums started to play, the sounds transformed the profane and mundane into the rhythm and motion of sacred time and place. The Olókun drums are not allowed to leave the Cabildo on Salamanca Street, for it is believed that bad luck will befall those who attempt to play the drums outside of historical home. For the procession to the ocean, the Lukumí batá drums are played as the faithful sing and carry offerings to the ocean. There are no religious restrictions as to where the batá drums may play.

Brazil

The grandest festival in the Orisha diaspora occurs on February 2, feast day of Our Lady of Navigators, on the beaches of Bahia, Brazil dedicated to Iemanjá (Yemoja) (see Daschke in this volume). Verger (2018, 198) identifies the festival with the feast day of Our Lady of Candlemas that is also celebrated on February 2. Thousands upon thousands of faithful and tourists line the streets, fill the beach, and travel out by boat to the ocean. The faithful, dressed in blue and white, bring flowers, sweets, food, perfume, and even mirrors to share with Iemanjá. It is the largest festival for Iemanjá in Brazil and in the Orisha diaspora. The sea has become the Lady's new home. The faithful flock to share in the mystical power of that sacred place for a moment, a day, and a lifetime. The African slaves may have seen more than a sacred place in the seawaters of Iemanjá; they may have seen revival, renewal, and the everlasting hope of return. The expression "All rivers lead to the ocean and all waterways are interconnected" is common among Orisha practitioners. It exemplifies the necessity of connectedness of nature in order to survive far from home. The exact year the Iemanjá festival started in Bahia seems to be unknown; however, public Orisha events did not occur until after the abolition of slavery in 1888. It is believed that practitioners celebrated these festivals within the *terrerio* prior to the early twentieth century. Both Carneiro (1936) and Rodriques (1935) document festivals that were held at the turn of the century at the lake of the Tororo Dam, where the Lucaia River originates. By the late 1910s and early 1920s, Candomblé practitioners seemed to have transitioned to the ocean for the annual festivals.[14]

While Bahia hosts the largest celebration for Iemanjá in Brazil, Rio de Janiero also hosts an annual event at the end of December where the faithful flock to the ocean, bringing offerings to Iemanjá in thanksgiving and petitioning for the New Year. The offerings at both festivals are similar: flowers, perfume, fruit, mirrors, boats, and combs.

Also present at both festivals is the now common image of Iemanjá as a white, sometimes tan, goddess or mermaid dressed in blue with long black hair emerging from the ocean. The statues are carried to the ocean in baskets filled with offerings, which are placed in small altars on the beach and fill the shrine to Iemanjá in Bahia. Verger's (1998) early research noted Iemanjá's Latinized form as a white mermaid with long, free-flowing hair.

CONTINUING THE ADAPTIVE PROCESS

The process of adapting and re-creating sacred spaces is ongoing across the Orisha diaspora (see Santos Rovira in this volume). Upon closer examination the traditions in Nigeria, Cuba, Brazil, and Trinidad are all undergoing dynamic changes due to the growing interest in Orisha worship across the globe. Another way of looking at this expansion is through the economic development of a worldwide Orisha marketplace in which new adherents can shop for a tradition that works best for their economic, social, and cultural realities.

The concept of "new places" is relevant due to the significant expansion of the Orisha diaspora outside of the original communities that developed a local structure of worship that maintained similar religious boundaries. This includes the Lukumí tradition in Cuba, the Candomblé tradition in Brazil, and the Orisha tradition (also known as Shango) in Trinidad. One example of this expansion is the growth of Lukumí practitioners outside of Cuba due to the exodus caused by the 1959 communist revolution. As the African slaves did before them, Cubans leaving the island brought with them their devotion to the Orishas. They again needed to identify new sacred spaces for worship.

UNITED STATES

Two of the earliest annual events dedicated to Yemayá started in New York City in 1988 and Chicago in 1990. Yvette Thomas Agongoloju, the leader of Ile Osikan, started the Chicago event at Lake Michigan as an annual homage to Yemayá. According to Agongoloju the first event was quite small, with a few godchildren and friends attending.[15] In 2005 the event was opened to other Iles in the Chicago area and developed into a community event. The establishment of the Oloshas United chapter in Chicago further solidified the community impact of this event. Lake Michigan became the ancestor home of Yemayá for Ile Osikan. The faithful of Ile Osikan include multiple ethnic groups but predominantly African Americans. While they are Lukumí practitioners, they are aware that Yemayá's ancestral home is the Ogun River. Nonetheless, the closest and largest body of water is Lake Michigan, dynamically transformed into a sacred place for Yemayá annually.

In the early 1980s Obatala possessed Tony Renaulds (adelola) at a drumming ceremony in New York City and requested that the children of each Orisha come together and establish an Egbe or community.[16] The goal of the Egbes was to bring together Olorishas (those who are fully initiated to an Orisha) from different households to honor the same Orishas and to nurture a larger community. Honoring the request of Obatala, the omo's (children) of Yemoja came together and established Egbe Omo Yemoja. In 1988 the first festival for Yemoja took place at Rockway Beach. During my conversation with the current leaders of the Egbe, I asked why they visited Yemoja at the ocean instead of the river. While they acknowledged the ancestral home of Yemoja as the Ogun River, and that they had participated in the festivals for Yemoja in Ibadan in 1990, they identify as Lukumí practitioners who honored the tradition of visiting Yemoja at the ocean. In 1990, through the intervention of Lloyd Weaver (a priest of Obatala) who was living in Nigeria, the Egbe Omo Yemoja funded the replacement of the Ogunleki statue for the Yemoja community of Ibadan.[17] As a surprise gift, the community in Ibadan commissioned an additional Ogunleki statue for the Egbe in New York that became part of the Odu Yemoja in 1991. One of the goals of the Egbe has been to educate the community that taking care of the ocean honors Yemoja. In a desire to honor her, the faithful brought numerous offerings to the beach. The sheer volume of the offerings and the various gifts created a trash problem on the beach and a pollution problem for the waterfront. To keep the beach clean and adhere to city guidelines, offerings to the ocean were restricted and adherents were encouraged to visit the Yemoja shrine and leave offerings to the Ogunleki image instead.

EVENTS HOSTED BY OLOSHAS UNITED

In 2013 a group of Oloshas was sitting in the Diaspora Cultural Center in Miami, Florida, discussing the current state of Lukumí Orisha practices across the globe.[18] The conversation turned nostalgic when talking about the grand processions that occurred in Cuba before the communist revolution and how historically unifying these events had been. These conversations sparked the development of Oloshas United in Miami. The original members, all olorishas of the Lukumí tradition, include Miguel Ramos, Jackie Ben, Raul Pielago, Eramo Acosta, Glen Corredeira, and Rita Guerra. I was also present at these early meetings. The idea of uniting the diverse Orisha traditions and practitioners across the globe evolved into an inclusive mission statement: "Oloshas United, promoting solidarity, tradition, and service for the preservation of our global Orisha community."[19] Ramos explained, "We seek unification and respect for a religion that has increasingly made its presence known in many areas of the world and continues to gain adepts."[20] The Orisha community yearned for this unification and communal celebration. The first event in 2014 was a tribute to Yemayá at the ocean in Miami Beach. I asked Ramos why they chose Yemayá as the first Orisha to venerate, considering that Elegua, the owner of the roads, would have been logical, given the Lukumí perspective that Elegua always receives the first sacrifices. He enthusiastically responded:

> Yemọja became the mother par excellence for a displaced population that sought succor and wellbeing in her. As the mother of all the Orishas, Yemọja protects humankind because we are her children. Her association with several Catholic manifestations of the Christian Mary seems to have further engrained her role as Divine mother. Crossing the waters safely, and the possibility of crossing them once again to return home, even after death, were the tasks deposited in Yemọja's arms. Thus, she became one of the most popular Yoruba Orishas in Cuba and Brazil.

Once the Orisha was determined, numerous Iles ("Orisha houses") came together to prepare for the large celebration.[21] The event, which was attended by faithful from numerous Orisha traditions, included singing, dancing, offering prayers and carrying a large raft out to sea with fruits and flowers. Ramos explained why Oloshas-United in Miami choose the ocean as the location for the Yemayá celebration, shedding light on how the Lukumí see their relationship with Yemayá and the ocean, which also addresses the ideas of homesickness and belonging that are characteristics of the development of sacred places:

> We took the idea from two earlier traditions: the Brazilian Candomblé Yemọja celebration, observed on the 2nd of February; and the Cuban Lukumí Cabildo celebrations that until 1962 were held annually during the second week of September in the town of Regla. Both traditions consisted of drumming, singing, and offerings to the seas, the place that in the Yoruba Diaspora is considered Yemọja's abode. While in Yorubaland Yemọja is mainly associated with rivers, in the Americas her association with the sea increased, possibly due to the horrors of the Middle Passage and the possibility of arriving in safe harbors in the Americas even if in chains.[22]

The enthusiasm quickly spread, with groups coming together to establish chapters in Central Florida, New York, Chicago, Atlanta, Houston, Los Angeles, the San Francisco Bay Area, Panama, and Trinidad and Tobago. Each of these communities determined where they would celebrate the festival for Yemayá. The communities in Atlanta, Los Angeles, San Francisco and New York chose the ocean; Chicago selected Lake Michigan; and Houston visited Rio Vista. In cases where the ocean was not readily available, the closest body of water dynamically became sacred space to worship Yemayá. These communities that practice the Lukumí system continue the traditions established by the African slaves and their descendants, transforming new profane locations into sacred places.

Pictures bring to life the communal aspect of these celebrations, showing the diversity of practitioners and offerings. The initial event dedicated to Yemayá generated significant enthusiasm and numerous chapters chose to add an event for Ochún. In 2017 several chapters hosted joint celebrations for both Ochún and Yemayá.

I attended the 2017 event of the Miami chapter of Oloshas United hosted at Oleta River State Park and dedicated to the three Lukumí mothers, Ochún, Yemayá and Oyá. It was a beautiful day, with the sun shining on the warm blue waters of the ocean and the river. This park provides a powerful landscape where the river and ocean meet. It is a natural spot to venerate both Ochún and Yemayá. The celebration began with offerings to Elegua, the orisha in charge of opening and closing the roads of life and destiny, and was followed by offerings to Oya, the Orisha of the winds, with singing and dancing. The atmosphere was festive and joyful as the group circled the offers to Oyá under the shade of a large tree. Next the group began the procession with offerings led by the beats of the bata drums to the intersection of the river and the ocean. The faithful delivered their offerings to the water's edge as the singing and danced continued, electrifying the air. For the next several hours, the practitioners returned to the hut and danced and sang to the Orishas until sundown.

TRINIDAD

The third wave represents the integration and expansion of Orisha traditions across the globe. Many are in closer proximity than ever before, which has led to integration and competition. Trinidad is an example of where the Orisha tradition established during earlier periods is now confronting practices from Nigeria, Cuba, and Brazil. In Trinidad the sacred space for worship referred to as an "Orisha yard" requires ritual preparation. Baba Awurela Adeloni Fakayode's temple in the Borough of Chaguanas, called Ojubo Orisa Omolu-Ijo Ifa Imole Osetura Temple, is an excellent example of how older established Trinidadian customs are merging with new or different Orisha practices from Nigeria. Baba Fakayode's temple opened in 1994 as a more traditional Trinidadian Orisha yard. According to Baba Fakayode, he underwent the Desunu and Sigbere ceremonies (head washing and gashing) as a youth.[23] Both ceremonies are part of the Orisha tradition established in Trinidad by Africans.

The first festival for Obalúayé was held in 1996 within the Trinidadian framework of Orisha worship. The festivals evolved after Baba Fakayode was initiated as a priest of Obalúayé within the Yoruba tradition. In 2006 he invited Yoruba priests to his temple in Trinidad for Itefa, the traditional Ifa initiation followed by a complete initiation to Obalúayé. In 2013 the temple started holding an annual festival for Yemoja and Ogun. Iya Omiyade Fakayode, the head priestess of Yemoja, hosts the annual festival officiated by Baba Fakayode. In 2017 members of the temple visited the ocean and the river as part of the annual festival. According to Baba Fakayode, Yemọja requested through divination that the faithful clean and reenergize their sacred icons at the ocean and then proceed to the river. I found this fascinating, since Yemọja seemed to support the integration of Nigerian and Diasporic traditions. These practices reflect a melding of Trinidadian and Nigerian traditions. There has been significant infighting among practitioners of differing Orisha traditions in the Americas over authenticity, especially where older, preestablished traditions exist. The temple of Baba Fakayode may be an example of successfully developing a new Orisha paradigm that integrates various traditions.

WHERE DO WE FIND YEMAYÁ, IJEMOJA, YEMỌJA, EMONJE?

With the expansion of Orisha traditions around the globe, there is a growing battle for authenticity and legitimacy. While Yourbaland is considered the ancestral home of the Orishas, the expansion of diaspora traditions has influenced the understanding of their origins and characteristics. Ease of travel and access to the internet have, at times, confounded and complicated the relationships between the traditions. Sacred spaces have also become contested spaces in the Orisha diaspora. One Orisha that seems to epitomize the growing struggle to define and delineate what is an appropriate sacred space is Yemọja, the guardian and owner of the Ogun River in Nigeria.[24] While practitioners in Nigeria recognize that any body of water is acceptable to venerate Yemọja, they emphasize the importance of the Ogun River as her primary home. In the Orisha diaspora, worshippers visit her at streams, rivers, and brooks, but the sea became her preferred home in both Cuba and Brazil. The importance of Yemayá in the traditions of the diaspora cannot be understated. The decimation of Oyo in the early nineteenth century brought a wave of Oyo and Egbado Yoruba with strong ties to the Sango Orisha complex. I contend that the large number of African slaves from the Oyo ruling areas, specifically the Egbado communities, emphasized the importance of worshiping Yemọja. They had to find a powerful new home for the mother Orisha who brought them safely to dry land. In Yorubaland she is Iya Olókun, a notion that celebrates the flow of rivers into the ocean. This interdependence between rivers and the ocean may have provided the connectivity needed to associate Yemayá with the ocean in the Orisha diaspora. In Bahia Yemọja is associated with Our Lady of Navigators, the Patron Saint of Bahia, and invoked by sailors and fisherman for protection. In Cuba the Church of Our Lady of the Rule faces the Bay of Havana, where she is also associated with the ocean and seafaring. Additionally, the imagery of mermaids found in Yorubaland may have strengthened her association with the ocean. The temples in Ilaro and Ibadan both displayed prominent mermaid imagery in the inner sanctuaries. This imagery continues in the Orisha diaspora —for example, the statue in front of Casa Yemanjá in Bahia and the Lukumí mermaids used in the sacred tools of Yemayá. Rodriques (1899, 252) had the opportunity to see two plaster mermaids in the Gantois Terrerio: one for Yemanjá in silver, and one for Oshun in bronze.

While the location of veneration may be a contested space across traditions, practitioners and the Orishas do not seem to mind the adaptive and transformative process exhibited in the diaspora (see also the introduction, Laughlin, and Benson in this volume). Yorubaland has become a significant player in the development of Orisha worship across the globe. This includes practitioners from the diaspora who have converted or adapted their practices to reflect the current definitions and boundaries of worship in Yorubaland. The location to worship Yemọja continues to be a prime example of the tensions that arise between traditions. Is it the ocean, or it is the river? Each tradition maintains its historic location.

CONCLUSION

The goal of this chapter was to present the diverse expressions of sacred places, emphasizing the adaptive nature practitioners of the Orisha Diasporic traditions employed to maintain a close association between nature and the Orishas. The Orisha diaspora continues to find new sacred places and to redefine others as they adapt to new communities and cultural realities. Clearly the adaptive process has not stopped. The variety of locations discussed in this chapter provides a glimpse of an expanding Orisha community settling in new locations across the globe. In each new location, practitioners continue to follow the example left by the African slaves, carving out new sacred places within the profane (see Benson in this volume). The diversity of images associated with Yemayá serves as an example of the adaptive process of religious and cultural survival. She may be associated with Our Lady of the Rule in Cuba, or Our Lady of Navigators in Brazil; she may be associated with mermaids in Nigeria and Brazil, or imagined as a white goddess with flowing hair and blue clothes in Rio and Bahia. Her festivals in Trinidad may be reimagined with an eye toward Yorubaland. Yet it is the adaptive nature of Orisha practitioners that this chapter brings to life.

Much work remains to be done, and many experiences to be documented, as the growth of the Orisha diaspora continue to emerge in new locations, within differing ethnic and cultural groups that work to integrate and preserve their Orisha traditions. A critical eye is needed to understand how modernity and technology are impacting the dynamics of the Orisha diaspora and how these influences are gradually impacting the landscape practitioners understand as sacred.

NOTES

1. The word "diaspora" comes from the Greek for "dispersal." The term was originally used to refer to the Jewish diaspora. The use of the term "Orisha diaspora" means to provide a unit of analysis for the movement of Orisha practices originating in West African and traveling around the globe.
2. Havana was one of the locations where the English and Spanish established a Court of Mixed Commission to arbitrate on slave ships captured on the high seas.
3. Orisha traditions survived across the Black Atlantic but not with the same complexity and organizational structure as seen in Cuba, Brazil, and Trinidad. See Simpson (1973) on the Kele Cult in St. Lucia.
4. Lukumí is now synonymous with Orisha practices that developed in Cuba. The original term was used to identify African slaves arriving from what now is considered Yorubaland. See Law (1997).
5. Each country in the Caribbean had differing laws that allowed slaves to buy their freedom. In the Afro-Cuban Orisha diaspora, slaves were able to buy their freedom or the freedom of their children. Additionally, the Mixed Commission housed in Havana also "freed" slaves.
6. Interview with author, November 5, 2017.
7. Interview with author.
8. The different spelling represents the influences of the predominant language that slaves were forced to learn——in the case of Cuba, Spanish; in Brazil, Portuguese; and, in Trinidad, English.

9. See Cabrera (1996) for a treasure trove of Lukumí stories about Yemaya. See Falola and Otero (2013) on an evolving dialog on the role Yemaya plays as mediator of gender relations.
10. Pedro Betancourt is a small town in the Matanzas Province of Cuba. See Cabrera (1993).
11. See Mason (1996) for a larger discussion of the Olókun cult in Cuba.
12. See Howard (1998) on the history of Cabildos in Cuba; Cuban spelling for those who are of Egbado descent.
13. The Cuban expression "children" refers to those initiated to a particular Orisha.
14. For additional perspectives on Yemọja worship, see https://orisabrasil.com.br/Loja/como-yemoja-passou-de-deidade-da-agua-do-rio-na-africa-para-agua-do-mar-no-brasil/?fbclid=Iwar2p0d7dbvhxYjuubyrxjko4qkbth0dcq3w3ksC-tthggoy1jG-jMbAarzY (accessed October 7, 2002).
15. The term "godchildren" refers to members of the religious household who may have varying degrees of initiation. These are aligned to the major Orisha of the household or shrine and participate as active members in all communal activities.
16. Interview with the Egbe Omo Yemọja, February 11, 2018.
17. The Ogunleki statue in New York is the twin of the one I saw in Ibadan during the festival.
18. The Diaspora Cultural Center was the precursor to Oloshas United.
19. Taken from Facebook on January 18, 2018.
20. Interview with author, January 17, 2018.
21. In Lukumí terms an Ile is an Orisha Temple based in the leader's home. This is in contrast to Brazil, where there are independent temples called terreiros.
22. Interview with author, January 17, 2018.
23. See Houk (1995) for an explanation of the head washing and incising ceremony.
24. While there is an ongoing struggle for authenticity related to where to venerate Yemọja, I believe this may be driven by academic inquiry and the power of social media and not a deep-seated conflict among practitioners.

REFERENCES

Ayorinde, Christine. 2005. "Santería in Cuba: Tradition and Transformation." In *The Yoruba Diaspora in the Atlantic World*, edited by Toyin Falola and Matt Childs, 209–30. Bloomington: Indiana University Press.

Barber, Karin. 1990. "Oríkì, Women, and the Proliferation and Merging of Òrìṣà." *Africa* 60, no. 3: 313–37.

Cabrera, Lydia. 1975. *El Monte*. Barcelona: Linkgua.

Cabrera, Lydia. 1993. *La laguna sagrada de San Joaquín* 2nd. ed. Miami FL: Ediciones Universal.

Cabrera, Lydia, and Rosario Hiriart. 1980. *Yemayá y Ochún*. 2nd. ed. New York: CR.

Durkheim, Emile. 2008. *The Elementary Forms of Religious Life*. Oxford: Oxford University Press.
Edison, Carneiro de Souza. 1936. *Religiões Negras: Notas De Etnografia Religiosa*. Rio de Janeiro: Civilização brasileira S.A.
Eliade, Mircea. 1961. *The Sacred and the Profane: The Nature of Religion*. New York: Harper & Row.
Frazer, James George. 2003. *The Golden Bough*. Salt Lake City UT: Project Gutenberg.
Gilroy, Paul. 1993. *The Black Atlantic: Modernity and Double Consciousness*. Cambridge MA: Harvard University Press.
Henry, Frances. 2005. "Reclaiming African Religions in Trinidad: The Socio-Political Legitimation of the Orisha and Spiritual Baptist Faiths." *Nova Religio: The Journal of Alternative and Emergent Religions* 9, no. 2: 115–16.
Houk, James T. 1995. *Spirits, Blood, and Drums: The Orisha Religion in Trinidad*. Philadelphia PA: Temple University Press.
Howard, Philip A. 1998. *Changing History: Afro-Cuban Cabildos and Societies of Color in the Nineteenth Century*. Baton Rouge: Louisiana State University Press.
Jackson, Richard H., and Roger Henrie. 1983. "Perception of Sacred Space." *Journal of Cultural Geography* 3, no. 2: 94–107.
Johnson, Paul Christopher. 2002. *Secrets, Gossip, and Gods: The Transformation of Brazilian Candomblé*. New York: Oxford University Press.
Lienert Bühler, Franziska. 2006. "Getting Touched by Oshun: An Orisha History of Trinidad." PhD diss., Studentendruckerei.
Lovejoy, Henry B. 2012. "Old Oyo Influences on the Transformation of Lucumí Identity in Colonial Cuba." PhD diss., University of California, Los Angeles.
Mason, John. Olóòkun. 1996. *Owner of Rivers and Seas*. Brooklyn NY: Yorùbá Theological Archministry.
Nina Rodrigues, Raymundo. 2010. *Os africanos no Brasil*. Rio de Janeiro: Centro Edelstein.
Olupona, Jacob K. 2011. *City of 201 Gods: Ilé-Ifè in Time, Space, and the Imagination*. Berkeley: University of California Press.
Otero, Solimar. 2010. *Afro-Cuban Diasporas in the Atlantic World*. Rochester NY: University of Rochester Press.
Otero, Solimar, and Toyin Falola. 2013. *Yemoja: Gender, Sexuality, and Creativity in the Latina/o and Afro-Atlantic Diasporas*. Albany: State University of New York Press.
Pals, Daniel L. 2006. *Eight Theories of Religion*. Oxford: Oxford University Press.
Parés, Luis Nicolau. 2013. *The Formation of Candomblé: Vodun History and Ritual in Brazil*. Chapel Hill: University of North Carolina Press.
Prorok, Carolyn V. 2003. "Transplanting Pilgrimage Traditions in the Americas." *Geographical Rreview* 93, no. 3: 283–307.
Thompson, Robert Farris. 1984. *Flash of the Spirit: African and Afro-American Art and Philosophy*. New York: Vintage, 1984.

Tylor, Edward Burnett. 1958. *Religion in Primitive Culture*. New York: Harper & Brothers.

Verger, Pierre. 2000. *Notas Sobre o Culto Aos orixás e Voduns Na Bahia De Todos Os Santos, No Brasil, e Na Antiga Costa Dos Escravos, Na áfrica*. São Paulo: EDUSP.

Verger, Pierre. 2018. *Orixás: Deuses Iorubás Na Africa e No Novo Mundo*. Salvador: Fundação Pierre Verger.

Vincent, Amanda. 2006. "Bata Conversations: Guardianship and Entitlement Narratives about the Bata in Nigeria and Cuba." PhD diss, University of London.

Warner-Lewis, Maureen. 1991. *Guinea's Other Suns: The African Dynamic in Trinidad Culture*. Dover MA: Majority.

Weber, Max. 1964. *The Sociology of Religion* 4th ed. Boston: Beacon, 1964.

CONTRIBUTORS

BENJAMIN HEBBLETHWAITE is associate professor in the Department of Languages, Literatures, and Cultures at the University of Florida, where he teaches courses on Haiti, Jamaica, and France. His books include *A Transatlantic History of Haitian Vodou, Stirring the Pot of Haitian History* (a translation of Michel-Rolph Trouillot's *Ti dife boule sou istwa Ayiti*, coedited with Mariana Past), *Stirring the Pot of Haitian History*, and the edited volume *Vodou Songs in Haitian Creole and English*. He is currently investigating Korean language and culture. Born in South Africa, he lives in Gainesville, Florida, with his wife and two daughters.

SILKE JANSEN is a professor of Hispanic and French Linguistics in the Department of English, American, and Romance Studies at the Friedrich-Alexander University of Erlangen-Nuremberg. Her research and teaching focus on language contact and variation in the Spanish- and French-speaking world, with a special focus on the Caribbean. Her publications include *Demystifying Bilingualism: How Metaphor Guides Research towards Mythification* (with Sonja Higuera, Jessica Barzen, Markus Opolka and Pia Reimann); *Fray Antonio de Montesino y su tiempo* (with Irene Weiss); and *La Hispaniola—Island of Encounters* (with Hanna-Lene Geiger and Jessica Barzen). She lives in a small village close to Nuremberg, with her husband and daughter.

Professor Emeritus of SUNY-ESC LEGRACE BENSON is currently an associate editor of the *Journal of Haitian Studies* and is a past President of the Haitian Studies Association. She is author of numerous essays on Haitian art and history and the book *Arts and Religions of Haiti: How the Sun Illuminates under Cover of Darkness*. A book on the Citadelle, Palais Sans Souci, and the associated nature preserve with coauthors Antonio Marcelli and Frederick Mangonès is expected in 2022. Her doctoral studies concerned perceptions as ecological systems and inform her work in progress with the Working Groups on Haitian Environment of the Haitian Studies Association.

ELEANOR A. LAUGHLIN specializes in the art of modern Europe and Latin America, particularly the politics of representation in multicultural contexts. Her research focuses on new social roles created for and by subjects using representational strategies such as allegory, portraiture, and costume in the late colonial and postcolonial periods. Dr. Laughlin's forthcoming book examines carte-de-visite photographs taken in Mexico of Maximilian von Habsburg's (1832–67) body and effects after execution as image-objects, arguing that the pictures fit into the vocabulary of Catholic relics and suggest alternative uses for photography in the nineteenth century. Additional research interests include textile traditions in Mexico and the Andes, especially those made by or depicting women.

DANIEL J. FRIM is a PhD candidate in Harvard University's Committee on the Study of Religion. His research focuses on Kwak'wala and other oral-traditional literatures within a comparative framework.

JOSÉ MARÍA SANTOS ROVIRA works at the Department of General and Romance Linguistics, University of Lisbon (Portugal), specializing in Spanish studies and sociolinguistics. He previously worked at the Guangdong University of Foreign Studies (China), the University of Macao, the International University (Indonesia), and the University of Nottingham. He is the author of the first monograph dedicated to Spanish in China, as well as the editor of many other works of linguistics.

ROBIN M. WRIGHT is associate professor of religion and anthropology at the University of Florida. He has a PhD from Stanford University (1981), and he worked as professor of anthropology at the Universidade Estadual de

Campinas (1985–2005). His areas of concentration are Indigenous histories and religious traditions, traditional forms of healing, and the ethnology of the Americas. He has published extensively, including several book-length studies of Indigenous religious traditions of the northwest Amazon in Brazil, where he has done most of his field research, and numerous articles and chapters on a variety of subjects ranging from Indigenous history Indian policy to a recent catalog of his digitalized research collection.

ANA MARIELLA BACIGALUPO, professor of anthropology at SUNY, works with Mapuche in Chile and mestizos in northern Peru. She has authored *Thunder Shaman: Making History with Mapuche Spirits in Patagonia*; *Shamans of the Foye Tree: Gender, Power, and Healing among the Chilean Mapuche*; and *The Voice of the Drum in Modernity: Tradition and Change in the Practice of Seven Mapuche Shamans*. Her new book project is titled "The Subversive Politics of Sentient Places: Collective Ethics, and Environmental Justice in Northern Peru."

IRITAMEI FRANCISCO BENÍTEZ DE LA CRUZ belongs to the Wixárika community and has been working for more than twenty years as a teacher in different communities in the Sierra Wixárika. He received his degree in teaching elementary school at the Universidad Pedagógica Nacional while working as a teacher. He continued his education at the Instituto Superior de Investigación y Docencia para el Magisterio, where he received his doctorate in applied educational research. His themes of interest are intercultural education, teachers' formation, and teaching the Wixárika language. Currently, Benítez de la Cruz is headmaster of a public primary school in the Sierra Wixárika.

ITXASO GARCÍA CHAPINAL graduated with a degree in history at the Universidad Complutense de Madrid, specializing in American history before the European colonization. She continued her training in the interdisciplinary program of inter-American studies at the Universität Bielefeld. Her first contact with the Wixárika community was during the field work for her master's thesis on Indigenous education in Mexico. At present she is developing her doctoral project on environmental knowledge and public education in Wixáritari communities at the Bielefeld Graduate School in

History and Sociology. During her academic training, García Chapinal has focused on oral history, education, and local knowledges of different Indigenous groups in Latin America.

DERECK DASCHKE is professor of philosophy and religion at Truman State University. His professional interests reflect various intersections of religion and mental health, including studies in shamanism, mind-body medicine, and apocalypticism. He is coeditor with W. Michael Ashcraft of *New Religious Movements: A Documentary Reader*.

JEFFERY M. GONZALEZ is assistant teaching professor at Florida International University and a doctoral student at the University of Reading. His areas of specialization include Orisha traditions in Brazil, Cuba, Nigeria, Trinidad, and the United States, as well as the impact of religion on marginalized communities.

INDEX

Page numbers in italics indicate maps; page numbers with F indicate illustrations

African diaspora: ancestral spirits of, 13; attitudes of Christians toward, 49; becoming Indigenous, 6; in Brazil, 282–83, 300, 303–4, 307–8, 310, 311, 312, 315; complexity of religions of, 5; convergences with Indigenous religious traditions, 26–43; in Cuba, 281–84, 302–4, 305–6, 308, 310–16; in the Dominican Republic, 145–71; fusing aspects of Western societies, 6; historical ideas of, 24–26; initiations among, 34; instruments of, 38; Marie Laveau's practice of, 101; in New Orleans, 83–109; ontology of, 16–20; and the Orisha diaspora, 282; political dimensions of, 10; problems with term, 2; role in Santo Daime, 278; role of colonial languages on, 315; role of publishing for, 50; role of sacred language for, 30; in Saint-Domingue, 61–81; spirits for, 8; surviving colonial conditions, 9–10, 12, 49; as a term of strategic essentialism, 8; in Trinidad, 282–84, 304, 308, 312–13

Agwe Tawoyo: fish-like possession by, 41, 52; lwa of the sea, 41, 63; represented by Saint Ulrich, 41

Aiamori (Yanomami xapiri), 32

Albert, Bruce: collaboration with Davi Kopenawa, 22, 37; study of Yanomami ontology, 50. *See* Kopenawa, Davi

altered states of consciousness (ASC), 22, 173, 204, 232, 252, 258, 266–67

Álvarez Chanca, Diego, 9

Anglo-Saxon settlers, 84

Arawak people, language, and religion: Amazonian, 30, 173; Baniwa as, 199; cultural matrix of, 4; ecology of the sacred, 15; Garifuna as a fusion of with Carib, 5; language and religions, 4, 30; migrations of, 3; northern Arawakan, 173; prophetic traditions of, 21, 36; shamans versus priests among, 36; topographic marking of, 3

ashe (ase, axé): accumulated in plants, 19; as sacred force, 20; as vital force, 26 ayahusca, 19, 39, 47, 50; and songs, 175, 257–58, 268; and visions, 265–67; use in Santo Daime church, 259–60, 265; use in Amazonian shamanism, 263

Aztec (Mexica) people, 4; diasporic identity of, 5; goddess Tonantzin, 42; rain god Tlaloc, 42; relationship with Wixárika culture, 236

Aztlán (Aztec homeland), 4

Babalorisa (priest in Nigeria), 301

Bahia, 5, 12, 16, 18, 24, 31, 52n6, 296F28, 300F35; Casa Yemanjá in, 314; feasts and festivals of, 307–8; mythology in, 305; Patron Saint of, 314; religious traditions in, 25, 26, 314, 315

Banisteriopsis caapi, 197

Baniwa, people and language: about, 199n1; biographical work with shamans of, 22; contemporary shamans of, 20; cosmovision of, 29, 175, 178, 197; cross-fertilization with Catholic traditions, 196; ecology of the sacred, 15; fusion of jaguar and human in ritual, 15; historical consciousness of, 23, 193, 198; Hohodene belief, 176; instruments of, 38–39; mythology of, 32, 216n12; ontology of, 15; the "other peoples" for, 175; *pajé* shaman of, 15, 32, 198; priestly chanters versus jaguar shamans in culture of, 36; prophets of, 20–21, 174, 196; role of DMT in culture of, 16; role of dreaming for shamans of, 196; role of sounds in, 180; songs in culture of, 173, 188–93; sorcery in the society of, 197; spirit Nhiãperikuli for, 28

baptism: of African kings, 147; of enslaved people, 10, 73, 75, 107n11, 147; of Marie Laveau, 97; as part of initiation to Vodou, 75

bata (drums), 306–7, 312

Beauvoir, Max: collector of Vodou songs, 24; oungan, 24; scholar, 50

behique (Taino shaman), 51

bisexualism: among machi, 227n15

Black Code: of 1685, 10, 107–8n11; liberal in Spanish colonies, 84; and Roman Catholic religion, 10, 41–42, 91

Black Nationalist movement (U.S.), 282

boarding schools, 11, 49; Franciscan in Mexico, 237

bòkò (Haitian Vodou diviner), 36. *See* oungan

Bororo, 40

Brazil: 1850s project of "civilizing" Indigenous people, 194, 199n1; Acre, 259; Afro-Brazilian spirits, 265; altar for Yemanjá, 300F35; Baniwa on frontier with Venezuela and Colombia, 194; Brazilian professionals and Santo Daime, 260; brotherhoods in, 149, 151, 163; Espiritismo in, 258; establishment of Orisha traditions in, 282; feast day of Our Lady of Navigators, 307–8; festival in Rio de Janeiro, 295F27, 296F29; importance of African cultural presence in, 164; impositions of, 196; Kawaiwete Tupi shamans in, 16; non-Brazilians in, 260; popularity of saints in, 94; popularity of Yemọja in, 310–11, 315; role of dance performance in, 17; rubber companies impact on, 11; sacred trees in, 20; Santo Daime in, 47, 257–80; *saudade* in, 269; social integration in, 31; spread of ayahuasca consumption, 259; stability of African diaspora religion in Salvador, Bahia, 12; state recognition of Yanomami people, 37; terreiro versus Ile, 316n21; Xangô traditions of, 25

British Honduras: deportation of non-Europeans to in 1797, 5

Brotherhood of the Holy Spirit of the Kongos of Villa Mella, 46, 145; African languages in, 156–58; and African vodun 160; Catholic religious celebrations in, 154; dances of, 157; funerals as celebrated by, 154–55; Haitian Creole in, 160–61; and Haitian vodou 160, 161–62; history of, 153–54; identity construction in, 161, 165; multiligualism in, 156, 162, 164; prayers and rituals of, 149–50, 155, 156–59; religious center of, 153; songs of, 158–59, 162–63; Spanish as main language of, 156; syncretic character of, 146, 148, 151, 156, 160; and the tradition of Catholic Black brotherhoods, 148–49, 163–64; Vodou/Vodun elements in, 159–60

Cabildo (Spanish government), 85, Cabildo Ewado (Cuba), 306–7, 311; history of cabildos in Cuba, 316n12

Candomblé religion, 5, 24; commonalities with other African diaspora traditions, 27, 308; festivals of, 307, 311; ideas of personhood in, 16–17; orixá in, 18; and Santo Daime, 278

cannibalism: accusing Indigenous people of, 9, 11; colonialism and industrializations as, 37; sickness as a result of cannibalistically eating animals, 40

Cão, Diogo, 147

Caribbean: early descriptions by French colonists, 76; Eastern, 4; enslaved people taken to, 146; hurricanes of, 62; hybridism of, 146, 148, 150, 159, 282; imposition of headscarf in, 87; influence of languages of, 12; manumission and its rarity in, 282, 285, 315; Middle Passage to, 303; Rastafari in, 166; trance possession in, 161

Caribs, Island Caribs: ancestors of Garifuna, 30; Black Caribs, 13; called "savages" by Spanish colonists, 25; ceiba tree in religion of, 38; combining with Arawaks, 5; territorial disputes of, 9. See also Kalinago

Caroline Code (1789), 156

Catholic religion: Bibles as ritual objects, 207; Black brotherhoods, 148–49, 163–64; Church, 11, 49, 77, 91, 97, 107–8n11, 237; churches in New Orleans, 95; churches in the Caribbean, 150; Creoles, 92; faith and Freemasonry, 43; faith and French colonial Black code, 10; faith and practices in Kongo kingdom (West Africa), 147–48; ideologies, 22; imagery in Haitian Vodou, 42; imagery in New Orleans Voudou, 96, 97–98; imagery in Santo Daime, 267–68; imposition of religion in colonization, 42, 105–6; influence in Wixárika culture, 237; Mass, 92; missionaries, 9, 62, 76; practices as disguise for non-Catholic religious practices 150, 305; priests, 72–73, 75, 80n15; privileges for religion, 10; and protestant domination of land, 49; rejection of influences, 43; religion and African religions, 148; religion practiced alongside spirit based traditions, 6–7, 159–60, 162; religious practice, 91, 149, 155, 163; saints in Candomblé, 18;

Catholic religion (*continued*)
saints in Costumbre, 42; saints in Cuban orixa/orisha tradition, 7, 305–6, 310; saints in Haitian Vodou, 24, 41–42, 76; saints in Lancandon religious traditions, 7; saints in Meso-American religions, 42; saints in New Orleans Voudou, 93–96, 105; saints in Villa Mella religious traditions, 162; schools, 11, 49; statues in Yoruba processions, 306; syncretism of practices with spirit based traditions, 6, 156; traditions blended with Baniwa traditions, 196; traditions blended with machi shamanism, 207; traditions in Santo Daime, 259; traditions in Villa Mella, 146

Catlin, George, 85–86; 90, 107n5, 107n7

ceiba pentandra (tree): possible syncretic origins of veneration of, 53n17; veneration of, 20

ceremonial language (Arawak), 30

chanting: and Dansé Calinda, 98; and healing, 184, 197, 225n6; to Orisha, 301; priestly chanters, 36, 53n20; in Santo Daime, 175; and shaping the past, 216; and using plants, 269

Chicago, *xvi*, 308–9, 311

Chile, *xv*; animal sacrifice in, 29; hegemonic knowledge in, 213; machi shamans of, 16; military of, 220; multitemporal trance techniques in, 21; "national history" of as ideological weapon, 22–23; political parties of, 226n12; shamanism in, 203–32

Chiriguano (Tupian language), 30

chromolithographs (of Catholic saints), 6; representing Vodou lwa, 41; Vodouists who reject, 42

Church of Our Lady of the Rule (Cuba), 305–6, 314–15

Colombia, *xv*, 30, 151, 163, 165, 194, 199n1, 207, 225

colonialism: chaos of, 213; crimes of, 49; hardships of, 23; history of, 6; legacy of in Mexico, 233; veneration of saints in, 106; white settler, 1, 22

coloniality: of reality, 7, 43–44, 233; values given to languages by, 248

Columbus, Christopher, 3, 6, 76; disproportionate structural violence after, 49; misunderstandings of, 3; religion after, 49; second journey of, 9

Congo Square (New Orleans), 84

Cora people and language: kingdom of, 237; neighbors of Wixárika people, 236

Coromantin (people), 75

Costumbre: initiation into, 249; among K'iche Mayas, 42; Protestantized, 43; syncretic practices of, 43

Creole language: in brotherhood of Villa Mella, D.R., 146, 156, 160; colonies where spoken, 6; as culture, 88; Haitian Creole (language), 24; in Louisiana, 90, 107; melding with Kikongo in Villa Mella, D.R., 162; opposition to in D.R., 161; pantheon of, 93; prestige of in religion in Villa Mella, D.R., 165; Taíno words in, 12; used in songs, prayers, and rituals; and Vodou, 12

Creole people: Afro-, 78; Catholic, 92; cleanliness of, 100; as race, 107; slave songs of, 100; as a status, 101; stereotypical treatment of, 103

Cuba: 1959 exodus from, 308; Abakuá ritual language in, 30; adaptive process in, 302, 308; African linguistic elements in, 164; Black brotherhoods in, 151, 163; Church of Our Lady of the Rule in, 314–15; commonalities with other African diaspora traditions, 26;

before communist revolution, 310; Cuban Revolution (1959), 282; festivals in, 305–7; Matanzas in, 295F26, 306; Ochún practices in, 304; Olókun in, 294, 316; orixas of, 7, 17; as part of Orisha diaspora, 47, 282, 315; procession in Regla, 293f24; religion in, 5, 17, 31; Sango worship in, 304; Santería in, 29, 52; *santeros* and *santeras* from, 19; technological limitations of, 282; waterways in, 303; Yemoja in, 283, 302, 310, 313

Cuneo, Michele da, 9

Danbala Wèdo (Danmbala Wèdo): accompanying captives, 63; calling people to initiation, 52; link to wealth and sexual health, 19; possession by, 41; represented by Saint Patrick (Saint), 41; serpent *lwa*, 18, 41, 97; yanvalou dance for, 33

Danwonmen Rite: from Fon people, 24; in Lakou Souvenance, 24. *See* Sèvis Ginen tradition

diaspora, diasporas: of African people in Americas, 5; of Afro-Cuban people, 315; among an-Other people, 61; caused by different types of mobility, 3; as a condition of multiple consciousness, 45, 61; cultural integration in, 156; deadliness of for enslaved Africans, 283; European, 51; festivals of, 307; Garifuna, 5; Greek origin of word, 315; Haitian, 75, 87; identity of, 5; Indigenous diasporas, 3–5; redefining deities in the, 304; of Yoruba Orishas, 281–84, 302, 304, 308, 311, 313–15

DMT. *See* N,N-Dimethyltryptamine, pariká

Dominican Republic: afterlife in culture of, 154; Black brotherhoods in, 46, 47, 145, 163; Black citizens in 152; blending of African and European cultural traditions in, 160, 164; denial of African cultural heritage in, 164

dreamer, 113; in Baniwa religion, 196, 197; in Kwakwaka'wakw religion, 136n5. *See* spy

dreams: in African diaspora religions, 17; as altered states, 204; in Baniwa religion, 173, 196, 200; finding remedies in, 207; foretelling the future with, 208; forgetting, 211; in Haitian Vodou, 35; in Indigenous and African diaspora religions, 1; interpretation of, 27; in Kwakwaka'wakw religion, 112, 113, 114, 132, 133; in Mapuche religion, 21, 205, 210, 215, 218, 222, 225; as means of communication with spirits, 8; in Tapirapé religion, 35; in Tupi religion, 35; in Wixárika religion, 234, 240; in Yanomami religion, 14, 30, 34

drums. *See* percussion instruments

Durán, Diego, 4

education: and Catholic Church, 49; of children, 240; civic and ethical, 246; and customs, 238; evangelization through, 237; and healing, 276; integral education, 251; intercultural bilingual, 241, 242, 248; and local knowledge, 248; by mara'akame (Wixárika shaman), 240, 246; in Mexico, 233; and orality, 241, 246; public among Indigenous people, 241–44; public system in Mexico, 241–42; and religion, 238; traditional and public, 245; traditional in Wixárika culture, 238–41; and the Western knowledge system, 233

Elegba (Cuba): owner of pathways, 306. See Legba, Atibon Legba (Haitian Vodou)

enslaved people, 146; adoption of Catholic rituals and saints, 150; from Bight of Benin, 165; buying freedom, 285; in colonial Santo Domingo, 146; creating languages, religions, and cultures, 6; creating meaning in landscape, 303; cultural resistance of, 285, 305, 311; dying on the Middle Passage, 305; edicts to identify with clothing, 87; escaping from ship wrecks, 5; forced to learn colonial languages, 315; history in Cuba, 164; imposition of Christianity upon, 10, 147; Indigenous replaced by Black people, 146; keeping order in chaos, 303; "Kongos," 152; manumission of, 84; masking the religion of, 105; in New Orleans, 84, 92; from Oyo, 303, 313; rituals of mentioned in Caroline Code of 1789, 156; from Senegambian region, 88; statistics about, 146; transformation suffered by, 283; versus "slaves," 282; ways of identifying, 315n5

enslavement: creating diasporas, 7; ecosystem of, 72; European colonialism and, 20; freedom from, 25; ideological dehumanization as basis of, 10; impacting African diaspora and Indigenous people, 10; ministers' views, 75; multigenerational, 43; surviving, 9, 283; in United States 1620–1865, 10; Villa Mella established by escapees of, 152

epistemology, 45, 46, 207, 233–35, 238–39, 240, 245–47, 250–51, 252

Èzili Dantò, 63, 73; etymology of, 24; represented by the Black Madonna Mater Salvatoris, 41

Èzili Freda, 63, 73; cycle of salutation for, 31; Saut-d'Eau and, 31; spirit marriage to, 28

Florida, 3

Fon people and language: concept of sɛ (vital principle) in, 53n18; contributions to Louisiana Creole, 90; language, 5; source of Danwonmen Rite, 24; source of Haitian Vodou's lexicon, 24; source of traditions in Villa Mella, D.R., 156, 158, 162, 166n6

Franciscans, 237

fraternities (religious), 149, 151, 153, 156, 163.

Fraternity of the Miracles of Our Lady of Carmen and Jesus of Nazareth, 149

Freemasonry: literature of in Haiti, 42; syncretized, 6, 43; syncretizing with African diaspora religions, 43

Garifuna: about, 5; accusations against, 11; Bantu words used by, 52n10; descendants of Island Caribs, 30; as diasporic people, 5; spirits of, 43

Gede Rite: from Gedevi people, 24; repellant insects of, 41. See also Sèvis Ginen tradition

gender: and colonial hierarchical relations, 226n9; and cultivation according to among the Wixárikas, 239; as modality of personhood of machis, 219, 227n15; in the representation of Marie Laveau, 103; and spirit possession, 52n8

Grenada, 12
gris-gris, 90, 96

Haiti: absence of anthropophagy in, 11; African diaspora initiations in, 34; anti-Vodou laws of, 10, 12; Archive of Haitian Religion and Culture, ix; camouflaging African beliefs, 93; *ceiba pentandra* tree, 20; Christian cultures in, 42; Dominican view of religion of, 160; government funding for Vodou, 38; Greek and Roman names in, 75; Haitian independence (1804), 6, 12, 79; Haitian tunnel period, schism (1804–60), 79; independence of, 6; indigenization in, 6; Kikongo influences on, 30; map of, xiii; preserving religious history in, 26; President Jean-Claude Duvalier, 38; revolution of, 67; rule in Dominican Republic (1822–44), 152; Saut-d'Eau, 31; wrapping style of tignon, 87. *See* Vodou

Haitian Creoles: influence in Villa Mella, 146, 165; *langaj* in, 30; language of sacred songs, 30, 160, 162; preserving linguistic heritage of in Dominican Republic, 165; Taíno words in, 12

Haitian people: anti-Haitian environment in Dominican Republic, 156; as bellwethers for civil rights, 78; conflicts with Dominicans, 164; discrimination of, 11; preserving identity of in Dominican Republic, 153

healing: ayahuasca and, 265, 267; Christ Consciousness in Santo Daime and, 268; combining Indigenous and African diaspora use of, 87, 101; combining service to spirits with, 8, 103, 112; community-based, 194, 195, 258, 265; diagnosis and, 34, 205; DMT and, 31; dreams and, 215; Dzuliferi and, 174; exorcism and, 221; function of for priests and shamans, 28; gift of, 217; as history, 205–8; honey for, 15; images for, 223, 264; knotted to unraveled, 221; Kwakwa̱ka'wakw shamanism and, 111–43; Lévi-Strauss's arguments about, 116–44; magical, 19; miração in Santo Daime and, 264; music in, 175; performances for, 114; plants for, 19, 50, 53n15, 175; psychological, social, and spiritual, 257; recurrence of illness, 210; reshaping the world with, 224; rites and rituals for, 122, 131, 174, 205, 218, 220, 224; sacred trees and, 20, 29; sacrifice and, 212–15, 226n10; Santo Daime and, 257, 261–62; as self-transformation in Santo Daime, 262; shaman's role in, 203, 205; sleight of hand and, 116, 118, 133; songs, chants, and hymns for, 184, 257–80, 268–70, 273–76; spirits and, 227; as stages of initiation, 121; symbols and, 271; Umbanda and, 278n7; *xapiri* and, 15; at a young age, 35

hinos (songs of Santo Daime), 258, 261, 276; about church's founders, 276; about and for Daime, 274; de cura, 267; and emotions, 269; and healing, 267, 271, 276; and miração experience, 267, 269, 278n7; and musical instruments, 269–70; and religious symbols, 267–68; structure of, 271, 273 *See* songs history: of Arawak and Tupi migrations, 3; of the Brotherhood of the Holy Spirit in Villa Mella, 153–54; building in Xangô traditions, 25–26; conception of among the Baniwa, 21; conception of among the Mapuche, 21, 225; of contacts between Indigenous and non-Indigenous people, 174, 193–94; in diaspora traditions, 13, 20; of Haiti's African religious legacy, 24; "history people" vs. "myth people" among Kwak'wala, 130, 141n37; as illness and healing, 205; of Kalinago (Garifuna) people, 4–5; machi spirits as repository of, 23; and multitemporal knowledge, 21; official of the Chilean State, 22; in official schooling, 246, 251; producing through religious practices, 203–4, 205; 210–11; seer-savants in, 197–98; of Vaudou in Saint-Domingue, 76; of Wixárika communities, 235; of Yoruba, 25

Hohodene (Baniwa subgroup), 173, 199n1; beliefs of, 176; cosmos, 174, 176–77; location of community, *xv* shamans, 15; trees in culture of, 29. See Baniwa.

Huitzilopochtli (Aztec patron deity), 4

Hurston, Zora Neale, 93–94

Ibadan, Nigeria, 281, 283, 291–92, 301, 309, 314, 316n17

Ibo Rite, people: people, 68, 75; Rite, 24, 74. See Sèvis Ginen tradition

icaros (songs), 268–69. See songs

Ile (Orisha Temple in home), 316n21

Ile-Ife, Nigeria, 281; dominant Orishas of, 304; Olókun's Well in, 288n19. See Map 1

illness: caused by modern life, 206–7; caused by not offering to gods, 250; caused by sorcery, 204, 211, 217; curing by shamans, 206–12, 222; curing with plants, 19; healing of in Santo Daime, 261–62; as history, 205–12, 225n5; learning through, 217, 224; narratives about, 116, 120; natural, 207, 209; as punishment, 217; to regain spiritual equilibrium, 261, 271; shamans fighting against, 27; as sign from a spirit, 35, 52n14; and social conflict, 206–7, 210; and spirits, 29, 30–31, 203, 207, 209; transforming into healing, 205.

Indians: Code of Indian Offenses, 11; in Dominican Vodou, 162; Indian villages in Wixárika territory, 236; portraits of by George Catlin, 85; relations with whites among Kwakwaka'wakw, 114; Removal Act of 1830, 11; St. Mary's Catholic Indian Boarding School, 11; U.S. commissioner of Indian affairs, 11

indigeneity, 4

Indigenous people: activists of, 50; Anglo-Americanizing of, 11; anticolonial revolts of, 237; apocalyptic conditions of, 9; Asian substratum of, 26; becoming over time, 5–6; and boarding schools in US, 49; "civilizing" of, 194; concept of place of, 3; consumption of entheogens among, 2, 50; conversion to Catholicism of, 10; cosmologies of, 135, 178; decimation of, 146; encountering African Americans, 13; enslavement of Spanish Crown, 10; essentializing of, 49; evangelization of, 237; forced migration of, 13; historical ideas of, 20–24; idealization of, 6;

imposing non-Indigenous agenda on, 246; languages of in school, 248; Marie Laveau's connection with, 87; medicine of, 28; Mexico's Law of Linguistic Rights of, 242; "military societies" or "age-group societies" of, 41; musical instruments of, 51; nationalist movements of, 43; notions of territory among, 222; ontology of, 13–16; political function of, 7; "priests" and "shamans" among, 27, 36; problems with term, 2; recognition of in Mexican Constitution of 1990s, 242; relations with non-Indigenous, 175, 193, 197, 235, 241–43; religion influencing Haitian Vodou, 43; religions of, 2; religious practices of, 11, 12; role of in the creation of Santo Daime, 259; role of sacred language for, 30; sacred animals of, 40; school curriculum for, 251; spirits in religion of, 8; structural violence faced by, 49; survival of, 37; traditions that pass to African diaspora ones, 7; versus settlers, 3

intoxication: ceremonial in South America, 28; ceremonial in the Caribbean, 28

Ìyá-Nàsó (Yoruba high priestess), 25

Jalisco (Mexico), xiv (M3), 47, 233, 235, 242, 246

Kalinago (Island Caribs), 4; diasporic identity of, 5; integration and capture of Africans, 5; language of 4

Kalina people, 4; from Guyana region, 4

kanzo (Haitian Vodou initiation), 24, 27, 34, 40; as an exhausting activity, 48

kariocha initiation (Santería), 27

katun cycles (Maya), 212

Kikongo language: connection to lwa Simbi, 46; in Haitian Creole songs, 5, 24; in hymns in Palenque, Colombia, 30; in Villa Mella, D.R., 156, 158, 162

Kongo, Kingdom of, 90, 92, 147; Catholicism in, 80n15, 147, 158; Indigenous religions of 80n15, 159

Kongolese people, 90, 147, 149, 152

Kongo Rite, 24. *See also* Sèvis Ginen tradition

Kopenawa, Davi (shaman), 14; biography of, 33; critique of invaders, 9; environmentalism of, 37, 50; global impact of, 37; narratives of initiation, 27, 30, 35; philosophy of, 14, 33–34, 50; relationship with xapiri, 34. *See* Albert, Bruce

kultrung (Mapuche instrument), 38, 214, 219, 221

Kwakwaka'wakw confederation, 111; attitudes to shamanism, 111–12, 114–15, 116–18, 123, 134, 136; attitudes to sleight of hand, 45, 135; George Hunt's initiation into culture, 112; intellectual property in communities, 123; narratives and Comox narratives, 137n15; narratives in shamanism, 124; number four in ceremonies of, 122; religious concepts and ideology, 135; research by Franz Boas with, 111, 115–16, 137n8; shamanism, 113, Winter Ceremonial, 126

Kwak'wala language: dialects of, 111; morpho-syntactic analysis, 124–25, 138n18; motifs in oral literature of, 131; narratives in, 111, 117, 118, 123, 125, 126, 135, 137n15, 141–42n41; personal names in, 118–19; term "spies" in, 136n5; transcription and translation of texts in, 136n6, 137n14, 137n17, 140n32

Lakou Nan Badjo: Nago Rite in, 24
Lakou Soukri, 34
Lakou Souvenance, Danwonmen Rite in, 24
Laveau, Marie: to African American lives in New Orleans, 84; calling Catholic saints, 95–96; caricature of with daughter, 83, 100–103, 106; as a caring figure, 106; and Catholic church, 97; Century Magazine's depiction of, 100–103, creation of gris-gris (charms), 90; dead of, 100; depiction as witch-like, 101–3, 106; dress of, 88; as a free women of color, 84–85, 106; in historical memory of New Orleans, 105; home altar of, 83, 96–99, 105; legends of, 84, 105; life of, 83–84; Native American heritage of, 87, 97, 97; painted portrait of, 83, 85–90; perception of, 84; possible second, 107n3; as a predecessor to present-day priestesses, 105; as a priestess, 83, 101; racist references to, 101; representation of, 45; spirit of, 103, 105; tarot card portrait of, 83, 103–5; Voudou legacy of, 83; and Voudou practice in nineteenth-century New Orleans, 90–91, 105; Voudou rituals and methods of, 93–95, 98; wearing a tignon, 87, 105
Legba, Atibon Legba (Haitian Vodou), 63, 73; represented by Saint Lazarus, 41; ritual of sweat droplets, 18; as Saint Peter, 96; *See* Elegba
Léogâne (Haiti): epicenter of Sèvis Ginen, 24
Léry, Jean de, 10
Leyes de Burgos, 10
Lukumí (practitioners): adaptive process in, 302, 308; batá drums of, 307; Cabildo celebrations of, 311; celebrations of, 311; continuity in, 311; disguised with Catholic saints, 305–6; dispersal after 1959 Cuban Revolution, 282; Elegua in, 310; in Florida, 310; Ile in, 316n21; mermaids in, 314; myths of, 304; Olókun in, 304; synonymous with Orisha practices, 315n4; waterways in, 284, 309; Yemayá in, 311, 316n9; Yemọja in, 309. *See* Cuba

machi (Mapuche shaman): about, 203–31; axis mundi for, 29; notions of history, 22–23; self-sacrifice of, 242n10; spirits of, 23. *See* shaman
Makaya Rite, 24. *See also* Sèvis Ginen tradition
manbo (priestess of Haitian Vodou), 7, 24, 36, 39, 72, 73; Mama Lola, 34; Manbo Inan, 34; plant-based healing of, 19; Tansia and ancestors, 18. *See* oungan, bòkò, Vodou
Mandinka, 149
mapou. *See* ceiba pentandra
Mapuche people: axis mundi in culture of, 29; evil in society of, 210; healing therapies of, 206, 207, 212; historical agency of shamans of culture of, 203–31; illness in culture of, 205; invoking deities of, 208; language of, 206; narratives about being civilized, 23; nonlinear telling of history, 22–23; sacrifice in ritual of, 29, 212, 226n10; shamans or machi of, 16, 21, 22–23; simultaneous temporalities of cosmogony of, 205, 216; sorcery in the culture of, 206, 212, 217, 221
Mapudungun (Mapuche language), 206, 207

mara'akame (Wixárika shaman): about, 239; attitudes about Western school, 245, 250; social roles of, 240
Maya people: cosmovision of, 20; Costumbre among K'iche, 42; katun cycles, 212; Lacandon people, 7; shamans, 51n4
medicine-men, 11
Mexica (Aztec) people, 4; ritual performances of, 4
Mexicanero (Nahuatl dialect), 236
Mexico, xiv, xiv: Aztec and Mexica people in, 4; gods of, 42; Maya people of, 7; Spanish chronicler in, 42; Wixárika people in, 233–56
military, 6; as aggressive outsiders, 196–97; assassination attempts by in Brazil, 196; in Brazil, 194–95; in Chile, 23, 220; defeats of Indigenous armies, 36; Indigenous societies for, 41; industrial domination today, 49; Nahuatl, 236; òrìṣà Ògún, 52; threat of African or Indigenous, 10; Trail of Tears and U.S., 6; U.S. occupation of Haiti, 11
milpa (Mexican crop growing system), 238
Mississippi, 6
Miwaxieti community, 233–56
Mixton War (1540s), 237
Moctezumah I (Aztec leader), 4
multinaturalism: definition of, 14. See also perspectivism
multitemporality, 21–22, 204; embodying of, 216–18, as a historical process, 204; and multiple gender, 220; and multiple personhood, 21, 226n11; and reordering the world, 225; and ritual language, 216; and rituals, 46, 215, 224; in shamanism, 173; and trance techniques, 21–22

N,N-Dimethyltryptamine, 21, 200. See pariká
Nagô, Casa de (House of Nago): temple in São Luis, 24, 26
Nago (Yoruba) people, 74; sea god Olokum, 305
Nago-Keto ritual, 52n8
Nago Rite, 24; headscarves in, 88. See also Sèvis Ginen tradition
Nahuatl language: links to Wixárika, 236; Mexicanero dialect of, 236; toponyms from, 236; workers, 236
neocolonialism, 48. See also colonialism
New Orleans, xvi, 45, 83–110
New York City, xvi, 308, 309, 311, 316n17
Ngünechen (Mapuche deity), different dimensions of, 220; forgiveness by 222; healing powers of, 221, 223; imploration of, 217; invocation of, 208, 211, 213; not offending, 218; possession by, 216; sacrifice for, 29; as spirits and ancestors, 219, 223
Nhiãperikuli (Baniwa deity), 28, 182
Nigeria, 24, 92, 259, 281, 283, 286, 287–92, 300, 304, 308, 309, 312, 313, 315
Niwetsik (Wixárika deity), 47, 235, 238–40
non-Indigenous people: compensating disadvantages of, 250; invasion by, 235; lack of awareness among, 243; privileged perspective of, 246; relations with Indigenous, 173, 175, 193, 197; role of teachers in Indigenous communities, 248
Norse adventurers, 9

Obatala (orisha), 281, 304, 309
Ogou (Haitian lwa), 7, 30, 32, 52n9, 63
Ogun River (Nigeria), 288, 301, 305, 309, 313

Ojibwes, 11
Oklahoma reservations, 6
Olókun, 288, 294, 295, 304–5, 306–7, 313, 316n11
Olorun (Yoruba Sky Deity), 18, 304
Omama (Yanomami xapiri): of metallurgy, 32
ontology: in African diaspora traditions, 16–20; animals in, 15; comparability of Indigenous ideas in, 16; definition, 13; in Indigenous traditions, 14–16, 50; peoplehood of diverse beings, 16, 41, 50; psychoactive tools of among Indigenous peoples, 21
Ordenanzas Reales, 10
oriki (Yoruba poetry), 302
Orisha: chanting to, 306; in communities, 285; communities of in Ibadan, 301; diaspora, 281–318; Elegba, 306; Emonje, 313–14; festivals in Brazil for, 307; Ijemoja, 313–14; Iles (houses of), 310; initiated to, 309; in Lukumí, 310; in New Orleans, 90; Ochún, 304; Ogun, 304; oriki (praise poetry for), 302; Oya, 312; sacred places for, 283–84, 303; in Saint-Domingue, 72; transatlantic slave trade and, 282; waterways, 286; worship as religion, 281; yard of in Trinidad, 312; Yemayá, 305, 313–14; Yemọja, 313–14; Yewa, 286
oungan, houngan (Haitian Vodou priest): ason of, 39; ceremonies of, 24; initiation and, 19; keepers of sacred knowledge, 73; *nganga* evolving into, 72; relationships with spirits, 17; scholars among, 50; style of consciousness of, 72; tracing *vèvè*, 7. See bòkò, Vodou, manbo
Oviedo, Fernández de, 9

Oyo Empire (Nigeria): decimation of, 313; deities of, 304; and influence of enslaved people, 304

Pacific Ocean, 239
Paiute people, 37
pajé (Baniwa shaman), 15, 32, 173–201; apprentice of, 181; curing, 175; domains of, 182; instruments of, 38; sacred snuff of, 178. *See* shaman
Pané, Ramón, 28
pariká: from berries, 182; as blood of Kuwai, 16, 178; 'dying' after consuming, 176, 195, 197; for a cure, 184; as psychoactive substance, 16; sniffing, 180; as tool of ontology, 21; for trance, 32; from tree sap, 29, 199n6. *See* DMT, N,N-Dimethyltryptamine
participant-observer, 2, 44, 46, 47, 145, 257
percussion instruments: in American Indigenous and African diaspora religions 1, 38–39, 50; in Baniwa religions traditions, 183, 186; in Cuban religious traditions, 294, 306–7; in Haitian Vadou, 39, 77; in Kwak'wala religious traditions, 114–15; in Mapuche religious traditions, 213; in Santo Daime, 164; in South American religious traditions 28; in Wixárika religion 249; at the Yemoja festival in Ibadan, 301; Yoruba abatá drums, 25
perspectivism: as basis for communication and metamorphosis, 14; definition, 14; as the interchangeability of "appearance" and "essence," 135; in Kwakwa̱ka'wakw culture, 111–36; as underlying commonalities among Indigenous religions, 135; as a universe, 135

petroglyphs, 3
Petwo Rite, 24. *See* Sèvis Ginen tradition
plants. *See* healing, ayahuasca
Port-au-Prince, Haiti, 12; bookstores with Vodou content, 42; major city for Sèvis Ginen, 24; as a meeting ground, 63
possession: in African diaspora, 31; agency of, 225; at age seven, 35; as altered state of consciousness, 204; and axis mundi, 16; as communication with spirits, 1, 2, 8, 28; cultural logic of, 226n9; to divine social and moral causes of suffering, 210; as an ecstatic practice, 34; by evil spirits, 206; hastening, 39; in Mapuche religion, 208–12; as multilayered ecstatic experience, 216; by past shamans, 22; as performance, 17; recognition for, 50; as reconnecting with the past, 23 205; shared between Indigenous and African diaspora religions, 161; as trance, 21; voluntary versus involuntary, 31
Price, Hiram, 11
prophetic religion: of the Arawak people, 21, 36; of the Baniwa people, 21; shamans, 36
psychoactive plants, 2, 15, 21, 29, 32, 176, 200; *See* entheogen, pariká, *Banisteriopsis caapi*
pyè tonnè (lightning stones), 7

Quran, 64

Rada Rite: over 100 lwa in, 24; cycles for Ayizan, 7; cycles for Èzili Freda, 31; foundational rite of Sèvis Ginen, 24; regal style of, 41; ritual assistant in, 34; serpent spirit in, 18. *See also* Sèvis Ginen tradition

Sacred Heart of Jesus, 65
Sacred Heart of Mary, 65
sacred language, 30
sacrifice (animal): in Cuban Santeria, 29; to Elegua, 310; in Haitian Vodou, 20; in Mapuche ritual, 29, 218; to placate ancestors and spirits, 50; in Wixárika culture, 249; to Yemoja, 301
Sacrum Cor Mater Dolorosa, 65
Sahagún, Bernardo de, 42
Saint-Domingue: anti-Vodou laws of, 10; archives in Aix-en-Provence about, 79; ecological approach to, 61–78; emergence of oungan and manbo in, 72, 73; estrangement of plantations in, 75; French retreat from, 78; history of Vodou in, 76; indebtedness of farmers, 62; Quran in, 64; religious treatises printed in, 79; Sacred Heart devotion in, 65; vector for lethal disease, 78
Saint-Marc (Saint-Domingue, Haiti), 63
saints, Sen yo (Haitian Creole): absence of Catholicism in, 41; Anthony de Padua, 94; The Black Madonna Mater Salvatoris, 41; blending of by Marie Laveau, 95–96, 105–6; as camouflage for African beliefs, 93, 305; Cosme and Damian, 149; enslaved people praying to, 150; Expedite, 94, 95; Father Arnaoud, 196; Francis, 66; Jerome, 7; Joseph, 94; Lazarus, 41; in Louisiana's mélange, 91, 93; Mary, 94; Mary (of) Magdalene, 94, 149; in Meso-America, 42; in Mexican K'iche Mayan culture, 42; Michael, 94; Our

saints, Sen yo (*continued*)
Lady of Navigators, 314; overlapping personality descriptors of, 18; *pajé* claiming to be, 195; Patrick, 41; Peter with and without the key, 94; put to work in Voudou, 93; in rituals in Villa Mella, D.R., 159–60; Sacred Heart of Jesus, 94; in Santo Daime, 268; Sebastião, 276; syncretism of, 6, 7, 24, 41, 96; Theresa, 66; Ulrich, 41

Ṣàngó, Sango (religious tradition), 5, 16, 18, 304; character of, 52n11; as a complex of spirits, 313; connection to thunder, 25; as king, 25, 52; as mixed-race, 52n11; as Orisha diaspora, 304; in Trinidad, 30; in Yoruba history, 25; as Xangô in Brazil, 25. *See* Xangô

santera (female practitioner of Santería), 19; using plants to heal, 19. *See* santero

Santería, 5, 16; animal sacrifice in, 29; commonalities with other African diaspora traditions, 27; dance performance in, 17; initiation in, 27

santero (male practitioner of Santería), 19; belief in bilongos and ebbos, 20; possession and gender ambiguity in, 52. *See* santera

Santo Daime, 47, 257; Amazonian shamanism in, 258; doctrine, 260–61, 266, 270–73, 277; founders of, 268; hinos sung in, 259, 267, 268–70, 270–76; miração experience in 262–66, 267; music in healing in, 173–74; pantheon, 274; participant observation in, 278n2; rituals, 267, 278n6; roots in Umbanda, 278n1, 278n8; shamanistic healing in, 257, 258, 261–62, 271; spirits in, 265; syncretism in, 258–59; use of ayahuasca in, 259, 260, 267; variety of churches in Brazil, 260

scalp-dance, 11

seer-savant (Baniwa), 193–97

self-sacrifice: in Mapuche ritual, 212–15, 217, 224, 226n10; in Wixárika religious system, 239–40

Sepúlveda, Ginés de, 9

serpent: as good and evil spirit, 16; in Kwak'wala religious traditions, 120; lwa in Haitian Vodou, 18–19, 33, 41, 52n14; in Santo Daime miração, 278n7

settlers (white, colonial), 3; Anglo-Saxon, 84; bringing suffering for Mapuche, 203; combating with shamanic logic, 206; as marauders, 23; monoculture plantations of, 16; right-wing, 22; wickedness of, 16

Sèvis Ginen tradition (Haitian Vodou): ceremonial rites of, 5, 24; demands of, 24; inclusion of African ethnonational traditions in, 24; kanzo initiation of, 24, 34; as a multidivinity tradition, 31; syncretism in, 5, 43

shaman, shamans: about, 174, 204; aggressive attacks of rivals, 198; anthropological understandings of, 223; Arawak, 3; ayahuasca, 26; Baniwa, 15, 21, 23, 28, 36, 173–202; biographies of, 22–23; Bororo, 40; Colombia, 207; coming into awareness of spirits, 33–4; consciousness of, 263; defending psychic integrity, 27; entheogens of, 16, 31, 35, 178; guardian spirit of, 133; guild of, 113; healing for, 28, 111, 116, 126, 131, 187, 194–95, 197, 265, 277; historical consciousness of, 23, 224; initiation into, 112, 113, 121, 130; instruments of, 38–39; jaguars as symbols for,

40; Kwakwaka'wakw, 111–44; Mapuche machi, 16, 21–22, 23, 203–32; marriage to spirits in Baniwa, 176; motivations of, 8; multitemporality and, 216; mythology of, 48, 124; narratives of, 22, 118, 125, 181, 212; nonsupernatural cure, 117; Paiute, 37; plant-based, 262; primordial, 184; problems with the term, 36; prophetic, 21, 36; reasons for becoming a shaman, 194; relationship with spirits, 30–31; reshaping history, 198; rituals of, 112, 136; sacrifice in, 212; Santo Daime and, 257–58, 268; seeking social harmony, 175; serving Moctezumah I, 4; skepticism and faith about, 112; sleight of hand in, 115–16, 123, 142n42, 111–44; songs of, 136n3, 173, 184–92, 221, 268; spies of, 133; spirit animals of, 222; sucking healing rituals of, 112; symbols of, 15; Taíno, 51; trance of, 31–33; transition to becoming, 35; Tukano, 40; Tupinambá, 16; use of trees among, 29; Wixárika, 233–55; Yanomami, 14, 20–21, 27, 29, 34, 37. *See* pajé, machi, mara'akame

shamanism: Indigenous attitudes about, 114–15, 118; problems with label, 26–27; sleight of hand and supernatural power in, 118, 126, 131, 134–35

silk-cotton tree. *See ceiba pentandra*

slaves. *See* enslaved people

sleight of hand: combined with masking, 130; concealing, 116; as controlling appearances, 118, 130, 131; described by Boas and Hunt, 111, 117; as distinct from shamanic power, 123; efficacious use of, 116–17, 121, 126, 131; elaborateness of, 129–30; as illegitimate, 134; integrated into shamanism, 115; in Kwakwaka'wakw shamanism, 111, 116; among modern stage magicians, 137n13; mythological past, 117; narratives about, 118–32; relationship to perspectivism, 135; and supernatural healing, 45, 117, 123, 125; as a technique for healing, 45, 114

songs, archaic, 30; of African captives, 146, 156–63; in African languages, 5; in African Vodun, 159–60; 157–58; in American Indigenous and African diaspora religions, 1; among the Baniwa people, 20, 32, 46, 173–74, 182, 183–93, 199n3; bodily effects of, 266–67, 274; in Candomblé, 18; Catholic, 42, 156, 162–63; among the Chemehuevi people, 39–40; and consumption of psychoactive plants, 268; of the Cross (Baniwa), 195; in Cuban Santeria, 17; and education, 241, 252; of European sailors, 66, 67; funeral, 158; in the Garifuna diaspora, 5; in Haitian Creole language, 30, 160; in Haitian Vodou, 17, 24, 47, 52n14; 53n15, 96, 108n15, 159–60; and healing/curing, 174, 178, 223, 257–58, 264, 277; among the Kwakwaka'wakw people, 112, 127, 128, 129, 136n3, 140n31; learning of, 269; as "long conversations", 68–69; among the Mapuche people, 203, 221–22, 223; in Navajo language, 30; in nineteenth-century Louisiana, 90; in nineteenth-century New Orleans, 95, 100; performative function of, 223; sacred 32, 112, 222, 267; as a sacred tradition, 49; of Ṣàngó, 25; in Santo Daime church; of the seer-savants (Baniwa), 193–97; of the shaman or priest, 27, 174, 178, 180, songs, archaic (*continued*) 183–93, 197–98, 221–22, 268; and spirits in African diaspora religions, 8; and topograms, 3; among the Tupi shamans, 35; in Umbanda tradition (Brazil), 278n8; among the Wixárika people, 240, 249; among the Yanomami people, 33; among the Yoruba in Trinidad, 284. *See hinos*

sorcery: accusations of, 206, 215, 217; affecting family, 214; amorality of, 221; in Baniwa stories, 200n12; and countersorcery, 207; and divination, 208; emetic medicine against, 213; in ethnographic accounts, 116; healing from, 173, 174, 186–87, 195–97, 204, 211; protection against, 222; as a source of back luck, 209; as a source of disruptions in the moral and temporal order, 210, 212; as source of sickness, 184; as a source of social conflict, 194, 211, 212; vulnerability to, 216

South America: ancestral homeland of Caribs, 4; ayahuasca in, 19, 26; ceremonial intoxication in, 28; drums and instruments in, 38–39; flawed comparison to Siberians, 26–27; map of, xv; marriage to spirits in, 28; mobility and diasporas on, 4; as origins of contemporary Western entheogen usage, 51n2; Pleiades constellation in, 183; spirit-based traditions of, 26; Taíno people fleeing to, 12

Spanish: administration in Mexico, 236; brotherhoods in colonies of, 149; chroniclers, 42; colonial empire, 10; colonial laws, 10; colony of Santo Domingo, 147; conquest of Hispaniola, 12; enslaved people with the names of, 147; in Florida, 13; imposition of Catholicism by, 105, 107n10; influence in New Orleans, 84, 85; influence in Villa Mella, D.R., 146; missionaries contribution to intercultural identifications, 42; numbers of enslaved people in, 146; rule of in Wixárika territory, 237; syncretism from, 43

Spanish Crown: authorization to enslave Indigenous people, 10; slave trade of in 1510, 146

Spanish language: African linguistic influence in Dominican Republic, 164; bilingual with Mapudungun, 223; bilingual with Wixárika, 244; books in Wixárika and, 242; as an imperial language, 234; name from in Wixárika territory, 252; prestige of, 164; problems with textbooks in, 246; in syncretic prayers, 156–57, 162; teaching Indigenous people in, 237, 243; tensions about the learning of, 245, 248; as tool for political and social integration, 24; as a tool of defense, 247

spirit-based traditions, 2, 9, 12, 20, 46, 51; in African culture, 148; convergences of, 26–43

spirits: as an ally, 18; ancestral, 13; animals of in Mapuche religion, 218, 222; appeasement of, 29; attacking traditions that worship, 9; attributes of, 8; blending human and animal attributes in, 18, 26; bringing with sprayed rum, 98; the call to, 34–35; canons of in Haitian Vodou, 24; Catholic condemnations of, 42; common features of the service to, 50; dance as symbolic representation of, 33; dances of, 126; direction to and from, 31; in Dominican Vodou, 159; as duplicating and transforming society, 211, 216; dwelling places of, 29; dyab or hot, 101; evil ones, 13, 203, 207, 208–9, 214–15, 217, 219, 220, 221; exerting influence on, 115, 117; exhaustion of working with, 27; facilitating contact with, 96; of the family (*Zany*), 18; Garifuna, 43; gender aspects of, 52n8; greeting in ceremonies, 17–18; group of performing Winter Ceremonials, 129; as guardians, 115, 133; in Haitian Vodou, 33, 75, 90; healing with, 19, 27, 31, 178, 183, 210, 223, 264, 268; horse of in Mapuche culture, 217, 218, 220, 222; horse of in Vodou, 17, 31, 32, 52, 162; imbibing entheogens to encounter and become, 31–32, 51, 279; inherited in families, 34; initiation and imprinting personality of, 17; instruments used to call, 38–9; jaguar shaman spirit, 178; of a killer whale, 112; living in trees, 20; Marie Laveau as, 105; Marie Laveau's calling upon, 88, 96; marriage to, 28, 176, 222–23, 224; methods of contacting, 17; mimicking Mapuche realities, 211; misbehavior and, 217; with national stature, 23; ones of Vodun origin in D.R., 150; of the Other World, 173; as owners of forests, 203; as the patrons of domains, 32; personhood of, 204; possession by, 31, 225, 226n9; possession performance as personification of, 17; priestly chanters invoking, 175; punishment for unfaithfulness to, 20; receptacle for holding, 90; as repositories of Mapuche history, 23; representation of with symbolic foods, 32; resingularization of, 23; retrieving songs from, 32, 35; role of in initiation, 19, 27; sacrifices for, 212; Santo Daime and, 261, 265; as serpent, 52n14; shamans assuming perspective of, 174; Simbi as an etymological pathway, 30; similitude with humans, 18, 204; spirit-peoples in Baniwa belief, 176, 197; spirit-wives or husbands, 28–29; as a substrate pattern, 51; as supernatural helpers, 28; of thunder, 205; types in Yanomami religion, 35; use of songs to counsel, 221; of the water, 19, 302; working with as a central theme, 8

spy, 113, 133, 136n5. *See* dreamer

Staden, Hans, 9

St. John's River (Florida), 3

St. Mary's Catholic Indian Boarding School, 11

St. Vincent, 5, 13

sun-dance, 11

superstition: anti-superstition campaigns (Haiti), 49, 77; labelling non-European religions as "superstition," 9

syncretism: in Africa and America, 146–48; of African traditions, 6, 24, 149–50; of Catholic saints, 41; combining disparate religious traditions, 5; Costumbre as, 43; degrees of accommodation, 5; festivals that display, 164; with Freemasonry, 43; Greek origin of, 165; Iberian, 149; identifications of spirits and saints as, 304; among Indigenous peoples, 42; in Meso-America, 53n17; in rituals of brotherhoods, 163; symbolized by brotherhoods, 151; in Villa Mella, D.R., 46

Taíno people and language: accusations about, 9; *behiques* of, 51; drums of, 38; emetic wands of, 51; *lua* of, 162; palm fronds in, 7; Pané's description of, 28; stone trigonal icons, 7; survivors mixing with Africans and Europeans, 12; words from, 12

Tatei Neixa (goddess of corn), 235; initiation ritual for children, 239, 249; Tatei Uteanaka, 238

Tatewari (Wixárika deity), 47, 235, 238, 240, 241

Tatutsi (Wixárika deity), 47, 238, 239

Tau (Wixárika deity), 235

Tenochtitlán (Aztec capital), 4

Thevet, André, 10

tignon (scarf), 85, 87–88, 89, 105

Timucuans (Florida), 3

Tlaloc (Aztec rain god), 42

Tlingit language, 111

Tonantzin (Aztec goddess), 42

topograms, 3

topographic writing (Arawakan), 3

traditions, compartmentalized, 1, 50

Trail of Tears (U.S.), 6

Trinidad: African Diaspora religions in, 5; Emanje (water goddess) in, 302, 304; English as predominant language in, 315n8; Ifa initiation in, 312; melding of Diasporic Orisha traditions with Nigerian traditions, 312–13, 315; Obalúayé festival in, 312; Ochún (water goddess) in, 304; Ògún worship in, 52n11; Orisha tradition in, 16, 26, 47, 282–83, 303, 308, 312–13, 315n3; and peoplehood of spirits, 16–17; personal relationship with Orishas, 18; sacred trees in, 20; Sango (Sàngó) worship in, 5, 52n11, 304; Yemayá festival in, 311;

Yoruba language in Sàngó temples of, 30; Yoruba people in, 284

Tucano (language), 30

tukipa (Wixárika religious center), 243

Tupinambá, Tupí (Kawaiwete), 3, 16, 35, 40

typological approach, 1, 2, 44, 48

Umbanda: Brazilian religion, 259; influence on Santo Daime, 267, 278n278; map 4, xv; orixás in, 259, 267, 278n5; songs in, 278. *See* Santo Daime

United States: attitudes about among Mapuche, 206; attitudes about "Voodoo" in, 106; Aztec and Mexica people in, 4; Catlin's travelling in, 85; enslavement in, 10; free port towns of, 84; influx of Haitians into, 90; Kopenawa's visit to, 37; Louisiana purchase of, 84; Map 5, xvi; Muslims in, 166n8; northern Plains culture in, 36; occupation of Haiti, 11; Orisha diaspora in, 47, 283, 308–12; reservations of, 11; stability of Vodou in Miami, 12

Venezuela, xv, xvi, 194, 195, 199n1

Vespucci, Amerigo, 9

vèvè (ground tracings), 7; as a magical practice, 24; for the serpent spirit, 52n14

villa, 145, 152

Villa Mella, Dominican Republic: xiii, 46, 145, 146, 150, 151, 152, 153, 155, 156, 157, 158, 160, 162, 163, 164, 165, 166n3

Virgen de la Altagracia, 162

Vodou (Haitian): accusations against, 11; afterlife in Nan Ginen-Vilokan, 74; altars in, 7; altars of, 73, 79; ancestors in, 18, 154; anti-Vodou laws, 10, 49; ason (shaker) in, 40; ayizan palm fronds in, 32; and the brotherhood of Villa Mella, D.R., 146, 156; and the Bwa Kayiman ceremony, 78; called to priesthood of, 34–35; candles in, 92; cardinal points in, 34; Catholic baptism and, 75; Christian-Vodou hybridity, 41; chromolithographs in, 41–42; color-coding clothing in, 88; contemporary services of, 65; creolization and, 6; Danmbala Wèdo in, 97; Dominican variety of, 159–62; double consciousness in, 72; drums and instruments of, 39; dyab in, 101; early history of, 76; and Fon and Kikongo,158; foula rum pulverizing in, 98; Haitian Creole as a holy language, 161; headscarves in, 88; healing plants in, 19; as indigenized, 5; inherited economic problems, 12; initiations in, 27, 33, 48; on the internet, 77; langaj in, 30; lexicon of, 24; links to politics, 38; lwa Ogou in, 7; Manbo Sallie Ann Glassman, 103; personhood of spirits in, 16, 17; potomitan (center post) in, 29; pubic louses and Gede, 32; roles of trees in, 24; shape shifting in, 41; spirits and environment, 65; spirits of, 74; St. Expedite as Bawon Samdi in, 94; syncretism of saints in, 41, 76, 96; syncretistic orientation of, 5; types of possession in, 31; vodouizing words, 43; water in, 34; Western traditions in, 28; as a worldview, 67; xenophilia of, 148; yanvalou dance in, 33

wanga, 90. *See* Vodou
war-dance, 11

Washington National Cathedral, 10
Watakame (Wixárika culture), 235
Western science, culture, and history: cultures, 8, 51n2; epistemology, 234, 252; ideas, 7; imposition of categories, 121; Indigenous nations, 40; knowledge systems, 233, 241, 252; medicine, 28; people, 209; problems with term, 7; scholars, 2; science, 234; societies, 6; thought, 43; traditions, 28
Wixárika (people, language in Mexico): about, 233–56; contacts with Aztecs, 236; corn in narratives of, 238; cosmology, 235; epistemic system, 234, 238, 245, 250–52; festivities of, 239; influence of agricultural cycle among, 248; language practices in schools, 246–47; origin of language, 236; public schools of, 233, 241–44, 250–52; religious system of, 238–39; role of shaman among, 240; sacred centers of, 235; traditional education, 246; use of land, 238; Wixárika and Spanish bilingualism among, 244
Wongòl Rite: from Angola, 24. *See* Sèvis Ginen tradition

Xangô (Ṣàngó in Brazil), 25
Xapawiyeme (Mexico), 235
xapiri (Yanomani spirits), 14–15, 30–31, 33–35

Yanomami people and religion: animal spirits in, 14; becoming a shaman in childhood, 34; becoming a spirit with *yãkoana* (DMT), 31; biographies of great shamans, 23, 33; Bruce Albert's work with, 22; dance and song in culture of, 33; encounter

Yanomami people and religion (*cont.*) with Brazilian army, 9; encounter with contemporary non-Indigenous people, 37; female water spirits in, 29; forest reserved for, 37; going under the water in, 33; initiation in, 29, 30; links between shaman, yãkoana, and xapiri 33; myths of, 15

Yemayá (Cuban Orisha): associated with La Virgen de la Regla (Our Lady of the Rule), 305, 315; celebration of, 299, 306, 308, 310–12; as an example of cultural and religious survival, 314–15; as goddess of the ocean, 304–5, 313–14; images associated with, 314–15; importance of in African Diasporic traditions, 313–14; Lukumí stories about, 316n9; migration to African diaspora, 303; processions dedicated to, 305; relation to Yemoja, 302; sacred tools of, 314; as universal mother, 305; as water goddess, 302; worship and sacred places of in the United States, 308–9, 310–12

Yemoja (Nigerian Orisha): animal sacrifice for, 301; associated with rivers and the sea, 311; in Brazil as Iemanjá, 307, 311, 314; ceremonies for, 301; chief priest of, 301; in diasporic traditions, 304, 313–14; and divination, 313; expansive nature of, 302; festivals dedicated to 281, 283, 301–2, 309, 312–13; integration of Nigerian and Diasporic traditions by, 313; as mother of all the Orishas, 310, 313; as "mother of fish", 301; in New York, 309; Ogun River as ancestral home of, 301, 309, 313; possession of Tony Renauld by, 309; praise poetry for, 302; relation to Yemayá, 302; river versus ocean as home of, 313–14, 3176n24; shrine of, 300, 309; worship at the ocean, 309, 310; worship of, 316n14; in Yorubaland, 311

Yorubaland, 47; developing the Orisha diaspora, 314; diversity of, 286; as a magical place, 285; origin of adaptive process, 302; photographs of sacred places, 287–92; residency of the divine, 285; river spirits in, 303, 311; source of Lukumí, 315; Yemoja festival in Ibadan, 301–2, 310

Yoruba people and language: *abatá* drums of, 25; in Brazil, 259; contribution to Haitian Creole, 24; Egbado, 313; festivals of, 305–6; Ìyá-Nàsó in, 25; language used in Trinidad, 30; Nago Rite from, 24; in New Orleans, 90; olorishas from, 72; plants for, 19; priests invited to Trinidad, 312; reestablishing sacred space, 303; in Saint-Domingue (Haiti), 74, 77; Ṣàngó worship among, 25; songs and dirges in, 284; songs surviving in language of, 5; source of the spirit Ogou, 30; subgroups creating Orisha diaspora, 282. *See* Nigeria

Youroumaÿn (Garifuna homeland of St. Vincent), 5

Yutoaztecan (language family), 236

Zapes (Sierra Leone), 149
zemi (cemí, Taíno statue), 12

www.ingramcontent.com/pod-product-compliance
Lightning Source LLC
Chambersburg PA
CBHW030604230426
43661CB00053B/1841